W9-BLF-225

STUDIES IN HISTORY, ECONOMICS AND PUBLIC LAW

Edited by the
FACULTY OF POLITICAL SCIENCE OF
COLUMBIA UNIVERSITY

NUMBER 434

THE REORGANIZATION OF THE AMERICAN RAILROAD SYSTEM, 1893-1900

BY

E. G. CAMPBELL

THE REORGANIZATION
OF THE
AMERICAN RAILROAD
SYSTEM, 1893-1900

*A Study of the Effects of the Panic of 1893, the Ensuing
Depression, and the First Years of Recovery on
Railroad Organization and Financing*

BY

E. G. CAMPBELL

AMS PRESS
NEW YORK

COLUMBIA UNIVERSITY
STUDIES IN THE
SOCIAL SCIENCES

434

The Series was formerly known as
Studies in History, Economics and Public Law.

Reprinted with the permission of Columbia University Press
From the edition of 1938, New York
First AMS EDITION published 1968
Manufactured in the United States of America

Library of Congress Catalogue Card Number: 76-76643

AMS PRESS, INC.
NEW YORK, N. Y. 10003

PREFACE

ALTHOUGH hundreds of books have been written upon various aspects of the history of the American railroad industry, there have been surprisingly few attempts to analyze its financial organization during the last half century. Yet the railway system in this country as we know it today is essentially different from what it was before the depression of the nineties. During that decade the first great transportation combinations were formed, simultaneously with the transfer of control over the industry to a small group of bankers. Nevertheless, the depression, per se, had less to do with these changes than might be thought; fundamentally they represented the culmination of trends already well established in the quarter century following the Civil War. It is the purpose of this study to analyze the effects of the depression on the railroads and to trace the beginnings of the new era in financial organization which had its origin in the depression years.

For their willing assistance in facilitating the research for this work, I wish especially to thank the staffs of the Columbia University Library, the New York Public Library, the Harvard College Library, the Interstate Commerce Commission Library and the Bureau of Railway Economics Library. Professor T. W. Van Metre of the Columbia School of Business and Professor John A. Krout of the Faculty of Political Science read the entire manuscript and made many helpful suggestions for its improvement; Professor Krout also very kindly helped read the proof. Thanks are also due to the many friends who have generously contributed of their time and efforts.

Above all I am indebted to Professor Allan Nevins of Columbia University whose invaluable aid has been liberally granted at every stage of my work.

E. G. CAMPBELL.

NEW YORK, 1938.

5

CONTENTS

CHAPTER I

POST-WAR BOOM TIMES AND CHAOS

THE decades following the Civil War were marked by an unprecedented industrial development in the United States. Even before the soldiers of the Confederacy had laid down their arms, a wave of war-time prosperity had swept the North and West. In the South the devastation caused by the war and the chaos induced by Reconstruction combined to prostrate economic life for several years. But, despite the essential precariousness of a prosperity which was accompanied by severe poverty in the South, the post-war period was one of rapid growth. Among the industries leading in both geographic and financial expansion were the railroads.

When Lee and Johnston surrendered their armies to Grant and Sherman in the spring of 1865, the total railroad mileage of the country was less than 35,000. Only thirty-six years had passed since the first steam locomotive in America had appeared in the Pennsylvania coal fields, and only thirty-five years had elapsed since the Baltimore & Ohio had opened its first division, 14 miles in length, on which horses supplied the motive power. When Andrew Jackson moved out of the White House in 1837 twenty-nine railroads were under construction, 400 miles of track had been laid and 1750 more were projected. State governments joined their efforts with those of private corporations, so that by 1850 most of the large Eastern cities were connected by rail and an embryo network was beginning to alter the economic map of the country.

The decade preceding the Civil War might have seen a transcontinental railroad bring California weeks nearer the other states of the Union, but political jealousies and hatreds, engendered by the slavery controversy, prevented the early realization of plans and hopes which already were mooted in the halls of Congress. While the feasibility of a transcontinental road

9

was debated, the construction of local lines continued apace, and the foundations were laid for that marvelous expansion which followed the war.

In 1862, after the Southern representatives and senators had left Washington, Congress voted to give land bounties and cash loans to any private corporations which would undertake to build the now badly needed transcontinental. When in accordance with this act the first rails of the Union Pacific and the Central Pacific were put in place, a new railroad boom period had started. In 1869, midway between the end of the war and the panic of 1873, the last spike was driven to join the rails leading east from the Pacific to those heading west from the Missouri River. The furious construction pace set by the transcontinentals proved contagious, and within two years, after a rapid and steady growth, the new mileage of railroad put in operation during the single year was more than 7300. During the panic of the early seventies, however, new construction slowed down to a mere 1700 miles in 1875.

In the latter half of the decade, as the country gradually recovered from the depression, construction of new mileage kept pace with the general revival. In 1882 a new peak was reached: in twelve months more than 11,500 miles of new line had been opened. From that record total there was a sharp drop the following year to about 6600 miles, itself a figure which would have seemed phenomenal a dozen years before. The rapidity with which the country's railroad system developed is emphasized by the fact that whereas in 1865 there was one mile of track in operation for every 1000 of population, twenty years later there was one mile for every 450 of population. While the population of the country had, very roughly, doubled, the railroad mileage had approximately quadrupled.[1]

1 *Appleton's Annual Cyclopedia and Register of Important Events of the Year 1884*, New York: D. Appleton and Company, 1885, pp. 677-87.

Partly because of the rapid growth that had already taken place, partly for other reasons, in the late eighties and early nineties construction of new mileage again diminished.[2] By 1893 the total mileage of the country was 176,461 and " the railroads stood ready to serve beyond the economic capacity of the country to support such service adequately ".[3]

The more prosaic additions of mileage in regions where there had been some roads before the War attracted less public attention than the development of competing transcontinental systems. In 1869 the Union Pacific and the Central Pacific had met. Many observers thought that this single track across the plains and mountains of the West would suffice to meet the economic needs of the country for decades to come, but in less than twenty-five years it had been paralleled four times. In 1881 the Southern Pacific was opened. Two years later the last spike on the Northern Pacific route to Puget Sound was driven. After another two years a rival to the Southern Pacific appeared in the Southwest, the Atchison, Topeko & Santa Fe. Finally as another panic was bringing a long period of prosperity to a close, the Great Northern pushed its tracks to Puget Sound and became a competitor of the Northern Pacific.[4]

At the same time that the railroads were penetrating what had hitherto been trackless forests in many sections of the West, a change was becoming apparent in the organization of railway companies throughout the country. Until shortly after the Civil War most of them had been local corporations, owning at most a few hundred miles of track which often connected with some other line at the terminals. But in 1869 Cornelius Vanderbilt gained control of the Lake Shore & Michigan

2 *Interstate Commerce Commission Report*, 1892, p. 72; see also *Commercial and Financial Chronicle*, January 7, 1893, p. 14.

3 *Interstate Commerce Commission Statistics*, 1894, p. 13; Miller, Sidney, *Inland Transportation, Principles and Policies*, New York: McGraw-Hill Book Company, Inc., 1933, p. 91.

4 *Ibid.*, p. 91.

Southern; he united it with his New York Central and thereby formed a through trunk line from the Atlantic seaboard to Chicago and the West.[5]

The advantages to be derived from having a long trunk line under one ownership, rather than controlled by several separate and diverse interests, soon became manifest and a new era had begun. The larger companies quickly expanded their systems by absorbing smaller roads. The history of the Pennsylvania system in the eighties typifies this phase of development. In 1880 the system represented an amalgamation of forty-four smaller companies, operating 3773 miles of track. During the next ten years twenty-nine more companies were absorbed, at least one every year and never more than four in any single year. Through these acquisitions by 1890 the parent company had increased its mileage to about 5000.

This growth was by no means peculiar to the Pennsylvania; most of the other large roads were engaged in expanding by the same methods. The Interstate Commerce Commission declared that in the nine years 1880-88 inclusive, 425 companies had been brought under the control of other roads either by lease, purchase, merger or some other legal means. In the single year 1880, 115 companies had thus lost their identity and the smallest number to be absorbed in any one year was twenty in 1884. The extent of this drift towards combination was evident by the nineties. At that time there were 1705 railway organizations in the United States; of these only 609 were independent. Fewer than 150 were owned by private individuals; the rest were subsidiaries or feeders in some relationship to the big independent companies.[6] For practical purposes, nearly two-thirds of the country's railroad companies had been absorbed by the other one-third.

This situation had not been brought about without liberal financial investments. A large part of the necessary capital had

5 Appleton, *Annual Cyclopedia*, 1884, pp. 677-87.

6 *Interstate Commerce Commission Reports*, 1889, p. 77; 1890, p. 58.

come from American sources, but there were few great systems which did not have many foreign stock and bond owners. Since railroads had first been built in the United States a steady stream of European money had crossed the Atlantic. The Union Pacific had been financed largely by English and Dutch interests; the Great Northern represented large amounts of Canadian and English capital; the Northern Pacific seemed at times to be an exclusively German company; three-fourths of the Louisville & Nashville stock belonged to Europeans. English investors had bought more than $2,000,000,000 of American railroad securities; so close was the connection between British money markets and transatlantic roads that when the London banking firm of Baring Brothers suspended in 1890, the reverberations of the catastrophe were felt just as severely by the Northern Pacific as by any London company. Dutch investors held about one-tenth as many securities as the English; and German, Swiss and French interests were also large.[7]

There were many times when these conservative Europeans were profoundly shocked by concomitants of the new trend to combination, which was partly the result, and partly the cause, of the methods and business ethics that accompanied the rapid expansion of railroad service. A chapter of the Atchison's history is indicative of the atmosphere in which many of the new lines were built. In the late seventies the Denver & Rio Grande Railroad had a monopoly of New Mexican freight and passenger traffic, but in 1879 the Atchison determined to push its tracks through New Mexico and on to the Pacific coast; tracks were to be built from La Junta through the Grand Canon of the Arkansas and thence westward. But the Rio Grande had paid spies in the ranks of the Atchison, and through them was kept cognizant of the latter's decisions. The Rio Grande's tracks were already laid to the entrance to the

7 Ripley, William Z., *Railroads, Finance and Organization*, New York: Longmans, Green and Company, 1915, pp. 5-6.

Canon, so President Strong of the Atchison, thinking his purpose known to only a few of his own subordinates, one day asked for a special train to take him to the Canon. The Rio Grande officials, knowing that Strong wanted the train to transport a construction gang, refused and instead dispatched a train carrying a gang of their own.

To head off the Rio Grande, Engineer Morley of the Atchison jumped on a horse and, by literally riding the horse to death, reached Canon City before the train. He found the people in the town so enraged at the exploitation which they had suffered at the hands of the Rio Grande, that he easily collected a construction gang of his own on the spot and got it started grading a right of way before the outraged Rio Grande gang arrived. When the latter came, the Atchison was indubitably in possession of the Canon and possession in the West of that time was more than nine points of the law. For a time an armed conflict seemed imminent and for two weeks state militia camped in the neighborhood, sleeping on their arms, while the opposing forces battled in the courts.

Finally, a counter-attack by the Atchison in another quarter brought an end to the dispute in the Canon, although not to the one in the courts. The Rio Grande, with a line from Pueblo to Denver, had refused the Atchison permission to use its tracks from the latter's terminal in Pueblo. Thereupon the Atchison began preparations for the construction of a new line between the two cities. The threat of a parallel line which would ruin its business was sufficient to force concessions from the Rio Grande. At once it withdrew from the Canon and permitted the Atchison to build without hindrance the line to Leadville at the western end. Once its line was finished the Atchison was safely esconced in the Canon, but the legal fight continued until a United States District Court put the Rio Grande into receivership.[8]

8 Appleton, *Annual Cyclopedia*, 1879, pp. 158-60.

Open warfare between construction gangs and races for rights of way were sensational phases of the struggles which characterized railroad history in the decades following the Civil War. But there were more secret and far more deadly phases of the same struggles. From the moment a railroad company was formed, it fought for its existence in a world characterized by anarchy and chaos. Despite the fact that transportation companies invited public subscriptions to their securities and were of a quasi-public nature, the only inviolable law was that of self-preservation. Common concepts of every-day honesty and fairness were ignored. Most of the great systems had been built by fraudulent construction companies, and if perchance a road had been honestly built, there was always an opportunity to correct this oversight by disreputable, but highly profitable, manipulation of its securities. Often railway companies were managed, or rather mismanaged, not with an eye to fulfilling their functions as transportation facilities, but solely with a view to making money from speculations in their securities. So many were the great fortunes quickly made in the railroad business that the public began to grow suspicious of all railway management.

In good part this suspicion was justified. A mania for construction had resulted in a railroad network far in excess of the country's needs. In part the over-optimism of promoters had led to unprofitable lines; in part tactical manoeuvres had led to the same end. Just as the Atchison was quite ready to build an unnecessary line from Pueblo to Denver simply for the sake of its nuisance value to the Rio Grande, many miles of road were constructed as moves in campaigns waged by one company against another. Since there was not enough traffic, competition was fierce and wasteful. As an inducement to shippers rebates were offered and paid; discriminations against one shipper and in favor of another were common. The most famous contract involving rebates was that of the Standard Oil Company in which a railroad agreed to make a uniform rate for shipping oil to everyone except the Standard company; ostensibly the latter would pay the regular rate but it would receive back nearly half of that amount as well as a similar portion of what its competitors had paid.[9] This was an extreme case, but the whole rebate system involved unjust discrimination between customers. As the system commonly worked, favored customers were secretly repaid a fraction of the rate which they had publicly paid. Any competitor shipping his goods at the published rate could easily be undersold and forced out of business by the company receiving the favors of the railroad.

Not only were there discriminations between customers, there were equally glaring injustices to localities and towns. If two or more roads had tracks connecting two cities, in an effort to get as much traffic as possible the rates between these two cities would be reduced so much that the roads were losing money. To recoup these losses, the roads charged as high rates as possible on freight to or from points where there was no competition. Thus often a rate for a point mid-way between two cities was higher than the rate for the longer haul between the two cities. For instance, in shipping goods from Buffalo to Cincinnati, it was cheaper to send the freight to New York City, and thence to Cincinnati via Buffalo than it was to send it directly to Cincinnati. The combined costs of the longer haul were much less than the charge for the one short trip.

Further, to get traffic, commissions were offered by the companies to private agents who would obtain freight for them. Had not all the roads paid commissions, some might have benefited; since all did, no road gained unless it paid more than its rivals, and then its own revenues suffered. The payment of commissions was essentially a form of rate-cutting, but far more important was the outright rate-cutting that was common. Often tariffs were not published and to every

9 *Industrial Commission Report*, Washington: Government Printing Office, 1900-1902, 20 volumes, I, pp. 609-16.

shipper was quoted a different rate, dependent on the price a rival was charging and almost regardless of the freight to be shipped and the length of the haul.

The inevitable result was that this management of the business had a direct and very decided tendency to strengthen unjustly the strong among the customers and to depress the weak . . . and tended to fix in the public mind a belief that injustice and inequality in public agencies were not condemned by the law, and that success in business was to be sought for in favoritism rather than in legitimate competition and enterprise.[10]

Railroad officials realized that the bitter warfare which characterized the industry was hurting it beyond any possibility of profitable return and tried to correct the evils which had developed. Time and again in the years after the war associations and pools were formed which were to end the need for unfair competition and to stabilize rates. Associations took various forms, some being so loose in their nature that they were little more than agreements between roads to cooperate when cooperation would be mutually beneficial. Pools were much more definite in their aims and provisions: they might concern freight, passengers or money, but all were intended to end needless competition by dividing according to a prearranged plan the railroad business covered by the pool. They originated in New England, but they were first of importance west of the Mississippi. A pool of passenger traffic between Chicago and Omaha was formed in 1870 and lasted until 1882; after a lapse of a year it was renewed until 1887 when the Interstate Commerce Act made it illegal. But this record was very unusual: most pools lasted only for a few months, or at most a few years. And even while the pools were in effect, the member roads were preparing for the period of bitter competition which would inevitably follow their dissolution; at most these brief periods of cooperation were similar to periods of

10 *Interstate Commerce Commission Report*, 1887, p. 1077.

armed neutrality, in which each road kept careful watch that a rival did not start breaking the rules of the neutrality before it did. The pooling agreements failed to last because they were essentially gentlemen's agreements in a time when railroads were operated under anarchic conditions. The courts held that pooling contracts were extra-legal, as are gambling contracts, so there was no way of enforcing them. Just before the Interstate Commerce Act made them illegal, the Southern Railway & Steamship Association, one of the best organized pools, attempted to make the agreements effective by providing a system of deposits and forfeits, but the experiment was too short-lived to prove its value.[11]

As time went on it became more and more obvious that the railroad situation could not be corrected unless some greater power than that vested in individual railroad executives were invoked. Railroads were of a quasi-public nature; not only the roads, but the public too were sufferers from the conditions existing, so inevitably there developed a demand for regulatory legislation. Several of the mid-Western states passed laws prescribing maximum rates for freight and passenger traffic and severely punishing unjust discrimination by the roads. But two factors rendered these laws ineffective, the efforts of the roads to control legislation and the decisions of the Supreme Court. Whenever hostile laws were proposed in any state legislature, a strong railroad lobby would quickly appear. One method of preventing the passage of reasonable laws was to have friends of the railroad introduce a huge number of bills each session; some of the proposals would be so stringent that no sane man could vote for them; some would be so favorable to the roads that only paid employees of the company could vote for them; but the very number of the proposals prevented a majority of

11 H. T. Newcomb, "The Present Railway Situation," *North American Review*, November, 1897, pp. 591-599; Langstroth, Charles and Stilz, Wilson, *Railway Cooperation*, Philadelphia: University of Pennsylvania, 1899, pp. 90-91.

the legislature from agreeing on any one. When this simple procedure threatened to fail, more direct methods were used: representatives who had been elected because of their promises to restrict the railroads were discovered to have voted in favor of the roads; that the representative might be defeated at the next election was unimportant: the roads would either give him a good job or else would set him up in a private business of his own. Even outright bribery was common: at times representatives were paid in cash and more often they were given free passes over the lines of the road. Before the Interstate Commerce Act became effective, it was estimated that one-tenth of all the passengers on the Union Pacific traveled on these passes.[12]

Despite the activities of railroad lobbyists, several of the mid-Western states had succeeded in passing restrictive laws and it seemed probable that the worst excesses of the roads could be ended. In 1876 and 1877 the Supreme Court had declared that a state could legislate maximum rates for grain elevators operated by railroads and that a state could regulate rates within its boundaries, even if such regulation affected persons outside the state, until Congress should legislate on the matter. But in 1886 the decision of the Court in another case reversed this stand and dashed the hopes of those who advocated state action to restrict the roads. In the Wabash Case the Court ruled that a state could not regulate rates even within its own boundaries for goods in interstate commerce; the Constitution delegated the control of interstate commerce to the national government.[13]

After state legislation had become futile, agitation for Congressional action brought the Interstate Commerce Act of

12 *Railroad Legislation in the Light of Past Experience, 1885-1905*, testimony of Edward Rosewater, editor of Omaha *Bee*, before Senate Select Committee, 1886, 23-page pamphlet.

13 Munn *v.* Illinois (1876) 94 U. S. 113; Peik *v.* Chicago & Northwestern Railroad (1877), 94 U. S. 164; Wabash Railroad *v.* Illinois (1886), 118 U. S. 557.

1887. Although overlooking the decision of the Supreme Court which had been the immediate cause of the passage of the Act, the Commission summarized the reasons for its creation in its first report:

Those who have controlled the railroads have not only made rules for the government of their own corporate affairs, but very largely also they have determined at pleasure what should be the terms of their contractual relations with others, and others have acquiesced, though often times unwillingly, because they could not with confidence affirm that the law would not compel it, and a test of the question would be difficult and expensive. The carriers of the country were thus enabled to determine in great measure what rules should govern the transportation of persons and property; rules which intimately concerned the commercial, industrial and social life of the people.[14]

The Interstate Commerce Act, however, proved only a mild palliative where some thoroughgoing reform was imperative. The Act had forbidden the railroads to charge more for " the transportation of passengers or of like kinds of property, under substantially similar circumstances and conditions, for a shorter than for a longer distance over the same line, in the same direction, the shorter being included within the longer distance." But the courts interpreted the qualifications in a broad sense, so that it was almost impossible for the Commission to find any cases where the law applied. Pools had been forbidden and the railroads protested that they could not make money if pools were not permitted. The few years immediately following the creation of the Interstate Commerce Commission proved less prosperous than those immediately preceding, and the roads laid the blame on the Act. Although the law against granting rebates, if observed, meant that the roads would thereafter collect full rates, and the section requiring publicity for tariff schedules was meant to prevent the irresponsible slashing of

14 *Interstate Commerce Commission Report*, 1887, p. 1074.

rates, nevertheless the roads continued to attack the Act because of the prohibitions on pooling and the long and short haul clause. And undoubtedly the Act had injured many roads, especially the smaller and less efficient lines. If each company had to charge its full, published rates and none could make special discounts to get traffic, most of the business went to those having the best terminals, the fastest trains and the largest systems. Strict enforcement of the Act might mean ruin for the smaller roads.

Perforce, within about a year of the passage of the Act, the roads began to practice all the former discriminations. The long and short haul clause and the prohibition on rebates were violated; tariffs were changed just as frequently, if a bit more secretly than before, and the annual commissions to brokers, often amounting to more than $100,000 for a single road, continued to drain away receipts.[15] Although it had been created to enforce the provisions of the Interstate Commerce Act, the Commission found itself powerless. Three decisions of the federal courts nullified all its efforts. The first decision had declared that a witness before the Interstate Commerce Commission need not testify if by so doing he might incriminate himself; not until 1896 did the Supreme Court approve an act which required witnesses to testify on condition that they be not prosecuted for their testimony. In another case a lower court decided that it might take up a case referred to it for enforcement by the Commission as though it were an original case; this decision meant that the Commission had no final authority to make decisions, and increased the already over-long delays in enforcing the law. A third decision denied to the Commission the right to prescribe what would be a reasonable rate for a road to charge; the Commission might only declare that a given rate would be unreasonable.[16]

15 *Interstate Commerce Commission Reports*, 1887, pp. 1071-1081 and 1888-1892, *passim*. Also, Langstroth and Stilz, *op. cit.*, pp. 72-3.

16 Adams, Henry C., "A Decade of Federal Railway Regulation," *Atlantic*

Despite the impotence of the Commission, companies claimed that it was because of the interference of the national and state governments that rates were steadily being forced down and that since pools were forbidden, they were unable to prevent further decline. It was indubitably true that freight rates were falling, and freight business brought in nearly three-fourths of the railroads' total income.[17] The cost of shipping a bushel of wheat from Chicago to New York by rail dropped in fifteen years from 42.6 cents in 1868 to 16.1 cents in 1883.[18] During the eighties the average freight rates between these two cities declined between one-third and one-fourth.[19] Average receipts per ton mile for the whole country declined from 1.99 cents in 1870 to 1.17 cents in 1880; a further drop brought the average to 0.91 cents by 1890, less than one-half of the figure of two decades earlier.[20]

Although they blamed the government for this decline, the roads continued to attempt so to organize themselves that rates could be stabilized.[21] The chaos which, despite the efforts of the Commission, was the rule rather than the exception, was described by J. N. Faithorn, Chairman of the Western Freight Association, in an interview which was copied into the annual report of the Interstate Commerce Commission:

The situation in the West is so bad that it could hardly be worse. Rates are absolutely demoralized, and neither the shippers, the passengers, the railways, or the public make anything by this state of

Monthly, April, 1898, LXXXI, pp. 434-443. Counselman *v.* Hitchcock, 142 U. S. 547; Brown *v.* Walker, 161 U. S. 591; Kentucky and Indiana Bridge Company *v.* Louisville & N. R. Railroad, 37 F. 567, 149 U. S. 777; Cincinnati, New Orleans & Texas Pacific Ry. Co. *v.* I. C. C., 162 U. S. 196.

17 Adams, Henry C. (special agent), *Report on Transportation Business in the United States at the Eleventh Census*, Part I, p. 12.

18 Appleton, *Annual Cyclopedia*, 1883, p. 152.

19 *Interstate Commerce Commission Statistics*, 1890, pp. 197-229.

20 Nimmo, Joseph, *The Railroad Problem, 1901-2* (volume of pamphlets, 1901-2), Section 7, p. 11.

21 Appleton, *Annual Cyclopedia*, 1884-1892, *passim*.

affairs. The profit is all secured by the middleman, the go-between. Take passenger rates, for instance. They are very low, but who get the benefit of the reduction? Why, no one but the scalpers, who have nothing at stake, everything to win and nothing to lose. In freight matters the case is just the same. Certain shippers are allowed heavy rebates, while others are made to pay full rates. Some of these shippers are constantly afraid of being hauled up before the Interstate Commerce Commission, but they need have no fear from that direction. The management of rates is dishonored on all sides and there is not a road in the country that can be accused of living up to the rules of the interstate commerce law. Of course, when some poor devil comes along and wants a pass to save him from starvation he has several clauses from the interstate act read to him. But when a rich shipper wants a pass, why, he gets it at once.[22]

The Interstate Commerce Act proved impotent to control the railroads, but no other authority was comprehensive or strong enough to do a better job. Undoubtedly some more stringent national law was needed, but not until the early years of the twentieth century did the demand for it become sufficiently strong to force action in Congress. Meanwhile railroads continued to operate amid the accustomed anarchic conditions.

Despite the complaints with which officials rent the air, the railroads in the late eighties and early nineties still constituted a profitable industry. In 1889, a normal year, the ratio of operating expenses to operating income for the roads of the nation was 65.34 per cent, leaving nearly 35 per cent of the roads' income with which to pay bond interest and dividends. Interest was paid that year on 78.31 per cent of the bonds outstanding. Although no return whatever was paid on $2,374,-200,906 of stock,[23] an average dividend of over 5 per cent was paid on 38.33 per cent of all the stock outstanding,[24] and some

22 *Interstate Commerce Commission Report*, 1890, p. 25.

23 *Ibid.*, 1889, p. 31.

24 *Senate Committee on Interstate Commerce*, 67th Congress, 2nd Session, III, table facing p. 1508.

dividends amounted to over 11 per cent.[25] What was, perhaps, of more importance, the percentage of stock-paying dividends was steadily increasing, and the amound paid out annually in dividends was rapidly growing.[26]

Railroads, rather than suffering unduly at the hands of aggressive state and national bodies, continued to prosper or be depressed in sympathy with the general business conditions of the country. In years of poor mid-Western grain crops, the Granger roads suffered; in years of poor cotton crops, the Southern roads showed losses, and the transcontinentals and Eastern trunk lines depended for their profits on the general business activity of the regions they served.[27] So in 1892 the Eastern and far Western lines were enjoying a moderate prosperity, and looking forward to a banner year in 1893 when the Chicago World's Fair would lead to an increase in traffic. The mid-Western roads were experiencing a boom period, carrying the huge crops of 1891 and the winter wheat of 1892. In the South, on the other hand, during the first half of the year the roads had a hard time making ends meet, but a rise in the price of cotton during the later part of the year brought a return of prosperity.[28]

Although serious problems faced the industry in the first years of the nineties, the prospects for the future were not particularly ominous. There was every probability that necessary adjustments would be made without undue effort. But instead of facing normal conditions, the roads were soon in the midst of one of the worst depressions the United States had ever known. Early in 1893 an epidemic of business failures swept the country: 573 banks, mostly local institutions in the South and West, closed their doors; in the first half of the year,

25 *Interstate Commerce Commission Report*, 1889, p. 31.

26 *Senate Committee on Interstate Commerce*, 67th Congress, 2nd Session, III, p. 1508.

27 Appleton, *Annual Cyclopedia*, 1879-1892, *passim*.

28 *Ibid.*, 1892, pp. 176-77.

8,105 commercial failures were recorded, nearly double the number for the same period the preceding year. Disastrous crop failures in 1894 and a slackening in the European demand for American wheat combined to involve the farmers in the general distress.[29] Bread lines formed in the cities; Coxey's Army moved on Washington; strikes were innumerable, and the bitter struggle in Chicago, originating in the Pullman Strike, served to make manifest the dangerous tension existing throughout the nation.

The panic itself, which preceded the long depression, lasted a scant ten months. In development it differed in no way from the pattern which was already familiar through frequent repetition: "One or two powerful corporations, which had been leading in the general plunge into debt, gave the first signals of distress."[30] The Philadelphia & Reading Railroad, capitalized at $40,000,000 and with a debt of over $125,000,000, acknowledged itself insolvent on February 20; eleven weeks later, on May 5, the National Cordage Company, with a combined total capital and liabilities of over $30,000,000, went into receivership. "The management of both these enterprises had been marked by the rashest sort of speculation; both had been favorites on the speculative markets. The bubble of inflated credit having been thus punctured, a general movement of liquidation started. This movement immediately developed very serious symptoms."[31] Panic spread quickly and throughout the spring, summer and autumn, failure after failure was reported from coast to coast. By late November this movement of liquidation had exhausted itself and the first essential for a slow resurgence of confidence in the business outlook was thereby achieved. Nevertheless the restoration of prosperity was of

29 Bogart, E. L., *Economic History of the American People*, New York: Longmans, Green and Company, 1930, pp. 725-726.

30 Noyes, Alexander D., *Forty Years of American Finance*, New York: G. P. Putnam's Sons, 1909, p. 188.

31 *Ibid.*, p. 189.

necessity very slow; the collapse had been too wide-spread to admit of a rapid return:

The record of business failures for the year gives some conception of the ruin involved in this forced liquidation. Commercial failures alone in 1893 were three times as numerous as those of 1873, and the aggregate liabilities involved were fully fifty per cent greater. It was computed that nine commercial houses out of every thousand doing business in the United States failed in 1873; in 1893, the similar reckoning showed thirteen in every thousand. The after-effects of the wholesale destruction presently appeared. So long as prices in every security and commodity were forced abnormally low by the necessities of domestic holders, foreign capital came into the markets in great amounts in search of panic bargains. But with prices moderately advanced above the lowest, bargain hunters left off buying, some them sold again to take profits, and domestic trade was left to the crippled consumer.[32]

The consumer was so thoroughly crippled that it was nearly six years before trade resumed its normal upward trend at the point from which it had been dizzily catapulted in 1893.

Severe though the panic and ensuing depression were for the general business interests of the country, the ruin among the railroads was singled out as indicative of the unheard-of destruction these years wrought in economic life in the United States. In its report for the twelve months ending June 30, 1894, which was roughly the first year of the depression, the Interstate Commerce Commission declared:

Never in the history of transportation in the United States has such a large percentage of railway mileage been under the control of receiverships as on June 30, 1894. There were on that date 192 railways in the hands of receivers, of which 126 had been consigned to receiverships during the previous twelve months, and 35 during the year ending June 30, 1893. The mileage of line operated by these defaulting companies was 40,818 miles. The total capitali-

32 *Ibid.*, p. 201.

zation of roads in the hands of receivers was about $2,500,000,000, that is to say, one-fourth of the total railway capitalization of the country. This, as a record of insolvency, is without parallel in the previous history of American railways, except it be in the period from 1838 to 1842.[33]

The *Commercial and Financial Chronicle,* in December of 1893 when the worst was already over, still could see very little that was encouraging in the railroad outlook:

That suspensions and reductions (of dividends) within the year have on the whole been so few comparatively, especially among the larger companies, is due mainly to two circumstances; first, the fact that not a few companies had already in previous years passed off the dividend list or greatly scaled down the rate of return paid, and, secondly, the fact that the effects of the unfavorable conditions now existing can hardly as yet be said to have fully developed to their full extent.[34]

Three weeks before the same journal had gotten cold comfort from the fact that the panic promised to reverse the two established tendencies which were hurting the railroads: the simultaneous decline of rates and increase in operating expenses.[35] The very necessity of seeking compensatory benefits in such dubious advantages, however, is indicative of the straits to which the railroads had been reduced.

Returns to investors in railroad securities steadily became more infrequent as the depression lingered. For several years before June 30, 1893, about 60 per cent of the capital stock of American railways had paid no dividends.[36] In the year ending then 61.24 per cent of the stock paid nothing [37] and in another

33 *Interstate Commerce Commission Statistics,* 1894, p. 10.
34 *Commercial and Financial Chronicle,* December 30, 1893, pp. 1108-9.
35 *Ibid.,* December 9, 1893, p. 961.
36 *Interstate Commerce Commission Statistics,* 1894, pp. 36-37.
37 *Ibid.,* 1895, pp. 68-73.

twelve months the percentage had advanced to 63.43.[38] For the year ending June 30, 1895, the figure had skyrocketed to 70.06.[39] This percentage varied little in the next two years;[40] however, by the middle of 1898 the worst was over.[41] Only 59.39 per cent of the capital stock made no return in the year that ended June 30, 1899,[42] and the steady return of prosperity was thereafter manifested by a constant shrinkage in the amount of stock in this category.[43]

While railroad capital was so unremunerative, it is small wonder that investment in new trackage shrank to a mere fraction of its yearly norm. From 1893 to 1897 less than 2000 miles were built yearly and in 1897 a low mark was reached with the laying of only about 1600 miles of new road. Only in 1900 did a revival in construction become marked; in that year about 5000 miles were laid. The falling off in this respect is emphasized by the fact that in 1890 there were 25.99 miles of railway track for every 10,000 people in the United States, and in 1900 there were only 25.44 miles per 10,000 of population.[44] The railroads of the country had failed to keep pace with the growth of population during the depression. Their total capitalization in the nineties showed strikingly the reluctance of the investing public to put more money into railroad securities. In 1894 the total combined capitalization of all roads amounted to $10,796,473,813;[45] four years passed before this figure was again equalled.[46] Not until about the turn of the century did capital freely flow into railroad securities again.[47]

---

38 *Ibid.*, 1896, pp. 51-55.   39 *Ibid.*, 1897, pp. 94-99.

40 *Ibid.*, 1898, pp. 76-81; and 1899, pp. 98-99.

41 *Ibid.*, 1900, pp. 58-64.   42 *Ibid.*, 1901, pp. 67-73.

43 *Ibid.*, 1902, pp. 53-61; and 1903, pp. 69-76; for the years ending June 30, 1900 and 1901, the percentages were 54.34 and 48.73 respectively.

44 *Ibid.*, 1900, p. 13.

45 *Ibid.*, 1896, pp. 51-55.

46 *Ibid.*, 1900, pp. 58-64.

47 *Ibid.*, 1901, pp. 67-73; and 1902, pp. 53-61.

Important and portentous as these factors were, however, the stagnation of railroad construction, the cessation of growth of railway capital and the diminished returns from capital invested, fail to convey quite so strikingly the severity of the depression as does the record of receiverships. But certain questions arise concerning the roads which acknowledged their insolvency: were these roads cut down in the midst of prosperity, by the sudden sweep of panic across the country, as their citation as economic barometers might presuppose? Or were they roads which were just struggling along and barely keeping solvent at best? Or were they roads which were bankrupt *de facto* before financial stringency brought *de jure* bankruptcy?

CHAPTER II
OVER-EXPANSION

When panic swept the country in 1893 the first prominent road affected, and one whose failure helped precipitate further liquidation, was the Philadelphia & Reading Railroad Company. After receivers had been appointed for this company in February, five months elapsed before the New York, Lake Erie & Western acknowledged insolvency. In mid-August the cumbersome Northern Pacific system, with its chief subsidiaries, the Wisconsin Central Railroad Company and the Chicago & Northern Pacific, applied for the protection of the courts. Almost exactly two months later a second transcontinental system, the Union Pacific, with its subsidiaries, the Oregon Railway & Navigation Company and the Oregon Short Line & Utah Northern, went into receivership; and on December 18, the Union Pacific, Denver & Gulf followed the rest of the system. Close on the heels of this failure came the bankruptcy of the Atchison, Topeka & Santa Fe. With the Atchison were involved the St. Louis & San Francisco, the Colorado Midland and the Atlantic & Pacific. After this violent storm of failure, a lull followed before the Norfolk & Western collapsed in February, 1895, and then more than a year elapsed before the venerable Baltimore & Ohio acknowledged insolvency. Three great transcontinental systems, one large Southern system and four prominent Eastern trunk lines had fallen victims to the movement toward liquidation. Innumerable lesser lines had failed, but these failures were for the most part of very minor importance to the nation as a whole and what importance they did have frequently lay in their absorption by the larger lines which reorganized many of them.

As receivership followed receivership during 1893 and the following years, economic critics and railroad officials advanced various theories calculated to explain the causes and meanings of the ruin which at times threatened to envelop the entire railroad industry of the country. One railroad periodical admitted quite frankly that:

The fact that the totals are so largely made up by a few great companies which had long been staggering under their load of debts and were at last obliged to confess insolvency gives reason to hope that the figures for the entire year (1894) will show a much less mortality than its ever memorable predecessors, 1893 and 1892.[1]

However, the majority of railroad men were not so ready to admit the validity of such a simple interpretation. The favorite explanations advanced were low rates and excessive regulatory legislation by state and national governments. Even the periodical quoted above had held very different views a scant six months before; at the end of 1893, reviewing the railroad receiverships of the year, it believed:

Ruinously low rates caused the fearful destruction of railway investments indicated by the record of receiverships in this issue. It was not lack of business; it was not bad management; it was not excessive cost of construction; it was not even the existence of too many railroads. At reasonable rates the hundreds of companies that in the last few years have gone into bankruptcy might have earned a fair return on the investment.[2]

Vice-president Frank S. Bond of the Chicago, Milwaukee & St. Paul stated in February, 1894, that:

There is a feeling on the part of railway men that the present is a good time for putting the position of the railways fairly before the public. That position they claim to be as follows: the railways are the most important industry in the country and represent far more capital invested than does any other industry. They are unable to return a fair interest on the capital, after making allowances for " water " in capitalization, and the reason is because they have been interfered with by legislatures, and have been refused the power to obtain fair rates by preventing senseless competition. They have now reached the point at which something must be done.

1 *Railway Age and Northwestern Railroader*, July 13, 1894, pp. 389-390.
2 *Ibid.*, December 15, 1893, p. 887.

The loss suffered by the community from the railways which have collapsed far exceeds the advantage gained from lower rates and competition.   The loss affects not merely capitalists, but also a far greater number of employes both directly of the roads and of the industries of which railways are the largest supporters.[3]

About the same time the Chicago *Tribune* printed opinions on the railroad situation from some of the leading railroad men of the mid-West, including President T. B. Blackstone of the Alton, President R. R. Cable and General-manager E. St. John of the Rock Island, President Stuyvesant Fish and Vice-president E. H. Harriman of the Illinois Central, Chairman H. H. Porter of the Chicago & Eastern Illinois, Vice-president E. P. Ripley of the Chicago, Milwaukee & St. Paul, George M. Pullman and J. W. Midgely, Chairman of the Western Freight Association. The consensus of opinion advanced by these men was that the depression had hurt the railroads, but that the failures were only the culmination of a long period of diminishing profits with lowered or passed dividends and defaulted interest. All these phenomena were caused by reductions in rates due, in turn, to cut-throat competition and state and national meddling with railroad matters, and to the building of unnecessary mileage which only increased the unnecessary competition. The higher costs of labor and the demands of the public for better service at lowered rates were of equal importance. Particularly, all agreed in emphasizing the unfortunate influence on railroad development of the Inter-state Commerce Act which had led to interference in railroad management by government officials who knew nothing of railroading.[4]

Simon Sterne, a recognized authority, had the temerity in 1894 to publish an article in *Forum* casting reflections on the railroad managements of the few preceding years. The *Commercial and Financial Chronicle* was horrified:

3 *Railway World*, February 24, 1894, p. 145.
4 *Commercial and Financial Chronicle*, February 3, 1894, pp. 206-207.

But the most surprising statement in Mr. Sterne's paper is the assertion contained in the following quotation: " The first explanation of the phase of the railroad problem presented by the events of 1893 lies in the fact that the railways have outgrown the ability of the community to furnish men of the high moral and intellectual order necessary for their proper administration." We should not have expected Mr. Sterne to venture such an assertion, for in our estimation, there is absolutely nothing in the history of railroad affairs in the United States to furnish even plausible ground for it. . . . That railroad men have been lacking in ability and fitness to manage the systems and that this is the cause of the recent failures—that is a view so utterly untenable we hesitate whether to take it seriously.[5]

But even if it could not take seriously the explanation advanced by Mr. Sterne for the troubles of the railroads, at least the *Chronicle* was unable to answer Mr. Sterne's comments on the absurdity of blaming these troubles on the Interstate Commerce Commission:

A commission, therefore, consisting of reasonable and intelligent gentlemen who are not even clothed with the power of a court; who are without authority to make any arbitrary rulings, or of enforcing them by direct action, if they should make them; whose investigating functions have, in large proportions, been nibbled away by the judicial interpretations of the last three years; whose decrees are disobeyed; whose mandates have in several instances been set at defiance; and who, since the enactment of the law, have year by year, been deprived by decisions in the Federal Courts of almost the whole of their controlling moral force—cannot be held responsible; nor can the Act which it is their function to interpret and cause to be observed be held, in any but a very remote and to an almost inappreciable degree, responsible for the extraordinary calamity which has overtaken the railway enterprise of the country. We must therefore look elsewhere for a cause.[6]

5 *Ibid., Investors' Supplement,* March, 1894, pp. 1-2.

6 Sterne, Simon, " Recent Railroad Failures and their Lessons," *Forum,* March, 1894, pp. 19-38.

Railroad critics a few years later had no trouble finding a cause for the failures in the very charge which the *Chronicle* had not been able to take seriously. E. S. Meade, writing in 1901, was even more outspoken than Mr. Sterne had been:

The panic of 1893 revealed the precarious condition of many of the largest systems . . . (and) the searching examination of their affairs which followed their efforts for rehabilitation revealed the facts that the bankrupt roads were greatly overcapitalized, that their bonds were improperly secured, that their traffic agreements and leases were often a burden rather than a help, and that in many cases they had been badly, even fraudulently, managed.[7]

Stuart Daggett after an exhaustive study of these failures, concluded that:

It is interesting to observe that the majority of the principal railroads which failed in the nineties had taxed their resources nearly to the point of exhaustion before the panic of 1893 finally drove them to the wall.[8]

The financial margins on which many of the bankrupt roads had been operating were far too narrow for safety: the Atchison, the Union Pacific, the Erie, the Reading and the Northern Pacific owed, for operating expenses and fixed charges in 1892, the year before the depression, over 95 per cent of their gross earnings; in other words, in each of these cases, a reduction of 5 per cent in gross earnings would bring insolvency even if no other obligations had to be met.[9]

Examination of the eight largest companies which failed during the depression leaves no doubt of the truth of these last assertions. All of these companies, except the Norfolk & Western, were bankrupt *de facto* before the depression forced them to admit the fact. Except for the Norfolk, all were

7 Meade, E. S., " The Reorganization of Railroads," *Annals of the American Academy of Political and Social Sciences*, pp. 205-43 March, 1901.

8 Daggett, Stuart, *Railroad Reorganization*, Boston: Houghton, Mifflin Company, 1908, p. 342.

9 *Railroad Gazette*, February 23, 1894, pp. 141-142.

over-capitalized to a greater or less degree; in several cases the management had looted the company, in others the true condition of the road had been hidden by manipulation of its annual balance sheets. In one case, that of the Erie, a defect in the conditions attached to the bonds prevented the raising of new capital when it was needed and thereby aggravated the troubles which a huge over-capitalization had initiated; in the case of the Atchison, serious mistakes in a previous reorganization had created an intolerable situation which was in good part responsible for the subsequent mismanagement of the system. In every case except possibly that of the Erie, the management had tried to expand so rapidly and so carelessly that the edifice soon became top-heavy. The financial foundations on which these great systems were reared were rotten at the core and eventually the strain proved too much in each case. The peculiar circumstances of the Norfolk & Western failure, although not characterized by the overcapitalization and near-criminal mismanagement of the other systems, indicated a similar weak financial structure just at the moment when panic swept the country.

The depression proved the last straw in each case, but to blame the several receiverships on that alone is to overlook more fundamental and important factors. While these underlying influences were inextricably mingled in the failure of each road, nevertheless it is possible to divide the bankrupt roads into three general categories: those failing primarily because of over-expansion, such as the Norfolk & Western and the Northern Pacific; those whose failures were fundamentally attributable to mistakes of past managements, which were publicly known long before the roads were forced into receiverships, the Erie, the Atchison and the Union Pacific; and those whose bankruptcies were followed by sensational disclosures of poor or even criminal management, the Baltimore & Ohio, the Richmond Terminal and the Philadelphia & Reading.

The failure of the Norfolk & Western presented one of the simplest problems of the depression casualties: a company which had been efficiently managed and had excellent prospects for the future, completed an expansion program just before the panic of 1893 swept the country, and in the weakened financial position which expansion had invoked the depression proved too much for it. Although not one of the great Eastern trunk lines, in 1893 the Norfolk & Western controlled about 1500 miles of track, mostly in Virginia with extensions westward. The history of the road went back to 1851 when the Virginia Legislature chartered the Norfolk & Petersburg line which was to be owned in part by the state. Later the state sold out its interest and the road became a part of the Atlantic, Mississippi & Ohio Railroad. The latter was unable to keep out of the hands of receivers and from the wreckage of this road the Norfolk & Western Railway was organized in 1880.[10]

In the years just prior to the depression of 1893 the Norfolk had indulged in a fairly rapid expansion of its system. This program had been characterized by the construction of an extension into Ohio and the building of other lines into the as yet unexploited mineral regions of West Virginia and the surrounding territory to the south and west. These regions were being slowly developed and coal and iron were being mined, but as the tonnage carried by the Norfolk increased, its revenues were not proportionally enlarged. The chief items of freight, coal and iron in this region and cotton on the southeastern parts of the system, were all low class freight, paying very low rates, despite the long hauls to markets. As a result net revenue was not improving at all.[11]

By 1891 conditions had begun to be somewhat alarming. Nevertheless an authority on railroad investments still foresaw a prosperous future for the system:

Some people anticipate a serious diminution of the surplus available for dividends in 1892; but even if this forecast proves

10 Snyder, Carl, *American Railways as Investments*, New York: The Moody Corporation, 1907, pp. 510-518.

11 *Commercial and Financial Chronicle*, March 31, 1894, pp. 534-536.

correct, there will be no cause for apprehension. There can be no doubt whatever that the system possesses such inherent strength and such brilliant prospects that it will resume its prosperous career as soon as it emerges from the state of suspense its affairs have been in since the commencement of work on the Ohio extension.[12]

Before the end of 1892, however, the pessimistic predictions were realized. Hitherto the preferred stock had regularly paid a 3 per cent dividend and in April the usual semi-annual 1½ per cent was voted. But in October only 1 per cent was paid, and that in a scrip which was convertible into debentures. Thereafter dividends on the preferred stock ceased entirely while earnings continued to fall.[13]

The company's annual report for the year ending December 31, 1892, revealed the difficult position in which the Norfolk found itself when the panic of 1893 occurred. The gross revenue for the year was the largest in the history of the system. More passengers and more freight were carried one mile during the year than ever before; the tonnage of iron ore, pig iron, coal, coke, stone and zinc established new records. But the net income showed a decrease from that of the year before. A decline in the price of cotton had created an acute depression in that industry, resulting in a 54 per cent loss in the number of bales transported by the road. The rates for carrying pig iron fell lower than ever and at the same time the tonnage of high class freight declined. The average rate received for freight was only 0.537 cents per ton mile for the system as a whole;[14] to this the 0.663 cent rate received by the other roads in the same region [15] offers a revealing contrast.

But despite the plight into which the road had fallen, it was

12 Van Oss, S. F., *American Railroads as Investments*, New York: G. P. Putnam's Sons, 1893, p. 760.

13 *Railway World*, February 16, 1895, pp. 132-133.

14 *Norfolk & Western Annual Report, 1892*; *Commercial and Financial Chronicle*, April 1, 1893, p. 519.

15 *Interstate Commerce Commission Statistics*, 1894, p. 64.

still solvent when a receivership was announced early in June. A creditor, to whom it owed $44,000, applied to a West Virginia court for the appointment of receivers for the system and the request was temporarily granted. When the circumstances of the claim were revealed, the receivership was hastily annulled three days later. The Norfolk was ready to pay the debt but the cash set aside for that purpose had been tied up by an attachment issued at the request of a creditor of the claimant, so that the money could only be paid over to the Norfolk's creditor on an order of the court. As soon as the order was forthcoming from the court, the money was paid. Meanwhile, however, during the three-day receivership the credit of the road had been damaged; that a great system, capitalized at $103,500,000, apparently could not pay a debt of a few thousand dollars seemed inexplicable and roused various rumors of imminent total collapse.[16]

Just before the temporary embarrassment of the Norfolk an arrangement was announced by which some much needed cash would be raised. The floating debt was not only mounting steadily, but the system also faced the maturity of $525,000 of 6 per cent debenture bonds early in 1894. To meet these needs and provide ample working capital, a syndicate had been formed which would guarantee the success of an offer of Norfolk & Western stock and bonds. $5,000,000 of 5 per cent gold mortgage bonds maturing January 1, 1900, and $5,000,000 of preferred stock were to be offered to the shareholders at a total price of $5,250,000. If the issue were not completely taken up by the stockholders, the syndicate would take the remainder at the same price.[17] The operation was successfully accomplished, but the necessity of giving such a premium in order to sell its securities revealed the weakness of the system's credit only too clearly.

A continued decline in freight rates, despite a further in-

16 *Railway Age and Northwestern Railroader,* June 9, 1893, p. 447.
17 *Railway World,* June 10, 1893, p. 542.

crease in the gross revenues, brought a still smaller net income in the year ending December 31, 1893, and for the first time in years there was a deficit, $99,742, under fixed charges. The net fell off to $2,833,157, having decreased more than $500,000 in three years. At the same time, because of the additional mileage that had been added to the system and other capital expenditures, the fixed charges were growing every year.[18] Contrary to the expectations of the management, the net did not increase with the gross receipts because of the increased operating expenses of the greater mileage and the concurrent steady decline of rates. In 1894 the average rate per ton mile for freight had fallen to 0.451 cents, a loss of 10 per cent from the figure the year before. This decline in rates, in turn, was due to several cooperating factors: the road's proportion of low class freight was constantly rising and that of high class freight as constantly dropping; although the Norfolk had to carry its coal twice as far as rival roads to transport it from the mines to tidewater, it was forced to cut its rates sufficiently to meet the retail market price its competitors charged; finally, about 439 miles of the 1567 mile total length of the system, 28 per cent, lay in regions which were yet to be developed and, since the depression prevented the rapid exploitation which had been expected there, rates had to be cut to get any trade. Had the depression been postponed until the Norfolk had had time to develop these regions, the system's strength would have been immeasurably increased, but instead the depression caught the system at the precise moment of its greatest weakness. The financial statement for the year 1894, in the face of these adverse conditions, showed alarming deficits. Operating expenses and fixed charges exceeded revenue by $325,376; in addition, $147,715 had been advanced to leased lines to cover their deficits. Further, the equipment mortgage of 1888 had required the purchase of $145,300 of these bonds. The total

18 *Annual Report*, 1893; *Commercial and Financial Chronicle*, March 31, 1894, pp. 534-536.

deficit for the Norfolk had been $618,392 for the year, and the prospects were that in 1895 it would be over $1,000,000.[19]

With the company hopelessly falling behind as every month passed, on February 6, 1896, a friendly federal court was petitioned to appoint receivers and promptly complied with the request.[20] As the *Commercial and Financial Chronicle* declared, the receivership was not unexpected, but nonetheless it disappointed financial circles. The road's management had succeeded for so long in staving off insolvency that hopes for a successful solution of its problems had been high. The system had been very well managed: within a few years it had built up such an enormous traffic as to rank as " one of the marvels of the time." [21] The integrity of the officers was further shown when the secretary of the bondholders' protective committee announced six months after the receivership that

at the instance of the Committee a thorough investigation and exhaustive report of the accounts of the company for the last three years has been made by the accountants, Messrs. Price, Waterhouse and Company, the result of which, save some modifications of minor importance, is considered by the Committee as confirming the accuracy of the company's reports and accounts.[22]

In contrast to the sorry showings so many railroad managements made, when their accounts were subjected to the impartial scrutiny of expert accountants, the Norfolk's officials had reason for self-congratulation when this report was published.

The immediate cause of the receivership was not difficult to find; as the petition for it pointed out, earnings had fallen off so badly that the deficit was increasing daily, while the depressed condition of the stock market precluded raising money by ad-

19 *Annual Report, 1894*; *Commercial and Financial Chronicle*, May 18, 1895, pp. 857-858.

20 *Railway World*, February 9, 1895, p. 101.

21 *Commercial and Financial Chronicle*, February 9, 1895, pp. 236-237.

22 *Railway Age and Northwestern Railroader*, August 16, 1895, p. 406.

vantageous sales of securities.[23] A year later, the reorganization committee succinctly stated the more fundamental causes of failure:

The recently constructed extensions, the full earning capacity of which could not be developed in so short a time (as elapsed after their completion and before the depression).

The general depression which resulted in the reduction of rates, especially those for the transportation of coal.

The heavy payments on principal of Car Trusts, which, as a matter of necessity, had to be provided for to a large extent out of revenue, there being no other means of paying the same.[24]

This latter payment amounted to about $150,000 annually for interest. In addition, during the next eight years about $3,-500,000 of the principal would have to be paid.[25] The only result of diminishing revenues and increased operating expenses and fixed charges must be failure, unless the trends could be reversed in time. Failing this, the inevitable happened despite the best efforts of a progressive and efficient management.

Like that of the Norfolk, the failure of the Northern Pacific late in the summer of 1893 was primarily attributable to the over-expansion of the system. But there the similarity ends. Whereas the gradual downfall of the Norfolk was visible to all observers, the crash of the Northern Pacific came suddenly, shrouded in mystery and accompanied by ugly rumors. Whereas the Norfolk's officials had made an enviable record for efficiency and honesty, the Northern Pacific management was widely accused of plundering the company, and at best was guilty of inefficiency and carelessness. Whereas the expansion of the Norfolk had been aimed at one objective which was reasonably certain of attainment, that of the Northern Pacific had often been frenzied and inexcusably blind. A little more

---

23 *Railway World*, March 9, 1895, p. 189.

24 *Reorganization of the Norfolk & Western Railroad Company, Plan and Agreement* and circular letter of submittal to security holders, dated March 12, 1896.

25 *Commercial and Financial Chronicle*, May 18, 1895, pp. 857-858.

time before the depression might have meant salvation for the
Norfolk; the Northern Pacific was tottering before the panic
came and would have been bankrupt soon with or without the
added problems financial stringency brought.

The road had been chartered by Congress in 1864 and immediately came under the domination of Jay Cooke, then at
the apex of his power. When Cooke failed in 1873, the Northern Pacific went into receivership. At the time only that section
of the line extending from Duluth to Bismarck, on the Missouri
River, had been completed, but a syndicate controlled by Henry
Villard bought this fragment at a foreclosure sale in 1875 and
pushed the construction of the line on to the Pacific Coast.
In 1883, with the ceremonial driving of a golden spike, the
continuous track from Duluth to Puget Sound in the Northwest was opened to traffic.[26] No sooner was the ceremony over
than the company was again forced into receivership; the completion of the road through the nearly trackless forests of the
Northwest had exhausted its credit and left it no working
capital.[27] The reorganized road did not include Villard among
its officials, but before long he returned as chairman of the
board of directors.

By the autumn of 1892 the system was again in difficulty.
At the stockholders' annual meeting October 20 a special committee consisting of Henry Clews, Brayton Ives, F. K. Sturgis,
William Salomon and Jay Cooke, Jr., was appointed to investigate the " conduct of business and affairs " of the company
by the current management which was dominated by Villard
and President T. F. Oakes. Salomon and Sturgis refused to
serve, so the remaining three employed William R. Rogers,
former chairman of the New York Railroad Commission, as
expert, and proceded with the investigation.[28]

26 Snyder, *op. cit.*, pp. 524-541.

27 Meade, E. S., " The Great American Railway Systems," *Railway
World*, 1905, pp. 397-399, 417-418.

28 *Report of Special Committee To the Stockholders of the Northern
Pacific Railroad Company*, New York: February, 1893, 29-page pamphlet.

The report of the committee first considered certain general characteristics of the Northern Pacific's situation, and then made a detailed study of the expansion program which had been pursued for several years past. A personal tour of the system had convinced the committee that the equipment was in good shape, although certain relatively minor improvements were recommended. The economic development of the regions traversed by the road promised a steady increase in traffic and the committee, very optimistically, saw no cause for apprehension on the part of the Northern Pacific in the competition which completion of the Great Northern to the Pacific Coast would soon offer.

After these laudatory opening remarks the tone of the report changed to one of distinct hostility and condemnation. The floating debt as of June 30, 1892, was $9,918,365.03. On over $8,000,000 of this amount the company was paying 6 per cent interest plus a 2 per cent commission. Recently a loan of $750,000 from the chairman of the board had been renewed at this rate of interest and commission, although at that time the general rate for demand loans was 2 per cent and millions were being offered in the country's financial markets for time loans at between 4 and 5 per cent. That the Northern Pacific should have had to pay the rate it did, despite the lower rates generally current, was typical of the state of the company's credit and the committee believed that Villard was guilty of poor taste at best in participating personally in this exploitation of the company's misfortune. All the bonds reserved for the improvement and betterment of the system had been posted as collateral for the floating debt, so the credit of the road was at a very low ebb.[29]

Although the investigating committee failed to point out the fact, the state of the company's credit could not be entirely blamed on mismanagement. The difficulties and subsequent liquidation of Baring Brothers in 1890 came just at a time

29 *Ibid.*

when the Northern Pacific had let a number of contracts for building extensions to its system, and cancellation of these contracts would have involved heavy losses. Because of the general financial panic the company's bonds could only be sold at a great discount, and rather than sacrifice them the board preferred to borrow at what rates it must, in the hope of re-funding the debt as soon as the panic was over.[30] However, to the remarks of the committee about the company's credit, the management answered that the refunding of the debt was only negotiated through the personal efforts and influence of the chairman, and that it was his example in taking such a large part of the total amount that permitted the negotiation to succeed.[31] This admission that the necessary funds could be gotten in no other way merely confirmed the hostile conclusions in reference to the Northern Pacific credit in 1892 and early in 1893.

The committee also made several criticisms of the condition of the Northern Pacific's branch lines. In all the Northern Pacific had had to make up a deficit of $1,229,961 for the preceding year. Traffic originating on these branches brought gross receipts amounting to $7,315,554 to the parent company. The auditor stated the cost of transporting this traffic was about 40 per cent, so that 60 per cent of this gross could be fairly estimated as profit. On this basis, the company had earned about $4,400,000 clear profit with which to make good the deficit. The report then took up each branch individually, condemning the acquisition of most of them for one reason or another.[32] To this detailed criticism the management replied in an open letter to the stockholders in which it defended its actions and justified its policies.[33]

30 *Railroad Gazette*, March 3, 1893, pp. 161-162, quoting letter from " Stockholder ".

31 *Commercial and Financial Chronicle*, March 4, 1893, pp. 354-356; also prints text of reply made by directors through Oakes, pp. 362-364.

32 *Report of Special Committee.*

33 *Commercial and Financial Chronicle*, March 4, 1893, pp. 362-4, reply of directors.

Until the company had gone into receivership and the many charges and countercharges were aired in court, the public had no way of telling which of the two versions of several transactions was the more accurate, but the report and the reply agreed on some very disquieting facts, especially in pessimistic remarks about the state of the company's credit. And the half-yearly statement for the period ending December 31, 1892, which was published in the middle of February, was not reassuring. Both gross and net receipts had fallen off, mainly because of the industrial depression in the Northwest and a decline in the price of silver in Montana. The effect of the completion of the Great Northern extension could not be accurately predicted.[34]

Continued rumors that the road would default on the bond interest due in June were sharply contradicted by President Oakes. The rumors, he charged, were instigated by Wall Street bears " who are just lying with more than usual vigor about the Northern Pacific ". He also declared that no part of the so-called " floating debt " of $10,000,000 would be due until September and that, before then, plans would have been matured to provide for its payment " without the interference in the form of pretended aid from persons who have sought to break down our property. We are able and shall handle our affairs for the best interests of the property." [35] His acrimonious concluding remarks were directed at Brayton Ives, of the investigating committee, whose offer to form a syndicate which would refund the floating debt of the company at 6 per cent for five years had been ignored by the management.[36]

True to his promise, in the middle of June Oakes announced a refunding agreement. The Northern Pacific would issue five year 6 per cent collateral trust notes, secured by Northern Pacific consolidated 5 per cent bonds, Chicago & Northern

34 *Ibid.*, February 18, 1893, pp. 266-267.

35 *Railway Age and Northwestern Railroader*, May 12, 1893, p. 372.

36 *Ibid.*, May 19, 1893, p. 394.

Pacific bonds, Chicago & Calumet bonds, St. Paul & Northern Pacific stock and Northern Pacific Express Company stock. The rate of interest was high for five-year notes, but on the other hand, it was below the rate usually paid to finance a floating debt. To safeguard the collateral trust notes, the railroad agreed that it would build no additional mileage while any of these notes were outstanding, unless it first received the approval of a committee of five trustees, which included: R. G. Ralston, J. A. Stewart, James Stillman, John D. Probst and Fred T. Gates. Similar provisions prohibited the road from guaranteeing, endorsing or buying the stocks, bonds or other obligations of any other companies. To bolster the Northern Pacific's credit, a final clause provided that the collateral which it deposited could not be sold below fixed prices: 90 for the company's own bonds, 95 for the Chicago & Northern Pacific bonds and 85 for the Chicago & Calumet bonds. Since each of these figures was far above the market quotation for that security, it was hoped that announcement of this contract would stiffen the market. The new bond issue was limited to $15,-000,000 par value, of which $12,000,000 was to be taken at once to refund the floating debt. Even before its public announcement, the issue was almost wholly subscribed by Henry Villard and his German-American friends and the Rockefellers, who took about one-third of the entire amount.[37]

Despite the success of the refunding operation, however, the company's affairs grew steadily worse, and on August 15, 1893, application was made to the court for the appointment of receivers. The court assented and appointed President Oakes, Henry C. Payne, of Milwaukee, a well known railroad man of the Northwest, and Henry C. Rouse, president and chairman of the Missouri, Kansas & Texas Railroad. The factors which had led to the receivership were summarized by Vice-president Williams:

37 *Commercial and Financial Chronicle*, June 17, 1893, pp. 984-5; *Railroad Gazette*, May 26, 1893, p. 398; and *Railway Age and Northwestern Rail-roader*, June 16, 1893, p. 471.

In consequence of the extraordinary depression and the stoppage
of business along its line, the Northern Pacific Railway Company
has been forced to acquiesce in an application for the appointment
of receivers. No company could long stand such severe pressure.
The falling off in earnings is due to several causes. The money
stringency prevents the marketing of crops, cattle and products
of all kinds; consequently the road's not getting the traffic usual
to this season of the year. The failures of banks have tied up
money upon which we depended for cash. The depression prevailing over the whole country has been exceptionally severe in
the younger states, so that general business along our main and
branch lines has been practically at a standstill. Payment of bond
interest under such circumstances could have been carried out
only by borrowing money and increasing the floating debt, which
would have entailed heavy sacrifices upon the bond and stockholders of the company. The receivership means, therefore, the
preservation of the property and a conservation of all interests
until better times.[38]

The troubles specified by the vice-president had led to the
development of a new floating debt of more than $1,000,000
since the refunding operation of June and to a shrinkage in
value of the securities the Northern Pacific had deposited as
collateral for various loans. Unable to check the growth of the
floating debt or to increase the margin on the loans, a receivership was the only way to preserve the system.[39]

But these facts, on which the immediate blame for the
receivership fell, were not the fundamental causes. Had the
road been in good condition when the depression began, the
story would have been far different. Its dividend record since
the reorganization in 1883 had been erratic. On the preferred
issues, 1 per cent was paid in 1883; nothing more was paid
until 1890 when there was a 4 per cent dividend. In 1891 the
4 per cent payment was repeated but in 1892 only 2 per cent

38 *Railway World*, August 19, 1893, p. 772.
39 *Railroad Gazette*, August 18, 1893, p. 622.

was paid in April and none thereafter. Of course the common stock had received nothing at any time during this period.[40] An average annual payment of 1 per cent on the preferred stock over a period of eleven years was not indicative of a very robust financial condition.

In the first place, the road was badly overcapitalized. The total capital and debt amounted to $259,141,608 which was represented by the operation of about 5400 miles of track, making a capitalization per mile of almost $50,000. The situation was made worse by the fact that the Northern Pacific was paying high rates of interest for the money it had borrowed. The annual fixed charges and sinking fund requirements aggregated $9,712,000, or roughly 4 per cent on the total capitalization of the road. Calculated on a mileage basis, the fixed charges were $1800 per mile yearly. If this capital had been invested in a section of the country which was densely industrialized, and if the equipment that represented it had been in a highly efficient condition, the capitalization might have been born successfully. But after a careful tour of inspection Receiver Rouse could not make a very encouraging report on the condition of the system. The rolling stock and the shops were in good shape and the terminal facilities and station buildings were frequently very good and in no case less than adequate. But the permanent roadbed of the main line presented a less optimistic prospect. About 1000 miles of rails had been in use for between nine and twelve years and were so badly worn that their replacement was imperative. The total length of the main line was 1908 miles and for 1073 miles light fifty-six pound rails would have to be discarded in favor of sixty-six or eighty pound rails, at an outlay of about $5,000,000. The reduction of grades on some sections of the line and the removal of excessive curves, costing about $1,800,000, were needed but could be temporarily postponed. The completion of ballasting the main line was an imminent need and would

40 *Railway World*, August 19, 1893, p. 772.

cost $555,000. Necessary replacements in the near future for bridges and trestles would cost at least $2,500,000.[41] Despite the vast sums of money which had already been poured into the road, $9,855,000 would be required to bring the roadbed to a point where it might be efficiently operated.

The importance of the high over-capitalization of the company and of the relative ability of equipment to operate efficiently had become manifest as James J. Hill's Great Northern pushed its way towards the Pacific. In the early months of 1893 a rate war with the Great Northern had further decreased the already declining gross receipts of the Northern Pacific.[42] In a report to German stockholders of the company in 1893, T. Barth emphasized the importance of Hill's competition and suggested what would at best have proved a drastic and dangerous manoeuvre:

Regarding the rate war with the Great Northern, the character of the manager and principal party in interest of this road, Mr. James J. Hill, has to be reckoned with. People who know him thoroughly assert that it needs only an energetic decision to defeat him with his own weapons. The most important territory of the Great Northern is the wheat district of the Red River Valley in which Hill is the successful competitor of the Northern Pacific. If the rate war could be carried to such a point that by a special reduction of freight rates in the Red River Valley the best business of the Great Northern would be threatened, peace could be quickly gained under a general restoration of freight rates. The very fact that the Great Northern traverses an immense territory —some 1500 miles—which has so far hardly been taken hold of by settlers, makes this system especially vulnerable at those points from which it gains its actual vitality.[43]

41 *Report of Receiver Henry C. Rouse*, December 11, 1893, 20 page pamphlet, New York: Evening Post Job Printing House.

42 *Commercial and Financial Chronicle*, August 19, 1893, pp. 272-3.

43 Quoted in Pyle, J. G., *The Life of James J. Hill*, New York: Doubleday, Page and Company, 1917, 2 volumes, I, p. 445.

Hill himself knew what bitter competition a bankrupt Northern Pacific, relieved from any necessity to pay the interest on its bonded debt, could give his Great Northern.[44] It was in full realization of this that he had extended his line to the coast, building and financing his extension in such a way that it would be prepared to meet such competition. The Great Northern had the lowest capitalization per mile in the country,[45] but at the same time the road was one of the most efficiently built and operated lines. Hill could make money at rates which would have spelled quick ruin for any other system.[46] Speaking of a new rate schedule which had just become effective, he wrote a friend on February 13, 1893:

This to our company is a higher rate than we would probably make if our line was alone in the business, as I believe the development and increased business from the growth of the country would give us a better revenue at a lower rate. At the same time, we thought better to keep the other companies on their feet at this time, although it seems certain to me that in the future they will be compelled to level down the great differences in their requirements over what the service can be performed for by a well-constructed road.[47]

Not only was the competition of the Great Northern already hurting Northern Pacific revenues, but far more important, the spectre to which Hill referred in this letter, of the future more deadly strife that was becoming inevitable, was ever present in the minds of the men controlling the destinies of the Northern Pacific. To forestall disaster when the Great Northern's extension to the coast would be completed, from 1889 until its receivership the Northern Pacific engaged in a frenzied expansion program which saddled it with several subsidiaries that

44 *Ibid.*, I, pp. 447-8.
45 *Ibid.*, I, pp. 464-7.
46 *Ibid.*, I, pp. 447-8.
47 *Ibid.*, I, pp. 486-7.

in the future might be profitable, but were meanwhile such heavy liabilities that even their eventual value was dubious.

The weakness of the system's branch lines was suddenly realized by Henry Villard, chairman of the board, when he took a trip over them in the fall of 1891. Describing his impressions, Villard wrote that:

The journey depressed him not only because of the popular silver hallucination, but also because of his observation of ominous factors in the Northern Pacific situation. First and most threatening of all was the loss of business by the competition of the Great Northern line to Spokane. There was also the paralyzing effect of the great fires at Spokane and Seattle. The decline of silver production in Montana and the Coeur d'Alene regions in consequence of the steady depreciation of that metal in the market also portended more and more loss of traffic. But the most alarming of all made upon him was the revelation of the weight of the load that had been put upon the company by the purchase and construction of the longer branch lines in Montana and Washington, which he then discovered for the first time. There was the Missoula Railway and Navigation, a mixed system of steamboats and rail lines; the Seattle, Lake Shore and Eastern; and the roads built into westernmost Washington, representing a total investment in cash and bonds of not far from $30,000,000 which together hardly earned operating expenses. The acquisition and building of these disappointing lines had in a few years absorbed the large amount of consolidated bonds set aside for construction purposes, which had been assumed to be sufficient for all needs in that direction for a long time. Under these circumstances Mr. Villard came back to New York with increased apprehension as to the future of the Northern Pacific.[48]

As a whole, for the year ending June 30, 1893, only two of the twenty-seven branch lines had earned any surplus over fixed charges, even after the earnings credited to the branches

48 Villard, Henry, *Memoirs*, Boston: Houghton Mifflin Company, 1904, 2 volumes, II, pp. 359-60.

had been most liberally calculated. Most of them barely earned their operating expenses. The bonds of these branches, guaranteed by the Northern Pacific, totalled over $45,000,000. The combined surplus of all the subsidiaries over operating costs for the year had been $583,209, against which stood a deficit in meeting fixed changes of $1,844,703. Traffic grossing $11,670,000 to the parent company had originated on these lines but most of them, even if they were not formally affiliated with the Northern Pacific, would still continue to interchange traffic with it. Negotiation of traffic agreements which did not include financial guarantees could net the Northern Pacific well over $1,000,000 per year in savings gained by the cancellation of all the guarantees.[49]

The policy of expansion by building branches or acquiring control of existing roads had been begun years before with the purpose, originally, of developing the territory penetrated by the Northern Pacific and thereby insuring the future prosperity of the line.[50] Later this object was subordinated to a more dangerous aim: the preemption of desirable natural sites for roadbeds and terminals before any rival company, specifically the Great Northern, could establish itself.[51] At no time were the branches expected, of themselves, to be profitable; the parent company would profit in the end by the increased traffic it obtained through the branch lines, so long as the deficits to be made up were not too large.[52] This line of reasoning was valid until, in an effort to head off the Great Northern, too many unprofitable feeders were absorbed at once. Of the companies absorbed in expectation of severe competition from the Great Northern, two particularly stood out as dubious investments, the Wisconsin Central and the Chicago & Northern Pacific.

49 *Report of Receiver Henry C. Rouse.*

50 *Railway Age and Northwestern Railroader*, March 10, 1893, p. 208.

51 *Commercial and Financial Chronicle*, March 4, 1893, pp. 354-6, reply to investigating committee.

52 *Railway Age and Northwestern Railroader*, March 10, 1893, p. 208.

The Wisconsin Central was leased January 16, 1890, in order to get an entrance into Chicago for the Northern Pacific. This purpose was gained, but at a high price: the Northern Pacific agreed to pay as rental 35 per cent of the gross income on the Wisconsin Central lines north of Altenheim and 37½ per cent of the gross on the rest of the Wisconsin system. The Wisconsin's entrance into Chicago was over the leased lines of a subsidiary, the Chicago & Calumet Terminal Company, and this lease was transferred to the Northern Pacific. Aside from the value of its terminal lease, the Wisconsin Central was in a desperate condition. Despite the increased traffic it carried as a result of the Northern Pacific alliance, it returned to the parent company an annual deficit of over $1,000,000. The company operated a line between Milwaukee and St. Paul, but had no terminal in either city. The leased Chicago terminal was very expensive and far in excess of the combined needs of the Northern Pacific and the Wisconsin Central, to say nothing of the latter alone. The road to St. Paul was not only in very poor shape, but was 462 miles long; the Chicago & Northwestern's parallel line was 400 miles long and so well constructed that its locomotives could haul 75 per cent more cars than could those of the Central.[53] On the same day that the Northern Pacific failed, the Wisconsin Central also went into receivership, and before a year had passed the court directed that the contract between the two roads should be cancelled in the interest of the Northern Pacific.[54]

The management of the Northern Pacific had not hesitated to admit that the Wisconsin Central lease by itself was not profitable; however, they contended that it was worth its cost because through it the Northern Pacific got control of the Chicago & Calumet Terminal system with its valuable properties in Chicago. That the terminals were valuable even the hostile investigating committee did not question, but whether

53 *Report of Special Committee.*
54 *Railway World,* April 21, 1894, pp. 315-6.

they were worth the price paid was another matter.[55] At the time the station was too large and expensive for the uses of the Northern Pacific system; and it was of doubtful wisdom to freeze the necessary amounts of capital, at a time when the Northern Pacific was definitely in need of cash, in an investment which would only be financially profitable at some future date.

The Chicago & Northern Pacific was another Wisconsin Central subsidiary taken over by the Northern Pacific. The parent company paid an annual rental of $350,000 plus a small percentage of the gross receipts from freight traffic, in addition to guaranteeing the funded debt of $26,392,000.[56] From the time of its transfer to the Northern Pacific until the latter's receivership this lease cost the parent company well over $1,300,000.[57] The court concluded that, in the interest of the parent company, it too should be cancelled by the receivers.[58]

That these leases were a potent influence in the insolvency of the Northern Pacific was generally admitted. T. Barth and G. Siemens, independently reporting to German stockholders after the failure, agreed on the importance of these contracts. Siemens went so far as to say that the depression and the consequent reduction in the system's earnings were not the causes of insolvency, but only the last straws; the causes of failure were the leases of the Wisconsin Central and the Chicago & Northern Pacific lines and the generally poor condition of the system's equipment.[59] The stockholders' investigating committee most emphatically blamed the embarrassment of the system in 1892 on the whole expansion program,[60] and in this opinion Henry Villard, one of the most important men

55 Report of Special Committee.
56 Ibid.
57 Railroad Gazette, September 29, 1893, p. 726.
58 Railway Review, September 30, 1893, p. 602.
59 Pyle, op. cit., I, pp. 444-5.
60 Report of Special Committee.

in the company's management, concurred.[61] Finally, an authority on the railroads of the Northwest has stated that " to that failure, competitive building of branch lines in the far Northwest very materially contributed ".[62]

The branch lines proved so unprofitable and the reasons for embarking on some of the ventures were so obscure that charges of corruption were freely aired both before and after the receivership. Brayton Ives, who was elected to the presidency of the road at the first regular stockholders' meeting after the appointment of receivers, led the attack on the honesty of the former Oakes-Villard management. He was a Wall Street stock broker, then in his early fifties, who had been prominent in New York financial circles for years. He had been graduated from Yale at the age of twenty-one and immediately joined the Union Army for the duration of the Civil War. After the demobilization he had become a broker, and twice was elected vice-president and twice president of the New York Stock Exchange; for a time he was president of the Western National Bank. Better educated than were many of the industrial leaders of the period, Ives was a well known bibliophile and at one time possessed a valuable library which included the Gutenberg Bible of 1450-5, the Columbus letter of 1493 in Spanish and the earliest folio of Shakespeare.[63]

Villard, about whose activities the controversy centered, was in many respects the exact opposite of Ives. He had been born in Speyer, Rhenish Bavaria, in 1835, when his father was a member of the supreme court of Bavaria. But two uncles were leaders of the 1848 revolt there and it was from them rather than his father that the young man absorbed his political ideas.

61 Villard, *op. cit.*, II, pp. 359-60.

62 Hedges, J. B., *Henry Villard and the Railways of the Northwest,* Cambridge: Harvard University Press, 1930, p. 208.

63 *Who's Who in America, 1899-1900,* edited by John W. Leonard, Chicago: A. N. Marquis & Company, 1899, p. 371 ; *Appleton's Cyclopedia of American Biography,* edited by James Grant Wilson, New York: D. Appleton and Company, 1900, VII, p. 148.

To cure him of his republican sympathies, he was sent to military school and then to the universities of Munich and Würzburg but the estrangement between father and son continued. At the age of eighteen the opposition of his family became unbearable and he suddenly fled to America, landing in New York in 1853. To prevent his family from tracing him and having him returned to Bavaria to do military service, the young man, hitherto known as Ferdinand Heinrich Gustav Hilgard, adopted the name of Henry Villard. He slowly proceeded west to Belleville, Illinois, where some sympathetic relatives lived, working at various jobs en route. So rapidly did he master the English language that in 1858 he was able to report the Lincoln-Douglas debates for the New York *Staats-Zeitung*. After the election was over, he travelled to Pike's Peak in the gold rush of 1858-9 and wrote a book describing his observations. He was back in newspaper work during the critical election of 1860, assigned to Springfield, Illinois, until Lincoln's departure for Washington. Upon the outbreak of war he became a war correspondent, first for the New York *Herald* and *Tribune* and then as a free lance.

Not until he was almost forty did Villard show any interest in railroading and then a combination of circumstances roused his interests. On a visit to Germany in 1873 he met members of the Oregon & California Railway protective committee and was persuaded to help them in reorganizing their company. For the next few years he worked in the railroad field without attracting undue attention but in 1879 he became nationally famous almost overnight: he reorganized the Oregon Railway & Navigation Company and in so doing came into conflict with the Northern Pacific. Villard sought quietly to buy a controlling interest in the latter but finding he had insufficient funds, he organized his famous " Blind Pool ": he invited the subscriptions to a project, the exact nature of which would not be revealed until later. Despite the very high premium thus put on his personal integrity, more than $8,000,000 was subscribed and he was enabled to gain control of the Northern Pacific and become its president in 1881. That Villard's sporadic successes in Northwestern railroading were not accidental but were rather due to an extraordinary capacity for visualizing future industrial possibilities was indicated by his interest in electricity, which was so great that he materially helped Thomas A. Edison during the eighties and founded the Edison General Electric Company in 1889.[64] Just as Ives was intellectually and culturally superior to the average native-born financier of the period, so Villard was one of the outstanding immigrants.

Unfortunately the controversies between the two were never thoroughly sifted in any court. A special master appointed by Judge Jenkins exonerated President Oakes from all charges of dishonesty, but in so doing he indicated his belief that Villard and some associates had swindled the company in the Chicago & Calumet deal and in some of the branch line construction in the far Northwest.[65] Villard disclaimed any greater responsibility for these transactions than was the share of all the members of the board individually and collectively and denied any wrong doing by himself or his associates.[66]

As early as October 20, 1894, Ives had petitioned the court to instruct the receivers to institute suit against Villard, Colgate Hoyt and Charles L. Colby, all former Northern Pacific directors, to recover nearly $2,600,000 alleged unlawful profits accruing to them from the acquisition by the Northern Pacific of several of its subsidiaries.[67] Nine months later Ives' request was granted in part. Judge Jenkins instructed the receivers to institute suit against Villard to recover about $550,000 which, according to the reports filed by the receivers, he had obtained illegally as a commission for negotiating the sale of the North-

64 *Dictionary of American Biography*, XIX, pp. 273-5.

65 *Railway World*, September 22, 1894, pp. 755-6.

66 *Ibid.*, November 11, 1893, p. 1068; *Railway Age and Northwestern Railroader*, November 10, 1893, p. 819.

67 *Commercial and Financial Chronicle*, October 20, 1894, p. 697.

ern Pacific & Manitoba to the Northern Pacific while a director of the latter and an agent of the former.[68]

Villard's side of the controversy is best summarized in his autobiography, in which he appears as the innocent victim of a struggle for control of the Northern Pacific. Although his long intended resignation from the board had been accepted June 21, 1893, he had foreseen that disaster was ahead for the Northern Pacific:

He was fully conscious that, in obtaining this release from official cares, he did not free himself from the heavy burden of anxiety with which the growing certainty of a catastrophe to the Northern Pacific oppressed him. The accelerated decline in the earnings, the increasing paralysis of silver-mining, and the fast-spreading stagnation of general business, convinced him that the breakdown of the company would come inevitably with the crisis which he expected would befall the country in 1893. It was perfectly clear to him, too, that the collapse of that company would again mean for himself discredit, calumny and abuse. It seemed a hard fate indeed that he should have to pass twice through the same ordeal and receive such severe punishment for once more loyally uniting his personal fortunes with the same ill-starred company. Considering default unavoidable, he advised making it as early as April, but the officers still believed in the possibility of early recuperation and managed to pay the April coupon.[69]

After the crash had come Villard at once strongly advised the Deutsche Bank, which had sold many junior securities of the Northern Pacific in Germany, to send a representative to the United States to care for the interests it represented. When a delegation led by Dr. Georg Siemens, the most influential director of the Bank, arrived, Villard explained the situation to them and then announced that he was going abroad for several years since

68 *Railway Age and Northwestern Railroader*, July 5, 1895, p. 325.
69 Villard, *op. cit.*, II, pp. 364-5.

owing to his failure in 1883 and the present crisis, his usefulness as a financial adviser and leader was obviously entirely gone, and that it was his firm belief that, in view of the bitter attack upon him, it would positively injure the work of the commission if he played a leading part in it.[70]

While Villard was in Europe two suits were finally begun against him, but neither was ever concluded:

He and his associates in the formation of the Chicago and Northern Pacific Railroad Company were charged in the press with having made millions for themselves out of it, and a small stockholder was even procured to bring suit for the recovery of these alleged ill-gotten gains. In his answer to the bill of complaint, Mr. Villard made an absolute denial of every one of the charges, and so completely that no further move was ever made in the case.[71]

In regard to the proceedings instituted by the receivers at the order of the court,

Mr. Villard had caused the receivers to be informed that he was ready to return and respond at any time to any summons in any suit against him, and in answer had received official information that they had been ordered to bring suit, but thought it proper to call on him first for certain explanations. He concluded to respond to this in person, and was able to notify the receivers early in May, 1895, that he was back and held himself at their disposal. Some correspondence with the receivers followed but nothing further was done in the case until the following winter, when the court renewed its order to bring suit, which was then commenced. But the suit never passed beyond the first stage— that is, the filing of the complaint and the defendant's answer. The case remained there until after the completion of the reorganization of the Northern Pacific company and the discharge of the receivers. Mr. Villard received then the fullest possible vindication by a dismissal of the suit without his solicitation, and a certification

70 *Ibid.*, II, pp. 367-9.
71 *Ibid.*, II, p. 369.

from the principal conductors of the reorganization, E. D. Adams, Francis Lynde Stetson and C. H. Coster, that no evidence whatever had been found to sustain the charges against him. This is the place in which to mention also that it was proved, through a most searching investigation of the Northern Pacific accounts made by order of the court, that not a dollar of the corporate funds had ever been improperly used.[72]

Lacking positive proof either way and in view of the bitter factional struggle which was being waged for control of the system, it is impossible to do otherwise than accept the verdict of Gustavus Myers, who was never over-charitable to the railroad capitalists:

So far as the court records indicate the facts, these allegations seem to have been part of a plan to discredit Villard, and cause his overthrow; when the charges were passed upon by the (lower) courts, Villard was personally vindicated. But that the railroad's treasury had been looted by previous groups of capitalists was absolutely clear.[73]

Certainly before the depression of 1893 appeared on the financial horizon, the Northern Pacific was a bankrupt road *de facto* if not *de jure*. Overcapitalized from the reorganization of the company in 1883, an expansion program had been pushed steadily and then as the threat of competition from the

72 *Ibid.*, p. 371. An examination of the Henry Villard papers in the Harvard Library substantiates Villard's contentions: certified copies of the charges against him and his answers thereto and incidental memoranda pertaining to legal controversies which revolved about his activities as chairman of the Northern Pacific board (boxes 15, 16, 34); carbon copies of the hearings before the special master upon the ouster suit instigated by the Ives faction against the receivers (box 34); and annotated clipping from the *Commercial and Financial Chronicle* of September 15, 1894, p. 473 (box 27); all these, together with his letter books, indicate that his claims are accurate. Also included is the original copy of the release signed by Edward D. Adams, Francis Lynde Stetson and C. H. Coster, dated January 15, 1897 (box 97).

73 Myers, Gustavus, *History of the Great American Fortunes*, New York: Modern Library, 1936, p. 683.

Great Northern grew more immediate, the expansion of the system became almost frenzied. Many of the branches acquired were perennial liabilities and many, which might have been invaluable in the future, were too great a strain to be borne by the flimsy credit of the Northern Pacific during the interim of unprofitable years. As had several other roads, the Northern Pacific had tried to expand too rapidly without regard to the fundamental weakness of its capitalization, and the result had been failure. The first adverse wind that came along found the house of cards more than ready to topple.

CHAPTER III

PAST MISTAKES

ALL the large systems which went into receivership during the nineties were characterized by precarious financial positions even in the opening years of the decade, but the New York, Lake Erie & Western, the Atchison, Topeka & Santa Fe and the Union Pacific failures were to a peculiar degree legacies of the past. In each of these three cases the troubles during the difficult nineties could be traced to specific earlier events, and when to initial financial vulnerability were added mismanagement and sometimes almost criminal falsification of reports and outright violations of the law, failure could be the only result.

Rumors concerning the imminent collapse of the Erie became insistent early in the spring of 1893, and with good cause. The past history of the road had been notorious. In 1859, as the New York & Erie, it had passed into the hands of receivers, to emerge two years later as the Erie Railway Company. Following this reorganization the road had fallen under the control of " Uncle Daniel " Drew and then that of Jay Gould and Jim Fiske. Its lurid history under the tender ministrations of these three financiers was a by-word in American railway history. The orgy of speculation of which the Erie was the core culminated in the second receivership of the road in 1875. Three years later the New York, Lake Erie & Western Railroad rose from the wreckage of the old Erie, and with an honest and capable management tried again to achieve the prosperity which had long been prophesied for it.[1] By 1890 the system included not only the main line and its branches, but also a network of leased mileage including the Buffalo, New York & Erie, the Buffalo & Southwestern and the New York,

---

1 *Railway Age and Northwestern Railroader*, July 2, 1893, p. 579. For details of the earlier history of the Erie, see Myers, *op. cit.*, pp. 407 *et seq.*, 423 *et seq.*, 437 *et seq.*, etc.

Pennsylvania & Ohio system, which, in turn, controlled the Chicago & Erie through a lease. The total mileage of the system was 1966 miles.[2]

The basis for the rumors circulating in the spring of 1893 was provided by the Lehigh Valley Railroad's construction of a competing line to Buffalo and the consequent abrogation by the latter of the old trackage agreement under which it had used the Erie roadbed from Waverly to Buffalo in return for a monthly rental of $100,000. President King of the Erie, however, publicly refused to see in this immediate loss of revenue to his company any ultimate financial loss. Rather, the new arrangement benefited the Erie, he declared, for it was more than making good the former rental payments by profits on coal which it sold along the line in towns where the Lehigh had hitherto enjoyed a monopoly of the anthracite business.[3]

As events proved, the loss of the Lehigh rental money was only one of several misfortuntes. On July 25, 1893, friendly receivership proceedings were instituted and President King and F. G. McCullough, president of the subsidiary Chicago & Erie, were made receivers. No dividends had been paid on the common stock since 1872 and, excepting 3 per cent in January, 1892, none had been paid on the preferred stock since 1884. With this record of prolonged financial stringency behind it the Erie's collapse roused no surprise and only a little protest.

As was so frequently the case, the immediate cause of the receivership was the existence of a large and constantly growing floating debt which was impossible of renewal in the midst of a nation-wide liquidation movement.[4] For once, though, the floating debt was not blamed on the management; critics declared the record of the King administration had been exemplary both in its honesty and in its efficiency. Physically the system was in excellent condition; traffic and gross earnings

2 Van Oss, *op. cit.*, pp. 211-34.

3 *Railway Review*, March 4, 1893, p. 143.

4 *Commercial and Financial Chronicle*, July 29, 1893, pp. 164-5.

were both increasing even during the period of panic and depression.[5] Strangely enough, it was largely this very growth in traffic and earnings which, because of a defect in the financial organization of the road, was responsible for the steady increase in the floating debt. The terms of the second consolidated mortgage of 1878 had practically precluded the issuance of any more bonds, no matter how great the need, since few investors would buy bonds on which the interest must be defaulted several times before foreclosure could be instituted. So although a period of rapid growth in the company's business necessitated a corresponding expansion of its facilities, the Erie could not increase its capitalization to pay for those betterments which were properly chargeable to the capital account.[6]

The dangers which had been inherent in this weakness for years, and which defied the efforts of a conscientious management to eradicate, had been pointed out by the New York *Evening Post* only a few months before the panic of 1893 swept the country:

No finer example of successful railway management under great difficulties exists than is afforded by the Erie Company. Its well nigh hopeless condition in 1884 and its gradual rise to the position of a road with established credit are well known. . . . Two years ago, in commenting upon the Erie Railway, the *Evening Post* . . . stated that more capital was the one imperative necessity for future prosperity . . . and it does not seem possible or politic to delay any longer the raising of additional and permanent capital.[7]

Another source of the increased floating debt had been the operation of several subsidiaries. The first annual report of the company under the receivers showed that the Chicago & Erie

5 *Railway World*, July 29, 1893, p. 709.

6 *Commercial and Financial Chronicle*, July 29, 1893, pp. 1164-5, and January 11, 1896, p. 54. See also circular letter to holders of New York, Lake Erie, and Western Railroad Company's second consolidated mortgage bonds, etc., dated January 2, 1894, signed by Board of Directors.

7 New York *Evening Post*, December 5, 1892.

Railroad, always assumed to return a profit to the parent company, on the contrary was a steady drain. The profit that it annually showed only existed after the Erie had paid its rental, which was based on a percentage of the gross receipts of the line. Taken by iself the road had a yearly deficit; after the rental had been paid, it had been able to declare a 2 per cent dividend. Similarly the Erie's control of the Union Steamboat Company had always been thought profitable, but it was now revealed that the company had a floating debt of $850,000. Further, after it had gone into receivership, the Erie was forced to write off its books over $500,000 advanced to this company to make up deficits in previous years. In addition certain entries hitherto carried as doubtful assets on the Erie's balance sheet were written off; the chief item in this group was $1,720,-125 due from subsidiary anthracite coal companies. The total thus written off the books after the receivership was $4,196,-020.73. If these losses had been credited to the accounts for the years in which they occurred, instead of showing a yearly surplus the Erie would have shown an annual deficit that would have been more truly representative of its financial condition than was the fictitious surplus.[8]

The result of the Erie's inability to sell more bonds and its costly subsidiaries had been the increase of the floating debt to nearly $9,000,000 and the creation of about $6,000,000 of car trusts.[9] To this should be added the $4,196,020.73 later written off the books; the total of the floating debt was a little over $22,000,000 when all the various parts were included. The unforeseen result of an attempt to prevent further over-capitalization of the road had been the necessity of a receivership while the road was still earning an annual surplus according to its books, and was showing a rather small yearly deficit according to the corrected balance sheets.

8 *Commercial and Financial Chronicle*, December 1, 1894, pp. 945-7.
9 Directors' letter, *op. cit.*

But although this defect in the financial organization of the road was one source of the large floating debt which, in turn, led straight to receivership, the ultimate cause of the Erie's failure was its colossal overcapitalization dating from the days of Drew and Gould. The historian of the Erie comments that

the company was bankrupt *de facto* when it passed to its new control (in 1878) and that the time when it must become bankrupt *de jure* was held off so long was a striking demonstration of the tact and resourcefulness which the new regime had been able to bring to bear in the management of the Company's unpromising affairs, and in judicious shifting and manipulating of the heavy burdens Erie bore upon its chafed and weary shoulders.[10]

A committee of the New York State legislature in 1880 had tried to discover what relation the value of the road bore to its capitalization, and their conclusions had been published only after careful and expert investigation. The estimated value of the system was about $65,000,000. Much less than this had been paid for its stocks and bonds, many of which had been issued as bonuses, yet the capitalization of the road was then almost exactly double this amount. In other words, just about half the capitalization was pure water.[11]

The New York, Pennsylvania & Ohio Railroad, one of the Erie subsidiaries which were an annual drain on the parent company, had one of the most weird capitalizations the railroad history of the United States had shown. Certainly no system in the country except the Erie, with its own grotesque capitalization, would ever have allied itself with a road situated as was the so-called " Nypano ". As the old Atlantic & Western, it had first, second, and third mortgages and an issue of prior lien bonds taking precedence over all mortgages. Interest on the

10 Mott, E. H., *Between the Ocean and the Lakes; the Story of the Erie,* New York: Ticker Publishing Company, 1908, pp. 273-4.

11 Parsons, Frank, *The Railways, the Trusts and the People,* Philadelphia: C. F. Taylor, 1906, p. 101.

prior liens was regularly earned and paid. At times the interest on the first mortgage was also earned and it was then paid in cash. When the interest was not earned, holders of the first mortgage received the treatment regularly accorded holders of the second and third mortgages: deferred interest warrants were issued to them and these were then capitalized and added to the total capitalization. The speed with which the capitalization mounted under such encouragement may be judged by the increase of the first mortgage indebtedness from $36,000,000 in 1880 to $72,000,000 in 1893. The total capitalization of the road in 1893 consisted of about $160,000,000 in stocks and bonds and $10,000,000 in prior liens, chiefly for car trusts. In return for this impressive investment, the stockholders had a single track road of 431 miles in not very good condition.[12] The Nypano was capitalized at approximately $400,000 per mile; even the Erie itself could show over 1100 miles of track at a total capitalization of about $180,000,000, or a capitalization of less than $165,000 per mile.[13] And with a road almost costly enough to have been built of solid gold, the Nypano annually showed a deficit in operating expenses to say nothing of ever meeting its fixed charges.[14]

Under such conditions it is no wonder that the Erie could not weather the financial storms of the summer of 1893. The failure was due to the depression in the sense that if there had been no depression the Erie might have been able to continue operating under its heavy burden indefinitely. But the *Economist* not unreasonably believed that " we cannot but think that a system is more or less to be condemned which is only designed to last in fair weather and which breaks down under the stress of hard times." [15] The criticism was, if anything, too

12 *Commercial and Financial Chronicle*, September 14, 1895, p. 449.

13 Van Oss, *op. cit.*, pp. 211-34; *Railway Age and Northwestern Railroader*, July 28, 1893, p. 579.

14 *Commercial and Financial Chronicle*, December 1, 1894, pp. 945-7.

15 *Economist*, July 29, 1893, p. 906.

mild; as Mott said, the Erie was bankrupt long before it went into receivership.

Equally bankrupt even before the panic was the Atchison, Topeka, & Santa Fe. Although its failure combined, perhaps more than any other, the various factors which contributed to the ruin of the several large systems, nevertheless the immediate cause of its bankruptcy, as in the case of the Erie, was an ineffectual earlier reorganization. First opened in 1870, by 1893 the Atchison had the greatest mileage of any railroad in the world. The line from Topeka to Atchison had been finished in 1872 and sixteen years later the extension to the Pacific coast had been completed. In 1890 the St. Louis & San Francisco and the Colorado Midland systems were added to the Athison by the latter's purchase of controlling blocks of stock in each.[16]

But even before the system had been rounded out financial difficulties had forced a reorganization. From 1883 to 1886, as the Atchison's mileage grew from 1820 to 3026 and fixed charges increased from $1,553,000 to $3,279,000, gross earnings per mile fell from $7755 to $3911 and the net per mile declined from $4048 to $1034. The resulting financial distress was intensified by an attack which Jay Gould launched against the road. Gould wanted to add the Atchison to his Missouri Pacific system and was doing his best to force the road into the bankruptcy which was imminent. However a reorganization was effected in 1889; President Strong was forced out and a completely new administration installed, which was dominated by President Allen Manvel and Chairman of the Board George C. Magoun.[17]

The reorganization, however, was a failure. The problems of the road, instead of disappearing, were increased by the inexpediency and dubious honesty of the policies which were adopted. In the first place, the reorganization failed to recognize the variety of values which the several liens on the road

16 Snyder, *op. cit.*, pp. 69-82.
17 Van Oss, *op. cit.*, pp. 566-73.

represented. Nearly all bonds were treated exactly alike, regardless of their security or the time they still had to run. This refusal to weigh the value of equities necessarily resulted in the issuance of $97,000,000 more bonds ahead of the common stock. After thus making it almost impossible for the stock to earn dividends, very inexpediently the control of the road was left in the hands of the stockholders. Inevitably there would be a temptation for the management to increase the value of the almost worthless stock it represented by manipulation of the books of the company; only by paying interest on the new income bonds could the stock's market value be increased, so a premium was put on payment of this interest, earned or not.[18]

Although the common stock had paid no dividends since 1888, expansion had been pressed. After 1888 the construction of branches had ceased, but purchases of controlling interests in already established companies had been made. Under this policy the mileage of the system had increased between three- and four-fold. The funded debt had risen from $127,140,000 to $220,832,000 in the same period, an increase of 73 per cent, which did not include the funded debts of the several lines whose stock had been bought. The net earnings, in the face of these increases, had risen $2,031,059, only 25 per cent, and therein the financial weakness of the road was accurately reflected.[19]

In the early months of 1893, however, the weakness of the Atchison was not so manifest as it rapidly became. When J. W. Reinhart was selected to succeed Allan Manvel in the presidency of the company, one periodical lauded the choice because

the credit for working out the great problem of reorganization which saved the Atchison company from default and placed it on the road to its present position of strength is due largely to Mr.

18 *Railroad Gazette*, April 19, 1895, p. 252.
19 Meade, E. S., " Great Railways," *Railway World*, 1904, pp. 687-8, 723-4.

Reinhart. His promotion by the interests which he has so well served is no surprise.[20]

The irony which later revelations attached to these words was wholly unsuspected by the writer, and not without reason.

Only forty-one years old, Reinhart was a young man to have thrust upon him the responsibilities of the world's largest road. But after his graduation from the Western University of Pennsylvania he had spent nearly twenty-five years in railroad work and had worked his way up from a clerkship in the office of the division superintendent of a small Pennsylvania company. By 1875 he was superintendent of transportation and rolling stock on the Allegheny Valley Railroad and five years later he accepted a position as auditor of the Richmond & Allegheny. After a short service in the same capacity for the New York, West Shore & Buffalo, in 1886 he became general passenger and ticket agent on the Lake Shore & Michigan Southern, helping reorganize the passenger department of that company. At the end of a year he resigned to locate in New York as a free-lance railway expert, and it was then that he first came into contact with the Atchison. In 1888 he investigated it and reported to its directors, recommending the amalgamation of scattered units of the system; as a result of the success of his suggestions, he was made fourth vice-president and head executive financial officer in charge of carrying out financial plans which he had formulated for the company. In 1890 he was promoted to first vice-president and three years later was elected president and made a director.[21] Although very young for so responsible a position, Reinhart was thoroughly experienced and had climbed step by step through subordinate positions to his hard-earned leadership.

The first disquieting signs to make their appearance were

20 *Railway Age and Northwestern Railroader*, March 10, 1893, p. 191.

21 *The National Cyclopedia of American Biography*, New York: James T. White & Company, 1929, VI, pp. 395-6.

several rate wars in the Southwest. Despite the efforts of the impotent Western Traffic Association, a bitter struggle between the Atchison and the Southern Pacific and other lines in the region broke out. The struggle flared up and died down in alternate spasms for over a year, and at times the rates which were in force seemed more characteristic of some philanthropic foundation than of capitalist railroads. In May a new swimming pool was opened in Glenwood, California. The Colorado Midland railroad, to increase its passenger receipts, early in the month announced a round trip rate from nearby points of $1. The parallel Rio Grande then announced a 55 cent rate. In retaliation the Colorado Midland threw down all bars and invited the public to make the trip free of charge as its guests. The Rio Grande, not to be outdone in generosity, countered with an offer not only to charge no fare for the round trip, but also to add a free ticket to the bathing pool. Only forty miles of road were involved in this war, but that ruinous rate struggles could not be confined to unimportant branches was evident when both lines announced a special $1 fare for the trip from Denver to Aspen or Glenwood in plate of the usual $12.85 rate.[22]

In less than a month this war was ended by the mutual agreement of the lines involved but conditions in the Southwest remained chaotic. In September a struggle with the Southern Pacific broke out in southern California. The Southern California railroad, a subsidiary of the Atchison, reduced its rates, and the Southern Pacific at once announced a reduction of $5 in the rates it would charge members of the Los Angeles board of trade who wished to visit the Chicago fair.[23] Before peace was made the Atchison had about halved its transcontinental through rates: from the Missouri River, Kansas, Texas and Colorado one way trips were reduced from $50 to $20 and

22 *Railway Age and Northwestern Railroader*, May 5, 1893, pp. 349-50 and May 26, p. 410.

23 *Ibid.*, September 5, 1893, p. 692.

round trips from $65.50 to $35.50; from St. Louis, over the St. Louis & San Francisco line, the $51 one way rate was reduced to $27.50 and the round trip price of $77.50 became $47.50; from Chicago passengers to the coast could travel one way for $32.50 instead of $57 and could make the trip both ways for $55.50 instead of the old fare of $85.50.[24]

Public suspicion that the Atchison could not pursue a suicidal rate-slashing policy for long had brought a statement from President Reinhart at the very beginning of the Rio Grande war. Remarkable though it sounded in the light of later events, he stated:

It will be the policy of the Atchison management to absolutely maintain rates. In competitive territory it will seek the cooperation of its neighbors to attain the same result. The Atchison management will be better satisfied with a financial net result based upon a fair and reasonable margin of profit and an economic administration than with a monumental showing of gross earnings with a heavy increase in operating expenses for hauling traffic at unsettled and unremunerative rates. The Atchison believes in stability of tariffs and will heartily support the best and strongest movement in that direction.[25]

If only the Atchison had pursued the policy indicated instead of one diametrically opposite, the outcome might have been better.

Throughout the summer months optimistic statements emanated regularly from the company's offices.[26] In August President Reinhart summed up the Atchison situation and harshly rebuked current rumors:

The last half of the year is by far our best half, and certainly not later than September 1 I look for the usual improvement. . . . The truth is that much of the financial distress is coming from those Wall Street pirates, to use no harsher term, who have been

24 *Ibid.*, February 23, 1894, p. 109.
25 *Ibid.*, May 5, 1893, p. 358.
26 *Ibid.*, May 5, 1893, p. 358; June 23, 1893, p. 487.

engaged in selling something they have not got, in order to buy it back at a profit. They have actually asserted that the Union Pacific, Missouri Pacific, Atchison and other roads, were going into the hands of receivers. The utter folly of the statement, as far as the Atchison is concerned, is that on July 1st we paid out in semi-yearly charges $3,700,000 in cash. . . . It is simply criminal to spread any story of receivers in view of such facts. I knew this financial depression was coming and we have prepared for it in consolidating offices and branch lines. A fair illustration is shown in the fact that we now have one vice-president, where we formerly had four. I thoroughly believe that September will usher in better times for Western roads.[27]

Three weeks later Reinhart reiterated his assertion that the company was in a safe condition:

The Atchison, Topeka and Santa Fe company has made itself financially easy again by securing a long extension on several millions of bonds which were due in November next and providing for the greater part of its January interest bonds by selling in London $3,000,000 of improvement bonds. To be able to sell new securities in these times indicates the existence of gratifying faith on the part of foreign capital in this great property.[28]

In October Reinhart explained the persistent rumors of the impending insolvency as a natural result of the recent Union Pacific failure; since the appointment of receivers for that system, as was only natural, other roads in the same part of the country had been suspect.[29] At the annual meeting of the stockholders late in November resolutions were adopted lauding President Reinhart and implying that the depression was a thing of the past: President Reinhart's " strong hand had been felt in carrying the company's finances safely through the most dangerous and distressful period which American railway finances have been called to meet." The road " has extended its

27 *Railway World*, August 5, 1893, p. 721.

28 *Railway Age and Northwestern Railroader*, August 25, 1893, p. 643.

29 *Railway World*, October 21, 1893, p. 994.

pressing obligations and although burdened with a large debt it also has a large and steadily improving field for support and in due time will be able to work out its complete salvation. Having passed through the panic without having passed through the hands of a receiver, as so many roads have done of late, the soundness of this company's financial policy" seemed to have been proved and "its prospects for the future are now more hopeful." [30] The smug satisfaction in the superiority of the Atchison over some of its rivals was a bit premature.

Early in December another of many attacks was made on Atchison securities on the Stock Exchange. Once again, this time from Europe, President Reinhart hastened to publish an optimistic denial that the Atchison was in dire straits. On receipt of Reinhart's message, the *Commercial and Financial Chronicle* declared: "It will be admitted, we think, that the finances of the company have been very skilfully handled, and that the property has passed through the late crisis and financial disturbances with credit to itself and its management." The basis of the rumors was the $7,250,000 floating debt, but, said the *Chronicle,* the company had sufficient securities in the treasury to pay it in full and was only waiting for the market value of these stocks and bonds to rise before doing so. This, together with about $9,000,000 of current liabilities, brought the total obligations of the system to about $16,000,000, but against that the company had on hand about $4,000,000 cash and $14,000,000 in its own and subsidiaries' securities. Conditions for the road were improving every month and the fact that it had survived the summer was in itself proof of its soundness.[31]

On December 23, 1893, the *Chronicle* announced the death of the chairman of the Atchison board, George C. Magoun, but

30 *Ibid.*, November 3, 1893, p. 801.

31 *Atchison, Topeka & Santa Fe Annual Report, 1893*; *Commercial and Financial Chronicle*, December 9, 1893, pp. 962-4.

discounted the effect this loss might have on the fortunes of the system. Acknowledging Magoun's financial power and the confidence he had inspired in the Atchison, nevertheless the *Chronicle* thought that since Reinhart had been handling the company's finances during Magoun's long sickness, his death would not affect the road.[32] However, on the very day of this expression of confidence, receivers for the Atchison and the St. Louis & San Francisco were appointed; for the moment only these two members of the system acknowledged their insolvency, but soon the Atlantic & Pacific and the Colorado Midland were also in receivership. The immediate causes of the Atchison's receivership were two-fold: the death of Magoun and an attack on the company's securities on the Stock Exchange had prevented Reinhart from concluding negotiations for a loan with which to meet $10,200,000 bond interest and loans due January 1, 1894. Reinhart had intended to deposit Atchison securities as collateral for the loan, but as their market value fell that became impossible and Magoun's death destroyed the last vestige of opportunity to finance the maturing obligations. So to preserve the system receivers had been appointed. Reinhart, as so often before, issued an optimistic statement to the effect that the company could earn its fixed charges and would have done so except for temporary conditions which would very soon be a thing of the past.[33]

The *Chronicle,* in view of Reinhart's many denials, reiterations and statements, commented sadly that the Atchison's failure was " the most serious event which has happened during the present crisis and a very great disappointment to its friends." [34] The *Economist* was not merely disappointed, its feelings were far stronger; it felt that the Atchison's

32 *Ibid.*, December 23, 1893, p. 1060.

33 *Railway Age and Northwestern Railroader*, December 29, 1893, p. 916; *Railway World*, December 30, 1893, p. 1236.

34 *Commercial and Financial Chronicle*, December 30, 1893, p. 1098.

downfall is of especial importance and significance. To start with, whilst the officials of other American railways have been extremely reticent in regard to the position of the undertakings which they direct or control—so much so, in fact, as to deserve apparently somewhat severe censure—those in charge of the Atchison have quite pressed views, opinions and what was assumed to be information upon the public. . . . But, as it turns out, practically nothing that has been said by the officials in regard to the company's position is deserving of belief; it has, in fact, been wholly deceptive in its character, although perhaps this was not intentional.

In the annual report recently issued

we have shown a balance of over three millions of dollars, and how is anyone, not an expert or an official, to be blamed if he regards that as proof of the stability of the company's position. . . . This is a specimen of the ordinary American railway balance-sheet, and embedded as it is in a mass of figures, we do not think that investors are to be blamed if they fail to discern what is the true position. . . . Why the directors do not state the case plainly in a few plainly-written lines, we cannot say, unless it be that it better suits their purpose to keep the shareholders entirely in the dark. One is loath to make such an accusation against the officials of the Atchison, for what is true of them applies more or less thoroughly to all American railway officials; and yet that is what we must believe, or else that the whole system of finance which they have adopted is entirely rotten. We know that financial conditions prevailing during the past few months have been extremely difficult, and also that great companies must necessarily have large floating balances, but these facts are not in themselves sufficient to explain the long series of disasters that has occurred. Primarily, we believe the difficulties have arisen out of the plan of borrowing money for capital purposes, not, as it were, openly and directly, but indirectly and secretly. The balance of revenue, which really belongs to the shareholders, is used up in this way, we suppose, and then further obligations are entered into on the strength of future revenue, paper in some form being issued temporarily as the security. Nothing is said to the bond or shareholders, who are compelled to remain in a state of complete ignorance, until the stress of circumstances discloses a floating debt which cannot be dealt with except by reorganization. And so the process goes on . . . to the great loss of the shareholders and to the profit of the officials, with their fat salaries, and whatever " pickings " may accrue besides . . . and to the still greater gain of the gamblers in Wall Street, with whom, it is feared, they too often work closely.[35]

The doubts which the *Economist's* editor cast upon the integrity of the Atchison's management were echoed by many commentators, because in no other way could the prosperous balance sheet of the annual report be reconciled with the failure of the road; obviously something was wrong somewhere.[36] However, it was not until Stephen Little, an expert railroad accountant, had examined the company's books and made this report that the full extent of the management's transgressions was revealed.

A forewarning that the Atchison's officials might not be very highly efficient or honest had been given the summer before by the discovery of pay frauds on the division between Topeka and Chicago. The conspiracy, which was costing the company about $17,000 every month, included employees ranking from the division superintendent down to section hands. Pay rolls were padded with fictitious names and the booty divided among the conspirators. A change in the method of paying wages that required all laborers to apply in person for their money at the pay car revealed an astonishingly large number of men too sick to leave their beds and meet the paymaster. Detectives investigated these suspicious circumstances and revealed the long existent fraud.[37]

The extent to which the highest officials of the road had been guilty of equally dishonest actions was summarized by Stephen

35 *Economist*, December 30, 1893, pp. 1558-9.

36 *Commercial and Financial Chronicle*, December 30, 1893, pp. 1100-02.

37 *Railway World*, July 29, 1893, p. 707.

Little under four headings in the report he made less than a year after the Atchison failure:

Illegal Payment of Rebates: despite the legal prohibition on granting rebates, the Atchison had paid $3,700,776.92 and the St. Louis & San Francisco $205,879.49 in rebates. This total of nearly $4,000,000 had not been charged to earnings, whence it came, but was listed in an " Auditor's Suspended Account— Special " which was included in the balance sheet as an asset. In 1891 part of this sum had been transferred to the Franchises and Property account because, according to a telegram signed with Reinhart's initials, it was to be considered as " representing net charges to Earnings and Operating Expenses properly applicable to the operation of the Company prior to the new Mortgage Indenture."

Additions to Earnings and Deductions from Expenses: on instructions from the Boston office of the company, $2,791,000 had been " credited from time to time to the Earnings and Expenses respectively, but these credits had no foundation in fact ". $2,010,000 had been added to the former and $781,000 deducted from the latter. The sum of the two items had been debited to an " Auditor's Suspended Account."

Improvements: Mr. Little contended that $448,000 was " transferred improperly " from Operating Expenses to Improvements or Capital account, which was finally closed into the Property and Franchises account.

Traffic Balance: a traffic agreement for the division of business had been formed in November, 1890, lasting until July, 1891, with " certain other companies ".[38] These other companies were listed as owing the Atchison a balance of $305,-

38 A typewritten copy of the report, addressed to the chairman of the reorganization committee for which Little was working, names these companies, the Southern Pacific and the Union Pacific, and lists the balances in each pool separately; the itemized statement is then crossed out with a pencilled line and the above phrase substituted, with the two amounts lumped together.

843.59. This sum was absolutely uncollectable and should have been written off the books several years before the receivership.

In all, Mr. Little found that in the three and one-half years preceding the appointment of receivers the Atchison had overstated its income $7,285,620.51 and the St. Louis & San Francisco had overstated its earnings $205,879.49, a total falsification of $7,491,500. To conceal this, the annual reports had been falsified in respect to the listings of cash on hand, bills payable and similar items. In addition to these positively fraudulent statements, Little considered that the actual assets of the company were overestimated in the annual reports. He advised writing off the books $1,201,050 worth of equipment which had been worn out or destroyed, $1,131,912 income from bad or doubtful investments and $642,917 in increase of interest on the unfunded debt. The total change in book value of the Atchison's assets which would result from the adoption of Mr. Little's recommendations was slightly more than a round $10,250,000.[39]

President Reinhart published a defense of the management on the same day that Mr. Little's report was published, but it failed to carry conviction. After complaining that he had not been given sufficient time to prepare his reply, he declared that the total error in the books was only $4,500,000, and therefore quite negligible. He then pointed to certain items in the balance sheet of the company which he claimed had been so far understated that a proper evaluation of them would transform the overstatement of income alleged by Mr. Little into an understatement. But Mr. Reinhart failed to meet any of Mr. Little's specific charges; he slid over the items which had been alleged

---

39 Typewritten report of Stephen Little, *Overstatement of the Income of the Atchison, Topeka & Santa Fe*, etc., addressed to " R. Somers Hayes, Esq., Chairman, and the Reorganization Committee." Also see, *Commercial and Financial Chronicle*, August 11, 1894, pp. 209-10; August 18, 1894, pp. 251-2; November 17, 1894, pp. 854-5.

fraudulent with no comment, and concentrated his attention on extraneous matters.[40]

The *Commercial and Financial Chronicle* considered the answer very unsatisfactory: it was convinced the charges were true and thought that they revealed an administration " without parallel in American railroad history." [41] The *Economist* again bitterly lamented the morals of American railroad management:

It will be remembered that when the Atchison recently fell into difficulties, a Committee representing the bondholders was appointed, and by this body Mr. Little, an expert of considerable reputation, was commissioned to examine the accounts and make a full report upon them. Very absurdly, as the *Economist* stated at the time, this self-appointed Committee drew up a scheme of reorganization before Mr. Little had made his report. It was assumed, without the slightest reason, for Mr. Reinhart had proved far from trustworthy, that the President's figures were correct, and that they would not ultimately need more than a little modification. The scheme, however, collapsed when Mr. Little reported that the company's accounts were entirely unreliable. Enormous sums, it came out, had been allowed as rebates—the Atchison thus dealing dishonestly with its competitors—which had never been debited to revenue account; considerable amounts had been improperly transferred from expenditure to capital; and, finally, the last named had been " jockeyed " to cover the policy which was being pursued.[42]

As time passed, it became obvious that all of Mr. Little's charges were true. Even after he had had sufficient time to examine the report and the company's books, Reinhart failed to issue a statement to prove his innocence. Rather, on the very day the report was published he quit under fire, stating that his resignation was due to a divergence between his and the directors' policies and to ill-health, and reiterating his certainty that

40 *Railway World*, August 18, 1894, pp. 653-5.

41 *Commercial and Financial Chronicle*, August 11, 1894, pp. 209-10.

42 *Economist*, November 17, 1894, pp. 1403-4.

his administration would be vindicated.[43] The Interstate Commerce Commission later prosecuted him for granting rebates when he was president of the road. Actually the rebates had been given during the Manvel regime when Reinhart was merely the auditor in the company's Boston office, so on this charge he easily proved his personal innocence without having to defend the annual reports he had permitted to go out over his signature or having to answer any of the charges Little had made.[44] Reinhart's failure ever to unearth any evidence that the annual reports were not fraudulent, in the face of the general acceptance by financial authorities of Little's report, makes it impossible to do other than admit the truth of the report.

Another important fact, which hitherto had been only suspected [45] but that the Little report made manifest, was the drain which the Atchison's subsidiary lines had made upon the parent company's treasury. The St. Louis & San Francisco, since its absorption, had more than paid its costs, but the Atlantic & Pacific and the Colorado Midland had both proved expensive investments. The former was described as a " wretched road, running, as it does, through an alkaline desert, where even the water for the locomotives has to be transported by rail." [46] The line was necessary to the Atchison, for it was the sole link between a network in southern California and the eastern roads of the system. But a 750-mile road crossing the sparsely populated regions of New Mexico and Arizona could only be made to pay if fixed charges were kept at a minimum. Despite the fact that ownership of a majority of Atlantic & Pacific stock assured it control of the line, the Atchison had entered a contract whereby it guaranteed the bonds and operating expenses of the subsidiary. The receivers, after a year's

43 *Railway World*, August 18, 1894, pp. 683-5.

44 *Railway Age and Northwestern Railroader*, November 2, 1894, p. 618; January 25, 1896, p. 43; May 23, 1896, p. 270; January 15, 1897, pp. 42-3.

45 *Economist*, January 13, 1894, p. 43.

46 *Ibid.*, November 17, 1894, pp. 1403-4.

further trial, cancelled this arrangement and controlled the Atlantic & Pacific through stock ownership without continuing to bear the unnecessary burden of paying the fixed charges.[47]

The Colorado Midland had proved another bad investment; it was so situated as to be a natural part of the Rio Grande system, not the Atchison, and the resultant competition prevented the Midland's paying dividends.[48] In 1893-4 these two subsidiaries had cost the St. Louis & San Francisco and the Atchison a round $2,000,000.[49] A reduction in the fixed charges of both these roads was necessary to the prosperity of the parent company and, lacking that, the credit of the Atchison would be subject to attack.

The credit of the system had been so weak since the 1889 reorganization that during the five years preceding the receivership it had paid over $1,100,000 in discounts and commissions to secure the renewal of its guarantee notes.[50] The final straw and the results were summed up by John Moody:

In 1892 an exchange of income bonds for fixed interest bearing bonds so increased the fixed charges of the company that, as a result of the panic of 1893, and its ensuing depression, the great Santa Fe system suddenly found itself in the hands of receivers. The president, John W. Reinhart, had persistently asserted throughout 1893 that the company was financially sound, but an examination of its books subsequently made in the interest of the security holders disclosed irregularities, dishonest management, and manipulations of the accounts.[51]

Although the fact had been concealed by the fraudulent manipulation of the company's accounts, the Atchison had been in a very shaky financial condition before the depression of 1893

47 *Railway Age and Northwestern Railroader*, December 21, 1894, p. 714.

48 *Economist*, November 17, 1894, pp. 1403-4.

49 *Commercial and Financial Chronicle*, November 17, 1894, pp. 854-5.

50 Meade, "Railroad Reorganization."

51 Moody, John, *Railroad Builders*, New Haven: Yale University Press, 1921, pp. 162-3.

swept the country. The death of Magoun, just when his reputation and financial resources were most needed, made impossible the task of longer hiding the true condition of affairs. A thorough financial housecleaning had been imperative ever since 1889 and the depression merely forced the reluctant management to acknowledge that fact.

The Union Pacific differed from the Erie and the Atchison in that its injurious inheritance from the past affected it in two ways. In the first place, it had been the victim of some of Jay Gould's later activities, at a time when he had been practicing the principles which had been perfected in his manipulations of the Erie; the natural and inevitable result for the Union Pacific had been the accumulation of a huge debt which had distorted the capitalization of the road out of all proportion to its value. Even more important in the nineties, the Union Pacific had been the recipient of large cash loans from the Government to aid in its construction, and these loans were due in the late years of the decade; since no adequate provision had been made for meeting them, as the time of their maturity came closer these Government subsidies became a disturbing factor in the company's affairs.

In 1862 Congress had chartered the Union Pacific to co-operate with the Central Pacific in the construction of the first transcontinental railroad line. The Central Pacific, a California corporation, was to build east from that state and the Union Pacific was to construct a line west from the Missouri River to meet the Central Pacific as it came eastward. The junction was made near Ogden in 1869, but the two lines were not operated for long as one continuous system. After the separation the Union Pacific built up its own system: in 1880 it absorbed the Denver Pacific and the Kansas Pacific; later the Oregon Short Line, the Utah Northern and the Oregon Railway & Navigation were added.[52] But despite the growth of the system, by the

52 Snyder, op. cit., pp. 696-717.

early 1890's it was in a bad way.   At that time an expert on
railroad investments summarized the problems of the Union
Pacific as three-fold and he was not overly optimistic of the
eventual result:

Within the next few years three events will happen the course
of which cannot at present be indicated in spite of the great importance that attaches to them. The debt to the Government will
fall due very soon, and there is no inkling as to the method of
payment the Government will propose or accept. The three years'
notes will be payable, and although they are amply secured by bonds
of subsidiary companies, they practically constitute a floating debt
which must either be paid or funded. In addition several descrip-
tions of bonds will mature and must be either extended or replaced by others. With three events of such magnitude impending
it will depend upon extraneous conditions, and still more upon
the performance of the property itself, and most of all, perhaps,
upon the attitude of the management, which, to aggravate matters,
has passed into the hands of Mr. Gould. If the next few years
provide a good business, and if, furthermore, nothing occurs which
unduly depresses the money markets, the company may be in a
position to reorganize its capitalization, to reduce its annual charges
and to propound a scheme which will provide for payment of the
debt to the Government; but the possibility of relief so much
depends upon a combination of favorable circumstances that it
seems to require some optimism to believe in a speedy establishment of the company's affairs upon a sound basis.[53]

The debt to the Government represented the amount of aid
that was extended to build the road originally. On the 1st of
July, 1862, Congress passed an act creating the Union Pacific
Railroad Company, granting the road land in proportion to the
mileage it constructed, and providing that the United States
would lend the company 6 per cent thirty year bonds to the
amount of $16,000 per mile on flat land, and treble that amount
in certain mountainous regions. The delivery of the bonds was

_____

53 Van Oss, *op. cit.*, pp. 636-7.

automatically to create a first mortgage on the whole line of the railroad thus aided, including the rolling stock and other equipment. The government, in the person of the Secretary of the Treasury, was empowered to take over the road if the company failed to pay the debt. This act failed to stimulate private capital sufficiently for the construction of the road, so another more generous act was passed July 2, 1864: the land grants were increased, the right of eminent domain under certain limitations was granted the company, certain restrictions which the earlier act had placed on the paying over of the bonds by the Governments were erased, and, most important, the company was allowed to issue prior liens ahead of the Government lien on completed sections of the road. This legislation contained what may be called the charter of the Union Pacific.[54]

By various acts of Congress after 1864 provision had been made for the burden of interest on these bonds to be carried by the Government until the bonds matured, at which time the whole debt, both principal and interest, would be due.[55] Under this arrangement the Union Pacific would then owe the Government $33,539,512 principal and $36,944,300 interest, a total of $70,483,812. The sinking fund to which the road had been depositing a small annual amount would not exceed $17,000,000 at most, so the balance due the Government would be over $50,000,000.[56] Since no provision had been made for meeting this huge debt which would be due in full January 1, 1899, the problem was fast becoming acute.[57]

Facing this large payment and with the company handicapped by a rapidly growing floating debt when Jay Gould regained control of the company in 1890 he had wanted to put

54 53rd Congress, 3rd Session, *Senate Report 830*, submitted January 28, 1895, pp. 2-7.

55 *Ibid.*, pp. 15-16.

56 *Railway World*, January 30, 1897, pp. 107-8.

57 *Commercial and Financial Chronicle*, April 29, 1893, pp. 693-5.

it into receivership at once in order to get it back on a permanently sound financial basis. However, he met objections to his plan from large financial interests in the East, particularly J. P. Morgan. Instead of resorting to a receivership, the floating debt was paid by the issuance of three-year collateral trust notes. Although these notes would be due in September, 1894, a brief breathing spell had been gained.[58] Under very favorable conditions the Union Pacific might be able to work out its own salvation.

But conditions were to prove anything except favorable and in addition the two most prominent financiers connected with the system were lost before the nation-wide panic had passed. In November, 1892, Jay Gould died and on September 13, 1893, Frederick L. Ames died. The loss to the road of these two directors meant that " from a financial point of view it was left like a ship without a commander in the middle of a storm." And this loss, in the opinion of the *Journal of Finance,* was a very important factor in the Union Pacific failure: " The company ought never to have passed into receivers' hands if at the most critical time the Union Pacific had not unexpectedly lost the support of two of its most prominent directors." [59]

However, the annual report for the calendar year 1892, issued late in the following April, presented a very encouraging picture. In contrast to a deficit in 1890, the company had earned 3½ per cent on the capital stock, which had been carried forward as a surplus of $2,069,757. Both the gross and net income had increased about $1,000,000 over the totals of the year before for the system as a whole. In this regard, a drop of about $1,500,000 in the gross receipts of the Oregon Short Line & Utah Northern, the Oregon Railway & Navigation Company and the Fort Worth & Denver City lines was a

58 *Railroad World*, October 21, 1893, pp. 996-8.
59 *Journal of Finance*, October, 1898.

disturbing element, but the general increase of traffic throughout the system more than over-balanced these losses.[60]

Before the end of the summer the situation was radically changed, and in mid-August the comptroller felt it necessary to announce that not only were economies being made by reducing the road's staff, but that:

We will be compelled to reduce our forces still further and may possibly have to cut salaries to meet the present exigencies. This last is a step which we will discuss very conservatively before taking action, but it will probably have to be considered. As to receivership it has not even been thought of. We are meeting our obligations as they fall due. Our credit is first class and physically we are in good condition. But there is nothing coming in. Commodities are not moving; corn is not yet harvested; wheat is practically a failure in Kansas and Nebraska. Colorado you know has shut down her silver mines and the country west feels the force of the situation.[61]

Admittedly to prevent a receivership, wages were drastically cut late in the month; but President Clark, returning from a summer vacation in the East, denied the current rumors of impending insolvency.[62]

Nevertheless the already familiar sequel to such official denials could not be postponed much longer. Announcement was made on October 13 that the courts had appointed as receivers President S. H. H. Clark, Comptroller Oliver W. Mink and E. E. Anderson, a Government director of the road. The immediate cause of the receivership was stated to be the catastrophic decline in the company's gross receipts. Starting the year with a surplus of over $2,000,000, in the first six months the company's revenues had dropped $800,000 from the figures of the

60 *Annual Report of Union Pacific, 1892*; *Railway Age and Northwestern Railroader*, May 5, 1893, p. 357; *Commercial and Financial Chronicle*, April 29, 1893, pp. 693-5.

61 *Railway Age and Northwestern Railroader*, August 18, 1893, p. 629.

62 *Ibid.*, September 8, 1893, p. 678; September 15, 1893, p. 693.

year before, declined another $2,000,000 in the next two months and in September had shrunk $1,500,000 more. In the face of such a decline of revenue, the company showed a deficit of about $3,000,000 in operating expenses and fixed charges, with no way of making it up. So the receivership petition had been filed to protect the system.[63]

But, rapid though it was, the decline in income was only the immediate, not the fundamental cause. Many roads in the country survived equally drastic reductions in revenue. The two-fold fundamental cause of the failure, with several contributory factors, are summarized by John Moody:

The financial failure of the system was due to a variety of causes. Its management had been extravagant and inefficient, and construction and expansion had been too rapid. The policy of building expensive branch lines where they were not needed and of obligating the company to finance them had been a grievous mistake and had contributed largely to the downfall of the company. Further than this, the credit of the Union Pacific was growing steadily weaker because the time was drawing near when its heavy debt to the United States Government would fall due. In all its history of more than twenty years the company had never paid any interest on the Government debt nor had it maintained a sinking fund to meet the principal when due. . . . Few were surprised when under the great pressure of the panic of 1893, the property was forced to confess insolvency. The Union Pacific had simply repeated the story of most American railroads: it had been constructed in advance of population and had to pay the penalty

when the limited amount of trade available to the five transcontinental systems was decreased by the depression.[64]

The inefficiency and extravagance of the management had been notorious from the very beginning of the road's history. Construction frauds and the resultant fictitious capitalization of

63 *Railway World*, August 21, 1893, pp. 996-8.

64 Moody, *Railroad Builders*, pp. 134-6.

the company had been the subject of numerous official and un-
official investigations. The revelations concerning the Credit
Mobilier had provided a chapter in American railroad history
only slightly less lurid than those involving the Erie.[65]

The Gould regime in the Union Pacific had continued the
looting of the unfortunate road. When Gould and his associates
got control of the company about 1873, without any ceremony
they at once issued two hundred thousand shares of common
stock. However, this was only a minor method of creating
fictitious capitalization for the Union Pacific and concrete
wealth for themselves. The most successful and remunerative
manoeuvre was the purchase of various railroads by Gould's
syndicate and the sale of these roads at exorbitant prices to the
Union Pacific. A typical operation of this kind resulted in the
acquisition of the Kansas Pacific. This company, after receiving generous aid from the Government, was plundered by its
officials and the stock fell to a low point. But rather than pay
even such a bargain price for control, Gould forced the stock
to practically nothing by threatening to build a competitive
parallel line. With control obtained for a mere pittance, he and
his associates proceeded to sell the road to the Union Pacific
for a fortune. In all, a Government investigating committee
declared, at a very conservatively estimated minimum Gould
and his associates pirated over $20,000,000 in this and similar
frauds practiced on the Union Pacific.[66]

In 1887 Congress had appointed the last of many committees
to investigate the subsidized roads; in a minority report Robert
Pattison, ex-governor of Pennsylvania, had retold the whole
familiar story in order to prove that the roads had misappropriated the money granted by the Government and that their

65 For a description of the Credit Mobilier, see Myers, *op. cit.*, pp. 441-5;
for a more detailed account, see *H. R. Report 1290*, 53rd Congress, 2nd
Session (contains Pattison's minority report on the Pacific railroads, 1888).

66 Myers, *op. cit.*, pp. 478-80; *Pacific Railway Commission, U. S. Executive
Documents*, 1st Session, 50th Congress, I, pp. 54-65.

capitalizations had been liberally watered.[67] In 1896 E. Ellery Anderson, one of the Government receivers of the road, declared that the value of the property was little more than half of the par value of the bonded debt; the stock represented no equity whatever.[68] Of the first $36,000,000 of stock issued by the Union Pacific, at most the company had received in cash two cents for each par dollar; the profits of construction were represented in the permanent financial statement by $43,929,-328.34 of outstanding bonds.[69] At the time of its failure, the company's total capitalization was $192,585,000, of which $131,717,000 consisted of the government debt and bonds and $60,868,000 represented the par value of the stock.[70]

The policy of the management in regard to branch lines had been a continuation of the extravagant and wasteful methods used in constructing the main line. Reference has already been made to the losses which the Union Pacific incurred from its relation to the Oregon Short Line & Utah Northern and the Oregon Railway & Navigation line. Within a few months of their appointment the receivers petitioned the court for permission to cancel the leases of fourteen subsidiaries. Ten branch lines were listed which had failed to earn even their operating expenses and taxes, to say nothing of the fixed charges which were guaranteed by the parent company. In two cases these deficits exceeded the gross revenues which the Union Pacific received from traffic originating on the branch lines: the Denver, Leadville & Gunnison had a deficit for operating expenses and taxes of $107,321 and from traffic brought to it by this branch the Union Pacific grossed $26,233.63; the

67 53rd Congress, 2nd Session, *House Report 1290, U. S. Executive Documents, Minority Report of the Commission.*

68 53rd Congress, 3rd Sessions, *Senate Report 830, U. S. Executive Documents,* pp. 35-55; also, report of Government Receiver Coombs, *Railway World,* September 14, 1895, p. 528.

69 *Railway World,* April 14, 1894, pp. 295-6.

70 *Commercial and Financial Chronicle,* May 29, 1897, p. 1025.

Kansas Central Company had a $99,035.84 deficit and the business the parent company derived from it brought a gross revenue of $18,096.[71] The receivers requested that all these branches be separated from the company as liabilities rather than assets, and their petition was granted.[72] Before receivers were appointed the Union Pacific operated 7691 miles of road; by mid-summer of 1895 the mileage had been reduced to a bare 3000 by lopping off unprofitable branches.[73] Into these unprofitable branch lines the Union Pacific had poured most of the $18,000,000 floating debt which had threatened to bankrupt the system in 1890.[74]

Considering the past history of the road, the plunder which had been extracted from the company at varous times by successive managements and the resulting over-capitalization of the system, it is small wonder that it was in a shaky financial condition by 1890. Even after the day of reckoning had been postponed by the funding of the floating debt the situation was only very temporarily relieved. Over the future of the road, like an impenetrable black cloud, hung the fast maturing Government debt. The mystery is not that the credit of the road had been weak for years, but rather that despite the names attached to its history it lasted as long as it did. The Union Pacific was one of the many roads which failed in 1893 that were badly in need of a reorganization to put them in a sound position. For the Union, reorganization had to be faced sometime and almost any pressure was enough to crystalize that need.

71 *Union Pacific Receivership Records*, 4 volumes, 1893, (?), pp. 149-95.

72 *Ibid.*, pp. 246 ff.

73 *Railway Age and Northwestern Railroader*, May 24, 1895, p. 248.

74 Dodge, G. M., *How We Built the Union Pacific Railway and Other Railway Papers and Addresses*, New York, 1910, p. 78.

CHAPTER IV

SCANDALS

As shown in previous chapters, some railroad systems failed during the depression of the nineties because they had expanded excessively; others failed because their past managements had made fatal mistakes which later administrations could not rectify. The failures of a third group of roads were characterized by revelations of mismanagement which shocked the investing public. These roads were in part victims of their own histories, in part victims of over-expansion, but their mistakes did not belong entirely to the past and the public had had no knowledge of what was taking place. The mismanagement which precipitated the failure of the Philadelphia & Reading could only be blamed on the regime in power at the time of bankruptcy and that regime had done its utmost to keep its actions secret. The management of the Richmond & West Point Terminal had changed somewhat but not completely since the worst plundering had taken place and the true condition of the several members of the system had been sedulously hidden. In the case of the Baltimore & Ohio the mismanagement had begun more than a decade before the depression of the nineties, but the regime in power had been placed there by the very interests which had formerly brought the company to the verge of ruin, for the purpose of preserving a discreet silence upon the former management's activities. Rumors which proved only too accurate preceded the acknowledgment of insolvency by each of these companies; nevertheless the disclosures which attended their receiverships and reorganizations startled all except the most cynical observers.

The Richmond & West Point Terminal system had been developed from the Richmond & West Point Railway & Warehouse Company, chartered about 1880.[1] The parent company had bought control of the Richmond & Danville Railroad, the

---

1 Snyder, *op. cit.*, pp. 670-680.

East Tennessee, Virginia & Georgia and the Central Railroad &
Banking Company of Georgia. Including the subsidiaries of
these companies, in 1892 the Terminal company controlled,
directly or indirectly, about 8400 miles of Southern railways
and was the most important system along the Atlantic seaboard
south of Washington. The three auxiliaries had been doing
extremely well and paying high dividends until in 1891 a
change set in, especially in the Richmond & Danville system.
Since the parent company, which owned and operated no mileage directly, was more deeply concerned in the affairs of the
Danville than in any of the other members of the system, a
crisis in the affairs of the Terminal company developed.[2]

In the face of rumors that the company's stock had been
manipulated for speculative purposes and that other discreditable machinations had taken place, a proposal was made that
$10,500,000, to pay immediate debts and provide working
capital, be raised through an assessment of $15 per share on
the stock. The stockholders, who were in nearly complete ignorance of the situation, refused to accept the proposal and instead
appointed a committee to investigate the needs of the system
and frame a plan to relieve the financial embarrassments which
were threatening its solvency. The committee proposed that a
syndicate for $30,000,000 be formed and the resulting funds
be used to pay the floating debt of the Terminal company, all
car trusts and the maturing debts of the Georgia Central.
Payment of these pressing obligations would place the system
on its feet again.[3]

But before the plan could be put into effect the Central of
Georgia was forced into a receivership which was highly complicated by numerous court litigations. The needs of the rest
of the system were too immediate to permit waiting for the
settlement of these legal problems, so another reorganization
plan had to be formulated. A new committee was appointed

2 Van Oss, *op. cit.*, pp. 774-787.

3 *Railway World*, May 14, 1892, p. 471.

by the stockholders, composed of Frederic P. Olcott, Oliver H.
Payne, Frederick D. Tappen, William H. Perkins, Henry
Budge, H. C. Fahnestock and J. Kennedy Tod.[4]

The group presented its recommendations on March 1, 1892,
about five months after the first appointment of a special committee. The plan proposed the issuance of $350,000,000 of new
stocks and bonds to replace the $394,500,000 of outstanding
securities of the Terminal Company, the Richmond & Danville
and the East Tennessee lines. The reduction in the amount of
outstanding securities, together with the proposed lower rates
of interest on the new bonds, would reduce the fixed charges
of the parent company to $6,400,000 per year. The rental of
the Cincinnati Southern line was $1,000,000 per year; that of
the North Carolina Railroad was $260,000. Adding these pay-
ments to the fixed charges, a total annual obligation of $7,-
660,000 would have to be borne by the company in contrast
to the former yearly $9,474,837. Basing their calculations on
the recent past earnings of the company, the committee believed
that this arrangement would permit payment of all outstanding
debts, provide ample working capital and leave a margin of
over $1,000,000 per year available for dividends. The Central
of Georgia was not included in the plan, but provision was
made for adding it to the Terminal system when it should
emerge from its legal difficulties.[5]

While the security holders were considering this proposal,
the committee organized a syndicate to underwrite the new securities, and to meet immediate needs raised $1,000,000 on
three-month notes of the Terminal and Danville companies.[6]
But the efforts of the committee were futile. Although the proposed plan was substantially that under which the system would
finally be reorganized, for a company which had not yet ad-

4 *Richmond & West Point Terminal Railway & Warehouse Plan of
Reorganization*, dated March 1, 1892, 28 page pamphlet.

5 *Ibid.*, and *Railway World*, March 2, 1892, p. 265.

6 *Railway World*, May 21, 1892, p. 495.

mitted that it was insolvent the terms proposed were too drastic to be acceptable to the several interests affected. Early in May it became apparent that the plan had small chance of success,[7] and before the end of the month the disapproval of holders of underlying securities led to its abandonment.[8]

As soon as the committe's plan had been definitely rejected, a new movement was begun to put the system on a sound financial basis. A petition, supposedly originating in the New York office of John Bloodgood and asking Drexel, Morgan & Company to undertake the reorganization, was circulated for signatures. Failure of the several previous efforts to put the system on its feet had convinced the bondholders of the need for a reorganization manager in whom all interests could put absolute faith.[9] But before an answer could be gotten from Morgan, the problem was further complicated by the receivership on June 15 of the Danville system and a few days later that of the Terminal company. As officially stated, the purpose behind the latter was to prevent a small minority of security holders from hampering the work of reorganization and the calling in of Morgan and to protect the system from dissolution.[10]

Insofar as the second of these objects was concerned, the manoeuvre proved a complete failure. On June 28 Morgan refused to undertake the reorganization. His letter declared that an investigation had assured him that a reorganization could be made, but because of " unparalleled complications and difficulties ", he wished protection " against any single interest " which might interfere with his proposals. To be sure of this protection, Morgan demanded that a majority of every issue of securities involved be deposited with Drexel, Morgan & Company; that all litigation concerning the receivership be

7 *Ibid.*, May 14, 1892, p. 471.
8 *Ibid.*, May 21, 1892, p. 495.
9 *Ibid.*, May 28, 1892, p. 506.
10 *Ibid.*, June 25, 1892, p. 615.

put under his control, and that a Morgan representative, Samuel Spencer, be substituted for the receiver already appointed. When the receivership had been announced, Morgan continued, he had asked W. P. Clyde if the suit which the latter controlled would be transferred to the Morgan firm and Spencer made the receiver. Clyde refused to give the required assurances and gave Morgan the impression that he would not be loyal to the latter's efforts in behalf of the system. In the face of this rebuff, Morgan felt his firm could not undertake the work.[11] Despite the harshness of these terms, repeated efforts were made by various groups interested in the fate of the system to get his help, but all to no avail. Morgan refused to retreat from his original demands, and meanwhile the company fell deeper and deeper into financial difficulties and danger of the dissolution of the system became more imminent.[12]

The immediate causes of the receivership of the Terminal Company are obvious. As officially announced, the protection of the court had been sought to facilitate the reorganization of the huge, ungainly system and to prevent its disruption.[13] These needs, in turn, had been the direct results of the accumulation of a large floating debt.

At the time, the bankruptcy seemed to at least one authority on railroad finance " to be connected more with speculative designs on the part of the powers that be than with real embarrassments ".[14] A report made to the court by Walter G. Oakman, the receiver, seemed to confirm this suspicion that the receivership was less the result of simple inability to pay the company's debts than of some more fundamental and mysterious machinations. The Terminal company, exclusive of subsidiary corporations, had a total capital stock of $75,000,000

11 *Ibid.*, July 9, 1892, p. 639 for text of letter.

12 *Ibid.*, July 9, 1892, p. 649; August 20, 1892, pp. 806-807. *Commercial and Financial Chronicle*, February 4, 1893, p. 178.

13 *Railway World*, June 25, 1892, p. 615.

14 Van Oss, *op. cit.*, pp. 778-779.

and funded debts totalling $16,500,000.[15] On June 22, 1892, it had $74,632,369.72 worth of securities of various other companies on hand. Of this amount, over $17,000,000 were deposited under a 6 per cent mortgage; almost $41,000,000 were included in the security for a 5 per cent mortgage and about $12,500,000 were earmarked for special use in intra-system financing. The unpledged securities on hand thus amounted to only $7,484,869.77; in addition the treasury contained about $2,500,000 of securities which had been redeemed and cancelled, and the property and bills receivable against which no lien existed were worth another $1,500,000.[16] So on the day when application was made for the appointment of a receiver, the company had over $11,000,000 worth of securities which could theoretically be realized at once in cash.

However, the existence of this unusually large balance for a bankrupt corporation is far from conclusive proof that the Terminal Company's difficulties were not genuine. As the application to the court pointed out, one of the chief motives in seeking the protection offered by a receivership was the preservation of the system. To have disposed of these securities, possession of which gave it control of its subsidiaries, would have meant the dissolution of the system; furthermore, such forced disposal would not have realized the values in cash at which these securities were carried on the company's books.

Late in August an advisory committee of fifteen representing the stockholders decided to investigate some of the rumors which were being bandied about in financial circles. Henry Clews, a Wall Street financier who was the leading spirit of the group, demanded that Receiver Oakman institute a suit against former officials to recover the funds which allegedly misappropriated from the company's treasury.[17]

Filing of the suit by the Richmond Terminal Company in

15 *Railway Age and Northwestern Railroader*, January 6, 1893, p. 2.

16 *Railway World*, August 20, 1892, p. 806.

17 *Ibid.*, August 27, 1892, p. 831 and September 3, 1892, p. 854.

the middle of December finally brought into the open the accusations which heretofore had not been publicly elaborated. Never adequately answered, these charges involved certain transactions in Central Railroad & Banking Company of Georgia securities. Since a Georgia court had precluded recovery from that company of the illegally appropriated money, the suit for recovery of $7,500,000 principal and interest was directed against all the individuals and corporations involved in the tangled web of transactions: Juneau, Swann & Company, H. H. Hollins & Company, August Belmont & Company, Lehman Brothers, Kessler & Company, I. & S. Wormser, Scholle Brothers, J. & W. Seligman, Blum, St. Goar & Company, Heidelback, Ickelheimer & Company, E. W. Clark & Company, Isaac L. Rice, John C. Calhoun, Patrick Calhoun and John H. Inman, who was the dominant figure in the syndicate.

Until 1865 Inman's had been a typical Southern life: born at Dandridge, Jefferson County, Tennessee, of English and north of Ireland ancestry, he had been raised on his father's plantation and gone to the neighborhood academy. He had preferred to work in a Georgia bank rather than go to college, and at the outbreak of the Civil War he was a clerk there. He joined the Confederate army, despite the preponderantly Union sentiment of his home county in eastern Tennessee, and fought from 1862 to 1865. His father was ruined by the War, so as soon as he was mustered out and had a few dollars in his pocket he went to New York and secured employment in a cotton house in which he was soon made a partner. In 1870 he organized his own house, Inman, Swann & Company and he was one of the founders of the New York Cotton Exchange, in which he was prominent until his death. It was while his headquarters were in New York that he became interested in railroading: he helped organize the Tennessee Coal, Iron & Railroad Company, which later became a part of the United States Steel combination. After this successful initial venture in railways he extended his interests to the Louisville & Nashville, the Central of Georgia, the Richmond & Danville and the Richmond Terminal. Although he held numerous directorships in these and other corporations, however, Inman was primarily a promoter rather than an administrator. His boast in later life was that he had been responsible for bringing $100,000,000 of northern capital into the South and his success in so doing was in good part due to his sincere belief in the industrial potentialities of the former Confederate states. At the time of his presidency of the Richmond Terminal he was in his late forties, a man of boundless energy, proven financial ability and considerable charm.[18]

The syndicate headed by Inman, the bill of complaint alleged, bought 40,000 shares of Georgia Central Stock for about $4,000,000, a price far above the market value of the securities. A corporation called the Georgia Company was then formed by employees of the syndicate members, with a nominal capital of $16,000,000, none of which was ever paid in. The Georgia Company bought from the syndicate the 40,000 shares of Georgia Central stock, and in payment turned over the whole of its own capital stock and $4,000,000 of its own collateral trust bonds, which were secured by a pledge of the Georgia Central stock. The contracts for this sale were signed January 1, 1888.

With these preliminary details out of the way, the Georgia Central stock was deposited with the Central Trust Company in New York as the collateral trust bonds provided. The capital stock of the Georgia company was reduced to $12,000,000 par value, and a voting trust formed by depositing 60,100 shares with the Central Trust Company. The remaining 59,900 shares were placed in a pool. In February, 1888, the syndicate tried to sell both the collateral trust bonds and the pooled stock in Europe. It was asserted that the $4,000,000 of trust bonds were secured by stock worth over $5,000,000 which for several years

18 *Dictionary of American Biography*, IX, p. 484.

past had paid yearly dividends of over 9 per cent. Despite the encouraging prospects thus attributed to the Georgia company, European buyers showed no interest in the securities and the attempt to sell them abroad was abandoned.

The efforts of the syndicate were then turned nearer home. On May 31, 1888, John H. Inman was elected president of the Richmond & West Point Terminal Company and John C. Calhoun was added to a board of directors which already included Simon Wormser and James Swann. A year later Patrick Calhoun joined the other syndicate members on the board of the unfortunate company. Late in October Emanuel Lehman, in behalf of himself and his associates, offered to sell the Terminal Company the entire 120,000 shares of Georgia Company stock at $35 per share. At this price the Richmond Terminal would be paying about $4,200,000 for stock worth absolutely nothing more than the value of the voting privileges attached to 40,000 shares of Georgia Central stock, since the Georgia Company's collateral trust bonds more than represented the market value of the Georgia Central stock. Nevertheless, the Terminal directors present at the October 22 meeting approved the purchase and appointed a committee to formulate plans for financing it. Four days later the committee announced that it had contracted with the syndicate to buy the stock and, also, that it had agreed to buy $1,000,000 of the Georgia Company's collateral trust bonds and either to buy the remaining $3,000,000 worth within ninety days, or else have the Richmond & Danville Railroad Company guarantee the interest on them.

The directors at once approved this remarkable arrangement. At their regular meeting on May 29, 1889, a committee of three to carry out the contract was appointed, to consist of Inman, Patrick Calhoun and one other director. To finance the purchase of the outstanding Georgia Company bonds, the committee was instructed to borrow the necessary funds from the Georgia Central.

The Georgia Central at this time was in need of cash itself

and was trying to sell $5,000,000 of Savannah & Western Railroad Company first mortgage 5 per cent bonds which it had guaranteed. A three-cornered contract was arranged between the Terminal company committee, the Georgia Central and H. H. Hollins & Company. Hollins & Company agreed to buy the Savannah & Western bonds at 95 plus accrued interest, on condition that the Terminal company committee conclude the purchase of outstanding Georgia Company bonds from the syndicate. The Georgia Central was to lend the Richmond Terminal committee $3,500,000 from the proceeds of the sale to Hollins, this money to be used for the purchase of the Georgia Company bonds. In addition, Inman and his associates were to receive a gratuity from the Georgia Central of $25,000 to help pay for the bonds, and a similar amount was to be paid Hollins & Company in settlement of its claims against the Richmond Terminal, the Georgia Central and the Georgia Company.

The contracts were carried out as arranged: the Richmond Terminal bought the Georgia Company stock; the committee bought the rest of the Georgia Company bonds. To meet the payments required by these deals, the Richmond Terminal issued 5 per cent collateral trust notes of the East Tennessee, Virginia & Georgia Railroad. At the conclusion of this sequence of events, the Terminal company found itself possessed of the entire capital stock of the Georgia Company, as well as that company's collateral trust notes. In return for these securities, the Richmond company had injured the credit of the East Tennessee, Virginia & Georgia to the extent that the latter's collateral trust notes had been issued; it had borrowed heavily from the Georgia Central at a time when that corporation could ill afford to lend any cash, to say nothing of paying out $50,000 in premiums for brokerage; the Georgia Central, further, was obligated to pay the interest on $5,000,000 of Savannah & Western bonds now in the hands of Hollins & Company.

In return for all these sacrifices, what had the Richmond Terminal company gotten? It had 40,000 shares of Georgia Central stock, which had cost it about $7,500,000. In 1889,

1890 and 1891 that company paid 8 per cent on its stock, but Receiver Comer in 1892 discovered that the money for these payments had all been borrowed, and that this dividend policy was responsible for the accumulation of a $6,657,302 floating debt. In other words, the Richmond company had bought stock which was practically worthless at the time of purchase, and its president and four of its directors had sold for $7,500,000 the worthless stock for which they had paid about half that sum.

Not only had the Terminal company been swindled, but the board of directors had not proceeded legally in approving the transactions. The Virginia law, under which the company was chartered, provided that a director could not vote on any transaction in which he was interested in any way other than as a director. The five Richmond directors did not vote on these transactions, but their abstinence prevented a quorum of the board from ever passing on the questions. At the meetings of the directors, Inman, the Calhouns, Wormser and Swann declared that they favored the purchases because of the high dividends paid by the Georgia Central, but when voting began they became officially " absent ". So the whole series of deals was illegal.[19]

The purchase of 40,000 shares of Georgia Central stock had carried with it control of that system, for only 75,000 shares were outstanding, but even the value attached to the voting power of the stock was dubious. In March, 1892, a Georgia Central stockholder sued in a Georgia court to prevent the Richmond Terminal from exercising its voting privilege. The circuit court upheld the plaintiff's contention that control of the Central by the Richmond would be a violation of the Georgia constitution, and enjoined the Richmond company from voting in the Central's election of officers.[20]

19 *Railway World*, September 10, 1892, p. 878; October 15, 1892, p. 999; December 3, 1892, pp. 1167-1168; December 24, 1892, pp. 1238-1239.

20 The receivership was only temporary, and was terminated as soon as stockholders had held a new election from which the Terminal was excluded;

Although a higher court reversed this decision in June, 1893, the question was not settled by the second decision. Litigation continued, and it was in the light of these legal complications that Receiver Oakman sued for restitution of the $7,500,000 fraudulently paid out by the Richmond Terminal Company and for the cancellation of all contracts involved.[21]

Former President Inman, in behalf of the defendants, made a statement as soon as the suit was filed. He did not deny that a gigantic swindle had been put over on the Richmond Terminal, but he did deny all knowledge of the details of the purchases made by the Terminal Company. Secondly, he pointed out that any action that had been taken, had been taken by the entire board of directors and, furthermore, all the actions of the board had since been approved by the annual meetings of the stockholders. In addition, Inman claimed that the suit was brought by stockholders who had bought their stock after the details of the swindle had become publicly known. By their purchases, he contended, they had implied approval of all previous actions of the company.[22]

Inman's statement was ingenious, but it fails to carry conviction. His final point may be ignored as at best a legal technicality which might bring an acquittal in court. His third point, the approval of the stockholders, is also inconclusive; the impossibility of stockholders' meetings doing more than give perfunctory votes of confidence in the management became notorious within a few years.[23] The attempt to shift the blame to the shoulders of the directors as a body is equally

it should not be confused with the receivership beginning October 7, 1893, which was caused by financial troubles.

21 *Railroad Gazette*, July 7, 1895, p. 506.

22 *Ibid.*, March 10, 1893, p. 197.

23 *Investigation of Financial and Monetary Concentration in the United States* (hereafter called *Pujo Investigation*), Testimony of H. P. Davison, II, pp. 828-831; after questioning by the committee's counsel, the witness admitted that he had never heard of a case involving a large corporation where common stockholders had been able to remove the management; only when a large block of stock could be voted, was it possible to do so.

unconvincing; a board of directors invariably approves any transaction which the special committee to investigate recommends. And in this case the defendants composed two-thirds of the committee and emphatically endorsed approval of the purchases. Inman's denial of detailed knowledge of the transactions is meaningless; he personally might not have known the full details and yet have been an important accessory to the swindle. Finally, Inman did not even deny a general knowledge of the affair, and even the most general understanding of what was being done should have brought violent and public protests from the president of the prospective victim-corporation. Unless Inman were to admit his guilt, no other course except a general denial of the charges was open to him. That this consisted of a denial of detailed knowledge and an attempt to shift to others blame for what he himself apparently considered a fraudulent transaction, only makes the statement completely inadequate.

It is indisputable that these transactions comprised an influential factor in bringing insolvency to the Richmond & West Point Terminal. In the first place, the receivership of the Georgia Central road was ordered to protect it during the litigation which originated in these deals.[24] And it was the receivership of that company which led to the abandonment of the earliest plans for reorganizing the Terminal company. Less tangibly, the failure of the Georgia Central roused a distrust of the system of which it had been one of the most prosperous-seeming members and was the starting point for rumors of a distinctly unfavorable nature about the integrity of the parent company's administration. More concretely and perhaps of far greater importance, these transactions increased the floating debt of the Richmond company and thereby helped destroy its credit.

The growth of the floating debt which these swindles caused might not have proved fatal, however, had the system been

24 *Railway World*, March 2, 1894, p. 265.

sound in other respects. But such was far from being the case. The physical condition of the system was so poor that huge expenditures would have to be made before it could be operated at a profit. It was still partially equipped with light rails, trestles badly in need of repair, unballasted roadbeds, bridges too weak to permit the use of heavy engines, engines and cars which were small, weak and old, and crude and wasteful repair shops. The extremity to which deterioration had progressed was illustrated in 700 miles of iron rails on the Richmond & Danville and 72 miles of them on the main line of the East Tennessee, and in the venerable age of some of the active locomotives, which had been used for from 22 to 33 years. To hide the true financial and physical condition of the system, its books had been improperly kept. Instead of charging repairs against operating expenses, they had been capitalized for the most part in the construction accounts. Some of the " assets " listed by the Richmond & Danville consisted of : bills receivable (worthless) $45,000; property destroyed by fires $32,043; property lost in East Tennessee & Georgia accident $16,466; worthless claims and balances, etc., probably $200,000; losses on certain traffic contracts $92,174.[25]

Testifying before the Industrial Commission in 1900, T. M. R. Talcott, assistant to the president of the Seaboard Air Lines, was asked: " What was the principal cause of the various receiverships of prominent railroads, such as the Norfolk & Western, the Richmond Terminal, etc., four or five years ago? Were they due to defects of management or to financial mismanagement? " Mr. Talcott replied:

Financial mismanagement, or, I would rather say, I do not know that that expresses it exactly. I might say that in their anxiety to build up a big system they bought properties and paid higher prices for them than should have been paid—more than they were worth. In other words, in the case of the Terminal Company, they diluted an exceedingly valuable stock by hanging on to it weak properties

25 *Commercial and Financial Chronicle*, May 23, 1893, pp. 858-860.

until they broke its back. I speak of the Richmond & Danville road. A more solvent institution never existed until they loaded it down —and it was not really bankrupt when they put it into the hands of the receiver.[26]

Although the last assertion, that the Richmond & Danville was not really insolvent when it was placed under the care of the court, is distinctly questionable, the rest of Mr. Talcott's analysis is confirmed and supplemented by the opinion of a later critic:

But as 1891 opened, the vast Richmond Terminal System was perilously near financial collapse. Notwithstanding the great value of many of the lines, its physical condition was poor; the liabilities and capitalization were enormous and much of the mileage was distinctly unprofitable. About this time many disquieting facts began to leak out: during the previous year the Richmond & Danville had been operated at a large loss, and this fact had been concealed by deceptive entries on the books; the dividends paid on the Central Railroad of Georgia stock had not been earned for some years; and the East Tennessee properties were hardly paying their way.[27]

The weakness of the system is well illustrated by the fixed charges of nearly $9,500,000 on less than 8500 miles of track. This mileage all lay in the South where cotton was the staple freight load. No road in an industrially undeveloped section of the country, with much of its tonnage carried at very low rates, could hope to remain solvent unless its management operated at a very high degree of honesty and efficiency. And both of these characteristics were conspicuous by their absence from the management of the Richmond & West Point Terminal Company.

The failure of the Richmond Terminal system occurred before the depression had enveloped the country. In February, 1893, the failure of the Philadelphia & Reading Railroad

26 *Industrial Commission Report*, IX, p. 636.

27 Moody, *Railroad Builders*, p. 187.

marked the beginning of the panic. The Richmond receivership
had been but a prelude to what was to follow, and antedated
the depression of 1893. The Reading failure, on the other hand,
was one of the great collapses which are frequently cited as
illustrating the severity of the economic chaos that swept the
country that year. It was important because it helped precipitate the panic that was developing; it was of greater importance
in that it ruined one of the most ambitious railroad-develop-
ment programs the country had seen before the early years of
the twentieth century. Finally, the Reading crash was of
national importance in its repercussions on the anthracite coal
industry and it marked the end of another attempt to solve the
chronic " anthracite problem ".

This anthracite problem had been acute almost constantly
since the railroads had begun to exploit the Pennsylvania deposits. The only known anthracite fields were concentrated in
four separate areas, whose size, if consolidated, would have
been less than 500 square miles. All four of these areas were
so situated as to facilitate cheap distribution of the coal to
factories in New York City, Philadelphia, Pittsburgh and
Buffalo, and to the millions of private homes in the rough
square formed by these cities.

First discovered between 1770 and 1790 by hunters who were
astounded to see the ground beneath them catch fire, the coal
seems not to have been mined at all until 1807, and little serious
effort to exploit it commercially was made until about 1820.
In the years following the Civil War the several railroad lines
which penetrated the region gradually brought up nearly all
deposits, although the immediate operation of the mines and
collieries was left to subsidiary companies.[28] In 1871 Franklin
B. Gowen, president of the Philadelphia & Reading, decided
that the Reading must buy some coal fields or it would soon
lose its coal trade, the chief item in its freight tonnage, to the
other railroads which were spreading their control over the

28 *Industrial Commission Report*, XIX, pp. 444-448.

mines. Extensive purchases were made and in May the Laurel River Improvement Company was organized to own and operate the mines. In December of the same year the name of the subsidiary company was changed to Philadelphia & Reading Coal & Iron Company, and under that name it continued to develop its holdings.[29]

The peculiar interest of the Reading in the anthracite industry was summarized by an investigating committee in 1900:

Since 1871, at least, the dominant railroad has been the Philadelphia & Reading, which affords the shortest and most direct connection between the field and Philadelphia. The peculiar position of this system is owing to the fact that it is a local road without through traffic such as is enjoyed by all the other lines. Thus, for example, the Pennsylvania, Erie, Lehigh Valley and other companies, all operate through lines to the West, to Buffalo, or other points on the Great Lakes, connecting them with the great Atlantic seaports. As a result, the coal mining industry is rather incidental to their other business, due to the fact that their lines cross or pass near the place of deposit of the anthracite coal. The Philadelphia & Reading on the other hand has no other interest, with the exception of the local freight and passenger business originating within its territory.[30]

Under these circumstances the maintenance of prosperity in the coal fields was a matter of life and death to the Reading. Depression in the industry would not only mean that the huge capital which the road had invested directly in anthracite would make no return to the parent company, but also the Reading's freight earnings would be severely reduced if coal shipments were slowed up. In 1883 the importance of this dependence became publicly manifest: to reduce the severe competition which was threatening to ruin the coal market by causing more tons to be mined annually than could be sold at a profitable

29 *Regulation of Stock Ownership in Railroads, House Report 2789*, 71st Congress, 3rd Session, III, p. 1216.

30 *Industrial Commission Report*, XIX, pp. 444-448.

price, the Reading leased one of its chief competitors in the
anthracite field, the Central Railroad of New Jersey, for a
period of 999 years. Upon the complaint of a stockholder in
the New Jersey road, this state's courts declared the lease illegal
and directed that it be surrendered. The New Jersey constitution forbade the lease of a corporation chartered in that state
by a company chartered in another state. But three years later
substantially the same ends were achieved. Both the Jersey
Central and the Reading were forced into receivership in 1886;
the former was reorganized by George F. Baker and his associates at the same time that J. P. Morgan was directing the
rehabilitation of the latter. The long-standing friendship and
business cooperation between the two men assured harmonious
relations between the roads as long as their control lasted.[31]

But in 1890 a new figure came upon the comparatively peace-
ful anthracite scene, A. Archibald McLeod. Born in New York
City of Scotch ancestry, he had left school at an early age to
become a rodman in the construction of the Northern Pacific.
After several years spent working on various roads in the
Northwest, he became general manager of the Elmira, Cortland
and Northern railway and in 1885 he advanced to the general
managership of the Philadelphia & Reading. Because of his
success in improving the roadbed and rolling stock to such a
point of efficiency that the Reading could compete with its
rivals, he was made vice-president in 1888.[32] Although comparatively unknown outside the Reading company, he was promoted to the presidency in 1890 and before four years had
passed he had experienced one of the most meteoric careers in
American railroad history.

While Morgan still controlled the road, Franklin B. Gowen,
the former president, formed a syndicate with the intention of
purchasing the reorganized company. Before the syndicate's
plans had an opportunity to mature, Gowen committed suicide,

31 *Stock Ownership*, III, p. 1217.

32 *The National Cyclopedia of American Biography*, 1906, XIII, p. 115.

but the purchase of stock continued until the syndicate had bought enough to assure control. Because of friendly feeling all around, Morgan permitted the voting trust, which he had established to operate the reorganized road, to be dissolved and the syndicate took over the road, electing McLeod to the presidency.[33]

Despite the fact that he owed his position to the syndicate, McLeod was a man who had views of his own and a notable determination to see them through. Perhaps as characteristic a remark as was ever attributed to him was his supposed assertion, on being told that J. P. Morgan frowned on some of his projects, that he would rather run a peanut stand than accept dictation from J. P. Morgan or anyone else. A strong-willed man, for three years he completely controlled the destinies of the Reading.[34]

For some time before McLeod took control of the Reading, the retail price of all anthracite coal sold along the Atlantic seaboard had been fixed under a loose agreement between the railroads chiefly interested in the industry. Periodically representatives of the several roads met in New York to discuss the financial situation and the problems of the coal trade. These very informal gatherings fixed the price at which anthracite was to be sold until the next meeting and appointed a time for that meeting. If a change in price were decided upon, a circular so stating was sent to all the roads involved; if no price change were approved, the meeting simply disbanded. There were never any legal contracts, official meetings, keeping of minutes, or attempts to organize a formal pool. The need to cooperate in order to maintain the price of coal, and thereby preserve the prosperity of the industry, was the only factor compelling obedience by the roads to the dictates of the meetings but that was

33 *Industrial Commission Report*, Testimony of Isaac L. Rice, a member of the syndicate, IX, p. 737.

34 Hovey, Carl, *Life Story of J. P. Morgan*, New York: Sturgis and Walton Company, 1912, p. 136; Corey, Lewis, *The House of Morgan*, New York: G. Howard Watt, 1930, p. 202.

usually enough.[35] And independent operators who proved recalcitrant were forced into line by a policy on the part of the
railroads of withholding the cars necessary to transport their
output.[36]

However, even with prices stabilized by this clumsy method,
the anthracite business was not prospering. So President
McLeod initiated an ambitious campaign of expansion for the
Reading, which was intended to give to this one company
virtual control of the industry. To avoid the New Jersey con-
stitutional provision that had invalidated the 1883 lease of the
Jersey Central, the Reading's first step was to charter the Port
Reading Railroad Company in New Jersey. This corporation
was to build a line from Bound Brook, hitherto the terminal
of the Reading system, to Port Reading on tidewater opposite
Staten Island. Before even that short roadbed had been more
than barely begun, the Jersey Central together with its subsidiaries was leased for 999 years to this corporation. The Port
Reading was to assume all the Jersey Central's fixed charges
and guarantee 7 per cent dividends on the capital stock. Any
earnings in excess of the sums needed for these purposes were
to be divided equally between the two companies. The whole
arrangement was guaranteed by the Philadelphia & Reading.[37]

On the same day that these contracts were signed, the Reading also leased the Lehigh Valley system, not only to further
the attempted corner of the anthracite industry but also to get
an outlet on the Great Lakes. The terms of this second arrangement were the same as those of the other lease. The Reading
assumed all the fixed charges of the Lehigh Valley, guaranteed
7 per cent on all Lehigh stock and agreed to divide equally
between the two systems any Lehigh profits over 7 per cent.[38]

35 *Investigation of Alleged Coal Combination, House Report 2278*, 52nd
Congress, 2nd Session, p. 6, Testimony of McLeod.

36 *Industrial Commission Report*, XIX, p. 457.

37 *Ibid.*, XIX, p. 456.

38 *Commercial and Financial Chronicle*, March 14, 1893, p. 352.

This lease also included all the subsidiaries of the lessee company, notably its coal companies.

While these negotiations were progressing a fourth of the anthracite roads, the Delaware, Lackawanna & Western, had been added to the combination.   J. Rogers Maxwell, president of the Jersey Central, and George F. Baker, the largest stockholder and the dominant director of that road, became heavily interested in the Lackawanna and were elected to its board of directors, replacing Russell Sage and Sidney Dillon. To complete the identity of interest between the two companies, President Samuel Sloan of the Lackawanna became a director of the Central.[39]   Further to strengthen the combination, the Reading proposed to bring in the independent coal operators. The railroads were accustomed to buy coal outright from these operators, paying them a fixed percentage of the price at tidewater, and then sell the coal through their own agents. To attract the independents, McLeod proposed to raise the percentage the combination would pay from the former figure of 55 to 60 and the operators were to be persuaded to sign long-term contracts.[40]

These leases and alliances radically changed the position of the Reading. McLeod had taken a little line entirely dependent on coal trade, controlling less than 1200 miles of track with no terminals, and transformed it into one of the major systems of the East, with a terminal on the Great Lakes and another on New York Harbor, controlling almost 4,000 miles of trunk line.[41] The dominance of the Reading in the coal trade had been made nearly absolute. Eight railroads entered the anthracite fields; of these only the Pennsylvania, the Erie and the smaller

39 *Report of the Senate Special Committee on Coal Combination ... of the New York State Legislature*, February 1, 1893, *Senate Document No. 21*, IV, 1893, pp. 3-5. Also see Jones, Eliot, *The Anthracite Coal Combinations*, Cambridge: Harvard University Press, 1914, pp. 52-53.

40 *Industrial Commission Report*, XIX, p. 456. See Jones, *op. cit.*, pp. 52-3.

41 *Railway World*, March 18, 1893, p. 245, quoting New York *Recorder*. Van Oss, *op. cit.*, pp. 307-337.

New York, Susquehanna & Western and New York, Ontario & Western remained outside the combination. The total annual capacity of the collieries was about 50,000,000 tons, but the total output was limited to a yearly 41,000,000 tons. Of this, about 35 per cent was carried to tidewater over these railroads. The rest of the mined coal went west to Pittsburgh, northwest to Buffalo or was used in Pennsylvania and nearby counties of New York. The combination controlled, directly or indirectly, about 70 per cent of the coal which reached tidewater.[42] Furthermore, competition with the independent lines was more theoretical than real.[43]

But as the Reading's power grew and as the effects of the attempted monopoly became apparent, seeds of disaster developed rapidly. A congressional committee, headed by Representative William J. Coombs, after investigating the combination presented findings of a disquieting nature. Even before the consolidation engineered by the Reading the railroads had charged rates for transporting coal nearly double those charged in other parts of the country for cotton and wheat. The Interstate Commerce Commission thought that $1.40 per ton would be a fair price for the trip to tidewater; nevertheless the current rate was $1.90 and the Commission had no power to lower it. The power given the Reading in the industry was reflected almost immediately by a rise in the cost to consumers. Grate coal prices advanced from $3.50 per ton in February, 1892, to $3.80 per ton in the following November; egg coal rose from $3.60 to $4.25; stove coal that had sold at $3.25 was priced at $4.60 and chestnut advanced from $3.25 to $4.50. Only on those sizes of anthracite which competed with bituminous coal was the price rise very slight.[44]

42 *Investigation of Alleged Coal Combination, House Report, 2278*, 52nd Congress, 2nd Session, p. 1; *Railway World*, January 21, 1893, pp. 49-50 and January 28, 1893, pp. 78-80.

43 *Investigation of Alleged Coal Combination, House Report, 2278*, 52nd Congress, 2nd Session, p. 1.

44 *Ibid., passim.* Also see *Railway World*, January 28, 1893, pp. 78-80.

This movement in prices only served to heighten the public apprehension which had been aroused when the formation of the combination was announced. In addition to the Federal investigation, the New York State senate had investigated for itself and the Pennsylvania legislature had conducted a third investigation.   Further, suits for dissolution of the combination were brought in New York, Pennsylvania, and New Jersey,[45] although only that in New Jersey had any direct effect. In January, 1893, the Chancellor of New Jersey upheld the decision of a lower state court which had declared the Central's lease to the Port Reading unconstitutional. The absurdity of leasing a system valued at over $70,000,000 to a tiny, half-built road worth practically nothing was too manifest.[46] That the creation of the Port Reading was merely a subterfuge to avoid the New Jersey constitutional law was so obvious that the chancellor ruled that in effect the Philadelphia and Reading was the lessor company, and therefore like its 1883 predecessor, the contract was illegal.[47] Even before this decision was published and while the case was pending, the two roads and their subsidiary coal companies had been operated separately,[48] but to make sure that both the letter and the spirit of the decision were observed, Ex-governor Ludlow of New Jersey was appointed by the Chancellor to make a report on the relations between the Reading and the Jersey Central.   Ludlow declared in his final report that the dissolution order had been obeyed by both roads and that the Jersey Central was no longer part of the combination.[49]

This defection from the ranks, however, still left the Reading in control of over 40 per cent of the anthracite reaching tidewater and, despite Ludlow's beliefs, competition between the

45 *Railway World*, February 4, 1893, pp. 99-101.

46 *Industrial Commission Report*, XIX, p. 457.

47 *Railway World*, January 7, 1893, p. 1.

48 *Ibid.*, January 7, 1893, p. 1.

49 *Ibid.*, April 8, 1893, p. 321.

Jersey Central and the Reading was only fictitious. There was no danger of the Central's waging a price war, or even making a gesture in that direction.[50] But with the maintenance of prices came a stagnation in the retail trade. The Reading could not begin to sell the coal it had carried to tidewater and as the supply grew, with it grew the amount of Reading capital tied up in temporarily frozen assets.[51] To solve the problem of marketing this huge store of anthracite, McLeod started the Reading on the second chapter of expansion under his direction.

New England, with its highly concentrated industries, seemed to offer a field for profitable enlargement of the anthracite trade if the charges for transportation could be kept low. The most direct way to achieve this end was to extend the Reading lines into New England, where a foothold had already been gained. In July, 1892, the Reading had gotten control of the Central New England & Western Railroad and the Poughkeepsie Railroad and had reorganized them as the Philadelphia, Reading & New England Railroad Company.[52] If connections could be formed with this line, New England would be open to the Reading and its surplus coal would find a market.

The roads which McLeod determined to add to the Reading system were the Boston & Maine, long a conservatively managed and highly prosperous local carrier,[53] and the New York & New England Railroad, a line whose financial condition was dubious, but which had the advantage of an entrance into New York City through a trackage agreement with the Vanderbilts.[54]

On the witness stand ten years later, McLeod denied that the presence of an unsalable surplus of coal was the cause of the Reading's ventures into New England, but the reasons he

50 *Industrial Commission Report*, XIX, p. 456.

51 *Commercial and Financial Chronicle*, February 25, 1893, p. 3113.

52 Van Oss, *op. cit.*, p. 306.

53 *Ibid.*, pp. 363; Meade, E. S., " Great Railways," *Railway World*, 1905, pp. 215-216.

54 Van Oss, *op. cit.*, pp. 367-369; *Commercial and Financial Chronicle*, March 11, 1893, p. 391.

gave by no means excluded that motive. To a question whether the Reading could have produced more coal than it did, McLeod answered: " Certainly, if it could dispose of it ". The next query was: " Did the existence of such a surplus have anything to do with the entrance of the Philadelphia & Reading into New England territory in 1892? " McLeod answered in detail:

No; my object in that move was to increase the Reading's tonnage without getting into such a row with my neighbors that the whole structure would go to pieces. There has been a well recognized rule among those companies for a number of years that where the transporting company owns the rails the tonnage distributed on those rails should be considered as belonging to that line, therefore, they would not precipitate a war that would be ruinous. My object in going into New England was to get, in that way, and under a well-recognized rule of the distribution of tonnage, an advantage that I could not get in any other way. The Boston & Maine and the New York & New England handle about 3,500,000 tons on their rails. That is the tonnage I intended to get for the Reading Railroad without a fight. If I could have carried out my plans I should have secured that large tonnage to the Reading, and the other lines would have had to give it up. It was a legitimate vantage I was securing for the Reading road.

Q. Which would have increased the tonnage very considerably?

A. Very largely; and would have enabled the Reading management to pay dividends on all its securities.

Q. Without increasing the price of coal in New England?

A. Yes; without increasing the price. Another thing I intended to do was to eliminate very largely the middleman. The amount of money between what the companies get for this coal and what it costs to the consumer when it is put into his cellar is simply outrageous. It is there that the greatest reform could be made in this business, and that is what I intended to do, and I have no doubt it will be done some day. I intended to erect large pocket depots in certain places in the city of New York and other cities where a man with a cart could go and get coal for the people. There would be nothing between the producer and the consumer but the man, the horse, and the cart. Instead of putting it into yards and reloading it at unnecessary expense, I would have simply a cart and horse between the producer and consumer, and the amount of money that could be saved would be enormous.[55]

These magnificent and philanthropic plans of the Reading president might have proved as beneficial as he expected, but from their very inception McLeod was working under the most stringent possible need for funds, and this lack finally contributed materially to the failure of all his hopes. When McLeod had been made president of the road, the syndicate in control had recognized that the Reading was heavily over-capitalized. To put it on a sound basis, a reorganization plan was worked out by Isaac L. Rice, one of the syndicate members. Mr. Rice then went to Europe to arrange for the necessary financial aid but while he was gone McLeod put an end to the chances of reorganization by paying up all the back interest on some income bonds, and thereby making those securities rise on the market sufficiently to preclude their voluntary surrender.[56]

By January, 1893, rumors of the approaching insolvency of the Reading were becoming more and more insistent. At the annual meeting of the stockholders early in the month McLeod emphatically contradicted the current reports that the system was not in a sound condition.[57] A few days later an official statement was issued which denied that the earnings of the anthracite combination had been disappointing and asserted that the exchange of traffic with the Jersey Central had continued since that road had been separated from the Reading system, just as it had for the past twenty-five years. Further, it was stated that the Reading treasury held nearly $20,000,000 in liquid assets, that the company was related to some New England roads only in that it had traffic agreements with them, and that it was having no difficulties with its bankers.[58]

55 *Industrial Commission Report*, Testimony of McLeod, IX, pp. 567-568.
56 *Ibid.*, Testimony of Rice, IX, pp. 737-738.
57 *Commercial and Financial Chronicle*, January 14, 1893, pp. 59-61.
58 *Railway World*, January 21, 1893, p. 63.

Unfortunately for President McLeod's plans, the last three of these assertions were absolutely false and the first one was distinctly misleading if not downright untrue. Had McLeod attempted his New England venture amid the financial surplus that this statement attributed to the Reading, the methods to which he resorted would not have been necessary. As the situation really was, the company lacked ready cash when, in the fall of 1892, McLeod launched his efforts to add the Boston & Maine and the New York & New England lines to the Reading system.

Without sufficient capital to buy control of the lines outright, he entered into a contract with the Pennsylvania Finance Company, which carried on large brokerage operations, whereby the latter was to purchase New York & New England stock. When enough to assure control had been bought, the Reading would assume ownership of the stock. After the first step had been taken, the New York & New England was to lease the Boston & Maine. Until a majority of the New York & New England stock had been obtained, however, the purchases were to be made in the name of McLeod personally. McLeod later stated that this circuitous method of purchase was adopted in order to keep the transactions secret, but it left room for less forthright interpretations when the value of the New England stocks fell.

As collateral for the purchases to be made in McLeod's name, Reading securities were deposited with the Finance Company. These securities were taken from the Reading treasury by Treasurer William A. Church on the presentation of an order signed by McLeod. Church later stated that on receipt of such an order he always assumed that the president was acting under the direction of the board of managers. However, it was not Church's duty to go behind McLeod's order: by a resolution of the board of directors some fifteen years before, the president had been given authority to use the property of the company to borrow money or to secure those from whom loans were made. Altogether from October 31 until the end of the year

Church turned over $300,000 of Reading first mortgage bonds
and about $700,000 worth of other Reading securities. These
securities ultimately came to rest in the coffers of two brokerage
houses, which were making the actual purchases of stock,
Prince and Ervin. Finally, on the day before the Reading
applied for the appointment of receivers, $250,000 was taken
from the Coal & Iron Company's treasury for deposit with
Ervin to protect the latter in the face of a drop in the value
of the New York & New England and Boston & Maine stock
it was carrying.

All the time that these securities were being drawn from
its treasury to serve as collateral for the purchase of stock in
other roads on margin, the Reading management was exerting
every effort to raise sufficient cash to keep the company solvent.
William R. Taylor, secretary of the road, was sent to Europe
to sell $5,000,000 of first mortgage bonds, and he returned in
mid-December with the proceeds from the sale of $1,000,000
of these. Isaac L. Rice also went to Europe with a portfolio
full of Reading securities, and succeeded in raising $13,000,000
of which $5,500,000 was paid in cash before February 1, 1893.
This relieved the pressure somewhat, but more cash was still
needed. Although Drexel, Morgan & Company had been the
Readings' bankers for years, early in January it was announced
that Speyer & Company had loaned the needed funds. No explanation of this sudden change in financial agents was given
at the time, and only later did its full significance become
apparent.[59]

The house of Morgan had long been banking agents of
the Vanderbilts and itself was heavily interested in the New
York, New Haven & Hartford Railroad. Neither of these
systems looked with favor upon the entrance of another major
trunk line into New England territory. So Morgan indicated

59 *Ibid.*, January 27, 1894, pp. 75-77 and February 3, 1894, pp. 96-97 re-
prints verbatim hearings before the special master who took testimony in
Rice's ouster suit against the receivers. See also testimony of Rice before
the Industrial Commission in its report, IX, p. 737.

that help from his firm would only be forthcoming if and when the Reading abandoned its New England plans.[60] McLeod refused to retreat, and negotiations with Speyer & Company had begun in October, lasting until January. The Speyers were equally reluctant to lend money to the Reading if the road were going into New England, but finally turned over $5,000,000 after repeated assurances from McLeod that he, not the Reading, was buying the New England stocks. S. A. Solomon, of Speyer & Company later declared: " I can tell you one thing, that is that if Mr. McLeod had not assured me that the Reading was not liable for the stock purchases of Boston & Maine and New York & New England, the negotiations for the loans never would have gone through." [61]

Even before the negotiations with Speyer & Company had been completed, McLeod's assurances were not only untrue in spirit, but they were equally false legally. In December the board of directors had assumed for the Reading the purchasing accounts with both Ervin & Company and Prince & Company. The board had been dubious about the transactions; some members wanted more specific details than the vaguely worded resolution gave and none realized the magnitude of the responsibility they were undertaking on behalf of the company; but the resolution was adopted, mainly because McLeod wished it and because he had been so successful in the Lehigh Valley and Jersey Central deals.[62] He told the directors, before they were satisfied, that the Reading's liability would be limited to $1,-000,000. The board had no way of knowing that they were assuming responsibility for 24,000 shares of Boston & Maine and between 20,000 and 30,000 shares of New York & New

60 *Industrial Commission Report*, testimony of F. E. Saward, editor of *Coal Trade Journal*, IX, p. 513; also, Hovey, *op. cit.*, pp. 136-137, 240.

61 *Railway World*, March 17, 1894, pp. 213-215, testimony before special master in Rice ouster suit.

62 *Ibid.*, January 27, 1894, pp. 75-77; February 3, 1894, pp. 96-97; February 10, 1894, pp. 116-117; February 24, 1894, pp. 153-157; March 17, 1894, pp. 213-215; more of hearings before special master.

England stock which had been bought on margin. Nor did they realize that about $6,000,000 of the Reading's own securities were involved in the transaction.[63]

As events proved, the New England venture was far more costly to the Reading than McLeod's estimate anticipated. After the Reading had gone into receivership the receivers closed out the two stock accounts. Altogether, according to the calculations of Stephen Little, the recognized authority on railroad accountancy, the New York & New England speculation netted the Reading a loss of $553,996 and the Boston & Maine venture cost $918,008.[64] The total loss of $1,472,004 was half a million larger than McLeod had stated the total responsibility of the Reading would be in the affair.

This abortive invasion of New England was an important factor in forcing the Reading into receivership. At least one director of the road believed that the company's floating debt, inability to pay which was the acknowledged cause of the receivership, grew to unmanageable proportions because all the Reading's negotiable securities were posted as collateral for these speculations.[65] Reference has already been made to the alienation of Drexel, Morgan & Company by McLeod's insistence on continuing the New England venture despite the opposition it aroused. But the damage done by this impractical ignoring of Morgan went beyond the loss of a financial agent, for the banker was determined to keep the Reading out of New England.

Morgan not only severed all relations with the road, he also let it be known in banking circles that anyone who came to McLeod's assistance need not expect to maintain friendship with Drexel, Morgan & Company. The hint was sufficient to freeze up all the wells of capital from which McLeod might

63 *Ibid.*, February 24, 1894, pp. 153-157; verbatim account of an interview with McLeod.

64 *Commercial and Financial Chronicle*, April 28, 1894, pp. 698-700.

65 *Railway World*, February 10, 1894, pp. 116-117, testimony of Director James Boyd before the special master in the Rice ouster suit.

have drawn help.[66] Finally, Morgan launched a devastating attack against Reading stock in the New York market. In the twenty days immediately preceding the receivership on February 20, 1893, Reading securities fell nearly $35,000,000 in market value.[67] On Friday, February 17, the attack became particularly vicious: 400,000 shares of Reading stock changed hands. On Monday the pressure was renewed with increased vigor and before the market had closed and the receivership became known, 958,000 shares were traded in. Since the total outstanding issue amounted to only 800,000 shares, the catastrophic effects of sales in such volume at constantly lowered quotations were inescapable.[68] At the time McLeod was accused of having precipitated the panic by selling his own company's stock short, but later evidence pointed to a concerted attack by banking leaders, led by Morgan, in which Ervin & Company joined to protect the marginal purchases which they were carrying for the Reading. Through Ervin the Reading's own holdings, posted as collateral, were sold in the mad rush but not by order or with the knowledge of the company's officers.[69]

Confirmation of the often denied rumors of the company's responsibility for the New England ventures [70] was only the first in a series of discreditable disclosures that the receivership brought to light. The lease of the Lehigh Valley, despite frequent assurance by McLeod to the contrary,[71] was revealed to have contributed materially to the bankruptcy of the Reading. Instead of the net profits of the Lehigh having increased over $1,000,000 within a year, as McLeod had declared,[72] during

66 Hovey, op. cit., p. 240.

67 Railway Age and Northwestern Railroader, March 10, 1893, p. 190.

68 Railroad Gazette, February 24, 1893, pp. 146-147.

69 Hovey, op. cit., pp. 136-137; Industrial Commission Report, testimony of Thomas H. Woodlock, editor of Wall Street Journal, IX, p. 466; Railway World, April 29, 1893, pp. 390-392 and February 24, 1894, pp. 153-157.

70 Railroad Gazette, February 24, 1893, pp. 146-147.

71 Railway World, January 14, January 21, 1893, etc.

72 Commercial and Financial Chronicle, January 14, 1893, pp. 59-61.

1892 that lease had cost the Reading nearly $1,500,000 and for 1893 the prospective loss was only about $100,000 less. Altogether Stephen Little calculated the net outright loss to be $2,786,673. Furthermore, on every ton of coal the Reading bought from the Lehigh it was losing money. It cost the parent company $1.58 per ton to mine its own coal. Under its contract with the Lehigh, $2.02 was paid for every ton bought from that company.[73] The contract called for delivery to the Reading of 1,500,000 tons per month, and this was far too much. In the first place, the Reading had not the facilities to sell such quantities, so a large stock accumulated; further, in frantic attempts to get rid of it many worthless debts were written on the company's books. Finally, the purchase of so much coal from the Lehigh left no alternative except a reduction in the output from the Reading's own mines, where it could be mined at three-fourths of the price the Lehigh coal cost.[74]

The exact extent to which an unsalable surplus of coal had been accumulating was not revealed until the receivers issued a statement in March. It was then discovered that the Reading held over 1,000,000 tons of coal which they had valued at $4.50 per ton, giving a book asset of $4,985,275.95. Actually it was by no possible stretch of the imagination worth that price and the loss was further increased an incalculable amount by the bad debts included in an entry for $5,291,829.21 entitled " due for coal sold on 30 and 60 days ". The total capital tied up in this unmanageable coal business was well over $10,-000,000.[75] That the Lehigh Valley lease was a costly mistake was tacitly admitted when the receivers first negotiated a reduction of the rental,[76] and then let the lease lapse without a protest.[77]

73 *Ibid.*, April 28, 1894, pp. 698-700.

74 *Ibid.*, January 13, 1894, pp. 58-60.

75 *Railway World*, March 18, 1893, pp. 253-254.

76 *Commercial and Financial Chronicle*, March 4, 1893, p. 352.

77 *A Statement of Isaac L. Rice Concerning the Affairs of the Philadelphia and Reading Railroad Company*, New York: C. G. Burgoyne (1895?),

Neither was the collapse of Reading credit disclosed in all its completeness until the receivers made their first report. This statement showed that the floating debt proper was about $10,-000,000 to which must be added about $8,600,000 current liabilities. Among the assets were only $29,241 cash and $89,966 in bills receivable. The rest of the $15,000,000 of paper assets consisted of over-valued coal on hand, debts of very doubtful value and materials which were necessary for the operation of the road, and therefore not rightly credited to the liquid assets account.[78] There could be little wonder that during the past year the Reading had been forced to deposit $12,000,000 of its own securities as collateral for a loan of one-sixth that amount.[79]

An important factor in the weakening of the Reading's credit had been a very unwise dividend policy which was adopted in 1891 to raise the market value of the road's securities. Under the 1886 reorganization, first and second preference income bonds had been issued. Since there was no prohibition in any of the indentures, the McLeod management had issued a new series of third preference income bonds, using them mostly as security for rentals accruing under the Lehigh Valley lease. This third lien on the Reading's income had partially destroyed the value of the preferred and common stock, of course, but it did not affect the liens prior to it. The conditions under which interest on any of the income bonds could be paid were carefully defined in Article IV of each indenture: net earnings were to be determined by deducting from the gross receipts the operating expenses, interest charges and all guarantees existing on January 1, 1888. Whenever there was enough net income, as thus defined, the income bonds were to receive interest in the order of their priority.[80] Despite these careful restrictions

a 41 page pamphlet summarizing Mr. Rice's objections to the receivers' management of the road.

78 *Commercial and Financial Chronicle*, March 16, 1893, pp. 437-439.

79 Meade, E. S., " Reorganization of Railroads."

80 Rice, *op. cit.*

on the right of these bonds to receive interest, in 1891 and early 1892 the company borrowed money with which to pay it, and then manipulated the books to show that it had been earned.[81] Further, in the latter part of 1892 this interest was not paid, although the guaranteed rental for the Lehigh Valley system was paid. The indentures explicitly stated that income bonds ranked ahead of any contracts thereafter made, but McLeod ignored this provision in order to preserve the coal combination.[82]

The *Railway World* summarized the downfall of the Reading in logical stages: first the coal combination was formed. As a result, the Reading was embarrassed by the huge accumulation of coal on hand and a growing floating debt, so it sought new markets for its coal. Since ready cash was lacking, this expansion took the form of buying the stock of New England roads on margin. The invasion of New England brought a retaliatory attack on Reading securities; since the collateral for the stock purchases consisted of these securities, interest had to be paid on them and their market value had to be maintained, so for these purposes more money was borrowed. Cash was still needed for the operation of the Reading itself but since all the road's assets had already been mortgaged to the limit, it was not forthcoming. The receivership was the necessary and logical final step.[83]

The Commercial and Financial Chronicle could also muster little surprise at the Reading collapse. Rather it seemed:

the natural and inevitable consequence of the development and operations of the last few months and of the magnitude of the task which the Reading management had assumed. The Reading has failed, just as it failed on previous occasions because it was carrying a burden of current liabilities beyond its ability to take care

81 *Commercial and Financial Chronicle*, April 28, 1894, pp. 698-700, Little's report; also see, *Industrial Commission Report*, Rice testimony, IX, p. 737.

82 Rice, *op. cit.*

83 *Railway World*, March 25, 1893, pp. 270-272.

of. The circumstances leading up to the creation of this debt have been different from those at former periods, but the outcome has been the same. A large floating debt is always a source of weakness, but especially where, as in this instance, the corporation concerned is spreading out and enlarging its operations rather than contracting them.[84]

As the full extent of McLeod's grandiose schemes had become apparent, the New York *Evening Post* expressed itself as shocked not at the Reading's failure, but at McLeod's policies:

It is hard to conceive of the conscience and business sense that led Mr. McLeod into business schemes that anyone could have seen would require for immediate use sums of money so large as to be beyond safe borrowing. The ventures into New England were seen from the first to be destitute of business foundation; when to this foolishness is added the method used to control the stocks of those railroad companies, the matter becomes in effect criminal.[85]

But these strictures were mild compared to those of the London *Economist* even before the receivership:

The American railway world has afforded abundant scope in the past for all kinds of financial trickery and apparently the "smart" operators, who have reaped such a large harvest in the past seem still disposed to look for further facilities for plunder in the future. The "crop of lambs" to be sheared, of course, varies from time to time, but, on an average, it would appear that the folly of investors may be regarded as a fixed quantity. That, at any rate, is the only conclusion we can draw from close observation of the policy which has been followed by the directors of the Philadelphia and Reading Railroad in the past three years. In this undertaking, which is now one of the most considerable in the United States, a very large amount of capital has been sunk by English investors, and yet their interests seem to count for nothing compared with those of the members of *le haute finance*, who

84 *Commercial and Financial Chronicle*, February 25, 1893, pp. 311-313.
85 New York *Evening Post*, May 19, 1893.

have temporarily a big speculative stake in the Reading securities. At least it is impossible on any other hypothesis to explain the action of the directors in regard to the payment of interest on the co-called Income Bonds. . . . To us it appears there has been an utter lack of all principle in dealing with the right of the Income Bondholders, and their securities have been made to serve as first rate gambling counters for the benefit of the big financiers who are in a position either to pull the strings or to obtain all the inside information. Superficially, indeed, we see little difference between the methods pursued by the Reading directors and some of those which the late Jay Gould employed in his dealings with the Wabash and other similar victims.[86]

The eventual news of the company's failure elicited no exclamations of surprise:

That the great and imposing combination which the Philadelphia and Reading had built up under the direction of Mr. McLeod, would ultimately collapse, has always seemed certain; for from the beginning a number of influences have been impairing its stability. . . . And the lesson is, as we have said so often, that investors in this country should entirely leave alone all contingent American railway securities, and should place their money solely in well-secured bonds.[87]

The gradual disclosures of the course pursued by Mr. McLeod in the management of the road brought from the long-weary editors another condemnation of American railroads:

Mr. McLeod, the late president, acted in a manner which, if it was not dishonest, affords a complete condemnation of the virtually despotic power possessed by too many American railway officials. . . . For apparently the directors and other officials — board of manager *et hoc genus omne*—often have no more power and are as inefficient in supplying the use of a drag on a reckless president, as any committee of shareholders on this side of the Atlantic. And,

86 *Economist*, January 14, 1893, p. 37.
87 *Ibid.*, February 25, 1893, p. 229.

unfortunately, it is not easy to discover a remedy . . . since an American railway is in nine cases out of ten essentially a fighting organism,

and therefore little time is available for consultation before a course of action must be adopted.[88]

The Reading collapse was recognized as inevitable after the secret machinations that preceded it had been revealed. Starting with a badly overcapitalized system in need of financial reorganization, President McLeod had sought to rear on this shaky foundation a monopoly of the anthracite coal trade and a railway network that would cover both the Middle states and New England. With each step he took, McLeod weakened the whole fabric; the coal monopoly roused a public outcry and tied up huge sums of capital; the need for expansion became more urgent the longer the coal monopoly lasted and the invasion of New England not only tied up more Reading capital, it also earned the fatal enmity of powerful financial interests which did not hesitate to ruin the Reading rather than see it succeed in the New England project. And to make matters worse, the management of the Reading was not endowed with a very scrupulous regard for the spirit of the law or for the niceties of business ethics. Behind him McLeod left a wide swath of deliberately misleading or downright false statements and transactions which, although not criminal, were none the less distinctly disreputable.

The last of the great systems to be forced into receivership during the depression, the Baltimore & Ohio, had always been considered the antithesis of companies like the Philadelphia & Reading, which had had a very checkered career and had always been definitely classed as a speculative investment at best. The Baltimore & Ohio, on the other hand, had always been conservatively managed by one of the established families of Maryland, or so critics thought, and had been in large part a

88 *Ibid.*, May 27, 1893, pp. 627-628.

civic activity which provided a reliable investment for the people of the city of Baltimore. The sudden disillusionment and the realization that the company had been as badly mismanaged, if not more criminally, than the Richmond Terminal or the Philadelphia & Reading, were distinct shocks to financial circles both in this country and in Europe.

Chartered by the Maryland legislature in 1827 in the hope of diverting to the port of Baltimore some of the trade which the Erie canal was taking to New York, the Baltimore & Ohio was the first American railroad to open its line when a trip was made in 1830. Although it was undertaken as a semi-civic project and liberally aided by the city, the road did not attain its modern preeminent position until, under completely private ownership and management, John W. Garret became its president in 1858. During his administration, which lasted until 1884, it became one of the great systems of the East and a highly profitable investment.

After 1884, however, the system rapidly lost ground. The policy of expansion by construction of new branches and by gaining control of established lines was continued so blindly that by 1887 the company was badly in need of financial help.[89] In this crisis a syndicate to refinance the road was formed, consisting of the British firms of J. S. Morgan & Son, Baring Brothers & Company and Shipley & Company, together with their American correspondents, most important of whom was Drexel, Morgan & Company. This syndicate contracted to sell $5,000,000 of consolidated 5 per cent bonds and $5,000,000 of preferred stock in order to permit the Baltimore & Ohio to pay its floating debt and refund its other obligations. The bonds were to be part of an issue of $29,600,000 of which $21,-423,000 were reserved to retire the main stem mortgage when it came due and the remainder was to be exchanged for securities in the sinking fund, the latter to be sold to pay off the

89 Snyder, op. cit., pp. 94-109; Van Oss, op. cit., pp. 268-288; Meade, "Great Railways," Railway World, 1904, pp. 843-845; 871-872.

company's unsecured debts. In return the syndicate made three demands: the company's statements must be verified by a certified accountant; the management must be placed in competent hands satisfactory to the syndicate; harmony must be established among the trunk lines running into New York to obviate the Baltimore & Ohio's building an unnecessary competing line parallel to the Pennsylvania tracks from Philadelphia to New York and to preclude the outbreak of rate wars.

The road's directors accepted the bankers' offer after making some changes: the exchange of new securities for those in the sinking fund was to be abandoned in favor of direct sale of the new issue. The stockholders objected to placing any more preferred stock ahead of the common stock; instead the company sold its express business for thirty years to the United States Express Company for $1,500,000 in stock of the express company, sold its telegraph business to Western Union for $5,000,000 of the latter's stock, and sold its sleeping-car business, equipment and franchise to the Pullman Company for twenty-five years for $1,250,000 cash. In each case the Baltimore & Ohio, in addition to the immediate purchase price, was to get a yearly percentage of the receipts of its former business.

In March, 1888, the syndicate agreed to these proposals, and further agreed to sell $2,500,000 more of the bonds, making a total to be handled by them of $7,500,000. At the syndicate's request Samuel Spencer was made president of the line, replacing the son of former president John W. Garrett, and a thorough reform of the system was initiated. As part of this program an investigating committee composed of directors friendly to the syndicate began a careful investigation of the past management of the road. But this was more than could be permitted by the Garrett family, holding as it did enough stock to control the system. The road had been managed by Garretts for forty years and, in the last few years, managed very poorly. Under the presidency of Robert Garrett, which began in

1884 and ended in 1887, the company had built a very expensive line to Philadelphia and had bought the Staten Island Rapid Transit Company in order to get an entrance into New York. These and other expansion schemes were carried out to the detriment of the company's financial position and even if President Garrett himself were blameless, revelations of carelessness and waste under his administration would inevitably reflect upon him. He was a very handsome, attractive man with unusual tact, affability and courtesy, but railroad administration was not suited to his talents and in 1887 he had resigned on account of ill-health, or so it was officially reported.[90]

Rather than let the committee complete its work and report whatever it might find, in November at the annual meeting of the shareholders the Garrett interests declined to re-elect seven of the twelve directors, including all the members of the investigating committee. Soon after, Samuel Spencer was ousted from what must have become a very unconfortable presidency and replaced by Charles F. Mayer, the nominee of the Garretts.[91] Although his presidency of the Baltimore & Ohio was his first venture in trunk line railroads, Mayer had been successful in the coal business in West Virginia and had dabbled in coal roads there since 1865.[92] Spencer had been in office long enough to reveal that the supposed surplus of the road was wholly fictitious and to advocate writing more millions of apparent value attributed to imaginary equipment and securities off the books, but the new Mayer regime ignored his recommendations.

Of course, after this refusal of the Garrett interests to meet its requirements the syndicate refused to go ahead with the refinancing scheme. Badly in need of new capital, the system proceeded to go from bad to worse for the next six years, until it acknowledged its insolvency in 1896. Before relief was

90 The Cyclopedia of American Biography, 1922, XVIII, pp. 4-5.

91 Daggett, Railroad Reorganization, pp. 11-16.

92 The Cyclopedia of American Biography, 1922, XVIII, pp. 5-6.

sought in a receivership, the road was in such wretched condition that serious consideration was given a proposal to abandon the passenger business because of an absolute lack of equipment. But in spite of the poor financial position of the company the old expansion program was readopted after the brief Spencer interlude; particularly in the western regions touched by the system a network of new lines was acquired.[93]

In the very first days of the panic of 1893 Baltimore & Ohio securities took such a drop in the stock market that rumors of an early receivership began to circulate. However, a plausible explanation was at once forthcoming, an explanation that accurately reflected the policies of the road: in order to get cash with which to finance some improvements, the Baltimore & Ohio had sold $5,000,000 of new stock to a syndicate; at the same time the pool had taken $2,000,000 of stock given in payment for the recently acquired Pittsburgh & Western Railroad; finally, the directors had just paid a 9 per cent stock dividend and much of this had also wound up in the hands of the syndicate. The sudden and simultaneous issuance of these three blocks of stock had glutted the market and Baltimore & Ohio securities had dropped.[94]

In the midst of this flurry in the stock market, the company was negotiating to assume new responsibilities. The Baltimore & Ohio completely dominated the Baltimore & Ohio Southwestern, and the latter proposed to absorb the Ohio & Mississippi system. The Southwestern ran from Marietta to Cincinnati; the Ohio & Mississippi extended from Cincinnati to St. Louis, with a branch running into Louisville and another to Springfield, Ohio. The proposed consolidation would round out the Baltimore & Ohio system in the middle west, give it the most direct rail route from Baltimore to St. Louis, and thereby enable it better to compete with the Pennsylvania and Vander-

93 *Railway World*, April 29, 1893, p. 395; Keys, C. M., "An Era of Better Railroads," *World's Work*, 1909, XIII, pp. 11238-11243.

94 *Railway World*, April 29, 1893, p. 395.

bilt systems beyond the Alleghanies. The negotiations were concluded with an agreement on the part of the Baltimore & Ohio
to issue its own bonds to replace all outstanding bonds of both
the subsidiary companies, except for a few Baltimore & Ohio
Southwestern terminal issues; present and future capital needs
were to be met by issuing mortgage bonds as required.[95] From
the viewpoint of rounding out the system, undoubtedly the
acquisition was more than justified, but the wisdom of assuming new bond guarantees when the parent company was in
dubious condition, even though its weakness was not publicly
known, was very questionable.

On the other hand, in May, 1893, the directors of the road
adopted a resolution endorsing a policy of strict economy. As
one director publicly phrased the reasons for the decision, the
Baltimore & Ohio was

confronted by a situation that demands prompt action. Legislation
both local and national towards railroad corporations has a tendency to greatly increase the expenses and thus necessarily cuts
off the gross income that will have to be made up from some source
to maintain an equitable balance between the company and its owners. The most notable instance in this direction is the recent passage
by Congress of an automatic coupler bill. An enforcement of this
law will entail an expenditure of millions of dollars on a corporation like the Baltimore & Ohio.[96]

Undoubtedly government regulation was heavily increasing
certain items of expense for the big systems, but as ever, the
road's policy could not be made consistent so easily. No sooner
had the retrenchment policy been made public than a new
announcement declared that the system's roadbeds were to be
improved. The whole Pittsburgh-Cumberland, Maryland, line
was to be reballasted with standard crushed stone to put it in a
condition far superior to what it had been. More improvements
were to be made in the following year, after having been post-

95 *Commercial and Financial Chronicle*, March 18, 1893, pp. 440-441.
96 *Railway Age and Northwestern Railroader*, May 26, 1893, p. 413.

poned when the panic struck the country.[97] However, wages were slashed on all parts of the system and an attempt was made to economize wherever possible.[98]

The annual report for the year ending June 30, 1893, was very optimistic. Dividends had been paid on all stock, and $750,000 had been used to reduce the principal of car trusts and similar obligations. A surplus of over $200,000 had been carried forward into the new year. And all this had been done after the costs of betterments made during the year had been paid out of earnings. Despite a decrease of 1 per cent from the figure for the year before in the gross revenue from freight, the gross earnings had been the highest in the company's history, owing to the growth of passenger income. The bills payable were just about equalled by the cash and cash assets in the company's treasury.[99] The next annual report was not quite so optimistic, but considering the depression it was not unduly alarming. The gross earnings had fallen 14 per cent, mainly because of a 21 per cent decline in freight revenues. But expenses had been slashed over 18 per cent so that the loss in net earnings was almost negligible, only $230,852. The loss in revenue from investments was enough to make a total decrease in net revenue of about $500,000. This decrease had been reflected in a semi-annual dividend on the common stock of only 2 per cent instead of the usual 2½ per cent.[100]

On January 1, 1895, the company paid in cash the fixed charges, car trust payments and sinking fund payments, about $1,000,000 in all, which were due. This achievement brought from the *Railway Age* a paean of praise for the Baltimore & Ohio which " under conservative management of President Mayer, has stood the financial storm remarkably well, and is in

97 *Railway World*, July 29, 1893, p. 705.

98 *Railway Age and Northwestern Railroader*, September 29, 1893, p. 725.

99 *Baltimore & Ohio Railroad Annual Report*, 1893, *Commercial and Financial Chronicle*, November 25, 1893, pp. 878-880.

100 *Annual Report*, 1894, *Commercial and Financial Chronicle*, November 24, 1894, pp. 900-901.

excellent shape for the future". President Mayer himself pointed with pride to this payment and added:

I name this fact because it is not unusual for us to make a loan for the unusually heavy payments January 1. I doubt if the Baltimore & Ohio has owed so small a floating debt for twelve or fifteen years, perhaps longer and it never had the large volume of stocks and bonds it now has, something over $16,000,000—not put down at their face value, but at their market value or far below their intrinsic value. I can safely say the road has not been in so strong a position as now for at least fifteen years.[101]

But despite President Mayer's ebullient confidence in the system's future, the board of directors on April 17, 1895, decided to pass the regular semi-annual dividend for the six months ending December 31, 1894, " in view of the unremumerative rates of freight prevailing since January 1, 1895, especially on through freight—the lowest perhaps ever known in the history of American railroads—and the uncertainty as to when the efforts of the more conservative companies will succeed in correcting this serious condition ".[102]

The annual report for the year ending June 30, 1895, showed improvement over the two preceding years in some respects, but in others it showed losses. Gross earnings, operating expenses and net earnings had all increased, the latter $74,165, but these gains had been more than offset by a drop of over $350,000 in income from other sources and an increase of $237,062 in fixed charges, for the most part due to the charges on terminals. The income account showed a surplus over operating expenses of $639,517, or 2½ per cent on the $25,000,000 of outstanding common stock, but because of the other discouraging factors no dividends had been paid.[103]

101 *Railway Age and Northwestern Railroader*, January 11, 1895, p. 26.

102 *Ibid.*, April 19, 1895, p. 198.

103 *Annual Report*, 1895, *Commercial and Financial Chronicle*, November 23, 1895, pp. 899-900.

Early in January, to the accompaniment of ever more persistent rumors, Baltimore & Ohio shares broke on the stock market. The *Railway World,* puzzled, was very pessimistic:

The break in Baltimore & Ohio, for example, which, so far, has receded from 44 to below 30, has more significance. It may mean a great deal more than now appears on the surface . . . (Bears) may have started the movement, but somebody else has secured certain facts regarding the company's financial position which are not at all favorable . . . (and) it may even be advisable to effect such rehabilitation (as is needed) through reorganization, the property in the meantime being placed under the protection of the United States courts.[104]

The day following this prediction receivers were appointed to operate the Baltimore & Ohio; the subsidiary Baltimore & Ohio Southwestern managed to remain solvent despite the strain to which the failure of the parent company subjected it. With this one exception, however, nearly the whole system collapsed. The parent company itself operated the 2094 miles of track between Philadelphia and Chicago, via Baltimore, and between Cumberland, Maryland, and Wheeling, Ohio, via Pittsburgh; it had $50,000,000 capital stock outstanding and its own bonds amounted to $84,000,000 at par; in addition it was the guarantor of about $10,000,000 of bonds of subsidiary roads. The Pittsburgh & Western, next to the Southwestern the most important subsidiary, was placed under a separate receiver despite the Baltimore & Ohio's ownership of a majority of its stock.[105]

The immediate cause of the receivership was the failure to pay $404,000 interest on bonds and a large amount of car trusts due March 1. But, of course, the inability to pay these obligations was itself the result of more fundamental causes. A few months earlier the management had appealed again to

104 *Railway World*, February 29, 1896, p. 193.
105 *Railway Age and Northwestern Railroader*, March 7, 1896, pp. 123, 124.

banking interests for help in a reorganization of the company's finances. The bankers had demanded, and received, representation on the board of directors in the persons of Louis Fitzgerald, president of the Mercantile Trust Company and a Morgan ally, Eugene Delano of Brown Brothers, William A. Read of Vermilye Brothers, and Howland Davis of Blake, Bossevaine & Company of London. John K. Cowen, general counsel of the company since 1876, had been made president. Before joining the Baltimore & Ohio staff in 1872, by reason of his eloquence, clarity of expression and sound judgment, Cowen had been one of the leaders of the Ohio bar. After moving to Baltimore he had continued his private corporation practice, as well as attended to the railroad's business, and had also had time to enter politics as a sound-money Democrat. He had been representative in Congress from Baltimore for one term, 1894-1896, and was highly thought of in the city in business, legal and political circles.[106]

The bankers had insisted on having Stephen Little audit the company's books and the task was nearly complete before the receivership. Although as yet no announcement of his findings had been made, it was rumored that the floating debt would prove nearer $15,000,000 than the acknowledged $6,-000,000. The former controller of the company supposedly had refused to sign the last annual report issued by President Mayer's regime (1892) because the books had been manipulated to hide the size of the floating debt. Further, it was said that Mr. Little had discovered that President Mayer sold $1,000,000 of the $5,000,000 of Western Union stock carried on the books without ever reporting the sale, and that the rest of the stock had been deposited as collateral for loans. The floating debt of the parent company itself, rumor continued, was as reported, between $3,000,000 and $4,000,000, but—and this had not been published—obligations of subsidiary lines for which it was responsible amounted to between $12,000,000

106 *Dictionary of American Biography*, IV, pp. 469-70.

and $14,000,000; the annual reports had been falsified to hide this fact.

It had been these rumors which prevented the payment of the March 1 obligations, for no bankers had been willing to lend the road any more cash until their truth or falsity had been established. And even the bankers represented on the board refused to advance any more money because they felt that the financial needs of the company were so great that the best possible solution would be a receivership.[107]

Wall Street had been predicting the bankruptcy of the road too long for anyone in this country to be greatly surprised. Rather the wonder was how the management had kept on so long in the face of all the difficulties confronting it; everyone agreed that except for its borrowing ability the receivership would have come two or three years earlier, since the financial and physical condition of the system had been getting progressively worse, primarily because of mismanagement originating during the administration of the younger Garrett.[108] However, the receivership was a distinct shock to London's *Economist:*

And now the Baltimore & Ohio Railroad has passed into the hands of receivers, and grave fears are naturally entertained by those whose capital is at stake. During the past two or three months there have been rumors afloat to the effect that the company was in serious financial difficulties, and that the following debt had been piled up to such an extent that a collapse was inevitable. But the rumors have been officially or semi-officially denied, while, though it was tacitly admitted that funds were needed, the expectation that they would be provided in ample time to pay the interest on the bonds was held out until the last; and as the Baltimore & Ohio had the reputation of being fairly and honestly managed, a large proportion of the holders of its bonds and common stock were reassured. . . . The effect of the announcement that receivers had

107 *Railway World*, March 7, 1896, p. 221; *Railway Age and Northwestern Railroader*, April 4, 1896, p. 337.

108 *Railway World*, March 7, 1896, p. 217.

been appointed was electrical, the bond issues declining dollars at a time, while the common stock which less than a year ago stood at 67½, changed hands in the market at 18, and disorganization for a time reigned supreme . . . but it is perfectly obvious that the state of the company's finances was not fully and accurately disclosed in the accounts to which we have referred, and there is only too much reason to fear that as in so many other cases, the amounts were " faked " so as to conceal the gravity of the situation. Otherwise the denouement is perfectly inexplicable.[109]

After the receivership months passed without the publication of the expected report of Mr. Little. The longer publication was delayed, the more persistent became rumors that it would be suppressed, so bad were the revelations it contained of the inefficiency and dishonesty of the road's past management.[110] When early in December the report was released to the public, it was damning enough, even if not quite up to the wildest speculations. Mr. Little summarized the causes of the Baltimore & Ohio's failure as:

Inflation or overstatement of net income from September 1892, to June 30, 1895, of $2,721,067.81, which was concealed in " two improvised profit and loss accounts . . . opened partly for this purpose ".

Mischarges of worn-out equipment to profit and loss instead of to income; the total mischarge since 1888 was $2,843,596.06.

Capitalization of charges to income under the title of construction, Main Stem, etc., amounting to $2,664,741.55 since 1888.

These items gave a total of $11,204,858.78 which, in Mr. Little's opinion, had been wrongly credited to the company's income account in the past five years.

Payment of unearned dividends: in November, 1891, a 20 per cent stock dividend, amounting at par to $2,056,920, had been declared and since 1888 cash dividends totalling $3,312,-

109 *Economist*, March 7, 1895, p. 295.

110 *Railway World*, April 25, 1896, p. 448; July 18, 1896, pp. 739-740; September 19, 1896, pp. 975-976.

087.75 had been paid. If no dividends had been disbursed, Mr. Little thought, the road would have remained solvent, for on June 30, 1895, the real deficit was only $294,043.61 and this would have been transformed into a surplus were it not for the payment of these unearned dividends.

Understatement of liabilities: the Baltimore & Ohio was responsible for about $3,500,000 of the debts of subsidiary companies but these had never appeared in the annual balance sheet.[111]

The reception accorded the report by the business press varied. The *Railroad Gazette,* accepting Mr. Little's figures, sadly commented:

What the present condition of the property would have been if it had been governed by a policy which would have been content with the results here shown (small annual surplus, but no dividends) and used the surplus for improvements instead of paying un-earned dividends is now a useless speculation.[112]

The *Commercial and Financial Chronicle* was more critical of Little's conclusions. It believed that he was wrong and the company right in the disposition of charges for improvements and depreciation. But it agreed that the liabilities on behalf of subsidiaries should have been shown even although few American roads included such obligations in their published reports, and it approved his calculation of the overstatement of income.[113]

The *Economist* found in the report just another proof of its long-standing thesis that American railroad stocks were not the proper investments for British capital:

Even, however, if it could be proved that some of the expenditure to which Mr. Little takes exception was reasonably chargeable

111 *Ibid.,* December 12, 1896, 1310-1311; and *Report* of Stephen Little to reorganization committee, July 11, 1896.

112 *Railroad Gazette,* December 11, 1896, p. 865.

113 *Commercial and Financial Chronicle,* December 12, 1896, pp. 1040-1043.

to capital, there is no dispute as to the inflation of the revenue accounts by practically false entries, nor can it be denied that dividends that had not been earned were declared and paid, and that a big floating debt, of which the security holders were kept in ignorance, was incurred. And when people here find that such malpractices as these have been carried on for a series of years, on what was believed to be one of the best-managed of the American railroads, and that, after they have been exposed, nobody seems to think of bringing those responsible for them to account, it cannot be wondered at if the small degree of confidence in American railroads that has been left them is still further impaired.[114]

A rival reorganization committee to that which employed Mr. Little had another expert accounting firm, Patterson & Corwin, check up on Mr. Little's findings. They severely criticized his statement that his discoveries were " causes " of the road's financial embarrassment, except in regard to the payment of unearned dividends, but their censures of the former management made Little's seem mild in comparison. The road had been financially embarrassed as far back as September, 1888, when it had a floating debt of $4,000,000. Little's estimate of the hitherto concealed floating debt incurred by the Baltimore & Ohio through subsidiary companies, failed to take into consideration the company's guarantee of some $40,000,000 of bonds of branch lines, a good part of which would have to be paid by the parent company. Further, Little himself had overstated the road's assets by $2,630,000: the cash on hand amounted to $5491, not $1,306,010; the offset to current liabilities was $41,145, not $1,348,899, for most of what Mr. Little had so classified consisted of securities specifically pledged for certain debts; he had omitted to include $945,240 owed by the company to subsidiaries; he had twice credited assets of $392,846. Because the whole system had no one set of books, nor even similar methods of bookkeeping, Patterson & Corwin believed that the true condition of the Baltimore & Ohio had

114 *Economist*, December 26, 1896, p. 1706.

not yet been revealed. The intra-system finances would have to be explored before that could be discovered, and they doubted if even then the true state of affairs would easily be found.[115]

Perhaps the truest indication of the company's condition was reflected in the actions of the receivers during the first year of their administration. In that time they had fictitious assets to the amount of $21,627,165 written from the books; this amount represented rolling stock no longer usable, equipment still in use but heavily over-valued, uncollectible claims against leased and subsidiary lines, and other bad debts. The result of this drastic operation was a reduction of the apparent balance to profit from $23,737,442 as listed June 30, 1896, to a more accurate $2,110,277. When it is remembered that during his brief tenure of the presidency in 1888 Samuel Spencer had similarly written $24,000,000 of fictitious assets off the books,[116] the almost criminal reluctance of successive Baltimore & Ohio managements to keep its accounts accurately becomes apparent. Within ten years, in two major operations, $45,000,000 of fictitious values had been removed from the company's balance sheet. Surely, there could be few more striking indictments of the road's management.

An important factor in this accumulation of worthless assets had been the over-expansion in which the company indulged. The Pittsburgh & Connellsville railroad was operated in 1896 at a loss of nearly $500,000 and the parent company also had to pay interest on $10,000,000 of bonds issued to gain control of it. In the same year the Philadelphia & Baltimore division of the system had cost $117,000 in addition to interest payments on $11,600,000 of bonds. Altogether, in 1896, the Baltimore & Ohio lost $1,142,812 on leased lines for which the annual rentals were $1,500,000. On the other hand on the original main line and branches of the company, embracing

115 *Railway World*, May 22, 1897, pp. 522-523, June 19, 1897, pp. 615-616; and *Review and Analysis of Reports on the Baltimore and Ohio*, etc., dated April 26, 1897, by Patterson and Corwin.

116 *Railway Age and Northwestern Railroader*, November 19, 1897, p. 635.

1500 miles from Baltimore to Washington, Cumberland, Maryland, and Parkersburg, West Virginia, in the same year there was a net profit of $368,000, nearly 10 per cent of the net earnings. Obviously the core of the system was sound but too great a burden of unprofitable branches had been added.[117]

Further, the inefficiency of the system had provided too great a handicap. Before the receivership, operating expenses had been very high because the roadbed and the rolling stock were in poor condition. From 75 to 80 per cent of the gross receipts had been needed merely to operate the system, whereas the ratio of operating costs to gross earnings of the Pennsylvania, one of its chief competitors, was about 65 to 70 per cent. When receivers were appointed, the system

was as much of a wreck physically as financially. Apparently nothing had been done of any consequence in keeping up the right of way, keeping rolling stock in condition or buying equipment. Most of the mileage was laid with badly worn rails. At every division headquarters were scores of locomotives and hundreds of cars, so badly in need of repairs as to be useless. Stations and other buildings were in miserable condition. Passenger cars in service, except between Washington and New York, were old, dirty and behind the times in other respects. Freight shipments were delayed five and six weeks for lack of facilities to move them and a large tonnage was lost to rival lines, also on this account.[118]

Although it had almost succeeded in weathering the storm, the Baltimore & Ohio was another of those roads which, because of mismanagement and subsequent efforts to conceal past and current errors, were bankrupt *de facto* before the depression began. John Moody, in commenting on the road's downfall, aptly states the case in declaring that:

As in the case of numerous other railroads, the financial breakdown of the Baltimore & Ohio Railroad was primarily due to a

117 *United States Investor*, April 23, 1898, pp. 577-578.
118 *Ibid.*, April 23, 1898, p. 577.

bad or reckless policy, for there was nothing inherently insecure in the railroad property itself. . . . But the steady increase in its debts over a number of years, its extravagance in dividend payments, and its painful efforts to keep down its operating expenses had so weakened the property that, when the hard times of 1893 to 1896 arrived it was in no position to weather the storm. The only wonder is that the management succeeded in keeping the system intact and apparently solvent as long as it did.[119]

But these censures were mild compared to those of the *Investor:*

Of all the railroad and other financial wrecks the country has suffered within the last quarter of a century, none is more hopeless or more pitiable than that of the Baltimore & Ohio, and its ruin was not due to natural causes, but to the almost criminal carelessness of its directors in blindly allowing the executive head to pursue plans of which they inexcusably remained in ignorance—at least they claimed ignorance.[120]

119 Moody, *Railroad Builders*, pp. 112-113.
120 *United States Investor*, April 23, 1898, p. 577.

CHAPTER V

MORGAN'S REORGANIZATIONS

ALTHOUGH the final great railroad failure of the depression, that of the Baltimore & Ohio, did not occur until March, 1896, the rehabilitation of bankrupt roads had been begun before then. In the hard times of 1893 and 1894 very little progress could be made, despite tentative efforts, because the necessary capital and confidence were lacking. The one road that was completely reorganized before the end of 1894 was the former Richmond Terminal system which was transformed into the new Southern, and this company had already been in receivership for a year when so many great systems were toppling in 1893. Most of the reorganizations were completed in 1895, 1896 and 1897, but the final reconstruction work was not done until the very eve of the turn of the century.

The process by which reorganization was achieved in almost every case has been succinctly described:

Foreclosure was in each case followed by purchase of the property in behalf of former shareholders, who, as a condition to their participation in the new company, were assessed pro rata to raise the needed cash resources, the bondholders submitting to lower interest rates, usually receiving stock in the new corporation as a solace.[1]

The ends almost invariably desired and usually achieved were a lowering of fixed charges, provision of new working capital, payment of floating debts, consolidation or separation of unprofitable parts of the system. Until nearly the end of the period of rehabilitation the reorganizing work was dominated by the firm of J. P. Morgan & Company almost to the exclusion of all other interests; only in 1897, after the Union Pacific had been put on its feet, did a rival to Morgan appear in the person of Edward H. Harriman.

1 Noyes, *Forty Years of American Finance*, pp. 276-277.

So frequently was Morgan called upon to come to the aid of bankrupt railroads that long before the depression was past stories of his activities had become current in financial circles. The *Wall Street Journal* published a typical one early in 1894:

Of Mr. Morgan and his fame and fortune as a reorganizer, a story of the late Wilson G. Hunt is revived. He said that Mr. Morgan reminded him of three men stranded in Missouri, too proud to beg and too honest to steal. One of them told the other two to go and contract a certain annoying but not dangerous complaint, mingle with the community, thereby circulating the complaint, when he would come along, cure it and receive fees for so doing. Within three or four months this amateur physician had all the money there was in that part of the country. Mr. Hunt thought so much of this scheme that if he was young enough, he said, he would set up a shop as a reorganizer.[2]

The first great railroad transaction in which the house of Morgan had made a reputation for itself was the sale of William H. Vanderbilt's New York Central stock in 1879. Public opinion was being aroused against the company and one of its most vulnerable points in the political forum was the nearly monopolistic control of its stock by the Vanderbilts. In order to democratize the ownership of the road and render it less susceptible to demagogic attacks, Vanderbilt asked Morgan to sell $25,000,000 of his stock. The sale was made in England with ease at $130 per share and netted Morgan a profit of about $3,000,000, in addition to inaugurating an alliance between the Vanderbilt and Morgan interests.[3] Morgan himself was made a director of the New York Central almost at once and the house of Morgan became the company's financial agents, to whom were referred all plans for expansion or consolidation.[4]

2 *Wall Street Journal,* January 3, 1894, p. 1.

3 Moody, *Railroad Builders,* pp. 30-40.

4 *Pujo Investigation,* II, p. 1014.

Morgan had gained experience in reorganizing railroads in his reconstruction of the Reading in 1886; and the sequel to his efforts, the ambitious designs of McLeod which ended in another failure, taught him an important lesson for the future: after the reorganization is completed, the work may prove to have been in vain if control is returned to the stockholders before the company is firmly established.[5] Another hard-learned lesson had been derived from his efforts to control the ruinous competition which was wrecking many roads in the West. After several fruitless attempts Morgan called a conference of Western railroad executives to meet in his home December 15, 1890. Sixteen representatives appeared, including Jay Gould, A. B. Stickney, C. P. Huntington, Thomas F. Oakes, James J. Hill and Russell Sage. An agreement, proposed by Morgan, provided for an advisory board, on which each road was to be represented by its president and one director, with power to appoint arbitrators and commissions. The board was empowered to establish rates between competitive points, and decide other controversies which might arise. The agreement was to go into force January 1, 1891, but any road might withdraw on ninety days' notice thereafter. However, there were no penalties provided for violations of the agreement, and therein lay its fatal weakness as an instrument to create harmony. At one of Morgan's conferences of railroad magnates, a president had stated that as gentlemen he respected every man present, but as railroad executives he would not trust any of them with his watch out of sight.[6] Because this remark was only too justified, Morgan's agreement did not accomplish as much as he had hoped, and the failure impressed upon him the need of some stronger bond than "gentlemen's agreements" to prevent wasteful and unnecessary competition.[7]

5 Moody, *Railroad Builders*, pp. 39-40.
6 Corey, *House of Morgan*, pp. 172, 173.
7 *Ibid.*, p. 175.

The Morgan reorganizations during the nineties all followed the same general pattern, manifesting three especially important characteristics. The immediate problems which had precipitated trouble—the finances of the road—were put on a sound basis. Secondly, Morgan was reluctant to surrender control of the roads after the reorganizations had been completed; by means of voting trusts his control was perpetuated and even after the trusts had been terminated, his representatives were usually to be found among the directors of the companies. The third feature of Morgan's railroad activities in the late nineties was the establishment of the Community of Interest idea, both in theory and in fact; to this end, of course, Morgan's continued control over the roads he had reorganized served as a nucleus about which to build.

To credit the reorganizations managed by the house of Morgan to the head of the firm alone would be to neglect several very important lieutenants. The most prominent of these was Charles H. Coster, a partner in the firm. He was given the work of weighing and sorting the various securities and assigning to each bond or share its proportionate equity in the new company. And he had no peer in this type of work but rather

was a kind of rare genius, a sort of financial chemist, and possessed a gift of analysis in this new and difficult field; it often happened, when everyone else was baffled, that he alone was able to lay before his chief solutions which made it possible for Mr. Morgan to go ahead with his plans for a new structure.[8]

On the roster of nearly every reorganization committee working under Morgan's direction appeared the name of Francis Lynde Stetson, as its attorney. Known as " Morgan's attorney general ", he reputedly received an annual retainer of $50,000 just to give Morgan first claim on his services at all times. He had first come into contact with Morgan through the latter's brother-in-law, Charles E. Tracy, a former partner in

8 Hovey, *Morgan*, pp. 233-234.

his law firm, and had rapidly become one of the foremost corporation lawyers in the country. He was credited with having invented no-par value stock and during the nineties he was instrumental in devising the form of future railroad mortgage indentures.[9] Stetson's work was seldom done in public, although he was a good trial lawyer, but the paucity of lawsuits originating in these reorganizations bears strong testimony to his legal capacities. Another member of a majority of the Morgan committees was General Louis Fitzgerald, president of the Mercantile Trust Company of New York, which was a subsidiary of the Equitable Life Assurance Company. Fitzgerald was usually the chairman and in that capacity he fulfilled nearly the same functions as public relations counsels of a later day.

The earliest of Morgan's reorganizations in the nineties was the creation from the ruins of the Richmond Terminal system of the Southern Railway. Factional quarrels among the security holders had led Morgan to decide against interesting his firm in the company's troubles, but successive failures of self-appointed reorganization committees to frame a practicable plan at last threatened to necessitate foreclosure of the mortgages. A forced sale would wipe out the value of many securities, so to avoid such a drastic step Morgan was again requested to manage the reorganization.[10] His demand that full authority over the plans and methods to be used be placed in his hands had been rejected by the security holders a few months before, but it was now accepted. The announcement early in February, 1893, that he would undertake to rehabilitate the Terminal system was greeted with the comment:

No announcement has been made for a long time containing so much of promise in an industrial way as that found in the correspondence made public Thursday between those in control of

9 *Dictionary of American Biography*, XVII, p. 598.
10 *Commercial and Financial Chronicle*, April 15, 1893, p. 596.

the Richmond Terminal properties on the one hand and Drexel, Morgan & Company on the other.[11]

The terms which Morgan had imposed virtually meant that the security holders accepted in advance any proposals which he might make, but so great was their desperation that they had acquiesced.

A little over three months later the reorganization committee, consisting of C. H. Coster, George Sherman and Anthony J. Thomas, announced a plan for rehabilitating the Richmond Terminal company, the Richmond & Danville and the East Tennessee. These roads controlled about 6,000 miles of track; the one other important member of the old Terminal system, the Central of Georgia, was not included because of the complicated litigation in which it was involved. The plan was very severe but it was equally thorough. All stockholders in the Terminal company were to pay an assessment of $12.50 per share, a much larger amount than had been expected. The assessments on East Tennessee shares were graduated: common stock was to pay $9, second preferred stock $6 and first preferred $3. In each case preferred stock was to be given in return for the assessments, but second preferred holdings were to be scaled down 25 per cent and East Tennessee common holdings were to be reduced 40 per cent. This latter provision was especially drastic because all East Tennessee equities had been subjected to this same treatment only seven years before.

The need of assessments was occasioned both by the physical and the financial condition of the system. Physical deterioration, already referred to as one of the factors contributing to the receivership, was so advanced that lavish expenditures would have to be made at once. The necessary cash was to be provided by these assessments and by the sale of new common stock. Bonds sold at 85 would realize $6,800,000; assessments

11 *Ibid.*, February 4, 1893, p. 178; also see, *Railway World*, February 11, 1893, p. 135; April 22, 1893, p. 374; *Railway Review*, May 26, 1893, p. 413.

would give $11,450,000; and an additional $5,000,000 was to
be raised by the sale of new stock with a par value of $33,-
333,000. This would bring the cash total to about $23,250,000,
which was to be allocated as follows: $10,100,000 for the float-
ing debt; $1,500,000 for notes issued by the receivers; $1,-
300,000 for equipment notes; $4,000,000 for new construction
in the next two years on the Richmond & Danville; another
$4,000,000 for the same purposes on the East Tennessee; and
$2,350,000 for the expenses of the reorganization and miscel-
laneous items.

The new company was to issue $140,000,000 first consoli-
dated mortgage and collateral trust bonds at 5 per cent (including in this total the $74,000,000 of Richmond & Danville
securities which were to be left undisturbed), $75,000,000 of
non-cumulative 5 per cent preferred stock and $160,000,000 of
common stock. These securities would replace outstanding
issues of the Terminal Company, the Richmond & Danville and
the East Tennessee; provision was made for issuing additional
securities to exchange for those of the Georgia Central as soon
as there was an opportunity to add it to the system. $35,000,000
of the new bonds would not be issued at once but would be used
as needed under careful restrictions; further reserves of the
preferred and common stock were also provided.

In the past the system had been paying fixed charges on
$153,847,000 of bonds and floating debt. The new company
would pay interest on only $104,617,000. The resulting reduc-
tion in fixed charges, from $9,500,000 to $6,789,000, meant
that the estimated net earnings for 1893, the first depression
year, would have given a surplus in place of the recorded deficit. The capitalization of the new company would be $55,000
per mile of road operated or controlled, but fixed charges per
mile would be less than $1,150 annually.

Drexel, Morgan & Company, as reorganization managers,
were to receive $100,000 in cash with which to pay office ex-
penses and $750,000 in stock, calculated at the same price, $15

per share, at which it was to be sold to the syndicate. The syndicate of $15,000,000 would guarantee the sale of the new securities and succeed to the rights and privileges of any former stockholders not wishing to pay the assessments. A voting trust consisting of three Morgan nominees was to be formed to manage the property for at least five years and for as long thereafter as the company failed to pay a 5 per cent cash dividend on the preferred stock in one year.[12]

The plan was well received in financial circles. The *Wall Street Journal* believed that

the only objection which Terminal security holders are apt to make will probably come from the 6 per cent bonds, which suffer severely, but the reasons given for this distribution are admitted to be very forcible. . . . Comment on the value of Terminal common stock is dismissed with the single statement that it has no value at all, active or prospective, except through reorganization.[13]

The New York *Evening Post* believed that most of the stockholders of the Terminal company and many railway experts approved the plan, but investors who had bought the common stock as a speculative venture opposed it since it meant the failure of their gambles.[14] An editorial emphasized four good points in the proposal: it was introduced with a frank statement of the company's position; those securities which were well secured were left undisturbed and the rest were to be exchanged for new, in contrast to the earlier attempts to lump all securities together; the reorganization was based on the principle of carrying a large traffic at low rates, which should be the guiding principle of railway operation; since the errors

12 *Plan and Agreement for the Reorganization of the Richmond & West Point Terminal Railway & Warehouse Company*, etc., dated May 1, 1893, 49-page pamphlet. Also see, *Commercial and Financial Chronicle*, May 27, 1893, pp. 858-860 for analysis of the plan.

13 *Wall Street Journal*, May 24, 1893.

14 New York *Evening Post*, May 24, 1893.

of the past had proved even worse than expected, only " heroic measures " could " work a remedy ", and these were provided.[15]

Despite the almost immediate approval of the plan by a huge majority of all security holders concerned,[16] after the annual report of the receivers was published some changes became imperative. The estimated amount of receivers' certificates was found to be far below the actual amount which had been required to finance the road through the year and a downward revision of the estimated earnings for the next few years was necessary.[17] In March, 1894, several modifications of the original plan were announced: a few minor lines were excluded from the reorganization because they did not and probably never would earn their expenses; this change reduced the mileage of the prospective system to about 4600. Fixed charges for the next few years, until the earnings would have increased, were to be reduced by funding the interest on certain junior bond issues; fixed charges in 1894 would then be only $4,-100,000 and in 1895 they would be $4,700,000; in 1896 and thereafter they would be paid in cash in full. None of these changes were drastic and considering the severity of the depression in the South they were really insignificant.[18]

When the reorganization was finally completed on September 1, 1894, the new Southern Railway operated about 4500 miles of road, of which all except about 500 miles were owned by the parent company. It included lines formerly operated by more than thirty separate corporations under various costly leases and agreements. The new company had been chartered in Virginia and careful legal work had been necessary to make it conform to the requirements of all the states its tracks

15 *Ibid.*, May 25, 1893.

16 *Railway World*, June 17, 1893, p. 566; *Commercial and Financial Chronicle*, June 24, 1893, pp. 1036-1039.

17 *Railway World*, February 3, 1894, p. 85.

18 *Richmond & West Point Terminal, etc., Plan of Reorganization as Modified*. Dated February 20, 1894. Also, see *Railway World*, March 17, 1894, p. 217, for analysis of the changes.

traversed. The reorganization had involved two trustees' sales, one receivers' sale, ten foreclosure sales, six conveyances without foreclosure and innumerable other contracts and agreements. A total of about seventy different mortgages had been reduced to less than half that number. And, perhaps most important of all, one management now controlled the whole system, replacing the innumerable semi-autonomous and quarrelsome local managements.

The system reached and served all the diversified interests of the South: the coal fields in Kentucky, Tennessee and Alabama; iron at Knoxville, Cleveland, Chattanooga and Birmingham; the lumber regions and cotton fields of North Carolina, South Carolina and Georgia; the tobacco industry in Kentucky, especially near Louisville, and around Oxford and Durham, North Carolina; and the garden-truck business in Florida. From Alexandria, on the Virginia side of the Potomac directly across from Washington, the main line went south into Florida and west into Alabama, and a network of branches covered the intervening regions.[19]

The rights of the bondholders were especially well protected in the new first consolidated mortgage. Rigid limitations governed the issue of any new bonds; the total of $140,000,000 could never be exceeded and the $20,000,000 of reserved bonds could only be issued at stated intervals after January 1, 1896. The trustees could certify these bonds solely upon instructions from the board of directors; after any of them had been issued and before more could be certified all previous issues had to be rigidly accounted for, with definite specification of the use made of them; finally, no new bonds could be certified until the company had received a guarantee assuring their sale at a fair price. The clauses governing the rights of foreclosure were equally definite: in case of default for six months, holders of 25 per cent of the bonds could declare the principal of the bonds due, but if the default were made up holders of a majority

19 *Railway World*, September 22, 1894, pp. 756-757.

might waive the foreclosure so begun. All foreclosure proceedings were to be directed by holders of a majority and four-fifths of the bonds could instruct the trustee to buy in the property at the foreclosure sale for their protection, or they might authorize an issue of prior liens to avoid foreclosure, so long as the latter did not alter the date or amounts of payments provided in the consolidated mortgage bonds.[20] The care with which these indentures had been drawn reflected the reaction of the Morgan firm to the chaos and vagueness that had been characteristic of the finances of the Richmond Terminal system. If forethought could prevent it, there was to be no repetition of the carelessness and fraud which had helped wreck the old system.

The growth of the Southern immediately after its establishment was phenomenal. Within a few months more than 3,000 miles of track had been added to the original 4500.[21] By far the most important acquisition was the Central of Georgia Railway, successor company to the old Central Railroad & Banking Company of Georgia. The Central had been put into the hands of receivers October 7, 1893,[22] while under the control of the Richmond Terminal Company. The earliest proposal for its rehabilitation was intended, by placing high premiums on all other securities, to force the Richmond Terminal to dispose of its majority stock interest and thus permit the Central to regain its independence. These measures were too extreme to succeed, however, and roused protests from New York and foreign stockholders as well as from the Richmond Terminal interests.[23] A second plan was announced by Samuel T. Thomas and Thomas F. Ryan in July, 1894: the Southern Railway was to retain control of the Central, but the latter was

20 *Commercial and Financial Chronicle*, November 3, 1894, pp. 761-2.

21 *Railway Age and Northwestern Railroader*, November 8, 1895, p. 547.

22 *Interstate Commerce Commission Statistics*, 1897, pp. 254-255.

23 *Railway World*, January 21, 1893, p. 49; *Railway Review*, January 28, 1893, p. 814.

to be operated separately.[24] However, the plan soon had to be abandoned because the Southern demanded further concessions.[25] About a year later Thomas and Ryan made a third proposal which finally satisfied a majority of the stock, several bondholders' committees, the Richmond Terminal reorganization committee and the Southern management. The great advantage of this plan over its predecessors lay in its reduction of the annual fixed charges from $2,750,000 to $1,815,000 by the substitution of three series of income bonds for securities with a fixed annual return.[26]

When it was added to the Southern after its reorganization[27] the Central of Georgia Railway owned 1120 and leased 385 miles of roadbed. Its capitalization consisted of $5,000,000 of common stock, $15,000,000 of first, second and third preferred income bonds and mortgage bonds whose par value should not exceed $18,500,000.[28] Of the bonds $16,500,000 were to be issued at once and the remainder " shall be used only for the purpose of betterments and purchase of equipment along, or appurtenant to the lines of railway covered by the mortgage ", in allotments " not to exceed five hundred thousand dollars in any one fiscal year, upon resolution of the Board of Directors ".[29] The strength of these bonds was revealed by the sale of a block not at once publicly subscribed to a syndicate of New York and London bankers at 96½.[30]

The management which was to direct the Southern was carefully chosen by Morgan. Of the voting trustees who exercised general control of the system he himself was one and the

24 *Railroad Gazette*, July 13, 1894, p. 500; November 23, 1894, p. 814.

25 *Ibid.*, March 1, 1895, p. 144.

26 *Ibid.*, June 14, 1895, p. 397.

27 *Railway World*, November 2, 1895, p. 683.

28 *Commercial and Financial Chronicle*, December 26, 1896, pp. 1139-40.

29 *Consolidated Mortgage*, Central of Georgia Railway Company to the Mercantile Trust Company, Trustee, dated November 1, 1895.

30 *Railway World*, November 30, 1895, pp. 778.

other two were entirely amenable to his wishes. To assure a satisfactory administration Samuel Spencer was made president. He was a native Southerner, having been born in Columbus, Georgia, in 1847. He began his education in the neighborhood elementary schools and from them went to the Georgia Military Institute in Marietta until 1863. He then joined the Confederate cavalry, first the Nelson Rangers and, toward the end of the War, Nathan Bedford Forrest's troop, with whom he was surrendered in April, 1865. He returned to Georgia to complete his education and in 1867 was graduated with first honors from the state university at Athens with a liberal arts degree. Two years later he entered the University of Virginia, from which he received a civil engineering degree in 1869. He worked for three years on the Savannah & Memphis Railroad, advancing to the position of chief engineer before he left to take charge of one of the transportation divisions on the Baltimore & Ohio. He left that company for a short time to serve as general superintendent of the Long Island Railroad Company but returned to it in 1879 as assistant to the president. After rising through the successive vice-presidencies in 1887 at the direction of the banking syndicate he was made president. At the conclusion of his short administration he became a railway expert for the house of Morgan and in December, 1890, was made a partner in the firm. For the next five years he had been in charge of the railway interests of the firm, in addition to holding directorships in the Chicago, Milwaukee & St. Paul and the Chesapeake & Ohio. The choice of such an experienced railroad man for president of the new system was universally approved.[31]

Morgan's achievement in reorganizing the decrepit Richmond & West Point Terminal Company into the Southern Railway was very aptly summarized by Messrs. Hambleton & Company of Baltimore:

31 *Railway Age and Northwestern Railroader*, August 10, 1894, p. 446; *Dictionary of American Biography*, XVII, pp. 453-4.

This corporation, which succeeds to all the benefits and advantages of the Richmond Terminal system, at the same time has been relieved of all its embarrassments. The theory of reorganization, as advanced by Messrs. Drexel, Morgan & Company, was that each individual property should receive an interest-bearing obligation, involving a fixed charge upon the new organization, only to such an extent as it was, unassisted, able to take care of from its own earnings. . . . The Southern Railway Company is the great trunk line of the South, and it will set the pace for other systems. Its management will be progressive and aggressive, and a new era in railroading will be inaugurated in this section.[32]

The prediction that the company would quickly assume the leadership in Southern railroading proved accurate: before the decade ended two new systems, the Atlantic Coast Line and the Seaboard Air Line, were formed in self-defense to compete with it. Samuel Spencer thought that his road had so benefited the territory it served as to be an active argument in favor of railroad consolidation:

The Southern Railway Company is probably as good an illustration of consolidation as exists in this or any other country. What is now the Southern Railway Company was, five or six years ago, something like thirty-five or thirty-six corporations. The rates have not been raised. The facilities I think every man who knows that country knows have been very largely increased. The properties are in better condition.[33]

On the other hand, Thomas H. Woodlock, railroad editor of the *Wall Street Journal,* thought that the reorganization of the Southern was one of those which were accompanied by undue increases in capitalization. Before the Industrial Commission he pointed out that

Mr. J. P. Morgan, in most of his reorganizations, estimated the minimum earning capacity and based the fixed charges, going to

32 *Railway World,* September 1, 1894, p. 685.
33 *Industrial Commission Report,* IX, p. 278.

bonds and preferred stocks, on that, but as regards securities dependent upon future prospects people could pretty much help themselves.[34]

He had estimated the minimum future earnings and then, on that basis, computed the capitalization bearing fixed charges, without reference to the value of the property and without limiting the amount of stock to be issued. This method of calculating capitalization was adopted by Morgan in most of his reorganizations but its importance in the case of the Southern lay in the fact that a precedent was set which would be widely followed.

The constructive phase of the rehabilitation of the old Richmond Terminal system was of tremendous value. One biographer of Morgan considers it his greatest achievement in the railroad field, a " reorganization which will always stand out as the prime example of his peculiar ability for mastering a bewildering and apparently hopeless situation ". When Morgan stepped in " the Richmond Terminal was a shocking exhibition of confusion and disorder, swayed by belligerents who acted as if unconscious of their bankruptcy " and then the Terminal company " with its annual tale of horrors in the balance sheet, vanished, and the Southern Railway took its place ".[35] A more impartial commentator agreed with these sentiments:

For a management to succeed in doing anything with such unpromising railway material, to take a collection, or rather a congeries, of poorly constructed, over-bonded roads, built to sell rather than to operate, and located in the most unpromising territory, from a traffic standpoint, in the United States and to weld this material into a great railway system which is not only solvent, but which holds out a reasonable prospect of dividends to its common shareholders, is one of the noteworthy achievements of American railroad history.[36]

34 *Ibid.*, IV, p. lx.
35 Hovey, *Morgan*, pp. 228, 229, 232,
36 Meade, " Great Railway," *Railway World*, 1904, p. 1236.

However, the prospect of common stock dividends became more and more remote as the years passed. Although the company was soon able to pay a dividend on its preferred stock,[37] dividends on the common were not begun for more than twenty years.[38] But the owners had no chance to make any effective protest; the voting trust which had been created as a supposedly temporary expedient while the new road was becoming established, seemingly became permanent. When questioned about this in 1912, Mr. Morgan assured the Pujo Committee that he would like to terminate the trust, but that it was against his principles to do so until a majority in amount of the stock requested the termination; since he had received no such request, the trust had been continued. Despite Mr. Morgan's disclaimers, one of his partners, Henry P. Davison, admitted that he could not name any case in which the stockholders in a great railway system had been able to oust the incumbent management; individuals such as Harriman, Morgan or Hill could buy control of railroads and oust the officials, but for ordinary stockholders to band together for that purpose was unheard of.[39] In other words, Morgan created a successful railway from the chaotic elements of the old Richmond Terminal, but the twofold price was the creation of so many securities ahead of the common stock that dividends became a mirage and the semi-permanent transfer of control over the property to the house of Morgan.

The second great system which the house of Morgan undertook to rehabilitate, the notorious Erie, offered problems in many aspects even more difficult of solution than those presented by the Richmond Terminal. The London *Economist* foresaw nearly insuperable difficulties ahead of the reorganization committee:

37 *Poor's Manual*, 1900, pp. 1268-1285.
38 *Pujo Report*, III, pp. 1828-1831, testimony of H. P. Davison.
39 *Ibid.*, II, pp. 1828-1831.

The simple old fashioned method of assessing the stock is apparently out of the question. Stockholders would not submit, and there is no effective means of coercing them, owing to the fact that the second consolidated mortgage contains a provision postponing foreclosure under its lien until six successive interest coupons have been defaulted. The only alternative is the scaling of interest charges by the creation of a blanket mortgage, a plan which, it may be noted, was pursued with success in the case of the Central Railroad of New Jersey, and with more success in that of the Atchison reorganization. . . . It would be only equitable that the provision of the bond in regard to foreclosure should be modified in their favour so that, should the occasion arise again, they would be entitled to enforce their rights more promptly, and be in a position to compel the stockholders to bear their fair share of the burden.[40]

However, J. P. Morgan no more chose to be dictated to by a mortgage provision than by the minority interests in the Richmond Terminal. Early in January a letter signed by the Erie directors declared that the receivership had been fundamentally due to this clause in the mortgage, and that discreditable though it might be, the interest on this mortgage would be defaulted the necessary six successive times to enable a foreclosure sale. The same letter announced that Drexel, Morgan & Company had agreed to help the directors carry out the reorganization plan which was published that day.[41]

A new second mortgage, eliminating the troublesome foreclosure provision and amounting to $70,000,000 was to be floated; with it the old second mortgage, funded coupon bonds and income bonds were to be redeemed. In exchanging their old securities for the new, holders of the second mortgage would be sacrificing 1 per cent interest annually, but because of the new foreclosure provisions they would be receiving far more valuable bonds. Of this new mortgage, $15,000,000 was

40 *Economist*, December 16, 1893, pp. 1500-1501.
41 Directors' circular letter, January 2, 1894.

to be reserved to purchase new equipment and pay for new construction, but not more than $1,000,000 was to be used in any one year unless the need for new cars became acute, in which case $500,000 additional could be spent for that purpose alone.[42] The common stock was to be assessed $20 per share and for this payment no return would be given. Preferred stockholders were to pay $25 per share, but would receive an equivalent in new preferred stock. If the dividends on preferred stock be considered fixed charges, this plan would raise the Erie's annual obligations over $82,000, but excluding them, it slightly lessened fixed charges through the reduction of interest rates on the new bonds to 5 per cent.[43] The directors' announcement of the plan concluded with the statement that the house of Morgan would decide when enough security holders had assented for it to be declared operative.[44]

A threat that recalcitrant interests would, if necessary, be coerced into accepting the proposal was implicit in the announcement that the bond interest would be defaulted until foreclosure were made possible. Nevertheless the plan aroused a storm of protest. The *Economist* of London was indignant at what it considered a deliberate attempt to make English investors pay for the receivership:

That the second mortgage bondholders should have to submit to some sacrifices is natural enough, for their lien is comparatively weak and they practically rank just before the preferred shareholders; but still it would be most unjust to cut down the rate of interest on the seconds from six to four per cent whilst at the same time impairing the value of the mortgage by increasing its amount. Moreover, it is said that no assessment is to be made on the shares. In other words, the bonds, which are held almost entirely in this country, are to be taxed for the benefit of the floating debt, who are, or should be, unsecured creditors, whilst the

---

42 *Railway World*, January 13, 1894, pp. 32-33.

43 *Railway Age and Northwestern Railroader*, April 27, 1894, p. 238.

44 *Railway World*, January 13, 1894, pp. 32-33.

shares, which are, we need hardly say, held to a large extent in the United States, are to be allowed to get off scot free. In other cases, we know, a similar policy has been followed, but no one can contend that it was in the slightest degree justifiable.[45]

The New York *Evening Post* believed the plan had some good characteristics, but its enthusiasm was very limited. The treatment to be accorded the bonds was legal and after all bondholders had no right to expect more than their indentures guaranteed. But the *Post* was not sure that the reputed surpluses of the Erie for the several preceding years had been bona fide and the plan depended on their actual existence. That the reorganization committee had done its best was obvious, since

We all know that proposals of this kind are matters of compromise, and no doubt the planners accepted what they thought they could get; but it will surely be regretted in after years that more discretion was not given the board of directors

because the provisions made for the future were sure to prove inadequate.[46]

These were not the only observers who looked askance at the new plan. Within a few weeks a protest sponsored by E. H. Harriman & Company, Kuhn Loeb & Company, August Belmont & Company, Vermilye & Company, Hallgarten & Company and other less known financial powers, was circulating in Wall Street.[47] These firms and J. C. Peabody, agents for the heavily interested Astor estate, published their criticisms in an open letter to Morgan: to bring fixed charges within the earning power of the road the new bonds should be made to pay 4 instead of 5 per cent interest; holders of the old second mortgage bonds should receive interminable, non-cumulative 4 per cent debenture bonds, interest to be paid only if earned; the new bond issues should be offered to present security holders at

45 Quoted in *Railroad Gazette*, January 5, 1894, p. 14.
46 New York *Evening Post*, January 4, 1894.
47 *Railway World*, January 27, 1894, p. 65.

a price below the expected market quotation, rather than offered at a higher figure in order to peg the market price; the new 4 per cent bonds should be based on a general mortgage large enough to finance future additions and improvements. These changes the signers of the letter believed, would both lessen the probability of a future foreclosure, which 5 per cent bonds might necessitate, and facilitate the reorganization by eliminating obvious injustices.[48]

Despite the strength of these protests, Morgan elicited from everyone except Harriman reluctant promises not to interfere with the reorganization,[49] and early in March he announced that since holders of a majority of each class of bond involved had approved, the reorganization plan was operative.[50]

Although Harriman was still comparatively unknown in Wall Street, he refused to be awed. Instead he formed a protective committee for dissatisfied holders of the second mortgage bonds which protested against the plan on the ground that it was unsound and unfair.[51] Personally Harriman had a very minor interest in the Erie, for he owned only a small block of bonds,[52] but he seemed determined to score a second victory over the mighty Morgan. In 1887 while he had been merely a director of the Illinois Central Railroad a lease which that system held on the Dubuque & Sioux City Railroad was about to expire, so he was authorized to get control of the latter either by negotiation or by stock purchase. A majority group of Dubuque stockholders, who knew of Harriman's instructions, placed their stock in the hands of Drexel, Morgan & Company in the hope of getting a better price for it that way than by individual

---

48 *Ibid.*, February 3, 1894, pp. 94-95.

49 Corey, *House of Morgan*, pp. 201-202.

50 Circular letter of March 6, 1894, signed by Drexel, Morgan & Company. Also, *Commercial and Financial Chronicle*, March 10, 1894, pp. 408, 430.

51 *Railway World*, March 10, 1894, pp. 192-193. The committee consisted of Harriman, Henry Budge, John J. Emory and Sidney Webster.

52 Corey, *op. cit.*, pp. 201-202.

negotiation. Harriman bought up as much of the stock as he could but he still had a minority and Morgan seemed in control of the Dubuque. At the stockholders' meeting, however, Harriman controlled a majority of the stock which was present and was able to reject all proxies on the ground that they were illegal in Iowa. After this preliminary stroke, " amid sheer amazement and indignation " Harriman rejected the stock held by Drexel, Morgan & Company because it was signed by the firm personally and not as trustee. Although Morgan took the case to court, Harriman had the upper hand and was able to force Morgan to accept his terms.[53]

In their struggle over the Erie reorganization Morgan defeated Harriman, but events proved it a pyrrhic victory. Until a law suit instigated by Harriman was decided, the actual execution of the plan was postponed, both to gain a sound legal basis for the transaction and to allow the worst period of the depression to pass.[54] On June 25, 1894, Morgan received the legal justification which he was awaiting. The Supreme Court of New York ruled that since holders of $31,000,000 out of a total $38,000,000 of the old bonds had assented to the plan and the plaintiff, owning only $40,000 of them, had not assented and therefore would have his lien damaged in no way by the new issue, the court would not interfere in the reorganization proceedings.[55]

But the emptiness of Morgan's victory was apparent before the end of the year. Whether or not the protests against the injustice of the plan were valid, there could be no doubt that the charge of financial weakness was true. In December Morgan asked the bondholders to approve a modification of the original proposal. The last annual report had shown that temporarily the net revenue of the system would be inadequate to pay the interest on the new bonds. Therefore they would be issued with

53 *Ibid.*, pp. 155-156.
54 *Railway World*, June 2, 1894, p. 425.
55 *Ibid.*, June 30, 1894, p. 516.

the coupons of June and December, 1894, attached, subject to a guarantee that they be paid as soon as practicable out of net earnings over interest and rentals accruing after December 1, 1894; in the event that a later default brought foreclosure, all original rights were retained by the bondholders. But if in June, 1895, the earnings of the Erie were still less than the requirements for interest on these bonds, Morgan reserved the right to take whatever action he considered best instead of delivering the new securities.[56]

The half-year probationary period showed that the plan would have to be abandoned and more drastic measures substituted, so on August 26 the new proposal was made public. The Erie system comprised the parent company, the New York, Pennsylvania & Ohio and the Chicago & Erie. The two subsidiaries had been operated under an agreement by which the Erie guaranteed that a fixed percentage of their gross receipts should be paid them as net earnings, regardless of whether or not they earned even their expenses. This arrangement which made the three members of the system rivals instead of partners, was a defect that the new plan corrected. The trustees of the Nypano had already promised, subject to the approval of their beneficiaries, to foreclose the mortgage on that road and permit the Erie reorganization committee to buy it in; the Chicago & Erie expected to make a similar agreement within a few days. All these properties were to be combined into a single corporation, both for financial and operating purposes. The new company would issue $175,000,000 of first consolidated mortgage bonds secured by a mortgage covering all property acquired under the reorganization; of these bonds, $35,000,000 were to be 4 per cent prior liens and the rest 3 and 4 per cent general liens. The company would also issue $30,000,000 of first preferred 4 per cent non-cumulative stock and $16,000,000 of second preferred non-cumulative stock, in addition to $100,000,000 of common stock.

---

56 *Commercial and Financial Chronicle*, December 15, 1894, p. 1031.

This $321,000,000 capitalization would be represented by a system embracing 1938 miles of track, valuable terminals in Jersey City, Weehawken, Buffalo and other large cities, and a one-fifth ownership of the Chicago, Indiana & Western Railroad Company. Also, $22,000,000 of the new bonds were reserved for betterments, additions and new construction. The ratios at which old securities would be exchanged for those of the new corporation were carefully worked out: Erie second mortgage bonds were to receive 75 per cent in general lien bonds and 55 per cent in first preferred stock; funded coupon bonds of 1885 were to get 100 per cent in new general lien bonds, 10 per cent in first preferred stock and 10 per cent in second preferred stock; Erie income bonds were to get 40 per cent in new general lien bonds and 60 per cent in new first preferred stock. The old preferred stock on payment of an assessment of $8 per share was to receive 100 per cent in second preferred stock, and the old common stock after paying a $12 per share assessment would get 100 per cent in the new common stock; neither stock would receive any compensation for the assessments levied.

The treatment to be accorded the Nypano's securities was noteworthy because this was one of the few roads from whose stock any water was wrung during the nineties. By dint of halving the value of the first mortgage bonds, exchanging preferred stock for new common at the rate of 50 to 1 and common stock for new common at the rate of 100 to 1, its total capitalization was to be reduced from about $160,000,000 to about $40,000,000, at which figure it was probably still heavily over-capitalized.[57]

As usual in Morgan's reorganizations, all the stock of the new company was to be placed in a voting trust. A syndicate of $25,000,000 had been formed to take $15,000,000 of the prior lien bonds and any stock on which the assessments were not

57 *Railway World*, August 31, 1895, pp. 490-1; *Commercial and Financial Chronicle*, September 14, 1895, p. 449.

paid. In addition to cash for all expenses Morgan was to receive a fee of $500,000 payable in common stock. The fixed charges of the former company had been $9,900,000. After two years those of the new company would be about $7,850,000, but meanwhile the general lien bonds were to receive only 3 instead of the usual 4 per cent interest, and this meant a further reduction of about $300,000 for those years. Although the net earnings of the system in 1893-4 were just sufficient to have paid these temporarily reduced charges, the average net for the past seven years would have left an annual surplus of about $1,-500,000 over the normal fixed charges of the new company, and that would have been enough to pay a 4 per cent dividend on the first preferred stock and 2 per cent on the second preferred.[58]

This second Morgan plan really tried to solve the problems of the road instead of merely supplying a minimum amount of necessary cash and glossing over the weaknesses which had led to disaster. And the reception accorded it was proportionally more favorable than that which had greeted its predecessor. The *Commercial and Financial Chronicle* thought the plan offered

little or no occasion for adverse criticism. It recognizes existing conditions, deals with the situation in a thorough and effective manner, and places the property on what promises to be an assured basis of solvency. The plan also possesses the merit which is characteristic of all reorganizations originating with the house of J. P. Morgan & Company, of exceeding frankness in dealing with the different classes of security holders.

The consolidation of the several parts of the system into one integrated company and the reduction in fixed charges were particularly commended.[59]

58 *Railway World*, August 31, 1895, pp. 480-1.
59 *Commercial and Financial Chronicle*, August 31, 1895, pp. 348-9.

The stock market reacted favorably to the plan despite its harshness, because the belief was prevalent that it would succeed and thereby renew confidence in American railway management both at home and abroad.[60] The New York *Evening Post* praised the same features of the plan which had attracted the *Chronicle's* attention.[61]

The *Wall Street Journal* also believed that

the Erie reorganization plan was well conceived. It is extremely drastic and such a measure was absolutely necessary. . . . The plan is a very shrewd one in more respects than one. The new bonds are given the right to vote when the voting trust expires, each bond rating as ten shares of stock. This is as it should be. . . . We venture the prediction that the Erie reorganization will be completed in fewer days from the issue of the plan yesterday than any other reorganization scheme in the history of the street.[62]

The *Economist* was considerably more restrained in its enthusiasm and inclined to weigh bitter memories:

The circular in which these proposals are made, and in a special degree the voluminous and elaborate pamphlet in which they are elucidated, are well calculated to conjure up a host of reflections anent American Railway securities—most of them unpleasant ones. One is, for example, likely to be struck with the somewhat quaint circumstance that the same company which four years ago had the audacity to pay a three per cent dividend on its preferred shares now reverses the customary order of things by exacting "dividends" from its shareholders. Then the scheme brings home to us with considerable force, that reorganization costs something besides the loss caused by " scaling down " or assessments. Messrs. Morgan state, with a candour which, as far as we know, has no precedent in such cases, that they are to get $500,000 cash for their trouble; and as, in addition the syndicate which guarantees the success of the scheme is likely to get a good commission on the $15,000,000

60 New York *Evening Post*, August 27, 1895.
61 *Ibid.*, August 30, 1895.
62 *Wall Street Journal*, August 27, 1895, p. 2.

bonds it purchases, the doctor's bill is sure to reach at least a million, and perhaps even two million dollars.

Yet, though this sum is no doubt enormous, and means at least a perpetual charge of $50,000, we are forced to admit that the scheme at any rate appears to be probably as good as could be devised. The essential qualities of a plan of the kind are adequacy, justice, and elasticity; and close scrutiny of the proposals before us fails to show a deficiency in any of these respects. . . . Messrs. Morgan, who had to deal with facts and not with ideals, have on the whole, acted wisely in accepting the situation and in making the best of it.[63]

The *Chronicle* found further cause for congratulation in considering the effect the new mortgage would have on the physical condition of the system; for years in a period of remarkable railway development the Erie management had been severely handicapped because they could not issue bonds to finance the purchase of needed equipment and additions. This condition had been eliminated and in the future necessary new capital could be obtained without accumulating an unwieldy floating debt in the process.[64]

After the new company had been launched, it was announced that the voting trust consisted of J. P. Morgan, Louis Fitzgerald and Sir Charles Tennant to represent the British interests.[65] Morgan influence was also predominant on the board of directors: at the first stockholders' meeting a board was chosen consisting of Charles H. Coster, James J. Goodwin, Abram S. Hewitt, Darius O. Mills, Alexander E. Orr, George W. Quintard, Samuel Spencer, Francis Lynde Stetson, E. B. Thomas of New York; John G. McCullough of Vermont; J. Lowber Welsh of Philadelphia and Samuel E. Williamson of Cleveland.[66] Of these men, Coster, Spencer, Stetson and Welsh had long been recognized as Morgan railroad experts.

---

63 *Economist*, August 31, 1895, pp. 1139-40.
64 *Commercial and Financial Chronicle*, January 11, 1896, p. 54.
65 Mott, *Between the Ocean and the Lakes*, p. 279.
66 *Ibid.*, p. 282.

Three years after the reorganization had been completed the Erie's historian pointed out that the annual reports issued since that time showed that fixed charges had thus far been earned.

According to the report for 1898 the net earnings of the railroad and income from other sources were $8,716,189.80, which provided for the fixed charges and left a surplus of more than $633,000. This, then, would seem to demonstrate, beyond dispute or cavil, the correctness of the claim of those who pressed the reorganization to success, that the Erie Railroad's earnings would easily be more than its expenses, if the Company were relieved of the incubi that had hampered it for a generation, and the subsidiary lines necessary for the Erie's traffic were changed from a warring irresponsible group to one uniform system, through a rational, business-like process of consolidation, by which they might be brought under the control and direction of one head. By such a consolidation of the Erie system, the days of loading upon Erie worthless and extravagant leases, the aftermath of corrupt stock-jobbery, and the cost and future responsibility of bad personal undertaking generally, have become, necessarily, a thing of the past. Those plunderings of Erie are represented today by not less than $100,000,000 of her tremendous debt. If the company and the railroad, conducted on correct principles of business and financeering and of operative management can show a surplus above the large sum of fixed charges made necessary by that unrighteous debt, what might not this highway of most unfortunate memory have done if it had not fallen into designing hands years and years ago? [67]

Undoubtedly Morgan had faced a difficult task in reorganizing the Erie, but it was unfortunate that no attempt was made to squeeze as much of the water out of the Erie's capitalization as came out of the Nypano's. Instead, the precedent set in creating the Southern Railway was followed and Morgan based the capitalization of the new company on its earnings, limiting the amount of bonds by the probable net earnings which would

67 *Ibid.*, p. 293.

be available for interest. But lacking any similar restriction on the amount of stock which the system might issue, hesitant interests were won over to the reorganization plan by liberal offers of preferred stock. The result of placing so many securities ahead of the common stock and then further reducing whatever value it might have by liberally distributing it, was that the system's shares sold at very low prices on the market. This meant that whenever the company wished to raise money it could not advantageously resort to the sale of stock; instead bonds were usually issued, and, of course, with each issue the value of the stock became less. During the first decade of the twentieth century the outstanding capital stock of the system did not increase at all; but the funded debt rose over 33 per cent, becoming considerably larger than the stock capitalization.[68] But whether Morgan could have squeezed very much water out of the capital, even if he had been so inclined, is very doubtful, of course, and the reorganization he actually carried through indisputably put the Erie in a better position than it had occupied for years.

The next system to be reorganized by the house of Morgan was the Philadelphia and Reading. Although he had been the system's financial agent until its abortive expansion into New England, and although his representative, J. Lowber Welsh, was made a receiver soon after the failure, the Morgan firm moved slowly in Reading matters. Several other interests hastened to propose reconstruction programs, hurl charges back and forth and finally force one another to a near standstill.

When the court appointed receivers for the Reading on February 20, 1893, it named President McLeod, President Wilbur of the Lehigh Valley and former Judge Paxson.[69] Almost immediately factional struggles for control began. The appointment of McLeod, who was almost universally held re-

68 Sakolski, A. M., *American Railroad Economics*, New York: Macmillan Company, 1916, p. 280.

69 *Railway World*, March 4, 1893, pp. 197-8.

sponsible for wrecking the property, was attacked immediately, although nothing more than rumors of his former activities had a general circulation.[70] At the request of Anthony J. Drexel, head of the Philadelphia branch of the house of Morgan, McLeod suddenly resigned April 4, 1893, the resignation to become effective May 1. Mr. Drexel had declared quite definitely that the necessary financial aid would not be forthcoming from banking circles as long as McLeod dominated the Reading and the public reaction to his retirement seemed to support this ultimatum.[71] The *Commercial and Financial Chronicle* believed the resignation had been wise and would facilitate the reorganization of the property.[72] The *Economist* of London thought that McLeod had " acted in a manner which, if it was not dishonest, affords a complete condemnation of the virtually despotic power possessed by too many American railway officials ".[73] A few editors were surprised; one was apprehensive because

McLeod originated and executed the brilliant moves which in a brief time expanded the Reading system into its present immense proportions and his retirement may signify abandonment of the bold plan of campaign which had not yet been completed when fiancial disaster overtook it.[74]

The more widespread feeling, however, was expressed by the St. Paul *Pioneer Press* when it remarked that " if President McLeod, of the Reading, feels aggrieved that he is out, he still has the consciousness that the stockholders are out also ".[75] His successor both as president and receiver was Joseph S. Harris,

70 *Ibid.*, March 4, 1893, pp. 193, 197-8; March 11, 1893, pp. 219-20.

71 *Ibid.*, April 8, 1893, p. 315; April 22, 1893, p. 361, etc.

72 *Commercial and Financial Chronicle*, April 8, 1893, p. 556.

73 *Economist*, May 27, 1893, pp. 627-8.

74 Quoted in *Railway Age and Northwestern Railroader*, April 7, 1893, p. 269.

75 *Railway World*, April 15, 1893, p. 341.

who was acceptable to Morgan and widely experienced in anthracite railroad problems.[76]

Among the first acts of the receivers was the termination of unprofitable contracts and ventures which McLeod had initiated. The brokerage accounts, through which New York & New England and Boston & Maine stock had been bought, were closed out despite the heavy losses the Reading suffered in the process.[77] Secondly, the rental paid to the Lehigh Valley was reduced in order to make the Reading's obligations more nearly proportional to the former's earnings. The original lease provided that the Reading should guarantee a 7 per cent dividend on all Lehigh stock, and that excess profits should be divided equally between the two companies. The new agreement reduced the rental to 5 per cent on the stock, with the additional provision that all earnings up to 7 per cent go to Lehigh stockholders and any return above that be split between the companies.[78]

As the outstanding manifestations of McLeod's presidency were obliterated, hopes for an early reorganization mounted. In April Messrs. Drexel, Morgan & Company and Brown Brothers & Company agreed to take care of approaching interest payments and several matured mortgages.[79] Estimates of the system's minimum needs were made and optimistic prophecies became more frequent.[80] Before the end of June a reorganization plan was published.[81] It imposed very easy terms on the various interests involved and demanded only three important concessions: stockholders were to surrender the voting power of their shares to a voting trust for seven years; the general mortgage bondholders must agree to the purchase of their

76 *Ibid.*, May 6, 1893, p. 409.

77 *Ibid.*, February 17, 1894, pp. 135-7.

78 *Ibid.*, May 6, 1893, p. 422.

79 *Ibid.*, April 1, 1893, pp. 289, 303.

80 *Ibid.*, April 15, 1893, pp. 342-4.

81 *Ibid.*, June 30, 1893, pp. 507, 509-10, 516-8.

coupons for five years if necessary; certain leased and guaranteed properties acquired since 1888 were to permit a reduction or funding of rental charges. New 6 per cent collateral trust bonds to the amount of $30,000,000 were to be floated and subscriptions invited from all security holders, but there would be no obligatory assessments and a syndicate would take up as much of the bond issue as was not wanted by security holders.

Compared to the terms which were offered to the holders of Richmond Terminal securities at about the same time, this plan was very generous. Richmond stock was to be assessed and lose its voting privilege; Reading stock was only to suffer the latter. Bondholders of the Reading were asked, if necessary, to waive their interest claims of five years and have the unpaid coupons added to the principal of their holdings; if any bondholder preferred, the syndicate would make the regular cash payments, in exchange for which it would receive a bond based on the coupons and redeemable at the discretion of the management at a price not exceeding 105.

The interest on the new bonds would be less than that on the floating debt, which was to be paid with proceeds from the sale of some of them. $8,000,000 of the bonds were to be reserved for working capital and improvements, to be spent in annual installments not exceeding $2,000,000. Assents must be received from at least 90 per cent of the bondholders and 60 per cent of the shareholders before the plan would become effective.[82]

Despite the generally favorable comment that greeted it, the proposal had one fatal defect: it was based on insufficient information. In a public letter to President Harris, Isaac L. Rice raised this point and added objections to the personnel of the proposed voting trust. The five men whom the plan named were four officials of the road[83] and one large stockholder. Rice protected that this meant men who had participated in the McLeod

82 *Commercial and Financial Chronicle*, June 3, 1893, pp. 905-7; *Railway Age and Northwestern Railroader*, June 9, 1893, pp. 446-7, 448.
83 Receivers Wilbur and Harris and two directors.

regime and had concurred in the latter's policies, were to be continued in control of the road. Further, Rice declared, according to the annual report which had been issued in January 20 no reorganization was needed. The stock ventures having been terminated, the balance sheet showed that the system should be solvent.[84]

The latter objection was indisputably valid: if reorganization were actually needed, proof of the fact should be presented in the form of a detailed report based on a thorough examination of the real condition of the company. Until definite knowledge was available all plans for rehabilitation would be based on guesses and hopes. In view of this situation, it is not surprising that within a month the plan had to be abandoned by its sponsors, the board of managers, because the assents required to put it into effect were not forthcoming.[85]

Before any more reorganization plans were proposed, considerable progress was made in consolidating the position of the road and in settling litigation roused by the receivership. In order to increase traffic, an alliance was formed with the Grand Trunk, effective August 1, 1893, by which the Reading would carry nickel ore from the Sudbury mines to the smelters in New Jersey.[86] An unsuccessful attempt was made to find a new market for anthracite coal in Europe: the coal was well liked by Europeans, but inasmuch as it required a stove different from that universally used, very little of it was sold. Some progress was made in establishing a market in London and other English cities but the receivers decided that the volume of sales did not justify paying the expenses of a permanent foreign representative.[87]

84 *Railway World*, June 17, 1893, pp. 563-5.

85 *Ibid.*, June 24, 1893, p. 578; *Commercial and Financial Chronicle*, June 24, 1893, p. 1035; *Railway Age and Northwestern Railroader*, June 30, 1893, p. 507.

86 *Railway Age and Northwestern Railroader*, June 30, 1893, p. 510.

87 *Railway World*, August 12, 1893, p. 752.

The Reading's relations with the independent coal operators were also clarified. There was a growing dissatisfaction on the part of the latter with the service provided by the Reading and its alleged discrimination in providing cars. For the most part Coxe Brothers & Company's collieries were supplied with transportation by the Delaware, Susquehanna & Schuylkill Railway and they had been working full time steadily, whereas other operators were working only about four nine-hour-days per week. During the summer Pardee Brothers & Company, shipping about 1000 tons of coal daily, had transferred their business from the Reading to the Delaware, Susquehanna & Schuylkill, and immediately they had been able to resume full time operation of their mines.[88] The Reading, on the other hand, had been equally dissatisfied with the former agreements. In forming his anthracite monopoly McLeod had made a contract with Coxe Brothers for 1,000,000 tons of coal per year. The agreement had necessitated the construction of a special branch line to the colliery, and the net profit to the Reading was too small to pay even the interest on the investment. So it was no surprise when the receivers abrogated this contract late in the summer.[89]

The most important of the Reading's alliances, that with the Lehigh Valley, had already been ended. Even after the rental had been reduced the lease was still attacked as constituting a liability to an already bankrupt system. When it was made in conjunction with the lease of the Central Railroad of New Jersey in order to dictate the prices of tidewater anthracite, there had been some justification for it, but after the termination of the Jersey Central lease had fatally weakened the monopoly that justification ended. The prospects of deriving any cash advantages from the lease were very poor, for the Lehigh must earn 7 per cent on its stock before the Reading began to share the profits. Meanwhile the Reading's unsold

88 *Ibid.*, August 5, 1893, p. 727.
89 *Ibid.*, September 2, 1893, p. 829.

supply of coal was still growing despite the curtailment of its own output. Other companies were expanding their production and distribution, but the Reading was afraid to push its sales lest retail prices be forced down and its investment ruined. Notwithstanding this situation and still hopeful that future results might justify them, the receivers had paid the rental the first time it came due.[90]

However, on August 8, 1893, the problem was unexpectedly solved: the directors of the Lehigh voted to cancel the lease because of " continued default on the part of the Philadelphia & Reading Coal & Iron Company in the payment of the sums due under the contract dated February 11, 1892 ".The Reading directors not unnaturally exhibited surprise at this culmination to their efforts. On June 30, they had paid the stipulated Lehigh dividend in order to prevent the lapse of this contract, although on the following day they had permitted the interest due on the Reading's öwn general mortgage bonds to remain unpaid.[91] The default which was used as a pretext for cancellation had been made on a debt contracted before the lease was signed. In respect to the consequences of the Lehigh's action one of its officials declared that

> The abrogation of the lease with the Reading does not mean a separation of interests. The two roads will continue to work together and their close intimacy during the past year will make it all the easier for them to agree upon traffic arrangements.[92]

Inasmuch as the lease had cost the Reading a cash loss of more than $2,000,000 in addition to injuring seriously its coal business, most security holders welcomed the Lehigh's action.[93]

Meanwhile Isaac L. Rice had sued to oust the receivers on the grounds that the lease of the Lehigh Valley and the coal

90 *Ibid.*, July 22, 1893, pp. 684-685.

91 *Ibid.*, August 12, 1893, pp. 754-757, 757-759.

92 *Railway Age and Northwestern Railroader*, August 18, 1893, p. 629.

93 *Railway World*, August 12, 1893, pp. 754-757, 757-759.

contracts should have been terminated as soon as they took office, and that they should have refused to accept responsibility on behalf of the Reading for McLeod's stock speculations. In their reply the receivers denied that their actions either provided grounds for dismissing them or implied approval of McLeod's policies:

> These transactions were based upon the advice of counsel and the opinion of the receivers that the title of Prince & Company and Ervin & Company to these securities (collateral for the accounts) could not be contested. The settlement with Prince & Company was made to carry through a reorganization of the company's affairs, and it was the intention of the receivers to do nothing that would imply a ratification of the purchases by Ervin & Company of the stock, and they carefully avoided doing so.[94]

The court referred Rice's petition to a special·master for investigation, and after long hearings he made a report which completely exonerated the receivers of any wrong-doing and asserted that there was no ground for ousting them.[95] Although he thought the facts disclosed by the hearings justified him in not assessing the costs against the plaintiff, the judge concurred in this judgment and thereby ended Rice's attempt to get control of the Reading through legal proceedings.[96]

While the troublesome struggle for control was being fought in the courts, little progress was made toward reorganizing the company. A supplement to the annual report for the year ending December 31, 1893, showed that when the receivers had been appointed on February 20, the balance on the wrong side of the ledger had been about $5,000,000. After they had operated the system for a year, this deficit was $8,000,000. The receivers added that:

94 *Ibid.*, December 23, 1893, pp. 1211-1214.
95 *Ibid.*, June 23, 1894, pp. 493-495.
96 *Ibid.*, January 12, 1895, p. 37.

various schemes have been suggested and elaborately discussed with the friends of the company, but as yet no plan has been formulated which the management has felt warranted in offering to the consideration of the security holders. The subject is under consideration and it is hoped that at an early day some method of adjustment may be agreed upon which will secure the approval and cooperation of the stockholders and creditors of the company.[97]

These hopes were aroused by a conference held on January 13, 1894, which was attended by the receivers, bondholders' representatives and the attorneys of both. A tentative draft of a plan had been agreed upon: bond coupons for the next five years were to be bought by a syndicate that would pay the holders in cash for them; the syndicate would hold the coupons as its security for their ultimate payment under the general mortgage. Elaborate plans had been worked out to fund the floating debt, which had grown to about $12,500,000: the Finance Company of Pennsylvania felt that the coal and coal accounts it held would be sufficient security for $6,000,000 of new 6 per cent ten-year trust certificates to be publicly sold at par. The Reading already possessed $10,000,000 of 5 per cent collateral trust bonds which had maintained their value because they were based on the stocks and bonds of subsidiaries; these could also be sold at a fair price to the public. The proceeds from these two operations would suffice to pay off the floating debt, the receivers' certificates and some car trusts which were approaching maturity. Funding of the bond coupons would provide enough cash to meet all maturing obligations, including equipment trusts, during the next five years. At the end of that period, under the terms of the Reading's reorganization the company would come into possession of $10,000,000 of 4 per cent general mortgage bonds, and these would provide working capital thereafter.[98] Although optimistic reports were published

97 *Ibid.*, April 28, 1894, p. 329.

98 *Commercial and Financial Chronicle*, January 20, 1894, p. 127.

about the progress being made under this program,[99] a suit was filed to restrain the receivers from entering into any reorganization arrangements and final court approval of their doing so was not obtained until autumn.[100]

Meanwhile the security holders were becoming disgusted at the long delays in reorganizing the company. On the grounds that the receivers had failed either to rehabilitate the road or to pay any interest on the bonds, a general mortgage bondholders' committee was formed early in May to protect the bondholders if necessary by foreclosing the mortgage.[101] Under date of October 1, 1894, this committee published its Readjustment Agreement, the third reorganization plan to be suggested. It provided for raising $8,000,000 with which to pay part of the principal and all of the interest on the receivers' certificates and the floating debt, and for raising another $2,000,000 with which to pay equipment notes and car trusts that could not be extended. This cash was to be contributed by stockholders and income-bondholders: each $10,000 of income bonds was to subscribe for $1,000 of collateral trust 5 per cent notes which would be due in 1912 at par plus interest; each 200 shares of stock was to subscribe an equal amount. For small security holders, scrip, exchangeable in lots of $1,000 for the notes, was to be issued. As an alternative to these provisions, any holder of stock or income bonds might pay 3 per cent of the value of his holdings in cash, for which no obligation of the company would be given. A syndicate had been formed to take up all the unsubscribed bonds at 75 per cent of par with a 2½ per cent commission. In case the reorganization were not successfully concluded, all contributions under the plan would be returned.

Control of the Reading was to be transferred to the bondholders until the defaulted interest had been paid. All stock was to be deposited in order that half the directors and the president

99 *Railway World*, February 10, 1894, p. 105.
100 *Commercial and Financial Chronicle*, November 3, 1894, pp. 757-758.
101 *Railway World*, May 12, 1894, pp. 366-367.

of the company could be elected by bondholders. As much as was needed of the $10,000,000 cash which was to be raised would be used to pay enough of the receivers' certificates, floating debt and balances on account of car trusts to bring the annual payments on these obligations below $500,000, or whatever figure might be set by the reorganization managers. A committee would be formed to buy the general mortgage bond coupons for five years, and this committee was to have the right of foreclosure in case of any future defaults on these bonds.[102]

Although adoption of the plan would obviate the necessity of a foreclosure sale, with its attendant destruction of the value of junior securities, early in January it had to be abandoned.[103] Among other criticisms, three were particularly emphasized by Isaac L. Rice as his reasons for opposing it. It would enormously increase the fixed charges which took priority over the general mortgage interest payments. It provided a ridiculously inadequate treasury reserve. And finally, the figures on which it was based were delusive in that they failed to allow for the losses sustained by the Reading Coal & Iron Company through bad debts, depreciation and similar factors [104]

The trenchancy of this final objection was revealed by the annual report for 1894 which was issued a few days later. The deficit in the amount needed to pay fixed charges was little less than $2,000,000. Although this shortage was in part due to extra large payments for equipment and improvements, nevertheless recent calculations had shown that on the basis of the year's revenue there had been a deficit of $148,000 towards paying interest on the prior liens alone, to say nothing of that on the general mortgage bonds. The receivers included with their statistical report for the year an observation that none of

102 *Readjustment Agreement*, dated October 1, 1894; also see *Railway World*, September 29, 1894, pp. 775-777 for analysis of the plan.

103 *Railway World*, January 5, 1895, p. 1.

104 *Ibid.*, January 5, 1895, p. 11.

the reorganization schemes thus far prepared had been drastic
enough:

> The falling off in the earnings of the Reading companies . . .
> is so great as to render necessary a larger contribution from the
> junior security holders, and possibly some concession from the
> general mortgage bondholders, unless a great and permanent im-
> provement in the coal trade shall promptly occur.[105]

Early in the fall the same committee which had prepared the
most recent ill-fated plan announced that it would soon have a
new proposal to lay before security holders. The committee,
headed by Frederic P. Olcott, was strong, including as it did
Adrian Iselin, Jr., J. Kennedy Tod, Henry Budge, Thomas
Denny, George H. Earle, Jr., Sidney F. Tyler, Samuel R.
Shipley and Richard Y. Cook; Messrs. J. P. Morgan & Company were cooperating and would manage the reorganization.
The plan which this group presented on December 15 for either
the reorganization or foreclosure of the property was intended
primarily to achieve five ends: protect the present general
mortgage; reduce fixed charge to a figure safely within the net
earning power of the company; adequately provide working
capital for the future; pay the floating debt and provide for the
car trust obligations; and vest control in a voting trust until
the road's financial status was satisfactory.

The new company was to have a total capitalization of $254,-
000,000 consisting of $114,000,000 of general mortgage 4 per
cent bonds, $28,000,000 of non-cumulative 4 per cent first pre-
ferred stock, $42,000,000 of non-cumulative 4 per cent second
preferred stock and $70,000,000 of common stock. Necessary
cash was to be raised, in part, by a 20 per cent assessment on
preferred income bonds and common stock and a 4 per cent
assessment on deferred income bonds. The new general
mortgage bonds were to be used to retire the prior liens and the
old general mortgage bonds as they came due; the new issue

105 *Ibid.*, December 7, 1895, pp. 802-803.

would also provide $20,000,000 for construction, equipment and similar expenses: $4,000,000 of them would be delivered to the underwriting syndicate and $875,000 reserved for contingencies. Provision was also made for $21,000,000 of additional bonds secured by the new mortgage; these could only be used to take up outstanding terminal and coal company bonds and if this were done those properties must be brought under the mortgage. The new first preferred stock was to be used as follows: $7,184,000 to retire first preference income bonds, $8,000,000 for delivery to the syndicate and $12,816,000 for a reserve. Of the second preferred stock, $40,286,000 was to be used in retiring the outstanding first, second and third preference income bonds and the remaining block would be used for contingencies. The new common stock would be exchanged for the old and the few extra shares would swell the amount held for contingencies. The bases of exchange for all the various securities were carefully adjusted: in every case except that of the deferred income bonds, which received 20 per cent of their par value in new common stock, old securities would be exchanged for 100 per cent or more of their par value in new securities.

Assessments would raise $20,800,000 cash and sales to the syndicate would add $7,300,000 more; after all obligations had been met, it was calculated that about $3,000,000 cash would be left in the company's treasury. Annual fixed charges would be about $9,300,000. The syndicate which was to sell the new securities and take up unpaid assessments included J. P. Morgan & Company. J. Kennedy Tod & Company, Hallgarten & Company and A. Iselin & Company. The voting trust was to be continued at least five years and thereafter until the company paid 4 per cent dividends for two successive years on the first preferred stock.[106]

106 *Plan and Agreement for the Reorganization of the Philadelphia & Reading*, etc., dated December 14, 1895; also *Railway World*, December 21, 1895, pp. 855-856 for analysis of the plan.

An implication which puzzled most observers was that the reorganization might be made without foreclosure. The advantage of so doing would be in the retention of the old charter: yet in 1886 it had been necessary to issue income bonds because that charter forbade the issuance of preferred stock; further, under that charter the new Pennsylvania constitution would limit the capitalization in common stock to $47,000,000, and the plan proposed a far greater amount than this.[107] The mystery was finally solved by a statement from the receivers. If unanimous assents from all the company's outstanding securities precluded a foreclosure, income bonds would be issued instead of the preferred and some of the common stock.[108] At most the problem was hardly more than theoretical, for the reorganization committee could always withhold consents from enough securities to assure a court order directing a foreclosure sale.

The plan was received with somewhat mingled emotions. The *Commercial and Financial Chronicle* believed that its best characteristic was the protection given the general mortgage bonds and regretted that the junior bonds and stock could not be more liberally treated. On the whole the *Chronicle* thought it was " drastic and radical and deals with the situation in a thorough and effective manner." [109]

The *Wall Street Journal* thought that considerable changes in the market value of Reading securities would be brought about by the proposal:

Nobody was surprised at the Reading plan, because it was precisely what had been outlined for several weeks. . . . If the common stock is worth 9, then first, second and third incomes are very much too low and so is the estimated value of the new first and second preferred stock.[110]

107 *Railway World*, December 21, 1895, pp. 855-856.
108 *Ibid.*, March 21, 1896, p. 274.
109 *Commercial and Financial Chronicle*, December 21, 1895, pp. 1084-1085.
110 *Wall Street Journal*, December 17, 1895, p. 2.

The New York *Evening Post,* while admitting that the plan might prove extremely drastic, yet saw hope that in the end it might be very lenient and was glad to see the income bonds eliminated:

> Thus the Reading plan is severe and radical or not, according as one views the situation. If junior security-holders are to find their losses permanent, the plan is drastic, though even then it but represents the existing limitations; if, however, success should follow, the plan permits the settling of present difficulties in order to make possible a success not now attainable. At any rate, it is to be hoped that we have seen the last of that financial monstrosity, an income bond.[111]

The company's annual report for 1895 confirmed the practicability of the new plan by showing a net revenue safely above the proposed fixed charges,[112] so its execution was rapidly pushed forward. Due to prolonged litigation in the courts, the foreclosure sale first ordered for the early summer did not take place until late in September, but J. P. Morgan and Company, as reorganization managers, then bought the road for $20,500,000.[113]

Under the plan the Philadelphia & Reading Railway Company and the Philadelphia and Reading Coal & Iron Company were made separate corporations both operated by the parent Reading Company. The latter operated under the old National Company charter which had been granted before the current strict Pennsylvania constitution had been adopted.[114] Joseph S. Harris was continued as president of the new company, but the board of directors was distinctly a Morgan group, consisting as it did of George F. Baer of Reading, Charles H. Coster and

111 New York *Evening Post,* December 17, 1895.
112 *Commercial and Financial Chronicle,* January 18, 1896, pp. 111-113.
113 *Railway World,* May 2, 1896, p. 466; September 26, 1896, pp. 998, 1000.
114 *Ibid.,* December 19, 1896, p. 1343.

Francis Lynde Stetson of New York, Thomas McKean, George C. Thomas and John Lowber Welsh of Philadelphia.[115]

The management proceeded at once further to improve the financial condition of the company. Former subsidiaries were retained, but on terms different from those hitherto in effect: the Reading would no longer guarantee interest on the bonds of several branch lines, and reductions in the rentals of five subsidiaries saved about $215,000 annually.[116] Another decrease in fixed charges was achieved by extending for fifty years the improvement mortgage 6 per cent bonds at an interest rate of 5 per cent. Altogether it was estimated that the changes made by the new management would reduce the annual fixed charges about $1,500,000 below the expectations of the reorganization committee.[117]

The bonds of the new company contained the restrictive provisions which, due to the frequency with which Morgan applied them to his reorganized roads, were rapidly becoming an accepted part of American railway finance. Of the new issue, $20,000,000 were reserved to be used for betterments, additions, construction and similar purposes only. No more than $1,500,000 were to be used in any one year except that in the year following the reorganization $2,000,000 might be spent; new issues were to be certified only after a strict accounting for all former issues had been made. A further clause in these indentures forbade the acquisition of any property which carried with it over $2,000,000 of liens; a reserve to take up the bonded debt of any new acquisitions was to be taken from the $20,000,000 fund within three years.[118]

Wall Street considered the reorganization so successful that predictions were freely made that dividends on both the pre-

115 *Ibid.*, November 21, 1896, pp. 1222-1224.

116 *Ibid.*, January 16, 1897, p. 64.

117 *Ibid.*, May 13, 1897, p. 262.

118 *Commercial and Financial Chronicle*, March 27, 1897, pp. 612-619 for texts and comments.

ferred and common stock would be paid in 1897. But the Philadelphia *Railway World* could not be quite so hopeful:

All this reads very nicely. It looks well in print. But when Reading pays a dividend on either its common or preferred stock, it will be a good time to get rid of these securities. It will mean either that some big interest is unloading or something worse is about to happen.[119]

Although these gloomy words proved groundless, the over-optimistic Wall Street prophecies were equally unfounded. Real financial success for the Reading only became apparent in 1901 when George F. Baer became president.[120] But the prosperity then was mainly due to Morgan's rehabilitation of the road. He had provided much needed funds with which to improve its physical condition; his efforts had definitely ended McLeod's ideas that the Reading was exclusively a coal road and had led to a successful attempt to secure a more diversified traffic. Finally, and perhaps most important of all, Morgan brought harmony into the turbulent anthracite industry. By his part in their reorganizations, Morgan controlled the Erie and the Reading; by his financial rehabilitation of the Lehigh Valley he had secured the controlling voice in that road's affairs;[121] the Jersey Central, already dominated by the friendly Baker interests, definitely came under Reading control in 1901 after the latter's large purchases of the former's stock;[122] finally, the Delaware & Hudson and the Delaware, Lackawanna & Western were dominated by the Vanderbilts, who were always ready to cooperate with the house of Morgan.

The cautious conclusion of the Industrial Commission in 1901 understated the situation, if anything:

It is not clear, either from testimony before the Industrial Com-

119 *Railway World*, December 5, 1896, p. 1290.
120 Snyder, *op. cit.*, pp. 595-609.
121 Meade, "Great Railways," *Railway World*, 1903, pp. 1383-5, 1411-13.
122 *Stock Ownership*, III, p. 1218.

mission or from other information available, what degree of actual
consolidation by exchange of stockholdings prevails among the
other roads in the anthracite field. Considerable evidence tends to
show that effective control by unity of stock ownership is given to
a large proportion of the entire output of the field. Thus the Lehigh
Valley Railroad, since J. P. Morgan & Company took up their
option on the stock of that company held by the Packer estate, is
quite certainly controlled by the same financial interests which entirely dominate the Reading Company. The Erie system also is
understood to be a Morgan road, despite rumors to the effect that
the Hill interests in the Northwestern transcontinetal lines had
secured control. The Erie road, through its acquisition of the
Susquehanna & Western, and the purchase of the Pennsylvania
Coal Company, now controls more than 11 per cent of the total
output. The Lackawanna road, with its 12 per cent of shipments
in 1900, is an important factor, but its definite relation to the
Morgan interests has not been made clear. Its substantial unanimity of interest with the roads previously named is, however,
apparent. While for many years the Pennsylvania Railroad has
persisted in independent action, and while the Delaware & Hudson
Company is usually credited with Vanderbilt affiliation, the proportion of the total output more or less directly controlled by the
Morgan interests is probably from two-thirds to three-fourths of
the entire shipment. The only roads which, it is maintained with
showing of authority, are entirely independent are the Ontario &
Western, and the firm of Coxe Brothers, which owns the Delaware,
Susquehanna & Schuylkill. These two roads together, however,
control but slightly over 7 per cent of the total shipments.[123]

Thus Morgan achieved by different methods what McLeod
had attempted before the depression. The Industrial Commission noted the irony of the situation:

It should also be noted that the same important financial interests which in 1892 caused the frustration of this attempted combination—J. P. Morgan & Company—have, since 1899, been in
charge of the renewed efforts at consolidation.[124]

123 *Industrial Commission Report*, XIX, p. 463.
124 *Ibid.*, XIX, p. 457.

CHAPTER VI

THE MORGAN-HILL ALLIANCE

MORGAN'S friendship with the Vanderbilts had helped him develop a strong influence among the railroads of the East and mid-West but until the nineties he had always lacked a powerful ally in the Far West. Conversely, James J. Hill had just established himself as the dominant figure in Northwestern railroading and was ready to expand westward when the panic of 1893 swept the United States. After viewing each other suspiciously over the ruins of the prostrate Northern Pacific, early in 1895 the two men joined forces. Their first and immediate objective was the rehabilitation of the Northern Pacific and this task could only be accomplished by harmonious co-operation between them. After they had successfully fulfilled their purpose and Morgan had established his influence among the transcontinentals, the same ' community of interest ' idea which they had evolved in the Northwest was applied to the Eastern trunk lines. The house of Morgan was the center about which a shadowy entente cordiale of Eastern roads was formed, and the systems he had reorganized, the Erie, the Reading and the Southern, together with the Baltimore & Ohio which he helped Hill rehabilitate, were the nucleus of the super-system that was developed.

The difficulties of the Northern Pacific resembled those of the Reading in that they were complicated by a bitter struggle, which was being waged among several groups of security holders for the control of the road.

At the first meeting of the stockholders after the appointment of receivers, a new board of directors had been elected. W. L. Bull and C. T. Barney, representing the German interests, were retained, but the other members of the old board were retired. The new directors were Isaac Anderson, August Belmont, J. H. Harding, Robert Harris, Marcellus Hartley,

Johnston Livingston, Donald Mackay, August Rutten, William F. Sanders, Winthrop Smith and Brayton Ives, who was elected president.[1]

As early as April 21, 1894, Judge Jenkins in Milwaukee, who had appointed the receivers, denied a plea from the new board, represented by Brayton Ives, to replace them. However, the court ordered an investigation of the specific charges against them: that they had been privy to deals in which the company had paid outrageous prices for properties in which some of the directors were interested. The plaintiff's claim that the company's policy of building branch lines provided in itself a basis for ousting the receivers was denied by the judge: even if these lines had proved unprofitable, the policy was a matter of judgment in which mistakes inevitably occurred at times; further, Ives himself and several members of the present board had formerly been directors and had approved the construction of some of the same branches which they were now criticizing.[2]

The demand for the removal of the receivers was based primarily on their nomination by the former management of the road and their endorsement of its various policies. Less than a month before the failure, the management had congratulated Henry Villard and his fellow directors on their excellent administration of the company's affairs. In verbal and published interviews officials had declared that the dividend on preferred stock which was due July 15, 1893, had been earned, was in the bank and would be paid; nevertheless at the last minute the dividend had been passed because it was "not earned". When a suit involving Manitoba land had been won the management declared that the victory furnished $1,000,000 with which to retire preferred stock, but bookkeeping sleight of hand diverted this money to general purposes. It had claimed that the Wisconsin Central and the Chicago & Northern Pacific were profitable acquisitions, whereas the court now confirmed

1 *Stock Ownership*, III, p. 1323.
2 *Railway World*, April 21, 1892, pp. 315-6.

the fact that they had cost the company $2,500,000. And, even when the application for the appointment of receivers had been pending in the court, it had claimed that a receivership was impossible.[3]

The bitterness and pettiness of the struggle between the receivers and the new directors was well illustrated by a public letter President Ives addressed to the receivers early in January, 1894:

Perhaps I should not be surprised, in view of past experience, at any action of yours, but I must confess I was not prepared for the statement: "For some reason of your own, and not because of any action of the receivers, you have stopped the transfer of stock and the registration of the bonds. We record our protest against this unwarranted and unnecessary action on your part."

The statement was unjust and untrue, Ives continued: transfers had been stopped because not only had the receivers taken the company's books and corporate seal, but they had also forced the secretary, the treasurer and the auditor to resign. These men could not work for both the board and the receivers, the latter had stated; since the receivers had all the company's funds, the directors could not pay salaries and were unable to retain these officers. Their signatures were necessary to transfer stock and register bonds, so these functions had perforce been suspended. Ives generously concluded that if the receivers would assent in good faith, he would try to have these officials reappointed to their former positions so that their work could go on. After this letter had been made public the receivers decided that it was a good time for them to assume a mantle of dignity; so in their reply they stated that the court was the proper forum for this discussion and since it would be heard there in a few days, they preferred not to imitate the company's improper procedure of public wrangling, but rather would wait and tell the true version of what had happened to the judge.[4]

3 *Ibid.*, October 7, 1893, p. 949, quoting letter from Charles D. Barney & Company.

4 *Ibid.*, January 27, 1895, p. 75.

After hearing both sides Judge Jenkins made permanent his former temporary endorsement of the receivers. He was fully convinced that they were not failing in their duty and in order to reorganize the railroad they would need, and therefore should keep, the company's books, seals and officials. However, the receivers and directors should cooperate to transfer stock and register bonds. In the final analysis, the judge pointed out, a receivership is instituted for the benefit of the creditors of a company and since the directors represent only stockholders, the receivers must be given precedence in the courts.[5]

Ives refused to be discouraged by this apparently final rebuff to his efforts to have the receivers ousted. And after eighteen months he achieved what seemed a definite triumph when Circuit Judge Gilbert in Portland, Oregon, handed down a decision which threw the whole case into endless confusion. Gilbert declared that Judge Jenkins, presiding over the circuit court of the Eastern District of Wisconsin, had no authority to appoint receivers for the Northern Pacific, since he had jurisdiction over none of its property. The receivers were ordered to appear before Judge Hanford of Portland to answer the charges filed against them by Ives. This decision, that the receivers had not been legally appointed, invalidated about $5,000,000 of receivers' certificates already outstanding, which would have no lien on the Northern Pacific property unless they were confirmed by Judge Hanford.[6] Further of course, the question of who was legally entitled to control the company was completely unanswered.

The reply of the receivers, Thomas F. Oakes, Henry C. Payne and Henry W. Rouse, to this decision was the submission of their resignations to Judge Jenkins on the plea that they could not be responsible to two separate and hostile courts at the same time.[7] Judge Jenkins accepted the resignations and

5 *Ibid.*, February 3, 1894, p. 86.
6 *Ibid.*, September 7, 1895, p. 510.
7 *Ibid.*, September 28, 1895, p. 563.

appointed in their place Frank G. Bigelow of Milwaukee and Edward W. McHenry of St. Paul, the chief engineer of the Northern Pacific. Circuit Judge Sanborn of the St. Paul, through whose district Northern Pacific tracks passed, followed Judge Jenkins' example and appointed the same two receivers, but Judge Hanford refused to accept the resignations since Oakes, Payne and Rouse had failed to appear before him as ordered. Instead he dismissed them and appointed Andrew F. Burleigh as their successor.[8] Judge Knowles at Missoula, Montana, and Judge Gilbert at Portland concurred in Judge Hanford's decision. But Judge Knowles also appointed Edward Bonner and Captain J. H. Mills to serve with Burleigh in his district and in every judicial district traversed by the Northern Pacific's tracks other than these three, the first set of receivers was still in office since their resignations had not been accepted.[9]

The spectacle presented by the company's multitudinous receivers was without parallel. If it were long continued, such a piece-meal management would soon complete the ruin of the company. At the same time the ridiculous side of the squabble could not fail to be evident:

Referring to the matter, together with a report that under probable conditions the transcontinental roads will ere long be taken out of the receivers' hands, the *Mississippi Lumberman* is moved to remark that for the sake of the army of gentlemen that now possess the title of receiver of the Northern Pacific road it is to be hoped that such a calamity will not occur; the throwing out of such a larger number of idle men would have a tendency to demoralize the labor market.[10]

The legal impasse was finally ended when Supreme Court Justices Field, Brewer, Harlan and Brown, in whose circuits the Northern Pacific lines lay, decided that primary jurisdiction over the road's affairs belonged to Judge Jenkins. By the time

8 *Ibid.*, October 5, 1895, pp. 587-9.

9 *Ibid.*, October 12, 1895, pp. 612-4.

10 *Railway Review*, October 19, 1895, p. 582.

this conclusion had been reached, it had lost much of its importance: impressed by the futility and foolishness of the situation they had precipitated, the various factions involved had begun to cooperate with each other to rehabilitate the company.[11]

The several committees and individuals who were interested in the reorganization proceedings had been making preliminary plans. A committee of consolidated mortgage bondholders had been formed in February, 1894, consisting of Edward D. Adams, chairman, John C. Bullitt, Louis Fitzgerald, Charles Lanier, J. D. Probst, James Stillman and Ernst Thaelman. It had invited the cooperation of other groups in forming an agreement for reorganizing the system,[12] but it had met immediate opposition from Brayton Ives. The chief criticisms the latter had to offer against the committee were that any proposal would be premature until earnings ceased to decline and an accurate financial statement had been made up, that the constitution of the committee was unfortunate in that its members owner or controlled only a limited amount of securities, and that it was dominated by friends of Villard.[13] The last charge was emphatically denied by Adams and by the Deutsche Bank, which added that it had no intention of giving Villard any voice in Northern Pacific affairs again.[14] Before the summer was over, a third mortgage bondholders protective committee, composed of representatives of New York banks and Charlemagne Tower of Philadelphia, entered the field.[15] The most important figure in the reorganization aside from J. P. Morgan, who was strongly represented on the Adams Committee, was James J. Hill, who worked independently of any committee. Rumors of a deal whereby the Northern Pacific would eventually become a subsidiary of Hill's Great Northern had been

11 *Railway World*, February 1, 1896, pp. 98-9.

12 *Bondholders' Reorganization Agreement*, dated February 19, 1894.

13 *Railway World*, March 10, 1894, p. 185.

14 *Ibid.*, July 7, 1894, p. 537.

15 *Third Mortgage Bondholders' Protective Committee Agreement*, dated August 15, 1894.

published and emphatically denied in the spring,[16] but he was already deeply interested in the reorganization plans.

Wall Street support for Hill's participation was not lacking. In a letter written October 26, 1894, Jacob Schiff, senior partner in Kuhn, Loeb & Company, had said:

> In my opinion your friends of the Deutsche Bank could do nothing better than to induce Mr. James J. Hill to interest himself in the affairs of the Northern Pacific Company. No one else so thoroughly understands everything concerning the traffic of the territory through which the Northern Pacific runs. . . . It would certainly be of immense advantage both to the Northern Pacific and the Great Northern if the two systems should come into close relationship, and it would increase the net earnings of both companies, but especially of the Northern Pacific,

if competition, which resulted in frequent rate wars, were eliminated.[17] Hill had been watching developments since before the receivership. At that time both he and Morgan had been approached. They were asked to help the road regain its feet, but Morgan refused until he should receive assurances that the Great Northern would not be hostile, believing that the latter could ruin the Northern Pacific any time it wished by virtue of its far greater efficiency.

Hill's interest had continued while the Northern Pacific sank lower and lower under the squabbles of conflicting interests. In October, 1894, he had explained his ideas in a letter:

> To handle the property in the courts and hasten reorganization would require actual control and a strong party. The amount of work to be done would be very great, and the men who could be of use are very few. The advantages to our company would mainly come from the freedom from competition and needless friction and expense in operation, all of which I think would be worth to

16 *Railway World*, May 25, 1894, p. 209.

17 Adler, Cyrus, *Jacob H. Schiff, His Life and Letters*, Garden City: Doubleday, Doran and Company, Inc., 1928, 2 volumes, I, pp. 85-7.

us about $600,000 or possibly $750,000. When they went into the hands of receivers a year ago, timid people said, " Now the Great Northern meets its Waterloo, with its competitors in the hands of receivers and released from fixed charges, etc."; but you will bear in mind our difficulties from serious floods, strikes, fires, etc., during the past year, and still we are prosperous and in good financial condition, while they are asking the courts to pay their shortages. I speak of this to show that we can get along without them and against their operating at an enormous loss. At the same time the control of an empire such as lies between Lake Superior and the Pacific Ocean, which is served by the lines of both companies, would render the future reasonably secure for both properties, and its value should not be overlooked. . . . However, I am reasonably satisfied that if the Berlin people or any other holders of Northern Pacific securities do not realize how much more we can do with the property than any other organization without exception, they will surely realize this before they are done.[18]

This last observation contained a veiled threat, but it was only too true : unless a reorganization squeezed millions of water out of the Northern Pacific capitalization and then rebuilt the system at enormous cost, the Great Northern could force it into bankruptcy at any time; the first requisite of a successful reorganization must be the cooperation of Jim Hill.

Although nothing was definitely known, rumors which quite accurately reflected the progress of the several committees were circulating long before Hill had made up his mind to help.[19] Only after long negotiations was an agreement finally formulated which the three dominant influences in Northern Pacific affairs, the Deutsche Bank, J. P. Morgan and Hill, could all approve. The plan was promptly adopted by the Adams committee and steps were taken to put it into effect. This London Agreement, so called because it was signed in Morgan's London home, provided that the Great Northern should guarantee a

18 Pyle, *Hill*, II, pp. 8-10.

19 *Railway World*, August 10, 1894, pp. 423, 425-6.

new Northern Pacific mortgage bond issue not to exceed $175,-
000,000 in principal and $6,200,000 annual interest. The reor-
ganized company was not to assume any other interest charges
without the consent of the Great Northern except those of the
St. Paul & Northern Pacific and the Northern Pacific Terminal
Company of Oregon, and the bonds of the former were to be
taken up at their maturity by new bonds reserved for that
purpose. More bonds might, however, be certified upon the
acquisition of additional mileage, although the maximum par
value of the entire issue was $200,000,000 and increases could
not be in excess of $20,000 for each mile added. The outstand-
ing bonds of branch lines were to be exchanged, if holders
consented, for the new parent company's bonds, but only to
such an amount as would not require more than $400 per mile
interest annually.

The new company was to be controlled by the Great Northern. The latter would receive half of the capital stock and have
the privilege of nominating at least five of the nine directors.
The minority stock could nominate four directors and elect the
chairman " so long as the majority capital remains en bloc, in
the interest of the Great Northern Railroad Company, but
not after Dividends at the rate of five per cent per annum shall
have been paid for two consecutive years upon the entire Capital Stock of the new Company, and not in any event for more
than five years." Finally, after the reorganization was completed the treasury of the new company must contain at least
$3,500,000 cash assets and $4,000,000 of the new 4 per cent
bonds, in addition to whatever securities had not been required
in the reorganization.[20]

Before going ahead with the execution of the plan, it was
determined to test the legality of this proposed merger of two
hitherto competing transcontinental lines. A suit to restrain the
committee from putting the plan into effect was instituted and
speedily prosecuted. In November, 1895, a state court declared

20 London Agreement quoted verbatim in Pyle, *op. cit.*, II, pp. 14-6.

the merger violated the anti-trust laws;[21] a few months later the Supreme Court confirmed this judgment[22] and the plan had to be abandoned. Even if the decision had been different, the plan was probably already doomed, for not only had there been an outbreak of public hostility at its announcement,[23] but the directors, led by Ives, had fought bitterly against unconditionally surrendering their property to their chief rival.[24]

The second and final plan proposed for reorganizing the company was assured of nearly unanimous approval from the security holders by the inclusion of the Ives faction in the negotiations which preceded its publication. The Adams committee continued to consist of the chairman, Adams himself, Bullitt, Fitzgerald, Godfrey, Probst, Stillman and Thaelman. A cooperating protective committee of stockholders included Brayton Ives as chairman, August Belmont, George R. Sheldon, and Charlemagne Tower, Jr. The managers of the reorganization were to be J. P. Morgan & Company.[25]

The new plan was agreed upon and ready to be put into operation even before the Supreme Court had definitely outlawed the first plan.[26] Fundamentally, it was the same as its predecessor except that the stock of the new Northern Pacific was to be held by individuals instead of the Great Northern.[27] According to its supporters it had a fourfold basis: the abandonment of Chicago as the eastern terminal of the system and the limitation of the region served to the west of the Mississippi River and the Great Lakes; this meant release from the heavy financial demands of the Chicago terminals. The ultimate integration of the main line, branches and terminal properties

21 Adler, *op. cit.*, I, pp. 85-7.

22 Pyle, *op. cit.*, II, pp. 16-17.

23 *Ibid.*, II, pp. 16-17.

24 *Message to the Stockholders* from Brayton Ives, October 17, 1895.

25 *Reorganization of the Northern Pacific Railroad Company*, March 16, 1896.

26 *Ibid.*

27 Pyle, *op. cit.*, II, pp. 24-26.

through direct ownership by a single company. A reduction of the annual fixed charges to less than the minimum earnings to be expected under probable conditions. Ample provision for any additional capital which might be required in a series of years for the development of the property and for the enlarged facilities necessitated by an increased business.[28]

The new company was to issue $80,000,000 of common stock, $75,000,000 of preferred stock and bonds not to exceed $130,000,000 at 4 per cent and $60,000,000 at 3 per cent; the bonds were only to be issued from time to time as they were needed.[29] Preferred stock was to be assessed $10 per share and common stock $15; in neither case would the holder receive any compensation in return for these cash levies. The basis for exchanging old securities for new was very liberal, varying from 100 per cent in the case of common and preferred stock to over 170 per cent in the cases of general third mortgage bond and dividend certificates, but this liberality was necessitated by the lowering of interest rates.[30]

The house of Morgan and the Deutsche Bank would form a syndicate which would be the financial agent of the company for ten years, marketing its securities and in return having the right to approve new issues and to examine the company's books.[31] Altogether the syndicate would subscribe about $45,-000,000 in cash for immediate improvements.[32] Hill was not a member of the syndicate but he and his friends were given the right to take up any stock on which the holders refused to pay assessments, and in the end this amounted to about one-fifth of the total issue. One clause, which was to prove of

---

28 *Reorganization Plan*, March 16, 1896.

29 *Ibid.* and Pyle, *op. cit.*, II, pp. 24-26.

30 Letter to security holders announcing plan, signed by J. P. Morgan & Company, March 16, 1896.

31 *Pujo Investigation*, II, pp. 1341-2, both text and minutes of meeting approving plan given in full.

32 Pyle, *op. cit.*, II, pp. 24-26; *Railway Age and Northwestern Railroader,* April 4, 1896, p. 326.

critical importance, reserved the right to retire the preferred
stock at par on any first of January in the next twenty years.[33]
A voting trust dominated by Morgan was to control the road
for five years after the completion of the reorganization.[34]

The immediate public reaction to the plan was for the most
part favorable. The approbation of the *Wall Street Journal* was
roused by the strong support it had from all the several hitherto
conflicting interests in the company:

> The remarkable thing about the plan is that it is practically ready
> to be declared operative, that is, the majority of all bonds have
> accepted it and are already deposited here and in Berlin. The stock,
> of course, is not in, but the largest preferred stockholders have
> accepted it, and those who do not accept will, of course, be wiped
> out.[35]

Further, the *Journal* emphasized the advantages of this proposal over that of the year before:

> The advantages secured to the preferred stockholders by the
> delay of one year is evident. The plan which it was proposed to
> put through a year ago was extremely drastic as far as it concerned
> the stocks. No secret was made of the intention of those who
> thought up the organization, to wipe out, to all intents and pur-
> poses, the common and preferred stock. The curious thing is the
> seconds and thirds receive now very much the same treatment as
> was proposed for them a year ago, while the consols and the stock
> are relatively much better off.[36]

The New York *Evening Post* concurred in praising the
treatment accorded the several classes of securities and commended the adoption of the theory that the stockholders, as
owners of the property, should pay for a receivership rather
than the bondholders.[37]

33 Pyle, *op. cit.*, II, pp. 24-26.
34 Letter to security holders, March 16, 1896.
35 *Wall Street Journal*, March 16, 1896, p. 1.
36 *Ibid.*, March 17, 1896, p. 2.
37 New York *Evening Post*, March 16, 1896.

That security holders in general agreed with these views was manifest when early in June the reorganization managers announced that enough assents had already been received to warrant their declaring the plan operative; June 30 was set as the last day on which bonds might be deposited under it.[38]

Despite this quick approval, the reception given the plan was not quite unanimously favorable. The ever-critical *Economist* was inclined to grumble a bit:

It is not proposed to force the conversion upon the holders of the General First Mortgage Bonds; but it is pointed out that the terms offered to those holders " while advantageous to the company, is manifestly to the advantage of the bondholders so converting." The bondholders, it may be added without going into details, are asked to sacrifice little in the way of interest, and for this sacrifice they are to be given longer-dated bonds, while the capital required for putting the road in order is to be provided from other sources. The scheme is certainly not unkind to the First Mortgage bondholders, nor have the holders of the Second and Third Mortgages any grounds of complaint under the circumstances. The position of the preferred and common stockholders is, however, different. . . . It is to be assumed that the scheme will pass, for the stockholders are powerless; but the lesson, coming as it does as one more in a long and dismal series, is not calculated to impress investors with the desirability of interesting themselves in the so-called securities of American railroads.[39]

The Commercial and Financial Chronicle was much more favorably impressed and pointed out three particularly good points; the plan had the adherence of every leading equity in the property, in contrast to the bitter conflicts which had been roused by every previous proposal. The syndicate headed by Morgan and the Deutsche Bank was to subscribe for an unusually large amount of securities, thus assuring the new company a plentiful supply of cash and a ready market for its future issues.

38 *Railway World*, June 6, 1896, p. 586.
39 *Economist*, March 21, 1896, pp. 360-1.

The plan included the whole Northern Pacific system, but it excluded the perennially costly Wisconsin Central and Chicago & Northern Pacific.[40]

Hill's authorized biographer was extravagantly enthusiastic about the plan when he looked back upon it some twenty years later:

In this was established the sort of community of interest which is all the more real and lasting because it rests on mutual understanding and confidence rather than on any formal stipulation. It gave practical effect to natural laws of railroad growth and development, in a shape that did not run counter to laws or court decisions. It was a long step forward in the adjustment of traffic facilities for the Northwest according to economic necessities. . . . It drew closer the relations between Mr. Hill and Mr. Morgan, which were to remain unbroken the rest of their lives.[41]

At Superior, Wisconsin, on July 25, 1896, the property of the Northern Pacific was sold at foreclosure to the reorganization committee [42] and at midnight, August 31, the new management took over the system from the surviving receivers, Edwin H. McHenry and Frank H. Bigelow.[43] The directors who were elected at the first meeting of the stockholders on October 6 clearly represented the interests which had reorganized the company. Edwin Winter of St. Paul was the new president and the board consisted of Edward D. Adams, Robert Bacon, C. H. Coster, Robert M. Gallaway, Brayton Ives, James D. Willis, Walter G. Oakman, Samuel Spencer, Francis Lynde Stetson, James Stillman and Eben B. Thomas of New York and Charlemagne Tower of Philadelphia.[44] The new capitaliza-

40 *Commercial and Financial Chronicle*, March 21, 1896, pp. 522, 527-9.

41 Pyle, *op. cit.*, II, pp. 26.

42 *Railway World*, August 1, 1896, p. 792.

43 *Ibid.*, August 29, 1896, pp. 894-5.

44 *Official Statement of the Northern Pacific Railway Co.*, December 1, 1896; see also, *Commercial and Financial Chronicle*, October 24, 1896, p. 1133.

tion was $235,000,000; fixed charges would be $4,853,000 less than before the receivership.[45] In addition to refusing to renew the agreements with the Wisconsin Central and the Chicago & Northern Pacific, the new management discontinued the leases of half a dozen other branches.[46] As a result the mileage of the system had been reduced to a little more than 4700.[47]

The mortgage indentures contained the type of restrictions common to Morgan's reorganizations but they reached a new level of precision in several respects. Enough of the new prior lien bonds were reserved to pay off the old bonds as they matured; however, if any of these latter were retired by payments from the sinking fund or from the proceeds of land sales, the same amount in the reserved bonds might be used only as carefully prescribed. Formerly the amount of the reserve represented by the value of retired bonds could be used in any way the directors wished. A fund of $10,000,000 was reserved to meet premiums on the old bonds, but the new indentures limited the price at which they could be bought to par and this was defined as the value at which $1300 of the old bonds would buy $1000 of the new; any savings made by buying at a lower ratio were to be applied to the " cash fund ". If the sinking fund retired bonds, the whole amount of prior lien bonds reserve for that purpose must be added to the " cash fund ". Before January 1, 1893, $3,000,000 of the $25,000,000 reserved for extensions, improvements and similar purposes might be set aside for some specific purpose. With this exception, only $1,500,000 could be spent in any one year and before a new issue was sold all former issues must be strictly accounted for; the obligations carried by any property acquired in the future could not exceed $2,000,000 and this sum must be reserved from the annual $1,500,000 within two years to redeem them.

45 *Railway Age and Northwestern Railroader*, July 24, 1896, p. 61.
46 *Railway World*, September 12, 1896, p. 958.
47 *Railway Age and Northwestern Railroader*, July 24, 1896, p. 61.

"Net moneys" were defined as the net proceeds from land sales and the proceeds from the sale of prior lien bonds released from the bond reserve by the operation of the sinking fund. One-half of this cash, but not more than $500,000 in any one year, was to be used to buy in outstanding prior lien bonds at not over 110, or if that were impossible, to buy general lien bonds at not over par or if that too were impossible, to buy securities in which New York savings banks could invest. The "cash fund" was to receive each year all "net moneys" not spent as provided and some other funds. It was to be used in annual appropriations of not more than $500,000 for improvements, extensions and similar purposes, under the same accounting regulations as applied to bonds reserved for similar purposes. Finally, the total of prior lien hundred-year bonds at 4 per cent was limited to $130,000,000: general lien mortgage bonds at 3 per cent were not to exceed $190,000,000 in par value, of which $130,000,000 could be issued only to retire prior liens when the board deemed advisable.[48]

The success of the Northern Pacific reorganization was apparent within a very few years. In 1898, the second year following its completion, preferred stock received a 5 per cent dividend and the following year it was paid 4 per cent and common stock got 2 per cent.[49] In 1901, the system was able to take half of the Chicago, Burlington & Quincy stock which Hill bought for it and the Great Northern,[50] in order to give the two very harmonious competitors an entrance into Chicago and a feeding network of lines in the Middle West.

The most prominent of the Northern Pacific's former subsidiaries, the Chicago & Northern Pacific, the Chicago & Calumet, and the Wisconsin Central, were reorganized separately. The Chicago & Northern Pacific Railroad Company and the Chicago & Calumet Company were consolidated into

48 *Commercial and Financial Chronicle*, December 5, 1896, pp. 988-90.
49 *Poor's Manual*, 1900, pp. 1268-85.
50 Snyder, *op. cit.*, pp. 524-41.

the Chicago Terminal Transfer Railroad Company, in which the Northern Pacific retained an interest. This company had a capitalization of $46,500,000 but the fixed charges were reduced from a combined total of $1,794,950 to $581,880, mainly by paying off many former bondholders in preferred stock.[51]

The Wisconsin Central reorganization was particularly difficult because the bonds, stocks and notes of thirteen different corporations were involved. When the system had been formed in 1887 the management had intended to replace all these with the securities of the parent company but unfortunately this had never been done and the reorganization committee had to take the task in hand. Each security holder claimed that his security was the strongest and should receive consideration in the new company proportional to that strength. This was the stumbling block which had prevented the redemption of these securities before, and the committee finally solved it by direct purchase of most of them.

Purchase, of course, necessitated large amounts of cash, in all more than $21,500,000, of which about $3,250,000 was contributed by income-bondholders and stockholders, and the rest by the sale of securities underwritten by a syndicate.[52] Income bondholders and preferred stockholders paid 20 per cent assessments and holders of common stock paid 10 per cent; all three groups had their holdings drastically scaled down. Altogether the new company issued $57,000,000 of new securities which were based on a unified system under the direction of one management. Fixed charges were $1,080,000, an amount safely within the net income the year before.[53]

About the same time that the reorganization of the Northern

51 *Railway World*, May 15, 1897, p. 495.

52 The syndicate consisted of Maitland, Coppell & Company, Brown Brothers & Company and Edward Sweet & Company, all of New York.

53 *Reorganization Plan of the Wisconsin Central System*, dated April 10, 1899; *Commercial and Financial Chronicle*, May 6, 1899, pp. 847-8; March 3, 1900, p. 401.

Pacific was being completed, the collapse of the Baltimore & Ohio had furnished another subject for the railroad and financial experts of the house of Morgan, but that firm itself played only a passive supervisory role in the reorganization proceedings. Although the accounts of the Baltimore & Ohio had been proven inaccurate before the receivership and were in a hopeless tangle, nevertheless it was apparent that the company was in much better condition financially than most of the other bankrupt roads, and at least the struggles for control which characterized several systems were lacking.

A few months after receivers had been appointed, the *Railway World* pointed out that

the case of the Baltimore & Ohio is somewhat remarkable among bankrupt roads in that, so far, the receivers have paid all the bonded interest practically as it matured. Where it has not been paid at maturity it has been paid later. At the same time the receivers have issued receivers' certificates bearing 6 per cent interest, which, of course, are practically being used to pay interest on 4½ and 5 per cent bonds. If the money were not paid away in interest it would be available for the purposes for which the receivers' certificates have been issued. The policy is the result, in part at all events, of the optimism of Receiver Cowen, who is said to believe that the property can be reorganized without assessment and with very little change of capitalization. There is, moreover, little or no doubt that Mr. Cowen's experience in the past as a lawyer has convinced him that it is often cheaper and better for a defaulting railroad or a railroad in receivers' hands, to pay the interest on its bonds, even though it has not been earned, than to commence litigation.[54]

There were also several encouraging aspects to the annual report for the year ending June 30, 1896, in the last four months of which the road had been in receivership. Excluding dividends on preferred stock and payments to retire bonds and other indebtedness, there was a surplus of $127,505 in place

54 *Railway World*, June 27, 1896, p. 663.

of the $1,700,000 deficit of the year before. Income from sources other than the road's operation had declined severely, but this was mainly because during the preceding year a book profit had been derived from the transfer of securities from one subsidiary to another and a further profit had been recorded when the sale of some bonds brought a surplus over the amount needed to pay a debt to Baring Brothers. The gross receipts had increased more than $1,000,000 during the year, and even a decline of $654,777 in net earnings was not as discouraging a factor as it might ordinarily have been. The decrease in the net was attributable to an increase of nearly $1,000,000 in the cost of maintenance and equipment, most of which had been spent in the months since the receivers had been appointed.[55]

Rather than a factor to rouse alarm, the large expenditures for maintenance and equipment were a cause for satisfaction. The very poor physical condition of the road had been one of the factors leading to the receivership, and the receivers had found, on taking charge, that before they could estimate the system's future earning power improvements must be made. Contracts had been let within two months for 5000 new freight cars and the rolling stock on hand was being repaired as rapidly as possible. When the receivers took control, 4500 cars had been out of use because of their need for repairs; this number had been reduced to 2800 by early May and was daily decreasing. Repairs were also being rushed on 400 locomotives which had been in such poor condition that they could not be used. Before the end of May the wisdom of these expenditures had been proven by an increase of about $3000 per day in gross earnings,[56] an improvement reflected in the annual report a few months later. Although the policy of the receivers was justified to most critics by the improved earnings, admittedly it represented a new theory of receivership: instead of merely issuing enough receivers' certificates to keep the system in about the

55 *Commercial and Financial Chronicle*, November 21, 1896, pp. 901-3.

56 *Railway World*, May 16, 1896, p. 518.

same condition it was in when they took it over, they had spent large sums to bring it to such a point of efficiency that it could compete with its rivals.[57]

As time went on and the improvements continued, the

statements by officials of the Baltimore & Ohio of the increased efficiency of the property, as a result of the improvements made, have been received with a good deal of interest by people who own the securities. The great question asked regarding all roads when they come to the point of reorganization is what can they be relied upon to earn year in and year out? Upon the answer to this question depends very largely the capitalization of the new company and the allottment of new securities. Nowadays earning capacity depends more upon physical condition, and ability to do business economically depends upon ability to carry full carloads and heavy trainloads. Consequently if it turns out that the Baltimore & Ohio can operate at as low a ton-mile cost as that of its immediate neighbors, the work of reorganization will be of greater simplicity than has heretofore been expected.[58]

From the very beginning of the receivership rumor had said that the reorganization could be made at a very slight cost to the security holders,[59] and when after a little over two years a plan was published it was comparatively generous. The plan had been formulated by a committee of which Louis Fitzgerald was chairman and which included August Belmont, Edward R. Bacon, Henry Budge, Eugene Delano, William A. Read, and Howland Davis; the reorganization managers were to be Speyer & Company of New York, Speyer Brothers of London and Kuhn, Loeb & Company of New York. The new company would issue $70,000,000 of prior lien 3½ per cent bonds, $63,-000,000 of first mortgage 4 per cent bonds, $40,000,000 of preferred stock and $35,000,000 of common stock. All holders of bonds and stocks were to receive between $1000 and $1500

57 *United States Investor*, June 25, 1898, pp. 902-3.
58 *Railway World*, November 27, 1897, p. 1172.
59 *Railway Age and Northwestern Railroader*, March 21, 1896, p. 151.

in new securities for each $1000 of old; the rank of new secur-
ity given would be determined by the value of the old.

The new prior liens would be secured by 1017 miles of track;
the first mortgage would comprise a second lien on this mileage
and a first lien on 570 miles not covered by the prior liens.
No leased lines were included in the reorganization plans; arrangements with them were to be made later. Common stock
was to pay a 20 per cent assessment for which it would receive
an equivalent in new preferred stock and it would then be
exchanged for new common stock at par. Second preferred
shares were to pay the same assessment and get in exchange 20
per cent in new preferred stock and 150 per cent in new
common stock. First preferred stockholders would pay 2 per
cent and then receive 52.5 per cent in new preferred stock and
75 per cent in new common stock. The voting privilege of all
stock was to be vested in a voting trust for five years.

The aims of the reorganization committee had been four-
fold: first, to reduce the fixed charges to an amount safely
within the net earning power of the system; the new annual
fixed charges would be $6,252,351, about $1,500,000 less than
the former amount and more than $1,000,000 below the net
earnings of the company in either of the two preceding years.
Second, adequate capital for the present and future needs of
the road: $36,092,500 in cash was to be provided from the
sale of Western Union securities in the company's treasury,
assessments and payments by the syndicate; debts immediately
payable included $19,192,225 car trusts, receivers' certificates
and other obligations outstanding and totalled $36,092,500;
although this figure was unusually high, it represented in good
part the cost of the improvements which the receivers had made
and as such it had already proved itself a good investment; after
January 1, 1902, the company would be permitted to issue
$5,000,000 more prior lien bonds, not over $1,000,000 in any
one year, for enlargements, betterments and additions; also,
the general mortgage could be increased from the initial $63,-

000,000 to a maximum of $90,000,000, though by not more than $1,500,000 in any one year from 1902 to 1906; and a further reserve of $12,000,000 was provided in mortgage bonds and preferred stock. Third, pay the floating debt which had been the immediate cause of the receivership. Finally, prevent disintegration of the system.[60]

The plan was assured of success from the start, for it was published with the expressed approbation of all the large interests involved, including J. P. Morgan & Company, Brown Brothers & Company, Baring, Magoun & Company, Speyer & Company, Vermilye & Company, J. S. Morgan & Company of London and Brown, Shipley & Company. The reception accorded it in the financial press manifested widespread approval. The *Economist* thought that

so far as we can judge, the plan has been devised on fair and equitable terms, and though Messrs. Speyer Brothers are mainly responsible for its presentation, it is published with the full approval of the whole of the issuing houses connected with the company, as representing the various classes of bondholders. . . . What strikes us as being one of the chief advantages of the scheme is the provision that by the creation of four new securities eighteen existing issues of bonds and stocks will be converted, thus greatly simplifying the present unwieldy capital account of the company. . . . Upon some of the bonds, even with the junior securities, which are to be given to the holders as compensation, the interest will be more or less reduced, according to the nature of the security held; but there seems to be no doubt that the concessions demanded of the bondholders, which are inevitable in any drastic scheme of reorganization, have been fairly adjusted; and moreover, the bondholders will be compensated, it is to be expected, for the loss of interest by the improved value of their securities in the market. . . . But perhaps the feature in the scheme which is most necessary in view of the past history of the Baltimore & Ohio Company is,

---

60 *Reorganization of the Baltimore & Ohio Railroad Company, Plan and Agreement*, dated June 22, 1898; also see, *Chronicle*, June 25, 1898, pp. 1215-7 for analysis of the plan.

that the by-laws of the new company will provide that its accounts shall be audited annually by accountants of established reputations.[61]

The *Wall Street Journal* was equally favorable:

The Baltimore & Ohio plan met the general approval of bond-holders. They regarded the method of creating one very high class bond and another good bond and then offering inducement for conversion by giving some of one bond some of another and a bonus in preferred stock as sound in theory and ingenious with reference to the probable objections to be met. . . . The saving in fixed charges of about $1,500,000 a year was regarded as all that could have been expected in view of the character of the bonds with which the committee had to deal.[62]

The plan was declared operative early in July [63] and less than a year later the new securities were ready for distribution.[64] An accomplishment almost unique in the nineties could be credited to the reorganization committee, for they had success-fully finished their work without a foreclosure sale of the road's main line. The value of this achievement has been pointed out by the historian of the system:

Yet, far more important than these great endeavors, was the successful accomplishment of the great goal of the receivers—the saving of the company from a foreclosure upon the property and a complete reorganization. In this point, very much more was at stake than might appear upon the surface. It will be recalled that the state of Maryland, in chartering the Baltimore & Ohio, had conferred upon it valuable tax exemption privileges. . . . After-wards, the commonwealth more than once had repented of its generosity and had gone into the courts to recover taxes from the railroad company, but the stout charter that John V. L. McMahon had obtained for the railroad in the very hours of its

61 *Economist*, June 25, 1898, pp. 938-9.
62 *Wall Street Journal*, June 23, 1898, p. 2.
63 *Commercial and Financial Chronicle*, July 16, 1898, p. 94.
64 *Ibid.*, May 20, 1899, p. 975.

birth firmly stood against these raids. There seemed to be no question at all in legal minds that foreclosure and reorganization would forfeit this ancient charter. And so force Baltimore & Ohio to begin life again; on an entirely new and far less satisfactory basis. So that charter was the one essential thing to be saved— at any reasonable cost. In the end, company and charter stood— as firmly as that old rock of Gibraltar. For one of the few times in all history, a great railroad was forced into bankruptcy and, within three brief years, emerged from it; with its honored name and charter alike unchanged, its shares and other securities higher in value than they had been for years before. Receivership for the Baltimore & Ohio had been changed from tragedy into victory.[65]

In view of the disclosures concerning the management of the company before the receivership, it is impossible to agree that the " honored name " of the Baltimore & Ohio had remained unchanged, but the premium to be placed upon retention of the charter explains the unusually liberal terms offered security holders. William Jett Lauck, an authority on railroad capitalization, a few years later stated that in his belief the reorganization had inflated the capitalization by $35,661,268 for which no consideration of any value whatsoever had been received.[66] But he was forgetting this highly valuable charter. Certainly it must have been invaluable if it was worth even a fraction of its price.

The board of directors, which was elected at the first annual stockholders' meeting after the reorganization had been completed, accurately represented the several interests which had been important in the company's rehabilitation. It included William Salomon, Jacob H. Schiff, James J. Hill, Edward R. Bacon, Louis Fitzgerald, Norman B. Ream, James Stillman, Edward H. Harriman, J. Kennedy Tod, Charles Steele, Alexander Brown, H. Clay Pierce, H. Crawford Black, John V. L.

65 Hungerford, Edward, *The Story of the Baltimore & Ohio*, New York: G. P. Putnam's Sons, 1928, p. 213.

66 *Senate Committee on Interstate Commerce*, 67th Congress, 2nd Session, V, p. 2271.

Findlay; the executive committee was especially strong, consisting of Salomon, Schiff, Hill, Bacon, Ream, Harriman, Steele, and President Cowen.[67]

But while the reorganization proceedings were still unfinished announcement had been made that a large and controlling block of Baltimore & Ohio stock had been bought by a group consisting of Philip A. Armour, Marshall Field, Norman B. Ream and James J. Hill. This investment by Chicago and St. Paul capitalists meant, primarily, the end of the Baltimore & Ohio as a " hometown " private Baltimore enterprise and its emergence into the national field of railroad finance.[68] Together with Coster's presence among the voting trustees, Hill's interest in the system further meant that henceforth the Baltimore & Ohio would join the Eastern trunk line community of interest being formed under the benevolent supervision of the house of Morgan. The voting trust, which was to be terminated at the end of five years or at the discretion of the members, reflected the predominance of the Morgan-Hill interest in the company: William Salomon, Abraham Wolff, J. Kennedy Tod, Louis Fitzgerald and Charles H. Coster.[69]

The Morgan-Hill alliance was indirectly influenced by the reorganization of one more of the bankrupt Eastern trunk lines: although comparatively unrelated to any other railroad group in 1896, the Norfolk & Western was soon brought into the newly formed community of interest through the purchase of a controlling block of stock by the Pennsylvania Railroad which later sold half its interest to the Baltimore & Ohio.[70]

As might have been expected in the case of a system which had failed only because the panic caught it just after it had finished a costly expansion program and which had been managed in an exemplary manner, the reorganization of the

67 *Railway Age and Northwestern Railroader*, April 27, 1894, p. 237.
68 *United States Investor*, September 24, 1898, pp. 1399-1400.
69 *Ibid.*, June 25, 1898, pp. 902-3.
70 Snyder, *op. cit.*, pp. 510-18.

Norfolk & Western was rapidly and simply completed. The road passed into the hands of receivers in February, 1895, and within fifteen months the final plan for its rehabilitation had been published. In August the secretary of the bondholders' committee had been able to announce:

The question of the reorganization of the property on a safe and permanent basis has been receiving the earnest attention of the committee, and the negotiations with the London and Amsterdam committees as well justify the belief that a plan of reorganization can certainly be submitted for the approval of security holders within a few months.[71]

True to this prediction, in April, 1896, the committee published a plan which the *Railway World* thought was " a very simple and comprehensive document " providing " an effective method for restoring the property to solvency ". Fixed charges, which had been $3,214,037 annually, were reduced to $2,-230,440, an amount more than $500,000 less than the average net earnings during the preceding five years.[72] The new company was to issue $62,500,000 of first consolidated 4 per cent mortgage bonds, of which all but about $4,000,000 were to be used to take up both securities which would not be effected by the reorganization and those which would be effected; the remainder of the bonds were to be reserved for improvements and additions. $23,000,000 of non-cumulative adjustment preferred stock bearing 4 per cent interest was to be distributed among the holders of bonds disturbed by the reorganization to compensate them for the loss of interest involved in the exchange of their securities. $66,000,000 of new common stock would be distributed in proportion to the strength of their equities, among the holders of the old preferred and common shares after they had paid an assessment of $12.50 per share.[73]

71 *Railway Age and Northwestern Railroader*, August 16, 1895, p. 406.

72 *Railway World*, April 11, 1896, p. 351.

73 *Ibid.*, April 4, 1896, p. 328.

The plan had been formulated after consultations among the London committee, the Amsterdam committee and the New York executive committee which did the actual work and included representatives of the other two groups.[74] Issued under such comprehensive auspices, it is not surprising that during the first week in May Chairman Louis Fitzgerald was able to announce that a majority of all bonds had been deposited under the plan; [75] by the middle of June holders of about 98 per cent of the outstanding bonds and over 87 per cent of the stock had approved.[76] Early in the fall all the preliminary steps had been taken and the new company, with the two former receivers, Henry Fink and F. J. Kimball, as president and chairman of the board, was able to succeed to the property.[77]

74 *Reorganization of the Norfolk & Western Railroad Company, Plan and Agreement*, dated March 12, 1896.

75 *Railway World*, May 9, 1896, p. 494.

76 *Ibid.*, June 13, 1896, p. 617.

77 *Ibid.*, October 3, 1896, p. 1059.

CHAPTER VII

HARRIMAN'S TRANSCONTINENTALS

EDWARD H. HARRIMAN played a minor role, indeed to the public eye an inconspicuous one, in railroad reorganizations after the depression, but within a decade he had gained almost complete control of the middle and southern transcontinentals. After the rehabilitation of the Union Pacific had been completed he rapidly became its dominating force; when Collis P. Huntington died, Harriman obtained control of the Southern Pacific and the Central Pacific; and by discreet purchases of Atchison stock in the open market during the early years of the twentieth century, he gathered a holding large enough to be transformed into a controlling interest almost at will.

The Atchison, Topeko & Santa Fe reorganization was the first to be accomplished during the nineties in which the house of Morgan did not take a prominent part. Several early attempts to formulate a practicable plan proved abortive, mainly because the only available information as to the true status of the company was insufficient and inaccurate. Within four months of the receivership, a general reorganization committee asserted that it would very soon submit a proposal " which it is confidently believed will be acceptable to all interests "; the committee had not called for the deposit of any securities because it thought that the reorganization could be accomplished without doing so.[1] This was an excessively optimistic view, however. Robert Fleming, who represented the London protective committee, was somewhat pessimistic. He was unable to get any positive and accurate information about the floating debt or the value of the main subsidiary properties. Although he publicly declared his assurance that the receivers were keeping the property in good condition, nevertheless he believed that fairly heavy assessments without compensation would be necessary unless the bondholders were made to pay for the

---

1 *Railway Age and Northwestern Railroader*, April 27, 1894, p. 237.

company's insolvency, and it was to prevent their doing so that he had come to the United States, for three-fourths of the bonds were held in England and on the continent.[2]

Despite the lack of definite information, a reorganization plan was announced June 19, 1894, by the general reorganization committee consisting of R. Somers Hayes, chairman, L. A. von Hoffman, Edward N. Gibbs, Frederic P. Olcott, Louis Fitzgerald, George C. Haven, Adrian Iselin, Jr., William Rotch, and B. Rodman Weld. The plan proposed foreclosure under the general or second mortgage and the organization of a new company having the same capitalization as the old. It would issue $35,000,000 of second mortgage bonds of which $5,000,000 were to be used to pay the floating debt and provide working capital. Not more than $3,000,000 more of them could be issued in any one year for improvements, equipment or general purposes. New income bonds were to be given in exchange for second mortgage A and B income bonds at par plus accrued interest. Stockholders were to pay an assessment of $12 per share, for which they would receive an equivalent in income bonds. The new income mortgage would be limited to a maximum of $115,000,000, of which $13,160,000 was to be reserved for the acquisition of outstanding securities of subsidiaries. To protect these bonds, a voting trust was to be formed in which their holders would have an equal voice with the stockholders; the trust would be terminated only after the income bondholders had received 5 per cent interest for three consecutive years. The plan made no provision for reorganizing any of the Atchison's subsidiaries, but it reserved the right to negotiate with them at a later date.[3]

Publication of the plan roused very little enthusiasm. The *Commercial and Financial Chronicle* pointed out that it called for the deposit of Colorado Midland and Atlantic & Pacific

2 *Railway World*, June 9, 1894, p. 447.

3 *Plan and Agreement for the Reorganization of the Atchison, Topeka & Santa Fe*, etc., dated June 19, 1894. Also, see *Railway World*, June 23, 1894, p. 485, for analysis of plan.

securities, but not those of the St. Louis & San Francisco. No explanation of the committee's intentions in regard to any of these companies was given, and the problem they presented was of the utmost importance; hitherto they had constituted a chronic liability to the Atchison and the success of any reorganization would depend largely on the arrangements made with them.[4] The *Wall Street Journal* thought that " the principal criticism of the Atchison plan, which we have heard, relates to the absence of a balance sheet, none having been published since June 30, 1893 "; until a more recent report would be available, the *Journal* hesitated to form an opinion.[5] The *Evening Post* regretted the omission but believed that the plan met " with considerable favor in Wall Street ", especially because it gave the income bondholders a voice in the management.[6]

A stockholders' protective committee which was formed to oppose the plan pointed out that it would increase the annual fixed charges; it seemed ridiculous to add $60,000,000 to a bonded debt already too large for the company to pay interest on. The committee also thought that the stock was being unfairly treated; it would not only be heavily assessed, but $35,-000,000 more securities would be placed ahead of it. Finally, the committee very cogently complained that the company's financial position was still unknown.[7] One stockholder discovered nine distinct faults which he felt justified his opposition to the plan; besides the criticisms being made in other quarters, he doubted that it provided adequately for the future needs of the company, that it was sufficiently comprehensive, and that either the market or the intrinsic value of the stock justified such heavy assessments.[8]

4 *Commercial and Financial Chronicle*, June 23, 1894, pp. 1054-5.

5 *Wall Street Journal*, June 21, 1894, p. 2.

6 New York *Evening Post*, June 21, 1894.

7 *Railway Review*, July 14, 1894, p. 407.

8 *Ibid.*, July 7, 1894, p. 393, letter from C. H. Venner.

One of the most vigorous protests was made by the London *Economist* in an article entitled " A Monstrous Reorganization ":

It is difficult to speak in measured language, and without heat, of the monstrous scheme which has been brought forward, with the endorsement of the London Bondholders' Committee, for the reorganization of the Atchison, Topeka & Santa Fe Railroad Company, which controls one of the greatest railway systems in the United States and in which English investors have sunk several millions to little profit. To appreciate at its real value what is now proposed, we must look back at the history of the past. About four years ago the Atchison, which had been growing like Jonah's gourd, experienced a set-back, and reorganization became necessary. A scheme was drawn up and carried through, which was, in most respects, entirely unsatisfactory. Then, as now, those who should have made the least sacrifice were called upon to give up most, and the shareholders—Americans mainly, we need scarcely say—got off more lightly than they had any just reason to expect. . . . Now, again, reorganization has become necessary, but the conditions are much more unsatisfactory. To start with, nothing is known in regard to the actual position of the company, which remains in the hands of those under whose guidance it has again fallen into a disastrous plight. The bondholders are once again asked, to use an American expression, to " carry the heavy end of the log." Finally, no provision whatever is made for better management in the future. Could anything be more fatuous? Would such an arrangement be entertained for a moment by ordinary business men in their daily transactions? We are willing to admit freely that the reorganization of such an enormous property as the Atchison, with all the conflicting interests which are involved, must necessarily be a work of great difficulty; but nothing, in our opinion, can excuse or justify the arrangement which the so-called London Committee of Bondholders has thought fit to recommend.[9]

A plan which convinced stockholders that they were being sacrificed to the bondholders and convinced junior bondholders

9 *Economist*, June 23, 1894, pp. 762-3.

that they were being sacrificed to the stockholders had no chance of success from the outset, and revelations of the Atchison's true financial and physical condition soon made the inadequacy of the scheme apparent. In the middle of August Stephen Little's report showed that the earnings of the system as a whole and the assets of the parent company itself had been overstated by millions of dollars. About four months later another bombshell was exploded in the announcement by Engineer Morse that expenditures of more than $14,000,000 in addition to ordinary expenses for maintenance were needed within the next five years to put the system into good condition.[10] These two disclosures ended all hope of putting the road on its feet merely by resorting to a little superficial patchwork; reorganization proposals must provide a completely new financial structure for the company or they would be impracticable.

Soon after the publication of these reports came a second plan for rehabilitating the road; although not complete in details, it seemed to have been based on realities. The Atchison had outstanding $150,000,000 of first mortgage 4 per cent bonds and $90,000,000 of second mortgage 4 per cents. In addition bonds of the St. Louis & San Francisco, the Colorado Midland and the Atlantic & Pacific to the amount of about $90,000,000 were outstanding; however, these could be bought in for about $45,000,000 cash. Thus the problem resolved itself into one of floating enough new bonds to care for about $285,000,000 of old and the latter probably could be scaled down about $50,000,000. A new $300,000,000 mortgage, it was estimated, would not only take care of these obligations but would also provide sufficient working capital to meet any exigency. Fixed charges would be $12,000,000 per year, and the past earnings of the road indicated that they could be met without difficulty.[11] The plan had the merit of reducing drastically the amount of subsidiaries' bonds guaranteed by the

10 *Railway World*, December 15, 1894, p. 996.

11 *Railway Age and Northwestern Railroader*, December 21, 1894, p. 726.

Atchison; but scaling down the bondholders' equities without exacting any equivalent sacrifices from the stock constituted a fault which would have to be corrected before it could hope to receive serious consideration.

In April the plan reappeared in amended and elaborated form with the endorsement of a joint executive committee which represented the New York general reorganization committee, the London bondholders' committee and Hope & Company of Amsterdam, who acted for the Dutch bondholders. The committee, consisting of Edward King, chairman, R. Somers Hayes, Edward N. Gibbs, George C. Haven, Adrian Iselin, Jr., C. Sligo de Pothonier, Robert Fleming, John Luden and Victor Morawetz, had five ends in view: first, fixed charges must be reduced to an amount safely within the earning power of the system. Adequate provision must be made for future capital requirements, subject to proper restrictions as to bond issues for this purpose. In the third place, the floating debt must be liquidated and provision must be made to take up the prior lien indebtedness which would soon mature. Existing securities must be reinstated upon equitable terms in the order of their priority. Finally, in so far as might be found practicable, the various parts of the system should be consolidated and unified in order to end the waste caused by the clumsy arrangements existing.

The general mortgage was to be foreclosed and a new company organized. It would issue $102,000,000 of common stock, $111,486,000 of non-cumulative 5 per cent preferred stock and $96,990,582 of general mortgage 4 per cent one hundred year adjustment bonds. Additional preferred stock not to exceed $40,000,000 might be issued under carefully defined restrictions to take up the bonds of subsidiary companies. If considered advisable, $17,000,000 of prior lien bonds might be issued; they would take precedence over the general mortgage bonds and could be used in place of some of the reserved preferred stock. The total capitalization of the new company would be

$233,486,000 in stock and $237,218,892 in bonds, a total of $470,704,892. Common stock was to be assessed $10 per share and in return for the payments there would be offered an equivalent value in new common stock. The second mortgage and income bonds were to pay a 4 per cent assessment and they would receive preferred stock as compensation. A syndicate would be formed to underwrite the plan.[12]

The treatment accorded the various bond issues was very harsh. First mortgage bondholders were to receive only 75 per cent of their old bonds in the new. Inasmuch as just six years had passed since the finances of the company last had been reorganized, this was a disappointment. All the system's divisional bonds, many of them always considered gilt-edged securities, would be consolidated and the interest rate reduced from 7 to 4 per cent. The readjustment bonds were to be so distributed that if the company earned enough, the various bondholders would receive the same return on their investment as they received before the receivership; however, the adjustment bonds ranked first ahead of the preferred stock, and only received interest if it were earned. Although the *Commercial and Financial Chronicle* admitted regretfully that this reorganization scheme was realistic and therefore looked sound and safe, for the sake of the foreign reputation of American railroads it was sorry to see such drastic treatment accorded to the bondholders.[13]

The severity of the plan was vindicated by the transformation it would work in the fixed charges. The system's total annual obligations would be decreased from $9,536,082 to $4,528,547. The bonded debt per mile would also be more than halved; and the new figure of $16,836 was over $3000 less than that of the system's chief rival. Annual fixed charges per mile

12 *Plan and Agreement for the Reorganization of the Atchison, Topeka & Santa Fe*, etc., dated March 14, 1895. Also, see *Railway World*, April 13, 1895, p. 291 for analysis of the plan.

13 *Commercial and Financial Chronicle*, April 20, 1895, pp. 685-6.

would be proportionally reduced from $1,433 to $680, as compared to $1,131 for the Atchison's competitor.[14]

The daily press did not give the plan a very enthusiastic reception and it emphasized three weaknesses. Nothing had been said about the annual rentals for terminals at Chicago and other important cities and these items should have been included in the estimated operating expenses. No definite provision had been made for the Atlantic & Pacific although $20,000,000 of bonds had been reserved for its acquisition. Finally, the par value of the new company's securities would be huge; admittedly, unless many security holders were to be frozen out, it was necessary to give compensation for scaled-down bond values in various grades of stock. Nevertheless that meant an enormous total capitalization.[15]

Remarkably enough, the *Economist* of London was favorably disposed towards the plan.

When a great company falls into such a desperate position as the Atchison—a position indicated by the fact that recently it has earned only about 60 per cent of its fixed charges, apart altogether from the huge losses incurred by the operation of two important subsidiary roads—it is evident that any scheme of reorganization which bids fair to be effectual must involve great sacrifices and that if salvation in any way is to be achieved, it will not do to be too critical and exacting. Taken altogether, the scheme that has been put forward appears reasonable.[16]

Before the middle of June a majority of each class of bond had been deposited and the plan was declared operative.[17] In two more weeks the approval approached unanimity as holders of nearly 95 per cent of the bonds and nearly 90 per cent of the stock had assented to it.[18] One of the most important an-

14 *Report of Receivers*, July 1, 1896 and *Railway Age and Northwestern Railroader*, September 20, 1895, p. 466.

15 *Railway Age and Northwestern Railroader*, April 26, 1895, p. 199.

16 *Economist*, April 13, 1895, p. 485.

17 *Commercial and Financial Chronicle*, April 20, 1895, pp. 685-6.

18 *Railway Age and Northwestern Railroader*, June 28, 1895, p. 312.

nouncements still to be made by the reorganization committee was its choice for president of the new company: Edward Ripley. He was "highly commended by the leading western railroad men, and also by the leading shippers and business men". He had been successively general Eastern agent, general freight agent in Chicago, general traffic manager and general manager of the Chicago, Burlington, & Quincy. Since 1890 he had been third vice-president of the Chicago, Milwaukee & St. Paul.[19] D. B. Robinson, who had been serving as the Atchison's first vice-president in charge of operations, was selected to continue in that capacity.[20]

On December 10, 1895, the greatest auction sale in history took place: Edward King of the reorganization committee bought in the whole system of 9343 miles for $60,000,000.[21] Exactly three weeks later the receivers turned the property over to the new owners, the Atchison, Topeka & Santa Fe Railway Company.[22] Some of the expenses incidental to the company's receivership and reorganization, which were made public when the court approved the allowances to those involved, were sufficiently large to emphasize the direct loss that any receivership inevitably involved. The judge ordered more than $470,500 distributed to the receivers, the various counsel and several banks for services rendered, and this was only the final settlement; a not inconsiderable sum had already been disbursed for similar purposes.[23]

The new mortgage indentures were very specific in the restrictions they imposed on the management. Prior lien bonds to the amount of $17,000,000 might be issued for only two purposes: $12,000,000 could be used to retire equipment bonds and car trusts at maturity and $5,000,000 might be spent for

19 *Railway World*, December 7, 1895, pp. 809-10.

20 *Ibid.*, November 23, 1895, p. 756.

21 *Ibid.*, December 14, 1895, pp. 830-1.

22 *Report of Receivers.*

23 *Railway Age and Northwestern Railroader*, January 20, 1896, p. 18.

betterments if general mortgage bonds could not be sold at 80 or above. Whenever any prior liens were issued, for every $1000 of them general mortgage bonds of $1250 par value must be reserved with which to redeem them as soon as practicable and to facilitate this operation it was provided that prior liens might be called at 103 plus interest at any time. Furthermore, the prior liens that were reserved for betterments could not be used after 1900, and the general mortgage bonds seemed destined to remain above 80 until then. This was a new kind of prior lien: one which could temporarily be of great service to the company but was very unlikely to remain outstanding long enough to become a detriment.

General mortgage bonds to the amount of $20,000,000 were reserved either to buy St. Louis & San Francisco, Atlantic & Pacific and Colorado Midland securities in order to retain control of those companies after they were reorganized, or to build 800 miles of new road to replace the connection which control of the Atlantic & Pacific had provided between the eastern and western networks of the system. Not more than $3,000,000 of these bonds might be used to buy branches of the three subsidiaries or to construct second tracks on them. Until February 1, 1897, this reserve could only be used if the written approval of a majority of the directors and two-thirds of the joint reorganization committee had been obtained; thereafter a resolution approved by a majority of the preferred stock and all the common stock present at a meeting called to consider the matter would be required.

Another $30,000,000 of the general mortgage bonds were reserved for improvements, extensions, second tracks and additional terminals on the Atchison. Only $3,000,000 of this could be used in any one year and of that amount only $750,000 could be used to build branch lines or extensions, and these could not carry a bonded debt of more than $15,000 per mile. When this reserve had been exhausted $20,000,000 of adjustment bonds could be used for the same purposes, but not more

than $2,000,000 of them could be used in any one year and a
majority of all outstanding adjustment bonds must approve
each new issue. The cash proceeds on hand at any time from
sales of either of these reserved securities was limited to
$500,000 and before more were certified, the proper disposition
of all former issues must be shown. Provision for the retirement of any liens on newly acquired property must be made
from these annual allowances.

Adjustment bonds were to pay 4 per cent whenever possible
and after June 30, 1900, interest on them would be cumulative.
In calculating the sum available for payment of this interest,
the permissible deductions from gross earnings were very carefully defined and if holders of one-half of the issue were dissatisfied, they might force the trustees to protect them by foreclosure, by investigating the company's books or by any similar
steps. If the Atlantic & Pacific or any other former subsidiary
were acquired by the use of general or adjustment mortgage
bonds, it must be treated as part of the Atchison in determining the amount of interest to be paid on the adjustment bonds;
however, if acquired in some other way its accounts should be
separate and any losses incurred by it would not prejudice the
rights of these bonds. Since the former bond indentures permitted payment of interest guaranteed to subsidiaries before
the payment of interest on the parent company's income bonds,
this particular restriction marked a definite improvement.[24]

The Atchison's reorganization had resulted in a drastic reduction of fixed charges but William Jett Lauck estimated that
it had increased the amount of unnecessary and fictitious capitalization nearly $240,000,000. This appraisal was based on the
exchange of securities of more than $383,000,000 par value
for ones worth less than $155,000,000 and the sale of securities
for cash at 100 when those same securities were selling in the

24 *Adjustment Mortgage*, dated December 12, 1895, to Central Trust
Company of New York; *General Mortgage*, dated December 12, 1895, to
Union Trust Company of New York; also, see *Commercial and Financial
Chronicle*, April 18, 1896, pp. 706-8 for analysis.

open market at 102 and higher.[25] Certainly the total capitalization of nearly $500,000,000 was of staggering dimensions and there was one dangerous provision which most of Morgan's reorganizations were carefully eliminating: interest on preferred stock was to be cumulative after 1900. This meant that in a period of prolonged depression such a huge amount of unpaid interest could accumulate as to make dividends on the stock absolutely hopeless for decades. But at best the task had been difficult and at worst receivership might easily have led to a disastrous disintegration of the system.

In the end the system was partially dissolved. Of the three important subsidiaries of the old parent company, only the Atlantic & Pacific was finally absorbed by the new, and this despite the fact that the relations existing between the two roads after the Atchison's rehabilitation were peculiarly apt to create a permanent impasse. The Atchison reorganization committee held $16,000,000 of the $18,000,000 of outstanding first mortgage bonds of the Atlantic & Pacific; the committee and the St. Louis & San Francisco between them held the entire issue of second mortgage bonds. Independent holders of the first mortgage were being urged to foreclose under that lien rather than let the Atchison foreclose under the second mortgage; by anticipating the latter's action, it could be made either to bear all the expenses of the receivership or else forfeit its interest in the second mortgage. Despite this threat the Atchison would not offer to pay more than 50 cents on the dollar to settle its guarantees of the bonds; rather than pay more it would let the first mortgage holders destroy the value of its second lien. This indifference was attributable to the clause in the Atchison reorganization plan which provided funds either to buy a controlling interest in the Atlantic & Pacific, or failing that, to build a competing line. Since the Atchison already owned the rolling stock used by the Atlantic & Pacific and the latter's main value lay in the connection its western division

25 *Senate Committee on Interstate Commerce*, 1922, V, pp. 2270.

afforded across the sparsely populated deserts which separated the eastern and western Atchison networks, a newly built competing line would make it absolutely worthless. So the companies were deadlocked: the Atchison refused to pay more than half the par value of the bonds and the first mortgage holders threatened to sell out the Atchison's second lien on the property.[26]

To obviate the necessity for building a second line which would be useless if it could acquire the Atlantic & Pacific at any reasonable figure, in January, 1897, the Atchison proposed to holders of the first mortgage that it buy $16,000,000 of the first mortgage 6 per cent western division bonds. The Atchison would pay 52½ per cent of their par value in its own general mortgage bonds carrying the April, 1897, coupon and 57½ per cent in preferred stock. It would also assume the floating debt of the other company. Altogether this floating debt and expenses incidental to the necessary foreclosure would cost about $1,200,000, but the Atchison would then be in an advantageous position also to acquire the central division of the Atlantic & Pacific if it wished. As an essential part of the bargain the Atchison was to be relieved from all responsibility for its former guarantees of Atlantic & Pacific securities and several court proceedings against it, which were based on these guarantees, must be withdrawn. The Atlantic & Pacific was to keep possession and control of the central division of its system and to retain one-sixth of the equipment hitherto used on the western division.[27] Thus in order to avoid building a new roadbed over the desert the Atchison was paying about $18,-000,000 in its own securities and thereby assuming an annual fixed charge of $400,000.[28]

The proposal was immediately accepted,[29] and on May 3 the

26 *Railway World*, January 11, 1896, p. 31.

27 *Ibid.*, January 23, 1897, p. 97.

28 *Ibid.*, March 6, 1897, p. 250.

29 *Ibid.*, January 30, 1897, p. 119.

road from Albuquerque to Needles was sold at foreclosure for
$12,000,000.[30] As soon as the final papers confirming the sale
were filed the Atchison deeded to the Southern Pacific its
Sonora division, an unconnected fragment of road entering
Mexico, and received in return the Mohave-Needles division
of the latter; each had been renting the section which it needed
and the trade simply ended the annual payment of rentals to
each other.[31] After this purchase had been concluded the
Atchison had a through line from Chicago to Los Angeles,
which, together with its branches, totalled over 9000 miles
and was the longest railroad track in the world under one
management.[32]

The central division of the Atlantic & Pacific finally passed
under the control of the reorganized St. Louis & San Francisco.[33] The latter's reorganization was carried through by a
committee consisting of Louis Fitzgerald, chairman, Isaac N.
Seligman, J. Kennedy Tod, B. P. Cheney, S. Alsberg, Charles
S. Gleed, S. C. Eastman and James A. Blair; it represented all
the bondholders except the Atchison. This committee and the
one representing the Atchison tried to agree to a mutually satisfactory plan, but the crucial problem of the road's future
control proved insoluble. Finally the Atchison sold its bonds to
the committee at 35 in order to end the deadlock.

The plan which was ultimately executed provided for a
reduction of the annual fixed charges from $2,436,982 to
$1,994,300, an amount well within the net earnings in even
the worst year of the depression. The new company would
issue $50,000,000 of consolidated first mortgage 4 per cent
bonds, $5,000,000 of non-cumulative 4 per cent first preferred
stock, $16,000,000 of non-cumulative 4 per cent second pre-
ferred stock and $29,000,000 of common stock. Enough cash

30 *Ibid.*, May 8, 1897, p. 470.
31 *Commercial and Financial Chronicle*, March 27, 1897, p. 586.
32 *Railway World*, May 8, 1897, p. 470.
33 *Ibid.*, December 25, 1897, p. 1265.

would be raised by assessments and the sale of new securities to pay off all arrears of interest, car trusts and the floating debt and to buy the bonds held by the Atchison; new bonds could be issued in amounts not to exceed $300,000 in any one year to meet future needs.[34] However, even before any additional bonds were issued, the capitalization of the new company exceeded that of the old by more than $12,000,000, despite the fact that common stock of the old company received no consideration in the reorganization. The treatment accorded the holders of first consolidated mortgage 5 per cent bonds dated June 11, 1891, was almost unparalleled: in return for the $1,000 bond and an 8 per cent assessment, the holder received $140 of first preferred stock, $1,000 of second preferred stock and $1,800 of common stock of the new company. Further, the holder was given the opportunity of subscribing to a new issue of consolidatd 4 per cent bonds to the amount of 67 per cent of his former holdings; on paying this subscription, each of these bonds brought with it $469 of first preferred stock, $670 of second preferred stock and $1,206 of common stock. The net result of depositing a $1,000 bond, paying the assessment of 8 per cent and subscribing the maximum $670 of new bonds was to get $670 of new bonds and $5285 of new capital stock.[35] Certainly the reorganization committee was offering bargains.

The new company, with an independent management under President D. B. Robinson, former first vice-president of the Atchison, took possession of the property at midnight, June 30, 1897.[36] In 1903 it became a part of the Rock Island system [37] and within a decade after the reorganization its mileage had been tripled, mostly through the purchase of new lines. This over-rapid expansion, coupled with the payment of unearned

34 *Ibid.*, April 25, 1896, p. 450.

35 *Investigation of Railroads*, by Interstate Commerce Commission, 63rd Congress, 2nd Session, Senate Document no. 373, p. 38.

36 *Railway World*, June 20, 1896, p. 643; July 4, 1896, p. 696; *Railway Age, and Northwestern Railroader*, July 3, 1896, p. 3.

37 Snyder, *op. cit.*, pp. 630-8.

interest on preferred shares, proved disastrous and the road was again in the hands of receivers in 1913.[38] An attempt to build a great system from a heavily over-capitalized road [39] ended in receivership again, just as had so many similar attempts during the depression of the nineties.

The reorganization of the Colorado Midland was also made independently of the Atchison, its former parent Company. The new Midland issued $10,000,000 of first mortgage bonds at a sliding scale of interest which was determined by the amount of earnings but was not to exceed 4 per cent, $6,000,000 of non-cumulative 4 per cent preferred stock and $4,000,000 of common stock. A voting trust was created to continue in control until 4 per cent dividends had been paid on the preferred stock for three consecutive years.[40] To provide future capital, the company was empowered to issue not more than $500,000 of 4 per cent prior lien bonds upon the approval of the trustees of the mortgage. This provision only applied until July 1, 1903, and if it were to be used an equal amount of mortgage bonds must be set aside to redeem the prior liens. The terms on which new securities would be exchanged for old, although not quite so generous as in the case of the St. Louis & San Francisco, were nonetheless liberal enough to saturate the capitalization of the new company with a large dose of pure water.[41]

The problems involved in rehabilitating the Atchison and its subsidiaries had been puzzling enough to tax the ingenuity of some of the countrys leading railroad experts, but the reorganization which finally lifted the Union Pacific out of the hands of receivers, both in its immediate and in its later consequences, was one of the most significant of all similar achievements. Of course the reestablishment of any of the transcon-

38 63rd Congress, 2nd Session, *Senate Document no. 373*, pp. 11-19.

39 *Senate Committee on Interstate Commerce*, 1922, testimony of William Jett Lauck, IV, p. 2272; claims $49,000,000 of water inserted.

40 *Railway World*, June 26, 1897, p. 640.

41 *Ibid.*, July 31, 1897, p. 758.

tinentals on a sound financial basis was a matter of great importance, but the reorganization of the Union Pacific was of especial interest because it marked the beginning of the end of the Government's partnership in transcontinental transportation after nearly forty years of trial and because it proved the starting point for the later career of Edward H. Harriman, who not only made the Union Pacific the most discussed and possibly the most efficient transportation system in the country, but also by creating a near-monopoly in transcontinentals rivalled Morgan's pretensions to dictatorship in the American railway industry.

The first committee to undertake the Union Pacific reorganization was one of the strongest ever formed. Calvin S. Brice, chairman of the Senate Committee on Pacific Railroads, was the chairman, and the rest of the group consisted of James A. Reilly, chairman of the House Committee on Pacific Railroads, Louis Fitzgerald, president of the Mercantile Trust Company and one of the most experienced railroad reorganizers in the country, General Granville M. Dodge, builder of the road and long active in its affairs, H. L. Higginson, a New York banker, A. A. H. Boissevain, a Dutch banker with long and arduous experience in the problems presented by insolvent American railroads, Samuel Carr, and, last but not least, J. P. Morgan.[42]

In December, 1893, this committee published its plan. Haste was necessary because two of the company's funded obligations were rapidly approaching maturity: collateral trust notes given in 1891 to fund the floating debt would be due August 1, 1894, and more important, the first instalment of the debt to the Government would be due November 1, 1895, and if this were defaulted the Government would have the road completely at its mercy.[43] There were outstanding $122,000,000 of primary and well secured bonds, the $56,000,000 due the Government,

42 *Outstanding Bonds and Stocks, June 30, 1894, and Particulars re: Default*, by the receivers, revised November 1, 1894, 112-page pamphlet. Also see, *Railway Age and Northwestern Railroader*, December 8, 1893, p. 875.

43 *Commercial and Financial Chronicle*, April 28, 1894, pp. 700-1.

which was not well secured except that the Government might take over the road if it were not paid, $55,000,000 of secondary issues and $5,000,000 of questionable issues, or a total of $238,000,000. The plan proposed that the stockholders surrender control of the system to the Government by allowing the latter to appoint seven of the twelve directors. The Government was to issue $300,000,000 of 3 per cent bonds at par, with which to pay all the company's debts and provide working capital. These bonds were to be perpetual and such that they might serve as a basis for bank note circulation.[44]

But the entire scheme was based on an assumption that the Government would concur in the committee's suggestions, and that supposition proved completely groundless. The plan was recommended by the committee in December and the following June it was still awaiting final approval or disapproval by Congress, despite the fact that it had the endorsement of both House and Senate Pacific Railroad committees and Attorney-General Olney.[45] Unable to reach any agreement with the Government, the committee finally had to abandon it.[46] The failure of the committee's efforts was disappointing, but it clearly showed that before any similar efforts in the future could succeed definite provision of one sort or another must be made for the Government debt.

The Government's connection with the road had originated in the demand for a transcontinental railroad that had been a major political issue long before the Civil War. Finally in 1862 and again in 1864 Congress had decided to give direct aid to anyone who would build the proposed road. In acts passed during those two years it had ordered that government bonds be sold and the proceeds loaned to private corporations constructing the line. At the time no provision had been made for the repayment of these loans, and before any action was taken

44 *Railway Review*, December 9, 1893, p. 741.

45 *Railway World*, June 16, 1894, p. 477.

46 Dodge, *How We Built the Union Pacific Railway*, p. 75.

in that regard the Credit Mobilier frauds had been thoroughly revealed. Moreover in 1875 the Supreme Court ruled that the companies could not be required to pay the United States for current interest on the bonds until the bonds matured. The construction scandals had strengthened the demand that the loans eventually be repaid to the Government in full and this ruling meant that the amounts due at maturity would be more than double the principal. So in 1878 Congress passed the so-called Thurman Act that provided for the establishment by the Treasury Department of a sinking fund which supposedly would contain enough money to pay off the subsidy when the bonds matured. The Act required that all compensation for use of the Government-aided roads by the Government should be kept by the Treasury, one-half to be added to the sinking fund and one-half applied to the payment of current interest on the bonds. In addition the sinking fund was to receive a yearly sum not to exceed $850,000 and 5 per cent of the net earnings of the subsidized companies. Altogether this annual contribution would amount to about 25 per cent of their net earnings, and it was to be invested by the Secretary of the Treasury in Government securities, preferably 3 per cent bonds, and the income from these investments was to be invested semi-annually in the same securities.

But the Thurman Act failed completely to accomplish its purpose; the courts decided that the companies could subtract money spent for new construction from their earnings before calculating the net and about that time they started to build branch lines: furthermore, the bonds in which the sinking fund was to be invested usually sold at premiums as high as 35 per cent, so that the interest rate on money invested in them was far below the expected 5 per cent.[47]

Long before the Union Pacific had been put into the hands of receivers it was apparent that some settlement of the debt other than that provided by the Thurman Act would be neces-

47 53rd Congress, 3rd Session, *Senate Report, no. 830, Report on Pacific Railroads,* submitted by Senator Brice, January 28, 1895.

sary. When the bonds matured the sinking fund would contain only about $17,616,000 whereas the total debt, principal and interest combined, would amount to over $70,000,000.[48] There seemed to be three possible modes of settlement. The Government might try to get as much of what was due to it as possible and write off the rest as a loss. Its interest in the roads was costly: in direct cash outlay, the Attorney-General had asked for an appropriation of $30,000 to pay the expenses of protecting this interest for the single year 1894. The litigation which it involved occupied the time and attention of the Government's legal experts, and both houses of Congress not only kept standing committees on Pacific Railroads but also spent many hours wrangling over the details of a possible settlement. Surely even an arrangement which failed by a wide margin to return to the Government all that it had lent would be worthwhile if it meant the end of all these expenses and annoyances, argued some exponents of a compromise settlement. And if negotiations failed the Government could always fall back on the right to foreclose its mortgage as a last resort.

A second proposal was to extend the period of the loans for fifty years, reduce the interest charges from the prevailing 6 per cent to 2 or 3 per cent and establish sinking funds which would provide enough cash for full payment when the bonds matured. The weakness of this plan lay in the fact that predictions of the potential earnings of any railroad over a period of fifty years were necessarily mere guesswork, and therefore it would be impossible to determine a fair rate of interest; furthermore, some critics believed that such a settlement would constitute implicit approval by the Government of the fictitious capitalization which had been created by the construction frauds. In favor of the proposal it was argued that at least

48 *Letter from the Attorney-General* transmitting, pursuant to House Resolution dated October 14, 1893, a draft of a bill to reorganize the Union Pacific Railway Company and to readjust and secure the claims of the United States against said Company, 53rd Congress, 2nd Session, House of Representatives, Executive Document, no. 203.

matters would be no worse than they already were and that
in the added time some better solution might be found.

The third suggestion was that the Government exercise its
right to assume control of the road and operate them itself.
If this were done it would have to pay off those claims which
preceded its own and perhaps more important, it would only
get fragments of the roads, for its lien did not apply to any
lines other than those built in part with Government subsidies.
In view of the stacks of Pacific Railroad reports compiled by
Government commissions and investigators, one of the objections which were raised to this solution was a bit ridiculous;
it might mean the railroads would be dragged into politics!
How they could be any deeper in politics than they were during
the nineties is hard to conceive. In favor of this plan it was
argued that Government competition with the other transcontinentals might force some of them to squeeze the water out of
their capitalizations and, secondly, it would imply a condemnation of the dishonesty which had so often characterized American railroad construction and management.[49]

In the period intervening between the receivership of the
Union Pacific and its reorganization all of these plans were
recommended to Congress and bills embodying each of them
were repeatedly introduced. Congressional committees, the
attorney-general, the secretary of the treasury, the Government
directors of the Union Pacific, special investigators and private
individuals all recommended solutions of the problem and Congress continually debated the subject, but it failed to take any
definite action.

While Congress was still receiving endless suggestions and
fruitlessly discussing them, in October, 1895, the formation of
a new and carefully constituted reorganization committee was
announced. Louis Fitzgerald, the chairman, represented the
Gould interests in the road; the rest of the group consisted of
Marvin Hughitt, president of the Chicago & Northwestern Rail-

49 Davis, John P., *The Union Pacific Railway*, reprinted in a 91-page
pamphlet from the *Annals of the American Academy*, p. 61.

way, and Chauncey Depew, president of the New York Central, both of whom represented the Vanderbilt lines which had traffic agreements with the Union Pacific; Jacob Schiff, of Kuhn, Loeb & Company, representatives of the foreign investors in the company and prospective underwriters and managers of the reorganization; Oliver Ames II and T. Jefferson Coolidge, Jr., representing the New England security holders, and Winslow S. Pierce as counsel.[50]

The plan recommended on the same day by this committee received a rather favorable reception; the *Commercial and Financial Chronicle* saw it as "a very clever contrivance and as containing within it the elements that are likely to insure its success." It included only the Union Pacific and its Kansas branches; the rest of the system was to be reorganized later when the parent company was in a better position to make alliances and enter into definite contracts. Bondholders, except owners of Kansas Pacific consols and trifling liens on the Kansas division, were to get 100 per cent of their holdings in new first mortgage bonds and 50 per cent in new preferred stock. The bonds excepted from that basis of exchange were to receive 80 per cent in new bonds, 50 per cent in new preferred stock and additional preferred stock for accrued interest. Stock was to be assessed $15 per share in order to provide needed cash. The bond issue, totalling $100,000,000, and the preferred stock, amounting to a par value of $75,000,000, were to be used to settle the debt to the Government and for extraordinary expenses, as well as to exchange for the securities of the former company.

The committee estimated that after the Government debt had been paid and the exchanges of securities made, there would remain about $56,000,000 as a reserve. The Government was to be offered its principal in full, about $33,000,000, and about $19,500,000 of interest, although the amount due was nearly

50 *Reorganization of the Union Pacific Railway Company, Plan and Letter of Submitted to Security Holders*, dated New York, October 15, 1895, 35-page pamphlet. Also see, *Railway World*, October 19, 1895, pp. 645, 635-6.

twice that sum. Despite the fact that it proposed paying only about 75 per cent of the total owed the Government, this offer was more generous than might have been expected from a committee representing the prior lien bondholders who had first claim on the system's property. The annual fixed charges would be about $4,000,000 and even in 1894, one of the worst years of the depression, the company had netted enough to pay this amount, whereas the average net earnings of the past ten years had been sufficient to pay it and also pay a 4 per cent dividend on the new preferred stock.[51]

Since the holders of the prior lien could, if they wished, foreclose under their own mortgage without paying the Government a cent, quite reasonably there was confident expectation that the Government would act quickly on this proposal.[52] Meanwhile the committee endeavored to gain the consent of security holders to the plan, and so successful were their efforts that before the end of the year a majority of all the first mortgage bonds that were involved had been deposited as well as large amounts of the junior securities and nearly half the stock. Fitzgerald announced that because of the strong support indicated by these deposits, the committee was proceeding to put the plan into operation as quickly as possible.[53]

Before the reorganization could actually be effected, however, acceptance of the terms offered the Government had to be obtained. As early as January, 1895, the Union Pacific directors had prepared a memorial to Congress offering to assess the company's stock enough to pay off all liens prior to that of the Government in return for an extension of the subsidy loans for fifty years at 2 per cent.[54] The Reilly bill then before Congress had provided for 3 per cent interest and amendments were introduced which would have brought this bill into agreement

51 *Commercial and Financial Chronicle*, October 19, 1895, pp. 683-4.

52 *Railway World*, November 16, 1895, pp. 732-3.

53 *Ibid.*, January 4, 1896, p. 5.

54 *Railway Gazette*, January 18, 1895, p. 46.

with the directors' proposal,[55] but to no avail; early in February the bill was defeated by a large vote, both with the amendment and without it.[56]

Despite the size of the vote by which the bill had been rejected, the New York *Evening Post* published a scathing arraignment of the demagogues who had felt it necessary to show their hatred of corruption by voting against what the *Post* believed was actually an excellent bill.[57] This attack was prompted by the announcement that a new reorganization plan would soon be published, and that news also inspired the *Wall Street Journal* to unhappy thoughts:

> The Union Pacific plan was regarded as a serious and business-like effort to deal with a complicated situation. There was very little definite criticism of the measures suggested, but a general feeling that it would take a good while to bring a body as powerful and unstable as Congress into acceptance of any reasonable plan. Members of the committee said it was evident from the plan itself speedy results were not expected.[58]

A year after the defeat of the Reilly bill, Winslow S. Pierce presented to the Senate Committee on Pacific Railroads the plan which had been formulated by the Fitzgerald committee in the meanwhile. He asked the Government to accept $35,-755,000 for the principal of the debt and $20,864,000 for accrued interest, payment to be either in Union Pacific securities which at par would be almost equal to the total face value of the Government's claim, or in cash proceeds from the sale of the same securities, which it was estimated would raise this amount of cash.[59] However, as had so often been the case before, the bill embodying this offer failed to win the approval

---

55 *Railway World*, January 26, 1895, p. 73.

56 *Ibid.*, February 9, 1895, p. 112.

57 New York *Evening Post*, October 18, 1895.

58 *Wall Street Journal*, October 16, 1895, p. 2.

59 54th Congress, 1st Session, *Senate Document no. 314, Notes of Hearings Before the Committee on Pacific Railroads of the Senate, etc.*, pp. 1-9 for testimony of Pierce.

of both houses and no action in regard to the Pacific Railroads was taken at that session of Congress.[60]

Hopeless of getting Congress to pass on the matter, President Cleveland acted under the authority conferred on the president by the past subsidy laws and instructed his attorney-general, Judson Harmon, to negotiate an agreement with the reorganization committee. After this decision delay was finally at an end. An accord was soon reached by which the Government, either in conjunction with the prior lien bondholders or separately as the courts might direct, would foreclose its mortgage; in return for so doing, the reorganization committee guaranteed that at least $45,000,000 would be bid for the property; in addition the Government was to keep the money in the sinking fund, which would amount to nearly $17,000,000. By this arrangement the Government would give up its claim against the Union Pacific and sever all connections with it. It would be receiving back the principal lent to the road, $33,539,512, and $36,944,300 interest, which, Harmon stated, was equivalent to interest at the rate of 3.45 per cent calculated to June 1, 1897.[61]

Before the agreement could be executed a new dispute broke out: Harmon asked whether the bridge in Omaha should not have been included under the Government's lien, and if so, was not that lien worth more than the sum agreed upon? In order to prevent an indefinite postponement of the reorganization, the committee gave affirmative answers to both questions and increased to $50,000,000 the sum in cash to be paid the Government.[62] However, even then its troubles were not over. There was a public hue and cry at the Government's acceptance of any compromise of the debt and after the McKinley administration had entered office new negotiations were initiated by Attorney-General McKenna. To prevent the nullification of all

60 *Railway World*, January 30, 1897, pp. 107-8.
61 *Ibid.*, January 30, pp. 107-8.
62 *Ibid.*, October 9, 1897, p. 998.

its plans, once again the reorganization committee raised its offer to the Government, and this time it agreed to pay the whole face value of the debt, principal and interest; no change was made in the price to be paid for the Government's lien on the Kansas Pacific division, which still remained what it had originally been, $2,500,000. Under this new accord, the Union Pacific committee was to pay the Government $74,591,046, representing the principal in full and interest thereon to October 1, 1897.[63]

After the first agreement had been made with Harmon the reorganization committee had announced that instead of the $100,000,000 of bonds originally proposed, the new company would issue only $75,000,000 of them.[64] Under the final arrangement with the Government this amount had to be raised to $85,000,000; the issue of $75,000,000 of preferred stock and $61,000,000 of common remained as expected. Interest on the new bonds would be $3,400,000 and dividends on the preferred shares would be $3,000,000, so that even after these changes in the plan there would be annual charges of only $6,400,000 ahead of a dividend on the common stock. Within the previous decade, only in 1894 had the yearly net earnings of the company fallen below this amount and the average for that period would have been enough to pay a 3 per cent dividend on the common stock.[65]

Between November 1, 1897, and February 19, 1898, a series of foreclosure sales took place at which the reorganization committee bought in the Union Pacific and its Kansas branches.[66] Under the original agreement with Harmon, the committee had agreed to pay $2,500,000 for the Government's lien on the Kansas Pacific but the public criticism which greeted this announcement forced it to raise its offer to $6,303,000,

63 *Ibid.*, October 30, 1897, pp. 1065-8.

64 *Commercial and Financial Chronicle*, May 29, 1897, p. 1025.

65 *Railway World*, December 25, 1897, p. 1269.

66 *Ibid.*, November 6, 1897, pp. 1090-3; January 15, 1898, pp. 61-2; February 19, 1898, p. 198.

which was the amount of the principal. There was still a strong public demand that the Government should also recover the interest, which would have approximately doubled the price, but the existence of a prior lien that amounted to as much as the principal of the Government debt, made this virtually impossible and the administration had to be content with the principal.[67]

The feelings with which McKinley viewed the results of the prolonged negotiations were reflected in an anecdote that General Dodge related: Dodge asked the president if he did not feel that the Government should raise a monument to " the man who built the road and paid the government debt, an unheard-of occurrence at that time. He answered, ' Yes ', but said, ' Don't you think, General, a monument should be raised to the President who made them do it?' ".[68]

On midnight, January 1, 1898, the new Union Pacific Railroad Company took over the property [69] in the midst of a general feeling that as a whole the reorganization had been achieved in a far more satisfactory manner than could have been expected a few years, or even months, before. The London *Economist* had raised a voice in opposition to the plan from the very start; it felt that the assessments being levied on the stock were far too large

and with regard to the necessity of providing for the Government debt, which the syndicate hope to settle at about 50 per cent of its total amount, a much more valid claim to favourable consideration could be shown if capital charges were cut down, as they easily can be by the compulsory conversion of the high interest bearing bonds which are now or will shortly become redeemable than if the present reorganization scheme, the essence of which is a grossly excessive piling up of new capital, is persisted. That

67 *Commercial and Financial Chronicle*, February 19, 1898, p. 359.

68 Dodge, *op. cit.*, p. 75.

69 *Railway World*, February 5, 1898, pp. 138-9.

scheme, we have already said, is one of which the reorganizers may make money, but it will benefit no one else.[70]

The *Journal of Finance,* thought, too, that the committee had been very generous, but the severance of the Government's relations with the road was something for which to be thankful. And

to be just, it has to be borne in mind that at the time when the plan was issued, and the syndicate had to be formed, the general conditions in the United States were still very unfavorable, and the syndicate obligations at that time involved a considerable risk . . . in judging the merits of the Union Pacific reorganization it has to be considered under the light of the conditions ruling in October, 1895, and not those of March, 1898, when the reorganization accounts were liquidated.[71]

William Jett Lauck testified, in regard to the water which construction frauds had inserted into the capitalization of the road, that

these fictitious securities were perpetuated in the capitalization of the Union Pacific Railroad in the reorganization of 1896 and involved at the existing rate of dividend disbursement upon its common stock an annual drain upon its resources of $5,000,000.[72]

However, the Government could well congratulate itself that the company, and not it, had paid for these frauds, because a compromise of its debt would have meant, in essence, that it was making itself pay the bill for these. The consensus of opinion in regard to the Government's part in the final settlement was epitomized in the statement of one critic:

For the government the whole outcome has been financially not less than brilliant . . . a result which, as has already been said, would have been thought a few years ago virtually impossible.[73]

70 *Economist,* May 15, 1897, pp. 708-9.

71 *Journal of Finance,* October, 1898.

72 *Senate Committee on Interstate Commerce,* 1922, V, p. 2272.

73 Myers, H. R., "The Settlements with the Pacific Railroads," *Quarterly Journal of Economics,* July 1899, XIII, p. 443.

On the board of directors and the executive committee of the reorganized company appeared the name of Edward H. Harriman, a name which had not figured in the news dispatches about the reorganization committee and its labors. Nonetheless Harriman had been an important factor in the success of those labors. Late in 1895 Winslow S. Pierce, then personal counsel to George J. Gould, had suggested to Jacob Schiff that Kuhn, Loeb & Company undertake the rehabilitation of the Union Pacific. Although not yet fifty, Schiff was at this time one of the financial leaders of the country. He had been born at Frankfurt-am-Main and educated in local schools until at the age of fourteen he was apprenticed to a business firm. Within a few years he was able to get reluctant permission from his father to emigrate to America and he arrived in New York in August, 1865. After he had been a licensed broker for less than a year he joined the firm of Budge, Schiff & Company in 1867. The firm was dissolved five years later but Schiff had meanwhile become a naturalized American citizen and as such he become manager of the Hamburg branch of the London & Hanseatic Bank. In 1874 he was invited by Abraham Kuhn, senior partner of Kuhn, Loeb & Company, to join that firm and in January of 1875 he accepted and once more moved to New York. To his new work, besides unusual energy and foresight, he brought his connections with banking leaders of London, Paris and Scotland and through these associations in the succeeding years he was instrumental in placing many American securities abroad. His rise in Kuhn, Loeb & Company was rapid and after ten years, at the age of thirty-eight, he was the head of the firm.[74]

Knowing that Morgan had been involved in the first abortive efforts to reorganize the Union Pacific, Schiff went to see him and asked if he were still interested in the task. Morgan answered that he no longer had any interest whatever in it and promised to give Schiff his fullest cooperation if the latter

74 *Dictionary of American Biography*, XVI, pp. 430-2.

should undertake the work. After he had been working for a
short time Schiff detected interference coming from some unknown source. He went to Morgan again, thinking the latter
might have changed his mind about the Union Pacific, but
was assured that Morgan had not been causing the trouble.
However, Morgan found out for him who was responsible;
Edward H. Harriman, then vice-president of the Illinois
Central, was the man.

Harriman was one of those American capitalists of the
nineties who exemplified all the traditions of the poor boy
working his way up in the world almost entirely by his own
efforts. He had been born in Hempstead, Long Island, in
1848, of parents neither wealthy nor poverty-stricken. At
fourteen he left school to become an office boy in Wall Street
and in seven years he had had enough experience to borrow
$3,000 from his uncle and buy his own seat on the stock ex-
change. His first connection with transportation came at the
end of the seventies through his purchase of a small boat running between New York City and Newburgh on the Hudson.
In 1879, after his marriage to the daughter of the president of
the Ogdensburg & Lake Champlain Railroad Company, his
interests broadened to include railroads. Two years later he
made his first independent venture in the industry: he bought
and rebuilt the bankrupt Lake Ontario Southern, renamed it
the Sodus Bay & Southern and sold it at a profit to the Pennsylvania, which needed it for a connecting link. In 1883 he
entered the directorate of the Illinois Central through his
friendship with President Stuyvesant Fish and thenceforth railroads were his chief interest.

Harriman was well equipped for the career he had chosen.
In his business relations he was cold and ruthless, sparing
neither friends nor foe if they blocked his plans. He had an
amazing grasp of detail, a shrewd ability to foresee and develop
new traffic resources and the stubbornness to make colleagues
agree with him. His leadership in the several ventures in which
he was involved was due not only to the respect aroused by his

successes but also to his dominating personality which, if not always pleasant, could never be ignored. The extent to which his ambition and foresightedness led him was revealed when he admitted to the Interstate Commerce Commission that if it were not legally impossible he would complete his semi-monopoly of transcontinental railroads and extend his transportation empire around the world. Death ended his plans before they could be fulfilled, but in the early years of the twentieth century he had taken substantial steps to bring them to fruition.[75]

When Schiff went to see Harriman the latter declared that he intended to reorganize the Union Pacific and make it a subsidiary of the Illinois Central; but a second conference between the two brought an alliance after Schiff had promised Harriman a place on the executive committee of the new company's board and thereafter they worked together. From mere membership on the executive committee, within a year Harriman advanced to the chairmanship and virtual control of the company.[76]

As soon as he had begun to establish his influence in the new Union Pacific, Harriman started an expansion and improvement program which soon made the road the talk of the country. Typical of the tactics that soon gathered into the system nearly all the subsidiaries which had been separated from it during the receivership, were those which brought back the Oregon Short Line and its subsidiary, the Oregon Railway & Navigation Company. In 1899 he had the dividend on preferred shares raised to 4 per cent and thereupon the value of all Union Pacific stock rose enough to convince the Oregon Short Line that it should exchange its own stock for that of the Union Pacific. Within a few years the whole system was rebuilt under Harriman's direction: within twelve months its

---

75 *Ibid.*, VIII, pp. 296-300; Kennan, George, *Biography of Edward H. Harriman*, Boston, Houghton, Mifflin Company, 1922, 2 volumes, *passim*.

76 *Stock Ownership*, III, p. 1225. Also see, Kahn, Otto, *Edward Henry Harriman*, address before the Finance Forum, January 25, 1911, 47-page pamphlet.

carrying capacity had been increased 75 per cent; the line was regraded to keep every grade below 44 feet to the mile, thousands of miles of track were reballasted, wooden trestles were replaced by steel and concrete or embankments, new cars and locomotives were bought.[77] The results of this program were summarized by General Dodge, the builder of the original line:

I was much impressed as I lately came over the Union Pacific by what these improvements have meant to the road. I had been staying for two months in the mountains where other railroads cross them, and I noticed that two locomotives could haul from fifteen to twenty cars only up their steep grades, while on the mountain division of the Union Pacific, a single locomotive could haul from thirty-five to forty-five cars, and from Cheyenne east they could handle fifty to seventy-five loaded cars. This shows where the great net earnings of the Union Pacific come from.[78]

Credit for reconstituting the Union Pacific system belongs to Harriman, but the rehabilitation of the individual branch lines had been independently achieved before he established his power in the company. The first important former subsidiary to be reorganized was the Oregon Railway & Navigation Company. Its existing first mortgage was not disturbed; a new second mortgage, secured by a second lien on the mileage covered by the first mortgage and a first lien on all the rest of the company's lines, was the basis for an issue of $24,-500,000 of fifty year 4 per cent bonds. The proceeds from the sale of these were sufficient to pay off the existing collateral trust bonds and finance needed betterments. A preferred stock issue of $11,000,000 was used to redeem the old collateral trust bonds at 70 per cent of their face value and consolidated mortgage bonds at 45 per cent, and to compensate common

---

[77] Keys, C. M., " Harriman," *World's Work*, XIII, pp. 8455-64, 8536-52, 8651-64, 8791-8803. Also see, Hungerford, Edward, *The Modern Railroad*, Chicago: A. C. McClurg & Company, 1911, pp. 139-41.

[78] Dodge, *op. cit.*, pp. 77-78; *Railway World*, August 31, 1895, p. 491.

stock holders for the 6 per cent assessment levied on their holdings. New common stock was exchanged for old at par. Under this plan fixed charges were reduced from $1,305,250 to $930,480 annually.[79]

Since the company had been separated from the Union Pacific, it had been fortunate in experiencing a remarkable return of prosperity. Consequently there was no reason to delay the rehabilitation of the company and at midnight, August 17, 1896, the new corporation took over the property.[80] Although it had no connection with the Union Pacific, it was by no means independent; a safe majority of its stock was held by the Oregon Short Line & Utah Northern just as before the receivership.[81]

A plan for the reorganization of the Oregon Short Line, which proved satisfactory to the security holders, was proposed on February 20, 1896. Bonds worth $36,500,000 were to be issued. They would be secured by a first consolidated mortgage with a first lien on all lines south of Ogden and on the Idaho Central mileage and a lien second only to the divisional mortgages on the rest of the system. The underlying divisional mortgages, having a par value of $21,775,000, were not to be disturbed. Two series of noncumulative income bonds totaling more than $22,000,000 were to be created and the common stock capitalization would be $27,460,100. Annual fixed charges would be $1,853,270 in place of the former $2,788,575.[82]

The new company was unattached to any other system and sought traffic alliances with all the transcontinentals. However, the Union Pacific had no intention of encouraging competition in its trade to Wyoming and Colorado, which control of the

79 Commercial and Financial Chronicle, September 28, 1895, pp. 536-8.

80 Railway Age and Northwestern Railroader, January 9, 1897, p. 29.

81 Railway World, January 9, 1897, p. 29.

82 Plan and Agreement for the Reorganization of the Oregon Short Line & Utah Northern Railway Company, dated February 20, 1896, 29-page pamphlet. Also see, Railway World, March 14, 1896, p. 251.

Short Line had formerly made its private monopoly. So in conjunction with one ally, the Southern Pacific, it boycotted the new system and forced it to rely entirely on the traffic it could get from Hill's Great Northern and Northern Pacific.[83] As Harriman and his associates had foreseen, the temptation to exchange precarious independence for the secured prosperity which the reinvigorated Union Pacific offered was too great to be resisted. Harriman held out the bait in the form of fast mounting dividends,[84] and the Short Line rejoined the system.

The Union Pacific, Denver & Gulf, the only former subsidiary not to rejoin the Union Pacific within a few years of its separation, was the last of the group to be reorganized. In 1898 a committee dominated by Granville M. Dodge proposed a plan which would reduce the yearly fixed charges from $1,-321,420 to $700,000 and the mileage from 1237 to 1086. Common stock was to be assessed $10 per share but holders would be compensated in bonds and preferred stock. The capitalization of the new company would consist of $20,000,000 of first mortgage 4 per cent bonds, $17,000,000 of non-cumulative 4 per cent first and second preferred stock and $31,-000,000 of common stock. Although this was considerably larger than heretofore, by paying off the former bondholders with only 80 per cent in new bonds and making liberal compensating allowances of preferred stock, the reduction in fixed charges was achieved.[85]

Successful as his efforts had been, Harriman was not satisfied with his extension and reconstruction of the Union Pacific alone. In 1899 he approached C. P. Huntington and unsuccessfully attempted to buy the latter's large interest in the Southern Pacific. After Huntington's death in 1901 he tried again and this time was able to acquire a controlling stock interest from the Huntington estate. Through this purchase he

83 *Railway World*, June 5, 1897, p. 567.

84 Daggett, *Railroad Reorganization*, p. 262.

85 *Reorganization of the Union Pacific, Denver & Gulf Plan*, dated September 29, 1898.

gained control not only of the Southern Pacific, but also of the Central Pacific. After many years of separate ownership and management the Union Pacific and the Central Pacific, which had been subsidized by Congress in the expectation that they would form a single transcontinental line, were finally to be combined into one system.[86]

In the same year, after being thwarted in his direct efforts to buy control of the Burlington by the success of Hill and Morgan in adding it to their transcontinental system, Harriman attempted to buy a majority block of Northern Pacific stock in the open market in order thereby to get control of the Burlington. His unsuccessful efforts precipitated a mild panic, and the net result of this Wall Street raid was the formation of the Northern Securities Company in which, with the blessing and cooperation of J. P. Morgan, Hill and Harriman pooled their enormous interests in northern transcontinental railroads.

When the Government had been paid its long-standing debt, critics thought that the Union Pacific reorganization had proved itself epochal; but that accomplishment was only one in a series of notable achievements stemming from the reorganization. As soon as Harriman had established himself in control of the Union Pacific, it became the nucleus of his attempts to form a railroad ' interest ' which would be greater in size and superior in efficiency to that of any other railroad operator in the country.

Before passing under the domination of Harriman, the Central Pacific had perforce emulated the Union Pacific by paying its debt to the Government. The former had remained solvent throughout the depression and if the bankrupt Union Pacific could pay in full, it would be necessary for the Central Pacific to do as well.

The Central Pacific Railroad Company of California had been chartered in that state June 28, 1861. The congressional act of 1862 empowered it to build from the Pacific coast east-

86 Keys, "A Corner in Pacific Railroads," *World's Work*, IX, pp. 5816-22.

ward to the State line, under the same conditions and with the same subsidies as had been granted the Union Pacific; an amending clause authorized it to continue building east as far as the Missouri River or until it met the Union Pacific. The act of 1864 restricted this eastward extension to 150 miles beyond the California state line, but another act in 1866 removed the limitation and restored the permission to work east until a junction was effected with the Union Pacific. The several later Pacific Railroad acts of Congress applied equally to both companies, the Union Pacific as well as the Central Pacific—indeed Congress always envisioned them as being two sections of one continuous transcontinental line.[87]

However, in 1885 the Central Pacific had been leased to the Southern Pacific under a very flexible contract which, if not mutually beneficial, was to be modified upon the recommendation of an arbitration committee. In accordance with this provision, on January 1, 1888, the annual rental paid to the Central Pacific was increased from $1,200,000 to $1,360,000, but the Southern Pacific protested that only in 1891 had it profited from this arrangement, so an entirely new lease, to be altered only by mutual consent, was made in 1894. The Southern Pacific no longer guaranteed the interest on Central Pacific bonds or paid any rental unwarranted by the latter's earnings. It agreed to apply Central Pacific earnings to that company's obligations in the order of their priority; any surplus was to go to the parent company. Out of this surplus the latter might compensate itself at 6 per cent for any improvements it made on the Central Pacific.[88]

Although the Southern Pacific had not underwritten the Central Pacific debt to the government, nevertheless the close financial and operating relations between the two companies and the near-identity of their managements and ownership made a settlement of nearly equal interest to both. Therefore

87 53rd Congress, 3rd Session, *Senate Document, no. 830*, pp. 10-11, 93-5.
88 *Commercial and Financial Chronicle*, March 31, 1894, pp. 365-6.

a tripartite agreement was announced in February, 1899, which accomplished three objectives: the debt to the government was to be settled; secondly, the relations of the Central and Southern were put on a definite and assured basis, thus removing the cause of chronic trouble between the roads; finally, provision was made for refunding the Central Pacific debt at lower interest rates and for raising needed cash to meet immediate and future requirements.

The primary purpose of the plan was to conform to an act passed by Congress requiring that the road's debt to the Government be paid in full and that provision for payment be made within a year. The Government was to receive twenty notes of the Central Pacific, one falling due every six months for ten years, secured by an equal amount of new first refunding mortgage 4 per cent bonds. The law passed by Congress had precluded tendering bonds directly to the Government, so this indirect procedure was adopted. Speyer & Company had agreed to buy the first three of the notes for cash; similar arrangements would be made as the rest of them fell due so that the Government would receive cash for its debt and its connection with the road would be completely terminated.

All existing bond issues of the Central Pacific were to be replaced by two new ones which the Southern Pacific would guarantee: a $100,000,000 first refunding mortgage 4 per cent bond series to run not less than 45 years and a $25,000,000 3½ per cent mortgage issue to run thirty years. The security for the latter was a lien second to that of the former on the physical property of the system and a first lien on the sinking fund assets of over $12,500,000. A new $20,000,000 issue of cumulative 4 per cent preferred stock was to be used mainly for betterments and additions; $5,000,000 of it could not be used at a rate exceeding $200,000 per year. None of it would be sold to the public; it would be taken up by the Southern Pacific and the latter would issue its own 4 per cent collateral trust notes against it. The common stock was to have the same par value, $67,275,500, as heretofore.

Due to funding both the principal and interest of the Government debt, annual fixed charges after the reorganization would be greater than before, but they were to be guaranteed by the Southern Pacific. The increase was only from $4,-269,905 to a maximum $4,875,000 after the notes held by the government had been paid and prior to that time they would be slightly less. At their highest the fixed charges remained less than the average net earnings for the past ten years and were safely below the net earnings for the previous fiscal year, so the Southern Pacific's guarantee seemed unlikely to weigh very heavily. A syndicate would pay cash to any security holders who did not care to avail themselves of the plan's liberal exchange offer, and would pay premiums on securities ranging up to 9 per cent. To provide cash for immediate needs the syndicate would also take a block of the new Central Pacific bonds and another block of the new Southern Pacific collateral trust notes.

Finally, the stock of the Central Pacific, upon payment of a $2 assessment, was to be exchanged at par for Southern Pacific stock. In this way the vexed questions arising from the relations between the two systems were to be permanently settled. The total increase in the fixed charges of the two companies would be $462,760 for the Southern Pacific and $135,000 for the Central Pacific, making a combined increase of $597,855.[89]

The plan won nearly unanimous approval from the security holders and the *Commercial and Financial Chronicle* thought deservedly so, because " the plan meets the situation exactly and it is difficult to see how the same happy results could have been attained in any other way." [90] Undoubtedly the reorganization accomplished at least two most desirable ends: it severed the connection heretofore existing between the Central Pacific and the Government and it defined and permanently established the relations between the Southern Pacific and the Central Pacific.[91] Just how much of the water which Central Pacific

89 *Commercial and Financial Chronicle*, February 25, 1899, pp. 352-4.
90 *Ibid.*, March 4, 1899, p. 397.   91 Daggett, *op. cit.*, pp. 425-6.

construction frauds and stock manipulations had inserted into the road's capitalization was perpetuated by the reorganization and just what the annual cost to the Southern Pacific stockholders of this water would be, were not mentioned.

The importance of the final severance of all special relations between the Government and the Pacific railroads, which this settlement achieved, can hardly be overestimated. A Congressional committee reporting in the nineties had wearily summarized the troubles to which Pacific roads had put the Government:

The subject has engaged the attention of all branches of the Government for many years. It has been almost constantly before Congress since 1878 when the Thurman Act was passed; various committees have investigated the condition of these bond-aided roads and have formulated plans for the settlement of their indebtedness to the United States; United States Railroad Commissioners and the various boards of Government directors have from time to time made their reports and recommendations; and a special investigating committee, appointed by the President under the Act of Congress approved March 3, 1887, made a most thorough and exhaustive examination of the properties of these roads and their financial condition, not only as to their present status, but also with reference to the construction of the roads and their subsequent managements, and submitted measures for the final settlements of the roads' indebtedness; and the attention of Congress has been called to this subject, at various times, by the President of the United States.[92]

At long last an end had been put to the problem. After more than thirty-five years of Government partnership, the Union Pacific and the Central Pacific were now completely separated from all relations to the Government other than those occasioned by the Government's regulation of interstate commerce. For Congress, the executive branches of the Government and even the judiciary, the removal of this constantly troublesome problem could not but be welcome.

92 53rd Congress, 3rd Session, *Senate Document, no. 830*, pp. 1-2.

CHAPTER VIII
PROSPERITY IN DEPRESSION

THE records of the bankrupt roads of the nineties comprise a sorry tale and a dismal commentary on American railroad management. But there is another side to the history of American railroads during that trying period. Although many of the largest systems collapsed, others equally great in the mileage they controlled and in the capital they represented and far greater in their ability to provide transportation efficiently and cheaply, survived with colors flying and, in some cases, emerged from the depression with larger and financially stronger systems than they had in 1892.

Of the roads which were able to take advantage of the depression to consolidate their positions, one of the most prominent was the New York, New Haven & Hartford. It had been formed in 1872 by a consolidation of the New York & New Haven with the Hartford;[1] by 1890 it was a prosperous little line, owning 141 miles of very well built road-bed and leasing 508 more miles, which had paid 10 per cent dividends for years past and had a bonded debt of $25,000,000. But in 1892 a most important addition was made to the board of directors in the person of J. P. Morgan.[2] Immediately thereafter the New York, Providence & Boston Railroad and the Housatonic Railroad were added to the system to increase its mileage to about 850.[3] The acquisition of these two new subsidiaries was a manifestation of the policy which was to transform the New Haven into one of the country's important systems before the end of the depression.

Early in February, 1893, the management announced a very notable addition to the system, the Old Colony Railroad. The

1 Snyder, *op. cit.*, pp. 487-500.

2 Brandeis, Louis, *Other People's Money*, Washington: National Home Library Foundation, 1933, pp. 121-2.

3 Van Oss, *op. cit.*, pp. 370-3.

New Haven possessed the only feasible entrance from New England into New York City, but at the other end of the line its trains entered Boston only by virtue of trackage agreements with three small independent roads. The mutual jealousy of these three was so great that if the New Haven wanted to add one train per day between New York and Boston, in order to retain friendly relations with all of them it was forced to add three, one to connect with each. To end this expensive procedure, the New Haven decided to buy one of these roads and thus get an entrance of its own into Boston. All three lines were considered, but the choice narrowed down to the Old Colony. The New York & New England served thirteen of the most important places which the New Haven already touched, so its purchase would mean a needless duplication of service. The Boston & Albany was passed over because its connection with Albany was more important than its Boston terminal and it was the latter in which the New Haven was interested. The Old Colony met the New Haven at Providence, only 44 miles from Boston; it owned or controlled every railway in southeastern Massachusetts, except those on two islands, and had branches to Lowell and Fitchburg. Altogether it operated 600 miles of track and, in addition, owned all the stock of the Old Colony Steamboat Company, popularly known as the Fall River Line, running between New York and various points in New England. Finally, the Old Colony had paid 7 per cent dividends for over ten years.[4]

At a meeting on April 4 the stockholders approved the transaction. The New Haven was to assume responsibility for all the fixed charges and rentals of the Old Colony and guarantee a 7 per cent dividend on its stock; if they wished shareholders could exchange their holdings for New Haven stock at the rate of ten shares of Old Colony for nine shares of New Haven.[5]

4 *Railway Gazette*, February 10, 1893, p. 114; *Railway World*, February 11, 1893, p. 135, April 8, 1893, p. 322.

5 *Railway World*, April 8, 1893, p. 322.

Both parties to the lease considered it only a temporary prelude to ultimate combination.

The advantages which the New Haven derived from the deal were obvious; the benefits accruing to the Old Colony were questioned by some of its shareholders but President Choate explained that although the company stood well in the region it served, " this was an age of combination and the efforts of the New Haven road to secure a line to Boston, which had been successful up to thirty miles from the city, had showed that if that road secured another line, it would result in a contest between the two roads ", in which obviously President Choate feared the Old Colony would be the loser.[6]

The New Haven's next achievement was an important agreement with the Boston & Maine providing for a division of New England between the two systems. The Boston & Maine agreed not to acquire either direct or indirect control of the Boston & Albany, or any line south of it; on the other hand, the New Haven might control it but not any line north of it. A third clause arranged for the interchange of traffic between the two systems and further stated that if the operation of through trains from New York to Bar Harbor and other northern points was begun, each company would provide a share of the cars and receive a share of the receipts proportionate to the mileage of its track traversed.[7] This alliance practically ended railroad competition in New England. Of the large roads not affected by the agreement, the Central of Vermont was controlled by the Grank Trunk and its traffic was mostly confined to local Vermont business and Grand Trunk through freight from Chicago to Boston. The Boston & Albany was a Vanderbilt road and the Vanderbilts were friendly to the New Haven; J. P. Morgan was heavily interested in both systems and would prevent any undue competition between them. The one road which might disturb the harmony

6 *Ibid.*, March 4, 1893, p. 193.

7 *Ibid.*, May 20, 1893, p. 467.

of New England transportation facilities, the New York & New England, was not left in that threatening position for long.

However, expansion proved expensive for the New Haven. In addition to the Old Colony acquisition, at the meeting April 4 the stockholders had approved ninety-year leases of the Berkshire Railroad, the Stockbridge & Pittsfield Railroad and the West Stockbridge Railroad.[8] Already in February the company had petitioned the Connecticut legislature for permission to increase its capital stock to a par value of $100,000,000, an amount at that time exceeded only by the Pennsylvania Railroad, the Atchison and the Southern Pacific.[9] In June there was a further indication that ready cash was not plentiful: the basis for the annual dividend was reduced from 10 to 8 per cent.[10] Soon afterward the legislature granted the company's petition and the New Haven proceeded to sell more stock as funds were needed.[11]

The system's next important acquisition was the New England Railroad. As the New York & New England it had been in financial difficulties as early as 1891. In 1892 a new administration dominated by Charles Parson had taken charge and revealed that the preceding regime had falsified certain accounts and concealed losses incurred the year before. The new management assured the stockholders that the company could and henceforth would be run at a profit if nothing interrupted existing traffic arrangements.[12]

In 1893 McLeod sought to gain control of the New York & New England in order to make it a part of the Reading's proposed New England network. Despite the receivership of the parent company at a meeting of the stockholders on March

8 *Ibid.*, April 8, 1893, p. 322.

9 *Commercial and Financial Chronicle*, February 18, 1893, p. 263.

10 *Ibid.*, June 16, 1893, p. 1010.

11 *Railway World*, June 29, 1893, p. 312.

12 *Commercial and Financial Chronicle*, March 11, 1893, p. 391.

14, 1893, McLeod was in control and was elected president.[13] But his triumph was short-lived for the road was forced into temporary receivership on December 27 [14] and on January 31, 1894, the receivership was made permanent.[15] A few months later a committee composed of John I. Waterbury and Henry W. Cannon of New York and T. Jefferson Coolidge, Jr., of Boston, announced the reorganization plan. Common stock was to be assessed $20 per share and no compensation would be given for this contribution; a syndicate had been formed to take up any assessments not paid by shareholders. Preferred stockholders were to pay a $25 assessment, for which new preferred stock would be given. The new company was to issue $20,000,000 of common stock and $5,000,000 of preferred stock with which to redeem outstanding issues of the same par value. The old bond issues, $10,000,000 of first mortgage and $5,000,000 of second mortgage were to be redeemed by an equal amount of new bonds and $2,500,000 more of new bonds were to be sold to finance needed improvements. These bonds and the assessments would provide $3,000,000 with which to pay the debts of the old company and another $3,000,000 for working capital. Despite the fact that fixed charges, if dividends on the preferred stock be included in that category, would be increased,[16] the plan was speedily put into effect [17] and at midnight, August 31, 1895, the company emerged from receivership as the New England Railroad.[18]

Rumor had said that J. P. Morgan was directing the reorganization but confirmation of this was lacking until almost a month after the new company had been established. Then

13 *Railway World*, March 18, 1893, pp. 252-3.

14 *Ibid.*, December 30, 1893, p. 1225; *Commercial and Financial Cronicle*, December 30, 1893, p. 1098.

15 *Railway World*, February 3, 1894, p. 86.

16 *Railway Age and Northwestern Railroader*, April 27, 1894, p. 238; *Railway Review*, February 2, 1894, p. 69 and April 28, 1894, p. 251.

17 *Railway World*, April 28, 1894, p. 384.

18 *Ibid.*, September 7, 1895, p. 511.

suddenly Morgan announced that he had bought control by open market stock purchases the previous spring. He intended, he added, to offer this controlling interest to the New Haven at the same price which he had paid for it.[19] At the October meeting of the New Haven President Clarke declared that a majority of the New England's stock " was in this building ", but refused to amplify his statement other than to indicate that the new member of the system would be separately operated at least temporarily.[20]

With this acquisition the New Haven became the dominant railroad system of southern New England, indeed nearly the only system in that region.[21] From a road controlling 508 miles of track and with capital liabilities of $25,000,000 in 1892, in five depression years it had grown to a system of 2017 miles capitalized at $80,477,600.[22] The bulk of its business consisted of goods and travel necessary to the everyday life of New England,[23] so that the amount of its traffic fluctuated very little and even in the worst days of depression it was able to pay the customary 8 per cent dividend.[24]

Just as during the depression years the New Haven established itself as the predominant transportation company of southern New England, so in northern New England the Boston & Maine was able to consolidate its position at the same time. It had started on a career of expansion in 1887 when it obtained control of the Boston & Lowell for 99 years in return for a guarantee of the latter's usual 7 per cent dividend until 1897, after which the dividend was to be 8 per cent.[25] In 1890

19 *Ibid.*, September 28, 1895, pp. 572-3.

20 *Ibid.*, October 12, 1895, pp. 615, 622-3.

21 Meade, " Great Railways," *Railway World*, 1905, pp. 235-6; 63rd Congress, 2nd Session, *Senate Document, no. 543, Evidence Taken before the Interstate Commerce Commission Relative to the Financial Transactions of the New York, New Haven & Hartford...*, 1914.

22 Brandeis, *op. cit.*, pp. 121-2.

23 Meade, " Great Railways," *Railway World*, 1905, pp. 235-6.

24 *Poor's Manual*, 1900, pp. 1268-85.

25 Van Oss, *op. cit.*, pp. 361-2.

it absorbed the Eastern Railroad of Massachusetts and the Portsmouth, Great Falls & Conway Railroad, which had formerly been leased. These acquisitions transformed what had hitherto been an unimportant local carrier into a major system controlling more than 1800 miles of track in northern New England.[26]

The company had been another of the roads which McLeod had dreamed of combining to form his future great Philadelphia & Reading system, and it had passed under his control early in 1893. He had been made president of the Boston & Maine at that time, but his regime did not last for long. When the Reading receivers sold the New England stock which had been acquired at such a bitter price, McLeod lost his influence in the Boston & Maine and immediately resigned both as president and director.[27]

In 1899 the company made another important acquisition: the Fitchburg Railroad was leased for 99 years. It had been subsidized to build a line from Boston to Albany where it met the Erie and the Delaware & Hudson.[28] One further addition to the system was made in 1901 when the Central Massachusetts Railroad was purchased,[29] but that was the last important change until it was absorbed by the New Haven in 1907.[30] Since the Boston & Maine had the same kind of business as the New Haven mostly freight and travel necessary to New England's daily life [31] it was able to continue paying high dividends throughout the depression. In 1894 8 per cent returns had to be abandoned in favor of 6 per cent ones, but in 1899 a 6¼ per cent dividend presaged the resumption of the former high rate.[32]

26 *Ibid.*, pp. 362-3.

27 *Railway World*, May 27, 1893, p. 481, June 10, 1893, p. 533.

28 Van Oss, *op. cit.*, pp. 364-6.

29 Snyder, *op. cit.*, pp. 110-7.

30 *Ibid.*, p. 110.

31 Meade, "Great Railways," *Railway World*, 1905, pp. 215-6.

32 Poor, *op. cit.*, 1900, pp. 1268-85.

Closely connected with the leading New England systems were the Vanderbilt interests. The Boston & Albany Railroad was the northeastern outpost of the Vanderbilt railroad empire and, through it and the New York Central, the Vanderbilts in 1896 bought $1,000,000 of stock in the New England Railroad to prevent the New Haven from encroaching too far south into their territory.[33]

The Vanderbilt system originated from the purchase by Commodore Vanderbilt in 1851 of the New York Central Railroad, and since the Civil War expansion had been a keynote of its policy; the Chicago & Northwestern, the Michigan Central & Canada Southern, the Lake Shore & Michigan Southern, the New York, Chicago & St. Louis, the Boston & Albany and a number of smaller roads, had been added to make the total mileage more than 15,500 by 1893.[34] Huge and diverse though it was, this system was one of the best managed in the country and every important link in it weathered the depression without undue difficulty.

The New York Central in the year ending June 30, 1893, had the largest gross and net earnings in its history, met its sinking fund payments, paid the usual 5 per cent dividend on its common stock and carried a small surplus over into the following year.[35] During the next twelve months the road began to feel the effects of the depression but because of the splendid physical condition of the roadbeds and rolling stock it was able to counterbalance a 7 per cent loss in gross receipts by an almost equal reduction in operating expenses. Net earnings decreased less than 3½ per cent and were still large enough to provide a 4¼ per cent dividend on the common stock; since the usual 5 per cent was paid, there was a deficit of $786,340 to be

33 *Railway World*, January 25, 1896, p. 74.

34 Snyder, *op. cit.*, pp. 471-80; Van Oss, *op. cit.*, pp. 192-210.

35 *Annual Report of the New York Central & Hudson River Railroad*, 1893; *Commercial and Financial Chronicle*, September 30, 1893, pp. 352-3.

taken out of accumulated surplus.[36] The comparative strength
of the New York Central's position was emphasized by the
contemporaneous losses of some of its chief rivals: while the
Central lost 6.60 per cent and 2.89 per cent in gross and net
earnings respectively in the first eleven months of the depression, the Erie, which relied to a large degree on the coal industry for freight, showed a decrease of 13.73 per cent in
gross and of 21.78 per cent in net; the lines of the Pennsylvania Railroad east of Pittsburgh and Erie, which depended
largely on the iron and steel industry and to a lesser degree
on coal for freight, lost 15.06 per cent in gross and 10.67 per
cent in net.[37] The Central, independent of any one industry and
gathering freight from widely scattered points, was able to
thrive while its rivals weakened as the depression struck coal,
iron and steel plants with especial severity.

The strength and stability of the Central was further proven
in May, 1895, when J. P. Morgan in one day sold 45,717 shares
of New York Central Stock in London at 105.[38] Despite a reduction of the dividend rate from 5 per cent to 4¼ in 1895 and
to 4 in 1896,[39] the faith exhibited by London investors was
merited. In the last quarter of 1895 considerable improvement
had been manifest in the gross earnings of the company. Operating expenses had risen almost as much as receipts, but this
was a sign of efficient and conservative management for improvements which had been postponed during the two previous
years were now being made in expectation of heavier traffic.[40]
In 1899 the dividend rate began to rise again [41] and by 1902

36 *Annual Report*, 1894; *Commercial and Financial Chronicle*, June 30,
1894, pp. 1090-1 and September 29, 1894, pp. 533-5.

37 *Commercial and Financial Chronicle*, April 7, 1894, pp. 573-5.

38 *Ibid.*, May 18, 1895, p. 952.

39 *Annual Report*, 1896; Poor, *op. cit.*, 1900, pp. 1268-85.

40 *Annual Report*, 1896; *Commercial and Financial Chronicle*, December
21, 1895, pp. 1086-7.

41 Poor, *op. cit.*, 1900, pp. 1268-85.

the Central was able to sell $17,250,000 of stock at 125, which represented a 25 per cent premium.[42]

The most important subsidiary of the New York Central, the Lake Shore & Michigan Southern, held jointly with the Great Northern, the Illinois Central and the Pennsylvania Railroad the distinction of being one of the few large systems not to reduce dividends between 1893 and 1898.[43] The efficiency of its management was reflected in a boast, which it maintained throughout the depression, that since 1884 not a cent had been charged to the Construction and Equipment capital accounts; all betterments and extensions had been financed out of income. Furthermore, the $50,000,000 total capitalization of the company had not been altered since 1871.[44]

Despite the already generally prevalent depression for the year ending December 31, 1893, the Lake Shore showed the largest gross and net receipts in its history, and earned 6.46 per cent on its stock, although only the usual 6 per cent was paid. The most encouraging factor of all was an increase of 240,459 tons in the amount of general merchandise which was carried.[45] This growth betokened the transformation of the region served by the company from an agricultural to an industrial community, and this change meant that the Lake Shore would no longer be as dependent as it hitherto had been on the wheat crop for its freight tonnage. Diversified freight meant a steadier income.[46]

The inherent strength of the company was well illustrated in 1894 when for the first time it felt the depression. Gross receipts fell 17.43 per cent but by reducing operating expenses

42 Sakolski, A. M., *American Railroad Economics*, pp. 262.

43 Poor, *op. cit.*, 1900, pp. 1268-85.

44 *Annual Report of the Lake Shore & Michigan Southern Railroad*, 1899; *Commercial and Financial Chronicle*, May 6, 1893, pp. 733-4; May 4, 1895, pp. 773-4.

45 *Annual Report*, 1893; *Commercial and Financial Chronicle*, May 5, 1894; pp. 754-5.

46 *Ibid.*, July 1, 1893, pp. 6-8.

23 per cent the loss in net was held to less than 3 per cent. After all fixed charges had been paid and all improvements charged against operating expenses, the 6 per cent dividend had been fully earned. That such a drastic reduction in expenses could be effected without impairing the road's operating efficiency was a tribute to the past efforts of the management. A large part of the saving was made simply by not buying any new equipment or constructing any new sidings.[47] Before the end of 1895 business again began to pick up and the Lake Shore gradually emerged from the depression without having reduced its dividends or having increased its capital by charging betterments to it.[48] The officials of the road had demonstrated what American railroad management could accomplish and had achieved results which rivalled those James J. Hill was achieving in the Northwest at the same time.

So well had the Vanderbilt system come through the depression that in the years immediately following it was able to inaugurate a new campaign of expansion. Between 1898 and 1900 not only was a large interest purchased in the Cleveland, Cincinnati, Chicago & St. Louis, but the community of interest idea was inaugurated in cooperation with the Pennsylvania and the Morgan-Hill interests in an effort to create a lasting harmony among the Eastern trunk lines.[49]

The Pennsylvania Railroad, which was the only real rival to the Vanderbilt system, passed through the depression with a similar degree of success. It had been chartered in 1848 and the main line, which was built by the state, was opened in 1854. The road lost money so steadily that in 1857 it was sold to the present company.[50] In 1893 the system consisted of two main divisions, the Pennsylvania Railroad Company, which operated

47 *Annual Report*, 1894; *Commercial and Financial Chronicle*, May 4, 1894, pp. 773-4.

48 *Annual Report*, 1898.

49 Meade, "Great Railways," *Railway World*, 1904, pp. 147-9, 175-6.

50 Snyder, *op. cit.*, pp. 542-65.

or controlled through stock ownership the lines east of Pittsburgh and Erie and held all the securities of the subsidiary Pennsylvania Company, which in turn either leased or controlled by stock ownership the lines of the system west of Pittsburgh and Erie.[51]

The annual report covering the whole system for the year ending December 31, 1893, showed that a policy of strict economy had been adopted until the depression should pass and listed several recent additions to the system. The extension of the second, third, and fourth tracks on the main line east of Pittsburgh and the doubling of the track west of Pittsburgh had been suspended as soon as the depression had become noticeable. Piers numbers 3, 4 and 5 on the North River in New York City, for which a large rental had hitherto been paid, had been purchased; the funds with which to pay for them had been raised by selling bonds which were secured by mortgages on the piers. A majority of the outstanding stock of the Clearfield County & New York Short Route Railroad had been bought in order to obviate the need of continuing an expensive lease. A controlling stock interest had been purchased in the Terre Haute & Indianapolis Railroad Company, which leased the St. Louis, Vandalia & Terre Haute Railroad; this road had been built jointly by the Pennsylvania and the Terre Haute & Indianapolis, but had been controlled and operated by the latter. This purchase gave the Pennsylvania a new 637-mile subsidiary, and extended the system to St. Louis. Control of the Toledo, Peoria & Western was bought to improve the connection between the Pennsylvania's southwestern lines and the Granger roads running into Chicago. Purchases of several other small lines rounded out the year's activities.[52] This expansionist policy, with its emphasis on the acquisition of various small roads which would serve as feeders or connecting

51 Van Oss, *op. cit.*, pp. 235-67.

52 *Railway World*, March 10, 1894, pp. 194-6; *Commercial and Financial Chronicle*, March 10, 1894, pp. 411-3.

links, was typical of the methods by which the great Pennsylvania network had been built up.[53]

Gross and net earnings had fallen in 1893 but in both cases the loss was less than 3 per cent and the figures which were included in the system's balance sheet were still almost astronomical: gross earnings of more than $135,000,000; net earnings of more than $39,500,000 and an accumulated surplus, after the usual 5 per cent dividend and a special 2 per cent stock dividend had been paid, of $26,478,152.[54]

During the following year gross income dropped about $16,-500,000 more but operating expenses were cut $13,097,186, so that the decrease in net earnings was only $3,429,384. Extraordinary repairs, such as elevating tracks to eliminate grade crossings in cities, cost $1,385,271. However, even after these expenses had been met the full 5 per cent dividend was earned and paid and a surplus of $895,100 was carried forward into the following year. The past conservative policy of the company, which had been to pay moderate dividends and use all surplus earnings to keep the equipment in good shape, was responsible for the dividends paid during the depression; only the excellent condition of the rolling stock and roadbeds in 1893 permitted a sharp decrease in renewal expenditures without an accompanying deterioration of the property.[55]

The conservatism of the management was further emphasized during the depression by its policy towards unprofitable subsidiaries. Unlike so many of its rivals, the Pennsylvania refused to pour its own profits into endless branch-line deficits; if subsidiaries could not pay their way it let them fall into the hands of receivers and then reorganized them on a profitable basis. When in April, 1893, the Western New York & Pennsylvania Railroad was unable to meet the interest payments on

53 *Interstate Commerce Commission Statistics*, 1889, p. 78, gives tabular history of growth of Pennsylvania up to 1890.

54 *Commercial and Financial Chronicle*, March 10, 1894, pp. 411-3.

55 *Ibid.*, March 9, 1895, pp. 412-4.

its second mortgage bonds, it was placed under the protection of the courts without waiting until the discretionary nine months' period of grace had expired.[56] Reorganization plans were formulated [57] at once and on February 5, 1895, the road was bought by the reorganization committee at a foreclosure sale.[58] The reorganization was drastic but it was correspondingly effective. The funded debt was reduced from $34,821,802 to $29,990,000; the par value of outstanding stock was reduced from $30,000,000 to $20,000,000. Fixed charges were cut from $1,114,060 to a maximum of $914,960. The advantages derived from these changes were reflected in a surplus over fixed charges and taxes of more than $300,000 in the following year, despite a drop in the freight rate per ton mile from 0.5662 cents to 0.4903 cents.[59] Since the road was an indispensible link in the Pennsylvania system and operated about 650 miles of track, its newly found prosperity was of major importance to the parent company.

The Grand Rapids & Indiana Railroad Company was subjected to similar treatment. As soon as it threatened to become a chronic liability its insolvency was acknowledged and foreclosure proceedings were instituted by the parent company. As the Grand Rapids & Indiana Railway Company, the line emerged from its receivership on August 1, 1896, upon a financial foundation better suited to its earning potentialities. Since it controlled nearly 600 miles of track in Michigan, the retention of a majority of its stock, to which the reorganization had given an intrinsic value, was distinctly advantageous to the Pennsylvania.[60]

56 *Ibid.*, April 8, 1893, p. 556; November 4, 1894, pp. 45-6.

57 *Railway World*, June 9, 1894, p. 456.

58 *Ibid.*, February 9, 1895, p. 101; *Commercial and Financial Chronicle*, October 26, 1895, p. 726.

59 *Interstate Commerce Commission Statistics*, 1895, pp. 94-6.

60 Schotter, H. W., *The Growth and Development of the Pennsylvania Railroad Company*, Philadelphia: Allen, 1927, 2 volumes, pp. 243-4, 253.

Without being forced to alter its customary dividend payments,[61] the Pennsylvania weathered the depression as well as any system in the country. Expenses had been reduced in large part by postponing repairs on the roadbed and rolling stock as long as possible. By 1897 the inventory showed that supplies were being exhausted and customers were becoming disgruntled at the resulting impairment of efficiency. So in 1899 under a new president, Alexander J. Cassatt, the Pennsylvania embarked on a rehabilitation and improvement program which would have bankrupted any company less sound financially.

As was usually the case with high officers of the Pennsylvania, Cassatt had worked his way up through the ranks, although at the time of his election to the presidency he had been in retirement for seventeen years. Born in Pittsburgh in 1839 of wealthy Scotch-Irish parentage, he had studied in Pittsburgh, in Europe at Darmstadt University and finally had been graduated from Rensselaer Polytechnic Institute as a civil engineer in 1859. He spent a couple of years as engineering assistant locating a railway right-of-way in Georgia, then joined the engineering department of the Pennsylvania Railroad in 1861. By 1870 he had become general superintendent of his department and he was among the first in this country to see the value of air brakes for railroads. In 1873 he was promoted to be general manager of the Pennsylvania's lines east of Pittsburgh and Erie and a year later he became vice-president in charge of transportation and traffic. In 1880 he was made first vice-president and was in line for the presidency but in 1882 he retired from active duty, although he retained his directorship in the company. Despite the fact that he had retired in order to indulge his hobby of stock-farming, he was persuaded to help build the New York, Philadelphia & Norfolk Railroad and was its president from 1885 to 1899, when the Pennsylvania directors recalled him to the presidency of their company.

61 Poor, *op. cit.*, 1900, pp. 1268-85.

His parents had been wealthy enough that Cassatt need never have taken his engineering career seriously had he not wished to do so and he never emulated some of his colleagues in excluding all other interests from his life. For nineteen years he was road supervisor in his home town, Merion, Pennsylvania, and he was one of the two or three leading patrons of the American turf. After racing fell into disrepute in this country he turned to horse breeding. Throughout his life he was interested in many sports, particularly cricket, hunting and yachting.[62]

When the directors called him in 1899 it was to guide the Pennsylvania on its rehabilitation and improvement program. In the next ten years half a billion dollars were spent to build a new freight line from Pittsburgh to the Atlantic coast, to enlarge congested freight yards, to elevate tracks in Pittsburgh, to build freight classification yards, to construct fourth and fifth tracks for long freight hauls, to build a new freight terminal in Pittsburgh, and last but perhaps the greatest achievement of all, to tunnel under the Hudson River and for the first time in its history permit the Pennsylvania to discharge passengers and freight in New York City at the New Pennsylvania Station. So well established was the reputation of the company that this huge program was financed entirely by the sale of bonds at low interest rates and of stock, some of which sold as high as 120. Before the work was finished, with the help of Kuhn, Loeb & Company, Pennsylvania securities had been sold all over the world, even in the Far East. And all this was done without changing the dividend rate.[63]

Although three of the large Eastern coal carriers, the Erie, the Reading and the Norfolk & Western, failed during the depression, a number of their smaller competitors fared much better. The two most successful were the Delaware & Hudson

62 *Dictionary of American Biography*, III, pp. 564-7.

63 Sakolski, *op. cit.*, p. 262; Keys, C. M., "Cassatt and his Vision," *World's Work*, 1910, XX, pp. 13187-204.

and the Delaware, Lackawanna & Western. The former owned, leased or controlled a canal and rail system of 727 miles: from Wilkes-Barre in the heart of the Pennsylvania anthracite region tracks ran to Albany and north to Rouse's Point; barges went down the Hudson River from Albany to New York City and through canals to Honesdale on the eastern border of the coal fields.[64] Despite the severe competition it faced, throughout the depression the company paid its usual liberal 7 per cent dividend without fail.[65] The Delaware, Lackawanna & Western Railroad was equally prosperous. It was connected through common directors and stockholders with the short-lived Reading combination but its branch tracks into the anthracite region near Scranton were less important than its Buffalo-New York City line which carried a prosperous local business. In 1893 the company became closely related to the Vanderbilt system through the purchase by the Vanderbilts of a large stock interest.[66] Aided by this new affiliation, it also was able to pay 7 per cent dividends all during the depression.[67]

After its reorganization in 1887 the Central Railroad of New Jersey had gradually increased its dividend rate until, in 1892 at the time it was leased to the Reading, it was paying 7 per cent.[68] Although the Reading lease was terminated by court order on August 31, 1892,[69] the dissolution had been of little importance to the Central. Its lines were fortunately situated in the densely populated parts of the Middle Atlantic states, with terminals in Philadelphia, New York City, and

64 Van Oss, *op. cit.*, pp. 302-4; Snyder, *op. cit.*, pp. 263-72; *Commercial and Financial Chronicle, Investors Supplement*, March, 1893, p. 50.

65 *Commercial and Financial Chronicle*, January 16, 1897, p. 107.

66 *Railway World*, October 28, 1893, p. 1019; *Railway Age and Northwestern Railroader*, November 3, 1893, p. 801; *Commercial and Financial Chronicle, Investors Supplement*, March, 1893, p. 52.

67 *Commercial and Financial Chronicle*, January 16, 1897, p. 107.

68 *Annual Report of the Central Railroad of New Jersey*, 1892; *Commercial and Financial Chronicle*, January 16, 1897, p. 107.

69 *Annual Report*, 1893; *Commercial and Financial Chronicle*, February 25, 1893, pp. 313-4.

the anthracite fields of Pennsylvania. Since most of its business was local, the effects of the depression were less severely felt than might have been the case if the company had depended on the anthracite industry for its prosperity.[70] The 7 per cent dividends were continued through 1894 but thereafter they had to be reduced and by 1896 only 5 per cent was being paid.[71] Gross earnings had continued to increase during 1893 and at the end of the year there had been a surplus of more than $500,000 to be carried forward.[72] However, in 1894 this surplus and more was needed to make up the deficit of $642,702 which had resulted from the payment of the regular 7 per cent dividend.[73] The reduction of dividend payments in the following year to an amount more nearly proportionate to earnings placed the company in a strong position which was maintained until the Reading bought control in 1901 and replaced the former management with its own officials.[74]

The last of the members of the Reading combination to regain its independence was the Lehigh Valley Railroad; it managed to survive the depression but it could not emulate the prosperity of its rivals in the anthracite trade. The company had begun to pay 5 per cent dividends in 1888 and it had increased the rate to 5¼ per cent in 1892,[75] but after the Reading lease had been cancelled dividends were suspended, not to be resumed for seven years.[76]

In an effort to increase the road's revenues, several through-traffic agreements were made in the months following its separation from the Reading system. The Lehigh's tracks ran from Buffalo and Fairhaven, near Oswego on Lake Erie, southeast

---

70 *Ibid., Investors' Supplement*, March, 1893, p. 23.

71 *Ibid.*, January 16, 1897, p. 107.

72 *Ibid.*, March 3, 1894, pp. 366-7.

73 *Ibid.*, March 2, 1895, pp. 369-70.

74 Snyder, *op. cit.*, pp. 147-55.

75 *Commercial and Financial Chronicle*, January 16, 1897, p. 107.

76 Snyder, *op. cit.*, pp. 396-405.

to the anthracite coal fields, where a maze of branch lines sprawled around Scranton, Mauch Chunk and Pottsville and met a connecting canal-rail link to Staten Island opposite New York City.[77] Soon after the Reading lease had been abrogated an accord was made with the Vanderbilts whereby Lehigh coal and other freight entered New England over the New York, New Haven & Hartford tracks. A second arrangement severed the former close relations of the Lehigh and the Jersey Central; instead of entering New York City over the latter's lines, a new alliance permitted the Lehigh to use the Pennsylvania's tracks for that purpose. The third agreement was with Coxe Brothers, the independent anthracite operators. They shipped most of their coal on their own subsidiary, the Delaware, Susquehanna & Schuylkill Railroad, but before the Reading's receivership the latter had carried any of it which was destined to New York City. Believing that the Reading was not getting a fair share of the profits, the receivers had abrogated the contract and for a short time the Jersey Central took over the job. By a new agreement between the Lehigh and Coxe Brothers, technically the former's tracks were to be used by the Delaware, Susquehanna & Schuylkill, but practically the contract increased the Lehigh Valley's coal output about 1,000,000 tons per year.[78]

Even after these new arrangements had been made the company was not in a very strong position; its floating debt was assuming inconvenient proportions, new capital was needed for improvements and too much of its paper was being traded in on the market. A controlling interest in the road was owned by the estate of Asa Packer, former president of the road; with these holdings as security the debts of the estate, amounting to about $2,000,000, had been funded and traded in on the stock market for over forty years but by 1897 these notes

77 Van Oss, *op. cit.*, p. 299.

78 *Annual Report of the Lehigh Valley Railroad*, 1894; *Railway World*, February 17, 1894, p. 125.

were beginning to depreciate. Just at that time an attack was made on Lehigh securities in the market, supposedly with the intention of forcing them down sufficiently to compel the Packer estate to sell its stock to prevent depreciation of the notes.

In this crisis a deal was made with Messrs. Drexel & Company, the Philadelphia branch of the Morgan firm, by which Morgan refunded the Packer debts and in return was given the voting power of the estate's Lehigh stock. In addition the finances of the Lehigh Valley were to be reorganized: a new series of 5 per cent bonds secured by all unencumbered assets was to be created; of these $5,000,000 were to be issued at once and $3,000,000 more as needed in the next three years; for seven years after 1899 the company was permitted to increase the issue by $1,000,000 annually. This last $7,000,000 could only be used to purchase property which would then be included under the mortgage. Proceeds from the $5,000,000 of bonds to be issued at once were to be used to pay the floating debt of about $2,500,000, to buy badly needed new equipment and to provide working capital. The Packer estate notes would be removed from the marked immediately and, in exchange, a voting trust would be created by Morgan to hold the estate's 150,000 shares, which constituted one-sixth of the outstanding Lehigh stock and was enough to assure control of the company. The voting trust would last as long as the collateral trust notes were outstanding; they were made for one hundred years but could be called at any time for 107½ plus current interest.[79]

This refunding agreement removed all danger of a receivership but it almost necessarily meant a change in the Lehigh's management. In July President Wilbur resigned and was succeeded by Morgan's nominee, Alfred Walter. At the same time, to fill vacancies created by resignations, three Morgan representatives were elected to the board of directors: Edward T. Stotesbury of Drexel & Company, C. H. Coster of Messrs.

79 *Railway World*, March 13, 1897, pp. 261-2, 264-5.

J. P. Morgan & Company, and former President Wilbur. The important finance committee of the new board consisted of the three new directors and one other.[80]

With his control of the Lehigh thus assured, Morgan came nearer to having an absolute monopoly of the anthracite coal industry than McLeod's Reading combination ever had. Together with the Vanderbilts Morgan controlled the Reading and the Erie after their respective reorganizations; the Vanderbilts and the Astors controlled the Delaware & Hudson, and with the First National Bank interests they controlled the Delaware, Lackawanna & Western; the First National interests controlled the Central of New Jersey. These railroads controlled 74.8 per cent of the anthracite which reached tidewater; the Pennsylvania Railroad, controlling 11.4 per cent more, was the only considerable factor in the industry not included in the group,[81] and the development of a community of interest between it and the Vanderbilt system in the course of the next few years made it a partner in the monopoly to all intents and purposes.

In the Mid-west one of the roads which rivalled the records of these Eastern lines was the Illinois Central. It had been chartered in 1851 and in 1867 started on a career of expansion which by the early nineties had given it control of more than 3600 miles of main line between Chicago and New Orleans and branches criss-crossing the Mississippi Valley.[82] In 1892 an expert believed that:

The property of the Illinois Central has until recently not been in particularly good condition; in fact the ultra-conservative management failed to introduce those improvements which were necessary to keep the road up to the requirements of the times. . . . Owing to its moderate capitalization the Illinois Central has always offered good returns upon its capital. Its bonds, the interest

80 *Ibid.*, July 17, 1897, pp. 712-3.
81 *Ibid.*, March 13, 1897, pp. 261-2, 264-5.
82 Snyder, *op. cit.*, pp. 360-9.

of which has invariably been promptly paid, rank among the gilt-edged securities, and its shares have always offered a good interest.[83]

The improvements which had been made during the eighties resulted mainly from the efforts of a new member of the board of directors, the still comparatively unknown Edward H. Harriman. He had been elected to the board in May, 1883, and almost simultaneously the hitherto over-cautious management began to made widespread improvements. By 1893 about 1500 miles of track had been added to the system; new passenger cars, locomotives and freight cars had been bought or built in large quantities; and the gross receipts had more than doubled. While this lavish outlay was being made the regular annual dividends on the stock were paid without fail. But after January, 1890, no new improvements were undertaken. Harriman, who had become vice-president of the company in 1887, had always favored generous expenditures for betterments. Now he astonished the directors by his strong opposition to a projected three and one-half year program which they had approved while he was temporarily absent. After some insistence he carried his point, much to the company's ultimate advantage; instead of being caught in the middle of a huge improvement program by the panic of 1893, the Illinois Central was well prepared to face a prolonged period of depression. It was so sound financially that in August, 1895, it successfully floated a $2,500,000 bond issue at only 3 per cent interest.[84]

The benefits which accrue to a strong company in time of depression were illustrated by the Illinois Central's purchase of the Chesapeake, Ohio & Southwestern late in 1893. This road which connected Louisville and Nashville, had been built by Collis P. Huntington in the expectation that it would form a link in his projected super-trunk line from Newport News to

83 Van Oss, *op. cit.*, pp. 731-2.
84 Kennan, *Harriman*, I, pp. 69-80, 88-95.

San Francisco. When his associates in the Southern Pacific later forced him to divert the main line to New Orleans, the Southwestern was left an isolated member of the system. As such it could not be made to pay and finally defaulted on its bonds. Huntington rid himself of the unprofitable investment and wholly withdrew his interests west of the Mississippi, by selling a controlling interest in it to the Illinois Central for $5,000,000. Thereby at a cheap price the Central acquired a nearly direct line to Memphis, 43 miles shorter than its previous route.[85]

Not only was the Illinois Central fortunate in concluding its long program for the betterment of the system just in time to face the depression in excellent physical condition and with a decreasing expense account, but the location of its lines provided a second advantage in the struggle against the hard times of the nineties. Because its main tracks ran north and south the Central tapped the cotton, rice and sugar regions of the South and at the same time penetrated the great Mid-Western grain fields and the industrial sections around Chicago. Therefore poor crops in one region or an industrial slump in another did not reduce the earnings of the system so much as otherwise might have been the case. Only when nearly all crops and industries suffered simultaneously could the income account decline seriously.[86] It was in good part due to this diversification in its freight traffic that the company was able to go through the depression without lowering its dividend rate.[87]

Although they were unable to rival the Illinois Central's dividend record, nevertheless the roads collectively known as the Grangers also weathered the depression without much difficulty. Among these systems, all of which centered in

85 *Railway Age and Northwestern Railroader*, November 10, 1893, p. 817; *Railway World*, December 23, 1893, p. 1203; Meade, "Great Railways," *Railway World*, 1904, pp. 433-5.

86 *Commercial and Financial Chronicle*, January 8, 1893, p. 103, September 30, 1893, pp. 533-4.

87 Poor, *op. cit.*, pp. 1268-85.

Chicago, the three most important were the Chicago & Alton Railroad, the Chicago, Burlington & Quincy and the Chicago, Milwaukee & St. Paul.

The Chicago & Alton controlled 843 miles of mid-Western tracks in 1892. The stagnation which had characterized it for nearly twenty-five years was indicated by the negligible growth of its mileage from 840 in 1881 to 843 in 1898.[88] But despite this ultra-conservatism, in 1892 an observer could say that " for many years past this company has been conspicuous as financially the soundest to be found in the entire West, if not in the whole country." [89] The success of this small system, surrounded as it was by larger and more enterprising lines, was attributed to its compactness, its good connections with larger systems at important traffic centers, its excellent physical condition, its policy of financing betterments out of income, its efficient management and last but by no means least, its small capitalization.[90]

So strong was the credit of the company and so highly valued was its stock, which for thirty years had paid dividends averaging a little more than 8 per cent, that in August, 1893, when the panic was still at its height the company was able to pay maturing bonds in cash which was raised by selling stock. That cash came from the sale of stock which had a par value of $2,500,000 and had been offered to shareholders for $114 per share.[91]

A year after the depression had begun, the *Commercial and Financial Chronicle* thought that:

It has been only the company's excellent physical and financial condition that has enabled it to maintain its dividends under these various adverse influences. . . . President Blackstone points out (in the company's annual report for the year ending December 31,

88 Meade, " Great Railways," *Railway World*, 1905, pp. 356-8.

89 Van Oss, *op. cit.*, p. 514.

90 *Commercial and Financial Chronicle*, March 4, 1893, pp. 356-7.

91 *Railway Age and Northwestern Railroader*, August 18, 1893, p. 627.

1893) that during the last fifteen years the company has not added to the length of its lines and has had no occasion to borrow money. It has, he says, in each year expended from $250,000 to $500,000 in increasing the capacity of the road and its equipment and in making such improvements as would add to the safety and comfort of its patrons and promote economy in maintaining and operating the company. While it can hardly be said that any American company ever is completed, the Alton, Mr. Blackstone thinks, may be considered as nearly completed as any road in the country.[92]

Even the London *Economist* praised the Alton's management:

It is a remarkable fact that about the most conservative of American railroad corporations belongs to the group of Western systems which, in the past quarter of a century have furnished so many instances of reckless and unprofitable extensions, of constant borrowing, and of perpetual anxiety on the part of investors. The Chicago & Alton Railroad Company, though an important member of the inharmonious family of " Granger " roads, has been managed by methods as different from those of its neighbors and competitors as night is from day. . . . The chief interest in the property is, however, found in the contrast which its management and their policy afford to those of the general run of American railways. The facts in this connection may be summed up by saying (1), that the executive officials and directors are heavily interested in the stock, and (2), that they operate the road with a view to earning and paying dividends on the shares. In this period in which so much has been and should have been written as to careless, inefficient, not to say vicious railway management in the United States, it may not be considered entirely out of order to point out the fact that while there is much to criticize in the management of some American railways, there are also some things to commend.[93]

Coming from the usually hostile *Economist,* this was praise of which any railroad official might well be proud.

92 *Commercial and Financial Chronicle,* February 24, 1894, pp. 323-4.

93 *Economist,* March 3, 1894, pp. 267-8.

The regular dividend rate of 8 per cent on all the road's stock was maintained until 1897; in the second quarter of that year it was reduced to 7, at which it remained for the next few years.[94] In 1899, after the management had piloted the road through the depression so successfully, it sold a controlling stock interest to Harriman, who paid $40,000,000 for stock of $22,000,000 par value and bonds worth $8,000,000 at par. The change of ownership was necessitated by the road's utter isolation in a period of great systems and by the cut-throat competition which they engendered. Under Harriman the company's capitalization was more than tripled in order to finance extensions and betterments.[95]

The Chicago, Burlington & Quincy had been chartered under the name of the Central Military Track Railroad Company in 1851. It had assumed its later name in 1856 and by the early seventies a period of steady expansion had brought it control of more than 6500 miles of track.[96] This system as did so many others, counterbalanced the decreased earnings which characterized the depression years with nearly proportional reductions of operating expenses. The *Commercial and Financial Chronicle* paid tribute to its capacity for adjusting itself to circumstances with the comment that:

The annual report of the Chicago, Burlington & Quincy for 1893 shows that this company has passed through a year of depression just about as we should expect in the case of a property of its strength and excellent physical and financial condition.

By careful management the company had been able not only to pay the usual 5 per cent dividend, but it also was able to carry a small surplus over into the succeeding year.[97] In the

94 Poor, *op. cit.*, 1900, pp. 1268-85.

95 Keys, C. M., "Harriman," *World's Work*, 1907, XIII, pp. 8455-64, 8536-52, 8651-64, 8791-803.

96 Snyder, *op. cit.*, pp. 191-8; Van Oss, *op. cit.*, pp. 494-502.

97 *Annual Report of the Chicago, Burlington & Quincy Railroad*, 1893; *Commercial and Financial Chronicle*, March 31, 1894, pp. 532-3.

third quarter of 1894 the dividend basis for the year was reduced to 4 per cent, but there was no further change in it until the middle of 1898 when the annual payments were increased to 6 per cent.[98]

The development most significant for the Burlington during the depression years was a transformation in the economic interests of the regions it traversed. In 1892 and 1893 bumper corn crops in the West had enabled it to show unprecedently high gross earnings, averaging $32,000,000 per year. Partial crop failures in 1894 and 1895 had been reflected in average gross earnings for those years of only about $24,000,000. But by 1900 the Burlington's dependence on the corn crop was a thing of the past: when a bumper crop was harvested in that year, the system grossed $47,000,000; although crops were even worse in the following two years than they had been in 1894 and 1895, the annual gross earnings jumped to $50,000,000 and then $53,000,000. The Burlington had ceased to be primarily a grain road and had developed a more diversified traffic as the mid-West became industrialized.[99] It was this diversified traffic which was gathered from the rich agricultural territories and equally wealthy iron and steel regions [100] in Nebraska, Kansas, Missouri, South Dakota, Iowa, Illinois and Wisconsin, that led to the abortive attempt by the Union Pacific to get control of the road in 1900 and to the successful efforts of Hill's Northern Pacific and Great Northern to buy a controlling stock interest at a price of $200 for each share of $100 par value.[101] The very fact that Hill was willing to pay so high a price testifies to the continuous success of the system throughout the depression.

The Chicago, Milwaukee & St. Paul Railroad had a less auspicious dividend record behind it than either of its two great

98 *Annual Reports*, 1894-8; Poor, *op. cit.*, 1900, pp. 1268-85.
99 Meade, "Great Railways," *Railway World*, 1904, pp. 899-900.
100 Pyle, *Hill*, II, p. 133.
101 *Ibid.*, II, pp. 103-133.

rivals. Organized during the Civil War,[102] in the middle eighties the road began to suffer from over-rapid expansion at a time when rates were rapidly declining. In 1888 it paid only a 2½ per cent dividend and in the next three years paid none at all because the board of directors refused to anticipate the development of new territory into which the road was expanding. This conservatism received its reward in the days of depression;[103] with a system totalling more than 6100 miles and governed by a board of directors which included Philip Armour, August Belmont and William Rockefeller,[104] the company survived the depression in excellent style. In 1892 a 2 per cent dividend had been paid; during the next two years this payment was doubled. In 1895 the road returned to a conservative 2 per cent basis but in 1896 4 per cent was paid and in the following three years this was increased to 5 per cent.[105]

The Chicago & Northwestern system, which controlled about 8000 miles of track,[106] made as good a record as did its Granger rivals. It was owned by the Vanderbilts and was managed on the same efficient principles that governed the New York Central and the Lake Shore. For the year ending June 30, 1893, net earnings had been double the combined total of bond interest and sinking fund payments.[107] Thereafter it suffered severely from the depression but still managed to show a profit each year. In 1894 the dividend payments were reduced from the former level of 6 per cent to only 3 per cent. However in 1895 a 1 per cent increase was voted and in the following year another increase brought the annual return up to 5 per cent.[108]

One of the great Mid-western systems probably least pre-

102 Snyder, *op. cit.*, p. 213.
103 Meade, " Great Railways," *Railway World*, 1904, pp. 1095-6.
104 Van Oss, *op. cit.*, pp. 463-77.
105 Poor, *op. cit.*, 1900, pp. 1268-85.
106 Van Oss, *op. cit.*, pp. 478-93.
107 *Commercial and Financial Chronicle*, August 19, 1893, pp. 275-6.
108 *Ibid.*, August 18, 1894, pp. 254-6, January 16, 1897, p. 107.

pared to face a prolonged depression was the Chicago, Rock Island & Pacific Railroad. In 1887 it had paid a 7 per cent dividend but thereafter the annual returns declined steadily for four years while the road transferred its field of major interest from the middle Northwest to the middle Southwest, in order to shift from a region thickly traversed by the Granger lines to one less exploited. A commentator testified to the wisdom of this change, despite the reduction of dividends it entailed, when he said:

this result was inseparable from a policy that cannot be designated otherwise than as expedient. The Rock Island was on the horns of a dilemma. It could continue its old course which would have led to slow financial deterioration; or it could change its policy any provide for a future supply of vitality by sacrificing part of its present prosperity. Which was the best it is easy to see.[109]

The transformation of the system was achieved by constructing new lines in the southern states. In 1887 the company had controlled 1384 miles of road; in 1892 it operated more than 3600 miles [110] and the expansion program had not yet been completed. On July 30, 1893, the last link in the new system was opened, a 1,112 mile line from Chicago to Forth Worth.[111] With this addition the Rock Island touched or traversed Illinois, Iowa, Missouri, Kansas, Nebraska, Colorado, the Indian Territory, Oklahoma and Texas. And in spite of the huge sums spent on new trackage, the company was capitalized at only about $29,000 per mile, a remarkably small amount considering the fine equipment it boasted.[112]

These new lines developed rapidly, especially in local trade which provides a sound basis for railroad prosperity.[113] Even

109 Van Oss, *op. cit.*, pp. 523-4.

110 *Railway Age*, June 16, 1893, p. 469.

111 *Ibid.*, July 28, 1893, p. 579.

112 *Ibid.*, June 16, 1893, p. 469.

113 *Commercial and Financial Chronicle*, June 17, 1893, pp. 992-4.

in the year ending March 31, 1894, which comprised the first twelve months of depression, the system showed increases in gross and net earnings and in surplus carried forward after 4 per cent dividends had been paid.[114] Nevertheless, as the depression continued it was forced to reduce its annual dividends to yearly payments of 2 per cent in 1895 and 1896.[115] However, in view of its unpreparedness for an extended period of hard times, the management did an exceptionally good job: entering a new territory, they not only enlarged their business so successfully that dividends were not suspended, but they also laid a foundation from which the company developed into one of the few great railroad systems in the country soon after the turn of the century.[116]

By expanding into the Southwest the Rock Island was poaching on the preserve which Jay Gould had marked out for his own in the later years of his life. The core of the Gould network was the Missouri Pacific, which had been chartered originally in 1849 and completed its main line to Kansas City in 1865. In 1876 a reorganization and the subsequent foreclosure sale gave Gould an opportunity to gain control of the company. He inaugurated an expansion policy which was temporarily halted in 1888 by the receivership of the Missouri, Kansas & Texas, one of the Missouri Pacific's more important subsidiaries.[117] Feeling quite rightly that the former's ruin had been caused by Gould's subordination of its welfare to that of the parent company, H. C. Cross reorganized it as a completely independent line. With terminals in Kansas City, St. Louis, Hannibal, Missouri, Houston and on the Gulf of Mexico, it was a natural complement to Gould's system but its

114 *Ibid.*, June 9, 1894, pp. 964-5.

115 *Ibid.*, January 16, 1897, p. 107.

116 Meade, "Great Railways," *Railway World*, 1905, pp. 27-8; Tittman, Edward D., "The Masters of Our Railways," *National Magazine*, Boston, 1905, pp. 65-82.

117 Snyder, *op. cit.*, pp. 456-68; Meade, "Great Railways," *Railway World*, 1904, pp. 491-3, 519-21.

new management preferred to ally it with the Burlington through an agreement for the interchange of traffic at St. Louis.[118]

This defection proved only a very temporary set back to Gould's expansion plans. After he had acquired the International & Great Northern in 1892, his system comprised more than 6100 miles of track. Its financial and physical condition was a mystery because

the Missouri Pacific is one of the very few companies that shirks publicity but there prevails a general belief that the dividend would not have been passed (in 1891) had not that course suited Mr. Gould's purpose. Fortunately that gentleman enjoys such a very small amount of confidence among bona fide investors that this class gives his securities a wide berth.[119]

The steady decline of dividends from payments of 7 per cent in 1887 to nothing in 1892 [120] indicated that all was not well. Under the circumstances the death of Jay Gould and the succession of his son, George J. Gould, to control of the system in 1892 [121] was probably fortunate. Public faith in the father had long since waned but the son was an experienced railroad man rather than a banker-pirate like his father.

As one writer phrased it, young Gould knew " his railways from ties to traffic, and from tariff to treasury ", having been active in railroad management from the age of fifteen. He had been born in 1864 and after finishing private school preferred entering business to going to college. Trained by his father to manage the family fortune, at twenty-eight he was in almost complete control of it after his father's death. The young president was a shy, unaggressive man, not entirely prepossessing; although never very strong, he was interested in

---

118 *Commercial and Financial Chronicle*, November 11, 1893, p. 786.

119 Van Oss, *op. cit.*, p. 594.

120 *Commercial and Financial Chronicle*, January 16, 1897, p. 107.

121 Titman, *op. cit.*

sports and did much to popularize polo in this country; in addition he showed an active interest in many other forms of athletics. In some ways his career resembled that of the legendary rich man's son; at one time he backed a musical comedy, was a director of the opera, kept up memberships in many clubs and successively married two actresses.[122]

Despite the change in administration the company narrowly escaped receivership; as early as April, 1893, insistent rumors had said that it would soon confess insolvency. Gould vigorously denied the truth of these assertions: the floating debt, he stated, amounted to only about $3,600,000 and it was held entirely by Russell Sage and himself; furthermore, there were enough securities on hand to pay it in full whenever the directors wished. The road was, he added, in better physical condition than ever before at that time of year. That Gould, in contrast to many of the railroad officials of the nineties, really meant his denials of impending bankruptcy was indicated a few weeks later when he filed suit against the St. Louis brokers who had started the rumors.[123]

Probably the road avoided a receivership only because Gould and Russell Sage held all of the floating debt.[124] Rates were steadily declining,[125] and despite rigid economy [126] the ratio of operating expenses and taxes to gross earnings rose from 78 per cent to a dangerously high $86\frac{1}{4}$ per cent.[127] As a result, the floating debt had increased to about $6,500,000 by the end of 1893 [128] and the rate of increase showed no sign of abat-

---

122 Parsons, *The Railways, the Trusts and the People*, pp. 236-7; *Dictionary of American Biography*, VII, pp. 450-1.

123 *Railway Age and Northwestern Railroader*, April 12, 1893, p. 330; *Railway World*, April 22, 1893, pp. 361-2.

124 Meade, "Great Railways," *Railway World*, 1904, pp. 491-3, 519-21.

125 *Commercial and Financial Chronicle*, March 25, 1893, pp. 484-5.

126 *Railway Age and Northwestern Railroader*, July 14, 1893, p. 547.

127 *Commercial and Financial Chronicle*, March 17, 1894, pp. 454-6.

128 *Ibid.*, March 17, 1894, pp. 454-6; *Annual Report of the Missouri Pacific*, 1894.

ing.[129] Early in March, 1895, the company finally announced a plan to provide for this debt which was inevitably a potential source of danger. The road would issue $13,000,000 of ten year 5 per cent collateral trust notes that were secured by assets which the company had held for years. These new securities would provide enough cash not only to take up the floating debt, but also to make good any losses which might be caused by poor traffic in the early months of the year.[130] When the Gould estate quickly agreed to take the whole issue, if any holders of the floating debt demurred at the proposed settlement, the success of the operation was assured.[131]

Dividends were not resumed until 1901 but this was a policy of sound, conservative management and not of necessity. Before any profits were divided the road was built up and expanded,[132] notably by the addition of the Central Branch of the Union Pacific and the Denver & Rio Grande.

The former was snatched out of the chaos which resulted from the collapse of the Union Pacific, but the latter was a still solvent and dangerous competitor.[133] The Rio Grande had been first organized in 1870; a default on interest payments brought a receivership in 1886 and " it was reorganized as the Denver & Rio Grande Railroad Company in such manner that no further financial embarrassments need be apprehended." [134] When the panic of 1893 occurred the road operated or controlled almost 1600 miles of track [135] under a conservative management. The year ending June 30, 1893, had been the most prosperous in its history and the floating debt had been

129 *Railway Age and Northwestern Railroader*, March 8, 1895, p. 122.

130 *Ibid.*, March 23, 1895, pp. 231-2.

131 *Ibid.*, July 19, 1895, p. 358.

132 Meade, "Great Railways," *Railway World*, 1904, pp. 491-3, 519-21.

133 Snyder, *op. cit.*, pp. 456-8.

134 Van Oss, *op. cit.*, pp. 677-8.

135 *Ibid.*, pp. 674-88.

completely paid.[136] But much of the road's traffic originated in the Southwestern silver states and soon the acute depression in that industry crippled the industrial life of the region. The Pueblo, Colorado, office had been very profitable, averaging gross monthly receipts of over $100,000; but by August, 1893, its income ranged below half that figure. Whereas formerly forty or fifty cars of freight were received weekly from Creede, and proportional numbers from other camps, now the mines were closed and none came through.[137]

On August 26 President Jefferies announced that

financial stringency, unsettled monetary problems, extraordinary depression in business and the temporary suspension of silver mining destroyed confidence, reduced traffic and revenues and forced upon the management immediate and radical retrenchments in every branch of service.[138]

But through careful and efficient management the road was able to meet all the demands made upon it. In July, 1893, as soon as the seriousness of the situation became apparent, dividends on the preferred stock were passed as a precautionary measure.[139] The year ending June 30, 1894, proved as bad if not worse than the management had foreseen. Gross earnings fell off 30.5 per cent and net dropped 37.96 per cent. But fixed charges were earned and paid and a surplus of $87,661 was carried over into the succeeding year; all expenses had been properly charged against income and the securities in the company's treasury had even been marked down to keep their book value proportional to market prices.[140] The annual report for the following year showed that the worst was over. Gross and

136 *Annual Report of the Denver & Rio Grande Railroad Company*, 1893; *Commercial and Financial Chronicle*, September 9, 1893, pp. 396-8.

137 *Railway Age and Northwestern Railroader*, August 18, 1893, p. 629.

138 *Ibid.*, September 15, 1893, p. 691.

139 *Commercial and Financial Chronicle*, July 8, 1893, pp. 41-2.

140 *Annual Report*, 1894; *Commercial and Financial Chronicle*, September 8, 1894, pp. 396-7.

net earnings both increased and the surplus over fixed charges rose to $528,690. No floating debt had been accumulated and $1,000,000 had been subtracted from the book value of equipment, although deterioration had not been allowed even to begin. At the end of the year the company could boast cash assets amounting to very nearly $2,000,000 [141] in excess of liabilities and a few months later it resumed the payment of dividends on preferred stock.[142]

The management had every reason to congratulate itself upon its success in piloting the system through difficulties greater than those of almost any other road in the country during the nineties. Nevertheless in 1901 the Rio Grande lost its independence; together with all its subsidiaries, totalling more than 2200 miles, it was brought into alliance with the Missouri Pacific in order to give the latter a better entrance into the silver and agricultural regions of the Southwest.[143]

The Eastern outlet for the Gould system was the Wabash railroad. Originally named the Wabash, an amalgamation was made with many small lines and the new company was called the Toledo, Wabash & Western. In 1879 Jay Gould became heavily interested in it and four years later he approved an outrageous lease which put it at the mercy of the lessor Iron Mountain, itself a Missouri Pacific subsidiary. In less than a year the lease was surrendered but the Wabash was already bankrupt. Foreclosure followed in 1889 and the subsequent drastic reorganization firmly established it in control of a system embracing nearly 2000 miles of track.[144] In 1893 a new line was completed from Montpelier, Ohio, to Hammond,

141 *Annual Report*, 1895; *Commercial and Financial Chronicle*, September 7, 1895, pp. 395-6.

142 *Ibid.*, December 14, 1895, p. 1038.

143 Snyder, *op. cit.*, pp. 283-91; Newcomb, H. T., " The Concentration of Railroad Control," *Annals of the American Academy*, 1902, XIX, pp. 89-107.

144 Van Oss, *op. cit.*, pp. 503-13; Snyder, *op. cit.*, pp. 722-35; Meade, " Great Railways," *Railway World*, 1903, pp. 1327-8.

Indiana giving a 267 mile track from Chicago to Detroit, which
was thirty miles shorter than the old route via Erie. Some
improvements on the Chicago-St. Louis division rounded out
a well-built road connecting the Southwestern Gould system
with the Canadian Pacific at Detroit and with the Grand Trunk
at its eastern terminal, Buffalo.[145]

Despite the high cost of these betterments, however, the
Wabash faced the depression in excellent physical condition
and without a floating debt. Expenditures had been confined to
the cash available.[146] This careful management had so strengthened the system that despite the depression, when Joseph
Ramsey became president in 1895 it was able to begin a long
and finally successful fight to bring its main line into Pittsburgh
and thereby share the rich middle Atlantic territory with the
Pennsylvania and the Vanderbilts.[147]

In this Eastern region there was one road which deserves
passing notice, the Pennsboro & Harrisville Railway. In 1892,
when critics thought that railroad conditions were not overly
favorable, it compiled a record that was the envy of the surrounding trunk lines. It was situated

in West Virginia, of three foot gauge and a total length of nine
miles, all under one management, and here is its last annual report
in brief: capital stock, $9,900; funded debt $14,000; gross earnings $8,490.83; operating expenses (64.7 per cent.) $5,514.71; net
earnings $2,976.12; interest on bonds $840; dividends paid (25
per cent.) $4275; deficit $338.39; surplus forward $3186.45; net
surplus (cash in hand) $2847.56. A railway that can pay 25 per
cent dividends in these degenerate and despotic times, and still
have on hand cash equivalent to more than half the year's operating expenses, is certainly remarkable. When it is added a woman

145 *Annual Report of the Wabash Railroad*, 1893; *Railway Age and
Northwestern Railroader*, June 2, 1893, pp. 342.

146 *Commercial and Financial Chronicle*, September 16, 1893, pp. 445-6;
Annual Reports, 1893-8.

147 Spearman, Frank H., *The Strategy of the Great Railroads*, New York:
Charles Scribner's Sons, 1904, pp. 97-111.

has just been made its president the peculiarities of the Pennsboro & Harrisville railway become still more notable.[148]

Although probably no other railroad in the country could compete with this pocket-size West Virginia line, there was one great system in the far Northwest whose name was fast becoming a by-word for efficiency and profitableness, James J. Hill's Great Northern. The Great Northern had been organized in 1889 under the charter of the old Minneapolis & St. Cloud Company, with stock half common and half preferred, of $40,000,000 par value. The Manitoba company which controlled more than 2700 miles of track and was the nucleus of the new system, was leased for 999 years through an agreement whereby the Great Northern guaranteed interest on all its bonds and 6 per cent dividends on all its stock, in addition to paying all taxes and assessments. By January, 1893, tracks had been laid to the Pacific coast and the Great Northern's main line was ready for business.

For 2000 miles the road paralleled the Northern Pacific and therefore was the latter's chief competitor. But because of watered stock and construction frauds the Northern Pacific's 2000 miles of track represented about three times as much capital as did the Great Northern's.[149] This situation had not occurred by accident. Partly it was due to Hill's moral code, which was far more strict than that of the normal railroad man of the time, and partly it was due to his conspicuous business ability.

He had been born in 1838 near Rockwood, Ontario, of north of Ireland descent. He attended the local schools and a nearby academy until the death of his father in 1852, when young James became a clerk in the village store, meanwhile continuing to study and read. His parents had wanted him to be a doctor but their hopes had been given up when the sight of an eye was lost by the accidental discharge of an arrow. At eighteen

148 *Railway Age and Northwestern Railroader*, January 20, 1893, p. 43.
149 Pyle, *Hill*, I, pp. 461-3, 472-3.

he left home for the Orient, going to the Atlantic seaboard in
hope of finding an opportunity to work his way on a ship.
Failing in this endeavor, he started west, planning to sail from
the Pacific coast. He arrived in St. Paul only to find that the
last wagon train to the coast for that year had left a few days
before and he must wait nearly twelve months before he could
continue his journey. By the time that year had passed Hill
was settled in St. Paul and had lost all wish to continue to the
Far East. He became clerk for a line of Mississippi River
packet steamers and in the course of his work had full charge
of shipping. When the Civil War broke out he tried to enlist
in the Union Army but his defective eyesight made him ineligible. In 1865 he embarked on an independent business venture,
forwarding and transportation. He continued his work in
transportation, gaining experience and accumulating some
financial resources, until in 1878 he entered the railroad field
by purchasing, in conjunction with three others, the St. Paul
& Pacific Railroad. Together with his colleagues, Norman W.
Kittson, Donald A Smith (later Lord Strathcona), and George
Stephen (later Lord Mount Stephen), Hill was then to be engaged in railroad work for the rest of his life. Nominally he
was general manager from 1879 to 1881, vice-president for the
next two years, president from 1882 to 1907 and chairman of
the board from 1907 to 1912, but actually he was the leading
spirit of the group from the start.

His great contribution to railroad management was his
emphasis on exact and complete knowledge of facts. " Intelligent management of railroads must be based on exact knowledge of facts. Guesswork will not do " was a dictum, and the
strength of his Great Northern lay in his careful application
of this principle. Physically Hill was of only medium height
but he gave the impression of great size and strength due to
his powerfully built frame, massive head and the impression
of great reserve of power. He was accustomed to command and
this characteristic showed in his direct and sometimes brusque

conversation which oftentimes deceived people into believing that he had no sense of humor. Withal he had a positive fanaticism for treating his stockholders fairly and at times leaned over backwards in his efforts to protect them.[150]

Acquisition of the segments which were combined to form the Great Northern system had been unaccompanied by the usual exorbitant profits and commissions. In a letter to Lee, Higginson & Company, written July 23, 1887, Hill outlined a procedure by which he proposed to gain control of the Montana Central and which was typical of his methods:

I hope to be able to settle with all subscribers for $3,000,000 of the Montana Central bonds, in which case I will turn over my contract with the Montana Central, or rather will close it up for the Manitoba account, paying the balance necessary to finish the road which will be from $2,000,000 to $2,250,000. . . . This, you see, will give the Manitoba the property, or at least the ownership of it. The stock will, I think, pay a dividend from the start and is certainly worth $3,000,000.[151]

Hill's expectations proved accurate and he secured a valuable piece of property at a bargain price for the Manitoba.

A few years later Hill wanted to penetrate the iron-ore fields around Duluth. The Duluth & Winnipeg, which had built part of a line from Duluth to Grand Forks, had issued $1,000,000 of stock and $800,000 of bonds and had floated a further loan of $1,000,000 on the security of the bonds. In 1892 some of Hill's friends became members of the board of directors and, as these loans matured, took them up with cash which he provided. In this way for $2,000,000 Hill acquired control of a road as valuable as the combined property of its two rivals, the Duluth & Iron Range and the Minnesota Iron Company, which were together capitalized at $18,000,000.[151]

---

150 *Dictionary of American Biography*, IX, pp. 36-41 ; Pyle, *Hill, passim*.
151 Pyle, *Hill*, I, pp. 472-3.
152 *Ibid.*, II, p. 464-7.

Completion of the extension to the Pacific Coast in 1893 did not put an end to the development of the system. Writing in 1907, a veteran railroad man stated that:

In 1890, when the total bond and stock capitalization of the Great Northern was $105,735,000, its 3,006 miles of railway were prairie lines in Minnesota and North Dakota. During the sixteen years between 1890 and 1905, in which its total capitalization increased $119,490,126, it has constructed 3,104 miles including the expensive lines over the Rockies and Coast ranges of mountains to the Pacific Coast, and expensive lines in the mountains, and has expended large sums of money in improving its terminals. It has built steamships which sail on the Great Lakes and on the Pacific Ocean. Its terminals at Minneapolis-St. Paul, at Duluth-Superior, and at Seattle are superior to all others. At Duluth-Superior, in my judgment, its facilities for handling grain, including elevators, are superior to the facilities of all the railways in the cities of Baltimore, New York and Boston combined. That Mr. Hill had the genius to build a line across the unsettled plains and the mountains to the Pacific in 1890-93, without a land grant or government aid—a feat never before accomplished—and to build in sixteen years over three thousand miles, and made the improvements specified by only doubling the capitalization, seems to the people of the West a wonderful exhibition of economic achievement.[153]

The essential strength of the system was indicated in its annual report for the first year of the depression. By dint of reducing salaries and personnel, as well as curtailing all unnecessary expenditures, the ratio of operating expenses and taxes to gross earnings had been reduced from the already low 1892 figure of 60.82 per cent to 57.29 per cent.[154] Hill did not relax his efforts to perpetuate the company's prosperity even after this remarkable achievement. In the fertile agricultural regions which were served by the Great Northern, the grain elevator companies gave the farmer cash advances on his grain

153 *Ibid.*, II, p. 482.
154 *Commercial and Financial Chronicle*, December 29, 1894, pp. 1125-7.

as soon as it was deposited in the elevator, thus permitting him to store it until it could be sold at a profitable price later in the year. As the depression continued it became gradually harder for the farmers to obtain loans of this kind. Realizing that if grain could not be moved the whole Northwest's industrial and economic structure must suffer untold damage, Hill came to the rescue and advanced sums up to 80 per cent of the value of the wheat which was in the company's elevators.[155]

By such efforts as these on the part of its management, the Great Northern was able to maintain its regular 5 per cent dividend level throughout the depression; in 1897 it paid an extra ½ per cent and in 1898 another increase brought the dividend rate to 5.75 per cent.[156]

In 1900 Thomas H. Woodlock, the railway editor of the *Wall Street Journal,* paid tribute to Hill's genius in enthusiastic words:

Mr. Hill was the first man in the United States to thoroughly lay bare the principles of transportation and put them in practice, and the result was his road has been a gold mine to those people who have stayed with it from the start and it works at lower rates than any road up there. . . . It runs at lower rates than others; it is not overcapitalized, and it has been splendidly operated and splendidly built from the start. Now Mr. Hill's stock has gone up from the basis of 100 to what is equivalent today to about 300. . . . The stock apparently sells for about 190, and there have been so many dividends and subscription rates in connection with it that it is really equivalent to 300.[157]

On the whole, " Mr. Hill is recognized, I guess, as the foremost railroad man in the United States," concluded Mr. Woodlock.[158]

So successfully had Hill's system survived the worst days of the depression that when the work of rehabilitating bankrupt

155 Pyle, *op. cit.,* I, pp. 488-9.

156 Poor, *op. cit.,* 1900, pp. 1268-85.

157 *Industrial Commission Report,* IX, p. 466.

158 *Ibid.,* IX, p. 456.

roads was begun, he was able to form the alliance with J. P. Morgan to reorganize the Northern Pacific. Before the panic of 1893 swept the country, Hill had an as yet incomplete line to the Pacific Coast. At the end of the depression he controlled the two northern-most transcontinentals and soon he annexed the Burlington to give them an entrance into Chicago. Of the five great transcontinental systems, three had gone into receivership during the depression, only the Great Northern and the Southern Pacific remained solvent, but the latter could not rival the record of Hill's system—indeed by the contrast they presented its difficulties served to emphasize the Great Northern's achievement.

The "Big Four", Charles Crocker, C. P. Huntington, Leland Stanford and Mark Hopkins, who had built the Central Pacific, had also built the Southern Pacific. After completing the latter they had leased the Central Pacific to it [159] and gathered a great system embracing 7000 miles of track around this nucleus[160] The company's main source of strength was its virtual monopoly of California railroad transportation. The Atchison had some mileage in southern California, but even there the Southern Pacific had the upper hand. The Union Pacific had at one time been expected to provide competition in northern California but this threat had been stifled when the Southern Pacific absorbed the Central Pacific, which was to have been the western end of the proposed Union Pacific system.[161] So complete was this monopoly that A. J. Vanlandingham, Commissioner of the St. Louis Traffic Bureau, stated in 1900 that "The Southern Pacific so far have been able to dictate all the rates to the Pacific Coast south of Portland" where it encountered Northern Pacific and Great Northern competition.[162]

159 Snyder, *op. cit.*, pp. 656-9; Van Oss, *op. cit.*, pp. 689-713.

160 *Commercial and Financial Chronicle*, April 28, 1894, pp. 702-3.

161 Meade, "Great Railways," *Railway World*, 1905, pp. 7-8.

162 *Industrial Commission Report*, IV, pp. 207.

An equally important source of strength to the Southern Pacific was its political interests. Speaking of the company's activities, William R. Wheeler, representing the Pacific Coast Jobbers Association, told the Industrial Commission:

The Southern Pacific is in politics. I might say that there has not been an office within the gift of the people or subject to the appointment of the governor or the mayors of the various cities or any other officials that they have not reached out and tried to grab.[163]

That the company was successful in these efforts was attested by a critic who wrote in 1892 that:

This company not only has absolute control of the railroads, but also " runs " the entire state, which it represents in Washington through Senator Stanford and " bosses " in Sacramento by means of its nominees and its influence. Having no competitor, the Southern Pacific is without inducement to pay much regard to the demands of the public, and consequently maintains an indifferent service and charges arbitrary rates.[164]

Despite the advantages of monopoly and political power, however, the Southern Pacific had difficulty surviving the first stages of the panic. Early in 1893 Leland Stanford's death had left C. P. Huntington the sole living member of the quartet which for so long had dominated California.

But although Stanford's death hurt the company, he had not been active in the management for some years. Huntington had made himself president in 1890 and from that time until his death he dominated the Southern Pacific. He was a New Englander by birth and always claimed that he had been fortunate to start life with neither a liberal education nor any money, since because he had been forced to do so, he had been ready to turn to any work he could get. At fourteen he had

163 *Ibid.*, IX, p. 743.
164 Van Oss, *op. cit.*, pp. 691-2.

begun to support himself by working for a neighbor in return
for $7 per month and his board. Within a year he left home
and began peddling merchandise through the South. By the
time he was twenty-one he had accumulated enough capital to
start a store at Oneonta, New York, and there he remained
until 1849 when he joined the gold rush to California. One
day of mining convinced him that he was not cut out for it;
so he returned to Sacramento and set up a jobbing and retail
store dealing in miners' supplies. A system of semi-barter
rather than a normal money economy prevailed and Huntington excelled in it by virtue of his shrewdness, great physical
strength, endurance and experience. In 1860 after a prosperous
decade of merchandising he became interested, with his three
partners, in the railroad industry and thenceforth railroads
were his lifework.

Of the Big Four, Huntington was always the dominant
force because of his inexhaustible energy, his shrewdness, his
independence of thought and his grasp of business problems.
He was a vindictive man and one of his firmest beliefs was
that his railroads were his private business only and that no
public interest inhered just because they were public utilities.
Throughout his life he was interested in little other than his
business, and even the political side of that was left to Leland
Stanford. In 1890 the two split over Stanford's political activities : in 1885 Stanford had been elected United States Senator,
as Huntington thought, at the expense of his friend A. A.
Sargent. When Huntington declared that Stanford was using
the Southern Pacific for political advancement without regard
to the best interests of the company, the split became irrecon-
cilable. In 1890 Huntington had himself elected president of
the road in place of Stanford and immediately announced a
change in the company's policies, thereby striking at Stanford's
management.[165]

In the spring of 1893 the company had a floating debt of

165 *Dictionary of American Biography*, IX, pp. 408-12.

about $15,000,000, mostly in the form of call loans secured by personal notes of Huntington, Stanford and their associates. Partly due to Stanford's death and partly to the depression, these loans were called during the early summer and the company was barely able to pay them. Since no available cash was on hand with which to meet the July 1 interest payments on both Southern Pacific and Central Pacific bonds, a default and subsequent receivership seemed inevitable but at the last moment Huntington was able to raise the necessary funds.[166]

By reducing drastically the amount paid out in wages,[167] the management confined the decrease in net earnings to $210,692 for the year ending December 31, 1893, and it was able to carry a surplus of about $1,000,000 over fixed charges into the succeeding years. But the system's weakness was reflected in the $15,000,000 floating debt which was offset by cash assets of only $10,000,000 and materials necessary to the functioning of the road which were valued at about $4,800,000.[168]

The company's solvency was more immediately threatened when the Government filed suit to recover from the stockholders allegedly fraudulent construction profits. The suit was directed against the Stanford Estate, and the Government asked for restitution of the subsidy money given to the Central Pacific to aid in its construction. Eventually the Supreme Court upheld the decision of a lower court that stockholders could not be held responsible for the debts and errors of the company, but a threat hung over the Southern Pacific's credit until the decision had been made final in 1896.[169]

The annual report for the system as a whole in 1894 showed

166 *Commercial and Financial Chronicle*, April 2, 1894, pp. 702-3; *Railway Review*, September 9, 1893, p. 560.

167 *Railway Age and Northwestern Railroader*, August 11, 1893, p. 613.

168 *Annual Report of the Southern Pacific*, 1893; *Commercial and Financial Chronicle*, April 28, 1894, pp. 702-3.

169 *Railway World*, July 20, 1894, p. 405; July 20, 1895, p. 373; March 7, 1896, p. 229.

several encouraging developments, especially in increased profits from branch lines,[170] but recovery was slow because vexatious problems were aroused by the rapidly approaching maturity of the Central Pacific's Government subsidy bonds. Until his death in 1901, however, Huntington continued to steer the system safely through all the threatening shoals and after his death a controlling interest was purchased by Harriman, who was building a vast railroad empire around his Union Pacific system.[171]

Severe though the depression was for the railroads of the country, nevertheless all those in good condition financially and physically passed through it safely. Indeed, as hindsight makes apparent the degrees of success achieved by the various companies fairly accurately reflected their strength. Study of the dividends paid and passed during the nineties sustains this impression. The percentage of all outstanding stock paying dividends declined from a high point of 40.36 in 1891 to 36.57 in 1894 and then dropped below 30.00 during the next three years. In 1898 it rose to 33.74 and in the following year reached a new high of 40.61, only to shoot further upward to 45.66 in 1900.[172]

The average rate paid on those shares paying any dividends rose to 5.45 per cent in 1890, slumped a trifle during the next two years, but in 1893, the first year of the depression, reached a high point of 5.58 per cent. The rate dropped to 5.40 per cent in 1894, but in the following year it rose to 5.74 per cent. In 1896 began a new decline which, by graduated reductions over the next four years, brought the average to a low point of 4.96 per cent in 1899. But the tendency was reversed the next year and the average dividend became 5.23 per cent.[173]

170 *Commercial and Financial Chronicle*, May 18, 1895, pp. 858-9.

171 Snyder, *op. cit.*, pp. 656-9.

172 *Senate Committee on Interstate Commerce*, 67th Congress, 2nd Session, III, table facing p. 1508.

173 *Ibid.*, III, table facing p. 1571.

Finally, the total cash value of all dividends paid on railroad stock throughout the country rose from about $80,000,000 in 1888 to almost $101,000,000 in 1893. In 1894 it declined to $95,500,000 and the next year dropped suddenly to only a little more than $85,000,000. In 1895 and 1896 payments amounted to about $87,000,000 but in 1898 they increased rapidly to a little more than $96,000,000. Thereafter the rise became meteoric: in 1899 dividends totalling approximately $111,000,000 were paid and in 1900 a new high water mark of $139,500,000 was reached.[174]

When considered together, these figures confirm the suggestions roused by study of the individual solvent roads. As soon as depression struck the weak roads were forced to reduce and then passed their dividends, thereby sharply reducing the percentage of shares paying a dividend. But the companies which were not in this marginal class were almost able to maintain their usual dividend rates. In other words, the depression separated the weak from the strong but failed to injure the latter seriously.

174 *Ibid.*, III, table facing p. 1569.

CHAPTER IX

SMALL ROADS

THE smaller railroads of the country struggled through the depression without attracting more than local attention to their triumphs and failures. Beginning in 1895 the Interstate Commerce Commission listed annually all the companies in receivership during the preceding years, and a few railway periodicals printed articles in which these casualties were tabulated. The reports invariably noted the number of companies involved, the mileage controlled by each and the capital it represented. Although the lists were of impressive length during the nineties, in evaluating them certain reservations must be kept in mind. Many of the small companies which were included were subsidiaries of larger systems and their failures were directly attributable to the receiverships of parent companies. Before valid conclusions can be drawn as to the effects of the depression on the country's smaller roads, the small independent roads must be distinguished from those affiliated with the bankrupt systems.

In 1893 for example, 76 railroads went into the hands of receivers; these roads controlled 29,476 miles of track, representing $1,060,913,000 of bonds and $697,923,000 of stock at par. But among these 76 companies were the Reading, the Erie, the Northern Pacific, the Union Pacific, and the Atchison, with their various insolvent subsidiaries. Excluding these large systems, the total mileage in receivership would have been only about 8000. In other words, five large companies contributed nearly 75 per cent of the total railroad mileage in receivership during that year.[1]

Although the insolvency of small companies operating more than 8000 miles of track indicated that local independent roads were not prospering, nevertheless when they are compared with

1 *Railway Age and Northwestern Railroader*, December 15, 1893, pp. 887-8; January 5, 1894, pp. 1-2.

the records of previous years those figures do not seem to be of catastrophic proportions. In the nine years before 1893 that total of bankrupt mileage had been exceeded three times, in 1884, 1885, and 1892. During these nine years, the average number of miles going into receivership annually throughout the country had been almost 5000 and this figure had not been swelled to an appreciable extent by the failures of any large systems. Only in 1886 and 1887 had fewer than twenty companies admitted insolvency, and the yearly average had been a fraction over twenty-six roads.[2]

During 1894 none of the larger companies failed, but many subsidiaries joined their parent roads in receivership when the support of the latter was withdrawn because of their own difficulties. In all, the five large systems which had failed in the preceding year contributed about 60 per cent of the mileage forced into receivership during the year.[3] In the following twelve months companies operating 4089 miles of track, representing a par value capitalization of about $147,000,000, were declared insolvent. But the Norfolk & Western and the New York, Pennsylvania & Ohio contributed 2299 miles and $104,000,000 of securities to these totals. As a result, the small roads in this group represented only about 1700 miles of track and $43,000,000, figures considerably smaller than the averages for the nine years before the depression.[4]

Taken collectively, the minor roads fared nearly as well during the depression of the nineties as they had during the more generally prosperous preceding decade. In 1893 an abnormal amount of their mileage had been put into receivership, but the havoc was not comparable to that created among the great systems. And despite the financial stringency still hindering business, after 1893 the annual lists of insolvencies among minor roads were smaller than those of the eighties.

2 *Ibid.*, December 15, 1893, p. 888.
3 *Ibid.*, January 4, 1895, p. 1.
4 *Ibid.*, January 3, 1896, p. 1.

Aside from the small companies involved in the failures of larger parent systems, the receiverships of local lines may be broadly comprehended in three categories: failures caused by the machinations of trunk lines contending for control of short connecting roads, like that of the Central Railroad of Vermont; receiverships directly attributable to the assumption of risky financial burdens during prosperous years, either in over-anxious efforts to expand or in the course of profitable financial manipulations, as in the case of the Louisville, New Albany & Chicago; and failures caused simply by an insufficiency of income. Failures of the latter type were not new phenomena, nor even of appreciably greater frequency during the nineties than before.

The Central of Vermont had been chartered in 1850 and almost at once absorbed the Vermont & Canada. In 1855 it was put into the hands of a receiver and not until 1883 was it reorganized. During these twenty-eight years there was a continuous repetition of costly litigation which together with the extreme wastefulness of the receivers, burdened the company with a debt much too large for a system of its size. The wreckage was finally sold at foreclosure and reorganized as the Consolidated Railroad of Vermont, which issued $7,000,000 of consolidated 5 per cent mortgage bonds. From then until 1892 an expansion policy was vigorously prosecuted by a series of leases and consolidations, in which the name "Central of Vermont" again appeared as the lessor and holding company. In the process of building up the system large debts were contracted, the most burdensome of which was the Consolidated's mortgage that had been guaranteed by the parent company; among the heaviest creditors was the Grand Trunk Railroad of Canada, which had acquired $700,000 of the Consolidated's bonds and $1,000,000 of the Central's 4 per cent bonds in addition to $100,000 of the floating debt and a claim for traffic charges.

The claim for traffic charges arose from traffic agreement

which the Central of Vermont had formed with the Grand Trunk. The former's tracks ran from Rouse's Point at the north end of Lake Champlain, where the Grand Trunk had a terminal, across Massachusetts to Boston and on to New London, Connecticut, on Long Island Sound.[5] On the one hand, the alliance gave the Central a share in the New England trade of the Grand Trunk, on the other it gave the Grand Trunk the most direct route from Boston to Chicago and the West. As the rapid development of traffic on this line became apparent the Canadian Pacific began to work into closer relations with the Central, and finally built a switch connecting the two roads near St. John in order to divert some of this traffic from the Grand Trunk to itself. It was after this manoeuvre had become known that the Grand Trunk suddenly sued the Central for $415,712.45, which was allegedly due on traffic charges. Furthermore, the Grand Trunk declared, the Central had about $22,500,000 of bonds outstanding on which interest had been defaulted.[6] Although the Central's management admitted the validity of the claim for traffic charges, it wanted proof of the amount; but without waiting to settle that point and without the knowledge of the Central's officials, he Grand Trunk asked the court to appoint receivers.

The tactics of the Grand Trunk were completely successful: receivers, one of whom was its own general manager, were appointed for the Central on the plea that the road could pay neither the traffic charges nor its floating debt, to say nothing of the bond interest; other creditors were about to force payment of their claims and this could only result in the dismemberment of the system, thus making it impossible for the company to pay its fixed charges in the future.[7] That the floating debt proved even larger than had been expected and that certain

5 *Commercial and Financial Chronicle, Investors' Supplement*, April 18, 1896, p. 31.

6 *Railway Review*, March 25, 1896, pp. 180-1.

7 *Railroad Gazette*, April 3, 1896, p. 235.

deceptive entries had been made in the books [8] were not of
decisive importance in determining the Central's fate. Over-
capitalization and the ever growing floating debt merely provided the opportunity for the Grand Trunk to get the system
under its control. When its profitable alliance was threatened
by the encroachment of the Canadian Pacific, the Grand Trunk
promptly used its advantageous position to assure retention
of its direct line between Chicago and Boston. The Central,
rotten though its financial structure was, failed only because it
was a valuable pawn in the struggle of the Grand Trunk and
the Canadian Pacific.

The ensuing reorganization proceedings were accompanied
by bitter struggles among security holders over the final disposal of control over the property. In September, 1897,
eighteen months after the receivers had been appointed, a meeting of the bondholders of the Consolidated Railroad of Vermont, which carried most of the Central's bonded debt, was
called to consider a reorganization plan. A new company would
be formed to take over the Central of Vermont and issue
new securities. Its bonded capitalization would consist of
$10,000,000 of first mortgage 4 per cent twenty-one year
bonds, $1,050,000 of second mortgage series A twenty-one
year adjustment bonds bearing 4 per cent interest which was
payable from net earnings only and $3,000,000 of second
mortgage series B bonds similar to the A bonds except in
having a lien secondary to theirs. Holders of first mortgage
5 per cent bonds of the old company would receive 85 per cent
of their holdings in new first mortgage bonds, 15 per cent in
series A bonds and accrued interest in series B bonds. Aside
from the rather harsh treatment given the bondholders, the
question around which discussion hinged was the part which
the Grand Trunk would play in the affairs of the new company.
The plan proposed that the two form an alliance which would
include a traffic agreement and also a provision that if the net

8 *Ibid.*, April 17, 1896, p. 279; *Railway Review*, March 20, 1897, p. 170.

of the new company were not enough to pay the interest on the new series of first mortgage bonds and series A bonds, the Grand Trunk would make up the deficit provided it were not required to pay over 30 per cent of the gross amount received from traffic interchanged with the new company.[9]

The plan was carefully considered in a frequently adjourned meeting before it was finally adopted by holders of more than two-thirds in amount of the outstanding bonds. The defect which had aroused the most opposition was the provision that the Grand Trunk's liability was so strictly limited; some of the bondholders wanted to see if a more advantageous agreement could not be made with the Boston & Maine, but upon assurances from the committee that they had already approached the Boston & Maine and it was not interested the opposition gave way.[10] Approval was by no means enthusiastic however, and a month after the plan had been adopted less than one-eighth of the bonds had been deposited.[11] After months of delay a new committee was organized in April, 1898, to put the plan into effect; it was a strong group, including as it did Richard Olney, T. J. Coolidge, J. A. Blair, James Stillman and Dr. W. Seward Webb.[12] It resumed negotiations with the Grand Trunk and made arrangements for the latter to pay interest for one year on bonds deposited under the plan; the Grand Trunk was to hold the redeemed coupons as security in case the reorganization failed.[13]

The security holders opposing the Grand Trunk had resorted meanwhile to political action in order to prevent execution of the plan. Early in May the governor of Vermont signed a bill which provided that: without the permission of the legislature

9 *Railway Gazette*, September 17, 1897, p. 660.

10 *Ibid.*, October 15, 1897, p. 738; November 12, 1897, p. 807; *Railway Review*, October 16, 1897, pp. 599-600.

11 *Railway Review*, November 20, 1897, p. 672; *Railway Gazette*, November 12, 1897, p. 807.

12 *Railway Review*, April 16, 1898, p. 208.

13 *Railway Gazette*, April 15, 1898, p. 286.

no alien company should be interested in the stock of any Vermont railroad hereafter organized under Vermont laws, nor should an alien corporation own or acquire title to any Vermont company.[14] Political and legal controversies resulting from this law continued throughout the summer while attempts were made to find a compromise acceptable to all parties.[15]

Preceded by many rumors,[16] a new plan was published early in the autumn by a committee headed by Ezra H. Baker of Boston. A new company would be formed to issue $3,000,000 of stock and $12,000,000 of first mortgage 4 per cent twenty-one year bonds. The Grand Trunk would guarantee interest on the bonds up to 30 per cent of the gross receipts it received from traffic interchanged with the Central. A reserve of $1,000,000 in the new bonds was to be set aside for improvements, additions and similar purposes, and a second reserve of $4,000,000 was set up for the acquisition of branch lines, settlement of preference claims and reorganization costs.[17]

Although the plan differed in very few respects from that previously opposed so bitterly, it was speedily put into effect. The Vermont legislature passed a law which would permit the incorporation of the company[18] if a few modifications were made in the plan. The bond holders quickly accepted these[19] and the plan was announced operative early in 1899.[20] The new company took over the system at midnight, April 30,[21] and the shareholders promptly ratified the agreement with the Grand Trunk; since the latter owned $2,180,000 out of a total stock

14 *Ibid.*, May 13, 1898, p. 349.

15 *Railway Review*, May 14, 1898, p. 265; July 23, 1898, p. 407.

16 *Ibid.*, October 8, 1898, p. 569.

17 *Railway Gazette*, October 14, 1898, p. 751.

18 *Railway Review*, October 29, 1898, p. 614.

19 *Railway Gazette*, November 25, 1898, p. 854; *Railway Review*, November 5, 1898, p. 628.

20 *Railway Gazette*, February 3, 1899, p. 95.

21 *Ibid.*, May 5, 1899, p. 325.

issue of $3,000,000, in addition to a large block of the new bonds, its control of the Central was assured.[22]

The Louisville, New Albany & Chicago was a local mid-Western road which ran from Chicago and Michigan City on Lake Michigan south to Monon, Indiana, where its main tracks divided into one line to Louisville and another to Cincinnati.[23] In 1889 the directors had exceeded their authority by attempting to interest their company in the Richmond, Nicholasville, Irwin & Beattyville line. The charter required that the stockholders approve by a two-thirds vote a guarantee of any other company's bonds, but the directors first assumed responsibility for $1,185,000 of Beattyville bonds, and then submitted the transaction to the shareholders for approval. However, they were forced to withdraw the guarantee when the approval was promptly refused.[24] Vice-president J. B. Carson and some of the directors had been interested in building the Beattyville and they had persuaded enough other directors to favor the project to obtain the board's ratification, notwithstanding the charter requirement. To make the transaction even more distasteful to the stockholders, the board meeting had been attended by only eight of the thirteen directors and the whole matter had been kept secret from the other five. Under these circumstances, and since the Louisville, New Albany & Chicago received no visible benefits from such gratuitous assumption of a large financial burden, the shareholders not only repudiated the contract, but they also turned the directors out of office.[25]

Although the guarantee was promptly cancelled, the Beattyville had already sold some of its bonds on the understanding that the Louisville, New Albany & Chicago was responsible for them. The purchasers paid far more for these bonds than they would have for securities backed only by the newly char-

22 *Ibid.*, June 9, 1899, p. 418.

23 *Commercial and Financial Chronicle, Investors' Supplement,* April, 1896, p. 87.

24 *Ibid.*, June 27, 1896, p. 1079.

25 *Ibid.*, August 15, 1896, p. 269.

tered Beattyville, so a suit was instituted against the Louisville, New Albany & Chicago in an effort to make it resume the guarantee. The litigation was intricate and prolonged, but the Louisville, New Albany & Chicago was uniformly successful at first.[26] However, the failure of the Richmond, Nicolasville, Irwin & Beattyville in the early days of the depression complicated matters even further. Attempts to reorganize the company made its extremely weak financial position only too evident and efforts were redoubled to force the Louisville, New Albany & Chicago to underwrite its bonded indebtedness.[27]

These efforts were rewarded with partial success in the decision of the United States Court of Appeals at Cincinnati on June 22, 1896: the court declared that although the Louisville, New Albany and Chicago directors lacked authority to bind the company, nevertheless the contract was made under the laws of Kentucky and was binding in that state. All the company's property which was situated within the jurisdiction of Kentucky officials was liable to secure the bonds which had been sold before the stockholders' disapproval of the contract had been made public. The guarantee was not valid in respect to bonds which were bought after it had been denounced; only innocent investors were to be protected.

The Louisville, New Albany & Chicago immediately prepared to carry the case to the Supreme Court, but meanwhile the company's officials attempted to minimize the importance of the decision. Under the conditions set forth by the court, at most only about $300,000 was involved, and they confidently expected the Supreme Court to invalidate the entire contract.[28] President Samuel Thomas issued a statement attacking the past management of the road and outlining its future prospects: its securities had suffered excessively from the adverse decision; it was hard enough to see the management's hitherto successful

26 *Ibid.*, June 27, 1896, p. 1079.
27 *Ibid.*, February 1, 1896, p. 234.
28 *Ibid.*, June 27, 1896, p. 1076.

efforts to preserve the company's credit nullified by the faults
of a previous regime, but even if the company had to assume
full responsibility for the Beattyville bonds its resources would
not be so exhausted as the market attacks on its securities would
indicate. Thomas was sure that the Supreme Court would acquit
the company of all liability but even if it should hold the contract valid, the resulting claims would come after the company's
own bonds as an unsecured debt which would not be large
enough to threaten stock equities.[29]

However, on August 24, 1896, the Louisville, New Albany
& Chicago resorted to a new manoeuvre to prevent an adverse
result: petition was made and granted for the appointment of
General Manager William H. McDoel as receiver for the company. A majority of the bonds were in friendly hands and the
management decided to take advantage of what seemed the
only sure way of escaping responsibility for the Beattyville
claims. Also, the floating debt amounted to about $900,000
and creditors were alarmed lest their interests be injured by
the payment of the Beattyville bonds. On August 3 holders of
these securities had served attachments on the Louisville, New
Albany & Chicago for $36,000 and this action had forced the
management to take the final steps into receivership.[30]

The road was in good physical condition and the annual
report for the year ending June 30, 1896, indicated that its
finances were almost equally sound. Net earnings in excess of
fixed charges had been $162,946 and there had been a deficit
of only $47,946 even after paying for additions and improve-
ments. Both freight and passenger earnings had increased and
the freight receipts per ton-mile had risen from 0.850 cents
to 0.875 cents.[31] The optimism to which this news gave rise
was justified less than two months after the appointment of a
receiver when a committee consisting of Frederic P. Olcott,

29 *Ibid.*, August 15, 1896, p. 269.
30 *Ibid.*, August 29, 1896, p. 357.
31 *Ibid.*, September 19, 1896, p. 500.

Henry W. Poor and Henry C. Rouse, announced a plan for reorganizing the company.

A new blanket mortgage at 5 per cent was to be issued. Limited to a par value of $15,000,000 it would be used to take up both the $6,109,000 of 5 and 6 per cent bonds outstanding and the $5,300,000 of divisional bonds; the rest of the issue would be sold to raise needed cash. A syndicate had been formed which would pay $2,100,000 for $1,500,000 of the new bonds, $680,750 of the new preferred stock and that part of the $10,500,000 new common stock not taken up by former common shareholders. Both common and preferred stock would be assessed $7.50 per share but this amount would be returned to holders in the form of preferred stock; preferred shares would then be redeemed by the syndicate at par and common stock at one-third of its face value. The old consolidated bonds and equipment were to be exchanged at par for the new bonds, but general mortgage holders would receive only one-fourth of their former holdings in new bonds and the rest, plus a small bonus for making the sacrifice, in preferred stock. Under this plan fixed charges, including the dividends on preferred stock, would be $1,108,450; during the preceding year the company had netted slightly less than this, but the average net earnings for the past ten years had been $1,182,384, so no difficulties were anticipated.[32]

The only important objection to the plan came from the holders of consolidated bonds. They protested that already they held what was practically a blanket mortgage on which they received 6 per cent interest. The new mortgage weakened their lien since it added more to the amount of the mortgage than to the security included under it; and also the new mortgage would lower their interest payments 1 per cent without providing any adequate compensation.[33] After they had negotiated for a short time, the reorganization committee and holders of

32 *Ibid.*, October 17, 1896, p. 702.
33 *Ibid.*, October 17, 1896, pp. 702, 712.

the consolidated bonds agreed on a compromise. The new bonds which were exchanged for these securities would bear the old 6 per cent interest rate and no bonus in preferred stock would accompany them. This change in the plan increased the fixed charges proper by $47,000, but by diminishing the amount of the issue of preferred stock, it decreased dividend requirements almost as much.[34]

Early in December enough securities had been deposited to enable the committee to announce that the plan was operative.[35] In March the property was sold at foreclosure and bought in by the bondholders;[36] less than a month later the new company was launched with the same officers as before the receivership.[37] The Louisville, New Albany & Chicago had been forced to acknowledge its insolvency because of the financial machinations of a preceding management; to escape the consequences of an illegal contract which had been abrogated long before, the company had resorted to a receivership from which it emerged with its credit preserved and its independence assured.

In addition to those small roads which failed during the depression, there were two minor systems for which the nineties were an especially momentous decade: they were at that time just inaugurating the expansion policies which would transform them from insignificant local carriers into great systems. Inasmuch as Southern railroading had been severely retarded by the Civil War and the ensuing period of Reconstruction, it is not surprising that both these systems were located in the old South. After the failure of the Richmond Terminal in 1892 the Southern Atlantic seaboard had been left without a single large solvent railroad system. In the early years of the twentieth century the same region could boast of three great systems, the Southern Railway, successor to the Richmond, the Atlantic Coast Line and the Seaboard Air Line.

34 *Ibid.*, November 14, 1896, p. 880.
35 *Ibid.*, December 5, 1896, p. 1010.
36 *Ibid.*, March 13, 1897, p. 517.
37 *Ibid.*, April 3, 1897, p. 664.

The Atlantic Coast Line Company had been incorporated in Connecticut on May 29, 1889, to consolidate a group of railways along the coast: the Wilmington & Weldon, the Charleston & Western Carolina, the Wilmington, Columbia & Augusta, the Richmond, Fredericksburg & Potomac and several smaller lines. No important changes were made in the system until March, 1897, when a financial reorganization took place: the par value of the capital stock was reduced from $10,000,000 to $5,000,000 and as compensation 5 per cent certificates of indebtedness were issued; at the same time it was agreed that the property would not be mortgaged without the consent of two-thirds of these certificates. A statement which was issued about three months later showed that the parent company controlled twelve small lines in Virginia, North Carolina and South Carolina, but it gave little other information. Five of these roads were consolidated into the Atlantic Coast Line Company of South Carolina on July 16, 1898, and two more small lines were rented at a cost of $31,000 per year. The consolidation was made by exchanging bonds of the new company for those of the several lines and, without waiting to see how profitable the new arrangement would be, a one hundred per cent stock dividend was declared less than four months later. Another consolidation, that of the Petersburg Railway into the Richmond & Petersburg Railroad, resulted in the formation of the Atlantic Coast Line Company of Virginia on November 21, 1898.

For the next year and a half both the Virginia and South Carolina companies steadily enlarged their systems and then on April 18, 1900, the two parent companies were merged to form the Atlantic Coast Line Company,[38] which owned 1701 miles of track and operated 1766 miles.[39] This mileage was multiplied several times in 1902 when a large block of Louisville & Nashville stock was purchased. In the midst of his speculations, John

38 *Stock Ownership*, III, pp. 1187-91; Snyder, *op. cit.*, pp. 83-93.

39 *Interstate Commerce Commission Statistics*, 1900, pp. 256-7.

W. Gates discovered that he possessed a controlling interest in
the company, and asked Morgan to sell it for him. Morgan
consented to do what he could and found a ready customer in
the Atlantic Coast Line.[40] Its tracks ran down the coast from
Norfolk to Florida; the new purchase gave the system control
of a much larger network which was shaped like an hour-glass
with the waist at Birmingham. The purchase increased the total
mileage controlled by the parent company to more than
10,200.[41]

The Louisville & Nashville was one of the oldest lines in
the South; it had been established in 1850 and had successfully
passed through the depression of 1873.[42] But in the early
nineties, despite its control of more than 4700 miles of track,[43]
it was not in a very strong position, Van Oss thought that:

there cannot be much doubt that for the third time in its history
the Louisville & Nashville has indulged in extension with more
energy than judgment, although the position of the company . . .
is so strong that this mistake will have no very injurious effect.
In 1891-92 the company earned a fair dividend in spite of the bad
state of trade and the great proportion of unremunerative mileage; it is easy to infer what the property will be capable of in
good times and with a better traffic on its new roads.[44]

Almost a decade was to pass before these optimistic prophecies would be realized. In 1893 dividends were reduced to
4 per cent and then because of the depression, they were passed
entirely until after the turn of the century.[45] Despite the fact
that recent losses had wiped out all the company's accumulated
surplus, late in 1893 the Louisville & Nashville directors pur-

40 Dozier, H. D., *A History of the Atlantic Coast Line Railroad*, Boston:
Houghton, Mifflin Company, 1920, p. 149.

41 Meade, " Great Railways," *Railway World*, 1905, pp. 171-2, 195-6.

42 Snyder, *op. cit.*, pp. 412-22.

43 Van Oss, *op. cit.*, pp. 736-48.

44 *Ibid.*, p. 744.

45 Poor, *op. cit.*, 1900, pp. 1268-85.

chased a controlling interest in the Chesapeake, Ohio & Southwestern, from C. P. Huntington and arranged to sell 50,000
new shares of stock to a syndicate in order to pay for it.[46]
But Chancellor Edwards of Kentucky decided that the purchase
violated the state constitution,[47] and the Louisville & Nashville
had to stand aside while the Illinois Central profited at its
expense by buying the Southwestern at a bargain price. The
system was involved in only one more important transaction
before its control passed to the Atlantic Coast Line: jointly
with the Southern Railway, it purchased a large and controlling
block of stock in the Cincinnati, Indianapolis & Louisville.[48]

After the acquisition of the Louisville & Nashville by the
Atlantic Coast Line, the latter took its place as one of the great
Southern systems. Two years after the merger which formed
the system had been completed a similar consolidation formed
the Seaboard Air Line. Lines formerly owned by eighteen different corporations and operated by three, the Georgia &
Alabama, the Florida Central & Peninsular and the old Seaboard
Air Line, were merged to form a new company whose tracks
paralleled those of the Atlantic Coast Line through the territory south of Washington.[49] The formation of this road was
not directly attributable to the depression but there was a
relationship: only by consolidating could small lines hope to
compete with the two giants which had been brought forth
during the depression, the Southern and the Atlantic Coast
line.[50]

Throughout the nineties hundreds of small railroad companies struggled along, some failing to weather the storms
because of their own mistakes, some falling victims to the

---

46 *Economist*, November 4, 1893, pp. 1310-1.

47 *Railway World*, July 14, 1894, pp. 556-7.

48 Snyder, *op. cit.*, pp. 412-22.

49 Meade, " Great Railways," *Railway World*, 1905, pp. 895-7.

50 Thompson, Slason, *A Short History of American Railways*, New York:
D. Appleton and Company, 1925, pp. 275-6.

cupidity of larger systems, some laying the foundations for future greatness and some simply enjoying an unheralded but none the less substantial and enviable success. These companies only attracted more than local attention when their interests impinged on those of the nation's great carriers. For the most part the public and even financial circles were wholly occupied by the larger and more sensational exploits and collapses of the major trunk lines. And this was natural enough, for the smaller roads unobtrusively continued their accustomed business, for the most part neither more nor less prosperous than usual.

CHAPTER X
DEVELOPMENTS DURING THE DEPRESSION

DURING the nineties American railroads experienced many changes. Large trunk lines were forced into receiverships and revelations attendant upon the reorganizations of some of them shocked the public. Of the companies which escaped receivership, some did so by the narrowest of margins, some took advantage of the nation-wide stringency to strengthen and enlarge their systems, and some met the exigencies of the depression with enviable success. Behind the scenes equally great changes took place: control of American railroads shifted from the hands of officials and owners to those of bankers with sufficient resources to influence and ally many systems at the same time.

Later writers have often blamed the difficulties of the railroads during this decade on the depression which lasted for about half of its length. But to do so is manifestly inaccurate. Even at the time very few experienced critics or officials were blind to the fact that the troubles of the companies antedated the depression. Many and conflicting explanations for these difficulties were offered, but there was a substantial unanimity of opinion that the industry had not been prosperous for years.[1] Undoubtedly the depression affected the roads both individually and collectively, but there is not a single case in which a receivership can be blamed on it alone. Financial chaos provided a test for the several companies and those which were weak almost immediately showed their vulnerability; those which were inherently strong and sound were able to adapt themselves to circumstances and emerge from the depression with increased efficiency and often enlarged facilities.

The reorganizations of insolvent companies all followed about the same pattern. Fixed charges were reduced in nearly

1 For some of these explanations, see above, pp. 30-35.

every case but there was seldom a simultaneous decrease in capitalization. Usually a number of securities which had borne fixed charges were transformed into contingent securities, frequently in the form of preferred stock with non-cumulative dividends. Almost invariably, too, the new bonds bore a lower rate of interest than had those which they replaced. A reorganization usually substituted one or two liens covering all the property of a company and bearing between 3 and 4 per cent interest for eight or ten or more different liens which had born 6 or 7 per cent.[2] The resulting simplification in financial structure was valuable, but the greatest benefits of these refunding operations lay in the reduction of fixed charges. This change invariably removed the difficulty which had been the immediate cause of failure—namely, inability to pay annual fixed obligations—and to that extent the reorganizations were wholly successful.

But when security holders were exchanging even junior bonds for new preferred stock or bonds bearing lower rates of interest, they demanded compensation for their sacrifice. This usually took the form of preferred or common stock; enough of these securities were distributed to give investors some prospect of receiving as great an annual return after the reorganization as before. This meant that although fixed charges were reduced, almost inevitably total capitalization was increased, sometimes to fantastic amounts. Since the demands of all investors in the old company were for

being remembered, and being remembered by a large amount in par value, the result (was) that through the reorganization you have got more stock and bonds than you had before you went into it; whereas the real cause of the receivership and of disaster was that they had too many stocks and bonds in the first place.[3]

The elements which entered into the increase of capitalization that characterized reorganizations were several in number.

2 *Industrial Commission Report*, testimony of W. Z. Ripley, IX, p. 298.
3 *Ibid.*, IX, p. 298.

Perhaps most important was the attempt to compensate investors for taking securities which gave a lower return or were less strongly secured than their former holdings. Frequently another factor was the capitalization of a floating debt which had been the immediate cause of insolvency. In only a very few cases did assessments raise enough cash to pay off the debt and even then preferred or common stock was often given to security holders in return for their contributions. Usually the cash thus raised was supplemented by the sale of new securities to a syndicate. Use of either or both of these methods meant that the floating debt had been capitalized.

A third important factor in this increase of capitalization was the cost of receivership and reorganization proceedings. The salaries of receivers, legal expenses caused by the almost endless litigation usually involved, and syndicate fees were eventually paid by the new company. The height to which the first two of these items could mount have been illustrated by the case of the Atchison; often the third was even larger. By 1896 syndicate operations had " become so profitable that certain banking houses have practically withdrawn from other uses of their money. They say it is the most profitable work they have been engaged in in recent years ".[4] The usual fee charged by underwriters for the formation of a syndicate was one per cent; in addition whatever profits attached to the sale of securities taken by syndicate members accrued to them in proportion to the share they themselves took.[5] The amount of profits to be gained from participation in these operations is illustrated by the experience of the Metropolitan Life Insurance Company, which was a member of several Kuhn, Loeb syndicates: it took a $5,000,000 interest in the underwriting of the Union Pacific reorganization, from which it derived a $131,-594.20 profit. In the Baltimore & Ohio refunding operations

4 *Railway World*, March 21, 1896, p. 274.

5 *Report of the Joint Committee of the Senate and Assembly of the State of New York Appointed to Investigate the Affairs of Life Insurance Companies*, testimony of Jacob Schiff, II, pp. 1337-8.

the much more modest total of $27,954.89 represented the profit from a $400,000 participation.[6] Both these and similar profits and the fees of reorganization managers, which often approximated $1,000,000 in reorganizations supervised by the house of Morgan, were added to the total capitalizations of the roads and helped account for the increases which took place in them during the reconstruction period of the nineties. Excluding the reorganization of the Baltimore & Ohio, which was notable for the increase of capitalization involved, the seven large systems which were rehabilitated during the decade levied assessments of more than $80,000,000, for much of which new securities were given, and realized nearly $50,000,000 in cash from the sale of new bonds and stock.[7] The combined total of about $130,000,000 represents the expenses which past mistakes and the ensuing receiverships and reorganizations cost these companies.

This situation had a very direct relation to the future financial structure of companies which had indulged in these generous stock issues. Since so many contingent and fixed annual obligations were given precedence over common stock, its prospect of ever receiving a dividend was very remote. Consequently its market value stayed very low. This meant that if a company needed capital it must issue new bonds and within twenty years after the turn of the century these circumstances had led to a disproportionate increase in fixed charges. In 1890 the funded debt of American railroads exceeded their stock capitalization by only $165,000,000. By 1918 this excess had grown to $2,929,000,000, an increase of 1675 per cent in the amount of difference. Total capitalization had risen 137 per cent, funded debts 165 per cent and capital stock only 108 per cent.[8] In other words, the plethora of stock issues in the nineties had destroyed

6 *Ibid.*, VIII, pp. 478-80.

7 Van Oss, S. F., "Recent American Railway Reorganizations," *The Journal of Finance*, April, 1898, pp. 345-55.

8 *Senate Commission on Interstate Commerce*, 1922, III, p. 1522.

stock values and thereby ultimately had caused an unforeseen and dangerous increase in fixed charges.

Because the greater part of the annual obligations of the new companies were contingent and not fixed, the immediate danger of future receiverships had been diminished, but a new problem had arisen which was destined to agitate the public mind for decades. The question was, to what extent could the public be expected

to pay a normal rate of interest upon that enormous aggregation of capital, some of which represents increase in the value of property, some of which represents pure water.[9]

Reorganization committees invariably based prospective fixed charges on net earning power for the few years preceding receivership; after they had thus determined the amount of bonds on which interest could be paid and issued as many as they safely could, then stock was issued in quantities sufficient to satisfy all equities. Since presumably all the net earnings would be needed to pay interest, the committees could hardly expect these shares to earn dividends except in unusually prosperous years. But earning power depended primarily on rates and there soon developed a demand that rates be raised enough to allow a fair return on all the capitalization, not just on the bonded debt. " The railroad declares itself to have a capitalization of $120,000,000 ", for instance. " They are entitled, as they contend, to earn a living interest and dividend upon that basis. The Interstate Commerce Commission answers, Not so; a large part of that capital is fictitious and we deny that you have a right so to earn." [10]

Since railroads had first been built in the United States there had been controversies over rates, but after the nineties the problem was distinctly different from what it had been before. Whereas in the seventies and eighties reformers had attacked

9 *Industrial Commission Report*, IX, pp. 291-2.
10 *Ibid.*, IX, p. 292.

the unfairness of existing rate schedules and the discriminations between places and shippers, and had sought to establish rates which would be fair to the customer, after the nineties the problem became twofold: to the old controversy was added one involving fairness to the investor. Few critics denied that the roads should be allowed to earn a fair return on their investment, but the crucial point lay in determining the meaning of these words.

In 1898 the Supreme Court had declared:

We hold, however, that the basis of all calculations as to the reasonableness of rates to be charged by a corporation maintaining a highway under legislative sanction must be the fair value of the property being used by it for the convenience of the public. And in order to ascertain that value, the original cost of construction, the amount expended in permanent improvements, the amount and market value of its bonds and stock, the present as compared with the original cost of construction, the probable earning capacity of the property under particular rates prescribed by statute, and the sum required to meet operating expenses, are all matters for consideration, and are to be given such weight as may be just and right in each case. We do not say that there may not be other matters to be regarded in estimating the value of the property. What the company is entitled to ask is a fair return upon the value of that which it employs for the public convenience. On the other hand, what the public is entitled to demand is that no more be exacted from it for the use of a public highway than the services rendered by it are reasonably worth.[11]

In these words the Court upheld the idea of a fair return on a fair value of the property and even suggested some of the factors to be considered in calculating the fair value, but it refused, and has continued to do so, to permit the use of any set formula in such calculations. In the Minnesota Rate Cases

11 Smith *v.* Ames, 169 U. S. 466, pp. 545-7; also see, Jones, Eliot, *Principles of Railroad Transportation*, New York: Macmillan Company, 1925, pp. 276-7.

in 1913 the Court declared that this was "not a matter of formulas, but there must be a reasonable judgment having its basis in a proper consideration of all relevant facts".[12]

The attempts to find a basis for estimating fair value have revolved especially around three possible standards: market value, original cost of construction and cost of reproduction. But none of these has been wholly satisfactory and the whole problem was complicated by a lack of impartially gathered information about the value of railroad property. In the late nineties a newly elected governor of Wisconsin, Robert M. LaFollette, was demanding that a physical evaluation of the railroads be made and that rates be based thereon; for ten years after he had become a senator, he continued his efforts to have the Interstate Commerce Commission undertake this work and in 1913 he was partially successful when President Taft signed a bill directing the Commission to do it.

The Railroad Securities Commission of 1911 defined a fair rate of return as "one which under honest accounting and responsible management will attract the amount of investors' money needed for the development of our railroad facilities".[13] But this definition contains several terms which would have to be carefully elaborated before it could be used in practice. What constitutes "honest accounting" and what is "responsible management"? Were the activities of the bankers during the nineties—activities which put so much water into railroad capitalization—included in these terms? The bankers and the holders of railroad securities naturally thought so and they demanded that they be permitted to earn enough to pay returns on all their securities.

However, the disbursement of the huge sums spent on reorganizations in the nineties was not entirely unproductive. Not only were the roads rehabilitated, but the care with which provision was made for future needs reflected a healthy reaction

12 230 U. S. 352, p. 434; see also, Jones, *Principles*, p. 277.
13 Jones, *Principles*, pp. 302-3.

to some of the mistakes which had led to the unprecedented number of failures during the depression. Because many of these insolvencies had been fundamentally due to abuses of credit and wild speculations in future needs, the mortgage indentures which were drawn in the nineties were carefully designed to prevent repetition of those same errors again. Francis Lynde Stetson, who was probably most influential in determining the form of these new indentures, said concerning them:

The panic of 1893 and the hard times ensuing led to defaults under many railroad mortgages, resulting in foreclosure sales followed by comprehensive reorganizations. In most cases such reorganizations involved the issue of long-time bonds of large amounts secured by all-embracing mortgages, and providing particularly for the increase of the initial debt by the issue of additional bonds for refunding and improvement purposes. The mortgages of the great reorganized companies, such as the Southern, the Erie, the Northern Pacific, the Atchison, and the Union Pacific, made from 1894 to 1896, were the result of comprehensive study of such instruments by many counsel, and they established the form of corporate mortgage now substantially followed.[14]

In carefully restricting the amounts of future bond issues and the purposes for which they might be made, these indentures were an immeasurable improvement over those which had formerly permitted the wildest sort of irresponsible financing.

Another reaction to the chaotic conditions that had preceded the depression was reflected in the extensive use of voting trusts which were created to retain control of reorganized roads until they were well established financially. Morgan's reasons for initiating this policy have already been explained, and similar motives were active in most other reorganizations: after having invested heavily in the railroads they reorganized, bankers were loath to return them to the owners and let anarchy rule the

14 Stetson, Francis Lynde, and others, *Some Legal Phases of Corporate Financing, Reorganization and Regulation,* New York: Macmillan Company, 1917, p. 13.

industry again. But the voting power of stock could be valuable and it could be used in a manner prejudicial to the equities from which a voting trust severed it. That " the voting power of stock is a valuable property right " and that " the right of control has a money value distinct from the right to receive dividends " was generally overlooked at first.[15] However, the Reading reorganization plan in 1895 and the Northern Pacific plan which was executed in 1897 at least partially recognized that it was necessary to provide some limits to the powers of voting trustees if the equities of security holders were not to be injured; both these indentures provided that " no superior rights, in the form either of additional preferred stock or of a new mortgage " could be created by the voting trustees without the consent of at least a majority of outstanding trust certificates.[16]

The bankers' acquisition and retention of control over railroads combined with several other factors to bring a new era in railroad organization and finance. Because of the almost fantastically high capitalizations of the several reorganized systems, bankers began to take an increased interest in railroad affairs just when railroad finance was becoming a matter of such huge operations that it could only be carried on with the coöperation of those who had unlimited resources at their command. Already in control of several great key systems, and able to dictate to other systems when they needed financial aid, the banks were in a position to protect their huge investments from the dangers which unlimited competition would bring:

Under the control of eastern bankers for the most part, the existing systems were treated as they had formerly treated branch lines. The securities of certain systems became centralized in certain banking groups which found their entire interest in ade-

15 Harriman, E. A., " Voting Trusts and Holding Companies," *Yale Law Journal*, XIII, pp. 109-123.

16 Cushing, Harry A., *Voting Trusts*, New York: Macmillan Company, 1915, pp. 45-6.

quate profits and not in the building up of one line at the expense of another. Only by large consolidations could a unity of action be effected and profits made secure.[17]

As banking interests extended their control over the railroads, the new era began; speculative profits would no longer be made by looting a single line in the manner of a Daniel Drew, a Jay Gould or a Credit Mobilier. Rather the stakes were larger: Harriman would fight Hill and Morgan in the open market for control of the Northern Pacific system although in so doing he would precipitate a panic, all for the sake of getting control of the Burlington. Similarly, the Louisville & Nashville would be speculated in by Gates until he had the whole system under his control, and this controlling interest would then be sold as a unit to the Atlantic Coast Line system. Trading whole systems replaced trading shares in a single company after the depression of the nineties.

This speculation in systems was partly the result and partly the cause of another trend which was best exemplified by Morgan's policies:

Starting as a financial problem of reorganizing bankrupt railroads (his) activity soon became an expression of the drift toward consolidation and combination. Community of interest was another form of combination, measurably contributing to unification of the railroads under definite financial control.[18]

The extent of Morgan's influence among the railroads of the country at the end of the nineteenth century cannot be stated absolutely, but by virtue of voting trusts, interlocking directorates and communities of interest, it was immense. By participating in its reorganization he had gained control over the Northern Pacific and allied himself with Hill and the Great Northern; he had entrenched himself in the Southern, the Erie,

17 Riegel, R. E., *The Story of the Western Railroads*, New York: Macmillan Company, 1926, p. 311.

18 Corey, *House of Morgan*, p. 176.

the anthracite roads, and the Baltimore & Ohio. He was the dominant figure in the New York, New Haven & Hartford, and by virtue of his membership on the New York Central's board of directors and his activities as financial agent, he was very influential in the Vanderbilt system. The creation of a community of interest between the Vanderbilts and the Pennsylvania, with which he also had close and important financial relations, extended his influence to the Norfolk & Western and the Chesapeake & Ohio. In the banking world, George F. Baker was a close ally and he controlled huge railroad interests through the First National Bank.[19] The National Bank of Commerce, the Chase National Bank, the Liberty National Bank, the New York Life Insurance Company, the Equitable Life and other financial powers were considered to be partly at least under Morgan's influence; and all these institutions had their railroad interests.[20] In its final report the Pujo Committee listed the companies whose reorganizations Morgan had been influential in shaping during the nineties: the Baltimore & Ohio, the Chesapeake & Ohio, the Cincinnati, Hamilton & Dayton, the Chicago & Great Western, the Erie, the Northern Pacific, the Pere Marquette, the Southern and the Reading.[21] All together, including those systems in which Morgan's control was apparent and also those in which it was less obvious, John Moody estimated that around the turn of the century the " Morgan railroads " embraced 47,000 miles of track [22]—and this was a conservative estimate. An expert railroad accountant testifying before the Pujo Committee stated that Morgan representatives were directors of railroads having a mileage of 48,000 and capitalized at $4,379,000,000.[23]

19 *Ibid.*, pp. 208-9.

20 Moody, John, *The Truth About the Trusts*, New York: Moody Publishing Company, 1904, pp. 492-3.

21 *Pujo Investigation*, pp. 148-50.

22 Moody, *Trusts*, pp. 492-3.

23 *Pujo Investigation*, testimony of Philip J. Scudder, pp. 985-6.

Morgan had gained his foothold in almost all of these companies after 1893. Before the depression he had been influential in the affairs of the Vanderbilt system and a few smaller lines, but beginning with his retention of control in the newly organized Southern Railway he had extended his railroad interests whenever opportunity offered. In doing so he was approximating, consciously or unconsciously, the policy for which President Alexander J. Cassatt of the Pennsylvania Railroad was to become famous in the opening years of the twentieth century. Cassatt, in his efforts to end rate-cutting, evolved his 'community of interest' idea. In accordance with it the several large Eastern trunk lines bought interests in each other and jointly purchased large blocks of the securities of smaller rivals. Through the interlocking ownership thus created there was developed a community of interest: it was to the best interest of all the roads that all be prosperous and the incentive for cutthroat competition was removed. Exactly the same end had been achieved among the companies controlled by Morgan: he would frown on any attempt by one road in which he was interested to benefit at the expense of another in which he held an equal stake.

The necessities of the reorganization period which followed the panic of 1893 had enabled Morgan to begin " collecting railroads " as a connoisseur might collect art; they had also given a start to the one man who, with more or less success, was to challenge Morgan's dominance in the opening years of the twentieth century, Edward H. Harriman. Before the depression Harriman had wielded an influence among mid-Western railroads because of his domination of the Illinois Central. But after his accession to control of the Union Pacific in 1897,

with these properties as a nucleus, and with the credit based on these assets, the Union Pacific in the last six years (to 1906) has so grown in power and influence that at this time it controls every line of railroad reaching the Pacific coast between Portland cn the north and the Mexican border on the south—a distance as great as that from Maine to Florida—excepting alone the Santa Fe, in which it has a large stock interest.[24]

By the time the Interstate Commerce Commission thus admitted its failure to maintain competition on the Pacific coast south of Portland, similar conditions existed in several other parts of the country. The reorganization of the Northern Pacific by Hill and Morgan had created a community of interest in the Northwest. Competition had been stifled in New England by the agreement between the Boston & Maine and the New York, New Haven & Hartford. The New York Central and the Pennsylvania had created such " an extraordinary concentration of railway interests " along the middle Atlantic seaboard that competition had been effectually ended.[25] Morgan domination of both the Southern and the Atlantic Coast Line precluded the maintenance of real competition in the South.[26] Only in the mid-West where these several groups of roads met was there anything resembling real competition and even there care was taken that rate-wars should not break out. The investments at stake were too huge to risk them when competition could be effectually smothered so easily.

During the nineties the railroads of the country had gone through a transition which was to be experienced by many of the other great industries of the nation in the period immediately following. At the beginning of the decade there had been innumerable great independent systems, each with its own group of subsidiaries, but each competing against rival systems in the same regions. At the end of the decade there were practically no independent systems; the various systems had been drawn into a few huge combinations which were dominated by a single man or a small group of men working in harmony

24 *Hearings in the Matter of Consolidations and Combinations, etc.*, by the Interstate Commerce Commission, 1906, *Report no. 943.*

25 Interstate Commerce Commission, *Report on Intercorporate Relationships of Railways in the United States as of June 30, 1906*, p. 40.

26 *Ibid.*, p. 41.

with each other. Just as a money trust existed some fifteen years later, a railroad trust had been formed in the nineties—and by interests practically identical with those which formed the money trust.[27] The railroad industry had been transformed from one dominated by hundreds of competing leaders into one controlled by a small group of financiers. For example, before the depression the Eastern trunk line business was divided among several independent and competing systems: the New York Central, the Pennsylvania, the Erie, the Baltimore & Ohio, the Philadelphia & Reading and the Norfolk & Western. At the end of the century a community of interest had been formed which included all these systems and competition between them was a thing of the past. In the South at the turn of the century there were three large systems, the Southern, the Atlantic Coast Line and the Seaboard Air Line—and Morgan dominated all three to the exclusion of competition. In trans-continental business there had been five competing lines before the depression: the Great Northern, the Northern Pacific, the Union Pacific, the Southern Pacific and the Atchison. Soon after the turn of the century competition between these five had been reduced to competition between two super-systems: Hill's two northwestern roads and Harriman's three lines to the south (if the Atchison may be included among the latter's lines despite the fact that he did not absolutely dominate it). Throughout the country competing systems had found it more profitable to form communities of interest and cooperate instead of competing and trying to ruin each other.

Before the Industrial Commission in 1900 Stetson had testi-fied that the reorganizations in which he had figured

had been rendered necessary by the inability of the corporations to meet their fixed charges, an inability which had been due largely to ruinous reduction of railway rates, partly through legislation and partly through ruinous competition.[28]

27 See *Pujo Investigation, passim.*
28 *Industrial Commission Report,* IV, p. 37.

Any future repetition of the disasters of the nineties was to be prevented if possible by the suppression of competition. Although legislative actions could not always be entirely controlled, ruinous competition could and would be ended permanently.

Building on the foundations so well laid during the nineties, by about 1905 the country was completely divided among a few great railroad empires. From the Atlantic coast to Chicago and St. Louis the Morgan-Vanderbilt-Pennsylvania group controlled practically every road of any importance. In New England the New York, New Haven & Hartford and in the South the Southern and the Atlantic Coast Line dominated the field; in the middle states and as far west as Chicago and St. Louis the Pennsylvania and the Vanderbilt Lines, together with the other roads in which they were interested, were in control. In the Northwest from Chicago to the Pacific Hill was in control and of course he worked in harmony with Morgan. The Union Pacific-Southern Pacific group was dominated by Harriman, and the Southwest was controlled by Gould and the Rock Island. Altogether these seven interests, Morgan, Vanderbilt, the Pennsylvania, Gould, Hill, Harriman and the Rock Island, controlled 85 per cent of the railroad earnings of the country—and these seven interests were in practice only four: the Morgan-Hill-Vanderbilt-Pennsylvania, the Harriman, the Gould and the Rock Island.[29]

Speaking in 1902 Interstate Commerce Commissioner Charles A. Prouty declared:

Five years ago the crying evil in railway operations was discrimination, mainly discrimination between individual shippers. While many rates were too high, the general level was low; and in view of competitive conditions which had for some time and then existed, little apprehension was felt of any general unreasonable advance. Not so today. The vast consolidations of the past few years; the use of injunctions to prevent departures from the pub-

29 Moody, *Trusts*, pp. 432-9.

lished tariff; the lesson which railroad operators themselves have learned, that competition in rates is always suicidal, since it does not increase traffic and does reduce revenues—these have largely eliminated that competition. That discrimination is disappearing, but in its place comes that other danger which always attends monopoly, the exaction of an unreasonable charge.[30]

Henceforth the problem would not be to curb the cut-throat competition of the railroads; it would be to regulate the great railway monopolies which had been formed during the nineties with so much water in their capitalizations.

At the time of their formation, the claim had been advanced that these monopolies would improve service as well as reduce the costs of transportation to the consumer. Nevertheless during the early years of the twentieth century it became evident that these benefits would only accrue if those who controlled the roads were forced to extend them. The insolvencies of several of the great systems had been partially caused by the poor condition of equipment and the financial rehabilitation of these roads was accompanied by similar improvement and reconstruction of the roadbeds and rolling stock. The Southern Railway, the Baltimore & Ohio and the Union Pacific particularly were characterized by comprehensive betterments at the time of their reorganizations and for a time it seemed that banker-control of railroads would usher in a new era of efficiency in the industry. However the promise was not fulfilled: in the first decade of the twentieth century the problem of adequate service came to the fore to rival in importance the older problem of rates.[31] Furthermore, the Illinois Central equipment scandal which became public just after Harriman's death in September, 1909, and the ruin of the Chicago & Alton showed that despite their loud protests against the looting of

30 Prouty, Charles A., *National Regulation of Railways*, American Economic Association Publications, 3rd series, IV, no. 1, February, 1903. Proceedings at 15th Annual Meeting, Philadelphia, December, 26-29, 1902.

31 Jones, *Principles*, p. 68.

railroads during the nineties, the bankers' assumption of control in the industry had not assured the millennium in railroading.[32]

Although in many ways American railroads were the best in the world during the early years of the twentieth century, yet the monopoly of control was permitting the appearance of disquieting symptoms. One commentator listed safety, speed, promptitude, adequate facilities fairly distributed, convenient methods and impartial treatment as the elements of good service and found that in all of these American roads were losing ground to those of other countries. In regard to speed, European roads were surpassing American and one former American official explained this fact: his line had never used their facilities for fast time between Chicago and New York to their utmost because if it had it would have precipitated a rate war. To prevent this, the roads had informal agreements limiting the speed with which the several runs would be made. The concentration of ownership in the industry facilitated and made inevitable such agreements concerning speed and other features of service.

In respect to promptitude American roads were easily second to those of Germany and the service offered in some parts of the United States, particularly in the South, did not compare favorably with the notoriously sloppy service offered on trunk lines in Italy before the government assumed control. Aside from the failure of American roads to train their railroad workers adequately, the cause of this evil often lay in preferential treatment accorded certain customers. For instance, it was not unheard-of for a crack passenger express train to be sidetracked to permit a freight train bearing Armour's beef to pass. Again, until Congress forbade the practice, officials were accustomed to refuse to permit the customer to specify the route by which his shipment was to go. The freight would often be sent by some unnecessarily long and slow route simply

32 Brandeis, *Other People's Money*, p. 115.

because by so doing mutual favors could be conferred by a group of roads. That the shipments were thereby made several hours late in arrival and at times spoiled on the way were ignored. A related difficulty was the monopolizing of cars by favored shippers to the misfortune or ruin of small business men.

The railroads further tended to ignore taking those steps which might have made travel more comfortable for the passenger. The checking of baggage through to a destination beyond the terminal of the railroad on which a journey was initiated, was at times impossible. Companies were lax in the ventilation and heating of cars. Service was so divided up and apportioned out as to cost the passenger the maximum of trouble and money rather than cared for economically by the railroads; for example, express service, dining service and similar correlative services were each cared for by a separate and irresponsible company to whose mercies the passenger was left.

Congress was trying to improve the standard of safety by legislation during these years and the very fact that it felt the need for such action indicated that American roads were not characterized by any too great attention to safety. After the turn of the century American roads surpassed only those of Canada and Russia in this respect and even in those cases the margin was very narrow. In Canada and Russia proportionally fewer persons were injured than on American roads, but twice as many were killed.[33] That safety was becoming an important issue was indicated by the gradually increasing proportions of the annual reports of the Interstate Commerce Commission which were devoted to discussing it; annually more and more detailed suggestions and reports were made on the subject to

33 In the United States 1 passenger in 1,957,441 was killed, 1 in 84,424 injured; in Canada 1 in 1,120,000 was killed, 1 in 158,000 injured; in Russia 1 in 1,080,000 killed and 1 in 250,000 injured. Judging safety by the number of passengers carried safely for every one killed, the order of safety in 1902-4 was: Belgium, Denmark, Switzerland, Germany, Austria-Hungary, Great Britain, Norway, Sweden, France, United States, Canada and Russia.

Congress. Congress replied with a set of laws providing in various ways for the safety of workers and passengers on the roads. The first such act, the Safety Appliance Act, became law on March 2, 1893; it required all railroads to equip their cars with automatic couplers and power brakes within five years. This and later legislation was necessitated by the reluctance of the roads to take sufficient measures to assure safety. The officials of the companies were not entirely loath to work for greater safety—for there were definite financial benefits to be derived from preventing damage suits, attracting customers by safety records and preventing the needless destruction of property in wrecks—but that they failed to take adequate action is indicated by the need for Congress to step in. Competition had disappeared and with it had gone the main stimulus to improve service in order to increase business.[34]

Despite the fact that the roads were not improving their service sufficiently to satisfy critics, rates were being steadily raised in the years after the turn of the century.

When the railroad combinations were being effected the financiers assured the public that railway rates would not be advanced; indeed, rates would be reduced, if anything, because of the economies of combination. Yet such is not the usual operation of unregulated monopoly; and the outcome was merely what might have been anticipated. Throughout the early years of the twentieth century, therefore, rates were considerably advanced. . . . These advances in rates, almost without exception, were the result of concerted action by the railroads. The advances in competitive rates were uniformly made effective by all the railroads on the same day and for exactly the same amount. As a rule the railway officials did not deny that they had acted in concert, but they maintained that there had been no illegal agreement. Yet whether there had been an illegal agreement or not, the significant feature of the advances was that the people had no adequate means of protecting

34 Parsons, *The Railways, the Trusts and the People*, pp. 425-51; Jones, *Principles*, pp. 375-410.

themselves against the injury resulting from the higher level of charges.[35]

In the face of rising rates, the railroad problem was continually before Congress and several different methods were tried in the efforts to solve it. The Interstate Commerce Act of 1887 had forbidden pooling and the roads had then turned to the formation of agreements to maintain rates in order to escape the consequences of competition. But in 1897 and 1898 the Supreme Court had held these agreements illegal under the Sherman Anti-Trust Act.[36] It had been in view of these decisions that the several railroad " interests " had been formed and, as soon as their formation was publicly known, agitation had begun for their legal banishment.

In 1904 and again in 1905 President Theodore Roosevelt included detailed remarks on the railroad problem in his annual messages to Congress. On December, 1904, he declared:

The Government must in increasing degree supervise and regulate the workings of the railways engaged in interstate commerce; and such increased supervision is the only alternative to an increase of the present evils on the one hand or a still more radical policy on the other. In my judgment the most important legislative act now needed as regards the regulation of corporations is this act to confer on the Interstate Commerce Commission the power to revise rates and regulations, the revised rate to at once go into effect, and stay in effect unless and until the court of review reverses it.[37]

A year afterwards Roosevelt reiterated and elaborated his demands:

35 Jones, *Principles*, p. 232.

36 In the Trans-Missouri Freight Association case (166 U. S. 290) and the Joint Traffic Association case (171 U. S. 505).

37 Richardson, J. D., editor, *Messages and Papers of the Presidents*, Washington: Government Printing Office, 1897-1925, XIV, p. 6902.

It has been a misfortune that the National laws on this subject have hitherto been of a negative or prohibitive rather than an affirmative kind, and still more that they have in part sought to prohibit what could not be effectively prohibited, and have in part in their prohibitions confounded what should be allowed and what should not be allowed. . . . What is needed is not sweeping prohibition of every arrangement, good or bad, which may tend to restrict competition, but such adequate supervision and regulation as will prevent any restriction of competition from being to the detriment of the public—as well as such supervision and regulation as will prevent other abuses in no way connected with restriction of competition. Of these abuses, perhaps the chief, although by no means the only one, is overcapitalization—generally itself the result of dishonest promotion—because of the myriad evils it brings in its train; for such overcapitalization often means an inflation that invites business panic; it always conceals the true relation of the profit earned to the capital actually invested, and it creates a burden of interest payments which is a fertile cause of improper reduction in or limitation of wages; it damages the small investor, discourages thrift, and encourages gambling and speculation; while perhaps worst of all is the trickiness and dishonesty which it implies —for harm to morals is worse than any possible harm to material interests, and the debauchery of politics and business by great dishonest corporations is far worse than any actual material evil they do the public. Until the National Government obtains, in some manner which the wisdom of Congress may suggest, proper control over the big corporations engaged in interstate commerce—that is, over the great majority of the big corporations—it will be impossible to deal adequately with these evils.[38]

The president's sermon finally had its effect and in 1906 the Hepburn Act was passed. Four years later the Mann-Elkins Act supplemented it. These two laws strengthened the Interstate Commerce Commission and greatly increased its power over rates but not until 1914 was a direct attack made on the railroad monopolies. One section of the Clayton Anti-Trust Act

38 *Ibid.*, XIV, pp. 6975-6.

passed in that year forbade a common carrier engaged in interstate commerce to acquire thereafter, directly or indirectly,
stock in another company engaged in interstate commerce, if
by so doing competition would be substantially lessened or a
monopoly created. A similar provision prohibited the creation
thereafter of holding companies, not themselves engaged in
interstate commerce, to hold stock in competing companies.

These various laws in the first fifteen years of the twentieth
century were designed, for the most part, to correct abuses
whose existence had been illustrated during the nineties or
which had grown up at that time. The punitive clauses of these
laws, if in effect during the last decade of the nineteenth century, might well have landed a number of high railroad officials
in jail. The attack on the community of interest, although not
applying to holding companies already organized, was designed
to prevent the furtherance of the existing monopoly in railroads. And, finally, the Interstate Commerce Commission was
given more power; not only were needed extensions of its jurisdiction granted, but its control of rates was made real. Concentration of control in the industry had made imperative some
positive control of rates instead of the former shadowy attempts
to prevent exorbitant charges.

The reluctance of the companies to provide better service
and the desire, at the same time, to raise rates indicated that
those in control were more interested in railroads as financial
pawns than as transportation companies. And the manipulations of systems in the early years of the new century confirmed this impression. The profits accruing to underwriters of
reorganizations have already been mentioned. But such profits
did not stop after reorganization had been effected. Kuhn, Loeb
& Company continued as the financial agents of the Union
Pacific after 1898 and continued to find the relationship extremely profitable. Although the Supreme Court refused to
approve Harriman's merger of the Southern Pacific and the
Central Pacific, nevertheless Kuhn, Loeb & Company received

their commission for having agreed to market the proposed new securities. And in the years following the bankers marketed millions of dollars worth of securities for the Harriman system, all at a nice commission. Similarly the House of Morgan made millions of profits marketing securities of the New York, New Haven & Hartford.[39]

Altogether the assumption of control over the country's railroads by banking interests who welded together huge monopolies failed to bring with it the benefits which had been promised. In the process of creating the monopolies large amounts of water had been poured into capitalization and there was constant agitation that the roads be permitted to charge enough to pay dividends on this water. During the nineties several companies had been rebuilt and a promising start of banker-control thus made, but after the turn of the century visible progress stopped: relieved of the pressure of competition, the roads did not make very serious efforts to improve their service and it is a significant fact that no important new inventions were introduced in railroading until the age of electrification and motor-bus competition began. The size of locomotives and cars was increased and half-hearted attempts to install block-signalling systems were made, but there were no great technical advances until competition forced the roads to act. Monopoly was not bringing the benefits expected of it, and on the other hand administrative scandals and stock watering continued.

Considered in the light of later developments, in two respects the depression of the nineties was particularly significant for American railroads: first, it was the final straw which forced several roads into the hands of receivers. These companies had been bankrupt *de facto* before 1893; the depression merely compelled them to acknowledge their insolvency a little sooner than might otherwise have been necessary. In this way the depression was distinctly purgative: in one mad destructive crash all the tottering financial structures which were stagger-

39 Brandeis, op. cit., pp. 18, 116-8, etc.

ing under too heavy burdens were relieved of these burdens and put back on their feet, ready to develop with fantastic rapidity in the early years of the twentieth century.

Secondly, the reorganization work which followed the crash laid the foundations for the consolidation movement which was to continue until it had combined into a few great railway interests nearly all the mileage of the country. In this reconstruction the men who would control this movement emerged from the common level of financial and official leadership to take preeminent positions. Of the three most powerful railroad men after the depression—Harriman, Hill and Morgan—none had been influential in the railroad industry before 1893. Harriman had had his Illinois Central, Hill his as yet incomplete Great Northern and Morgan his interests in the Vanderbilt and a few other systems. After the depression was past, these three together with the Vanderbilts and the Pennsylvania dominated the transportation facilities of the country.

The depression had brought an unprecedented number of railroad failures. But the receiverships had been those of companies already essentially bankrupt. Without irreparably harming the well-managed roads, the depression had forced the crippled companies to reorganize on a sound basis and it had laid the foundations for the new movement towards the consolidation of railroad properties to the exclusion of competition —a tendency not yet completed.

BIBLIOGRAPHY

PERIODICALS

Commercial and Financial Chronicle, 1892-1899, New York City.
The Economist, 1892-1899, London, England.
The Evening Post, 1892-1899, New York City.
Railroad Gazette, 1892-1899, New York City.
Railway Age and Northwestern Railroader, 1892-1899, Chicago, Illinois.
Railway Review, 1892-1899, Chicago, Illinois.
Railway World, 1892-1899, Philadelphia, Pennsylvania.
United States Investor, 1898, New York City.
Wall Street Journal, 1892-1899, New York City.

ANNUALS AND ENCYCLOPEDIAS

Appleton's Annual Cyclopedia and Register of Important Events of the Year, 1879-1899, New York: D. Appleton and Company.
Dictionary of American Biography, edited by Allen Johnson and Dumas Malone, New York: Charles Scribner's Sons, 1928-1936.
Lamb's Biographical Dictionary of the United States, edited by John H. Brown, Boston: James H. Lamb Company, 1900.
The National Cyclopedia of American Biography, New York: James T. White and Company, 1922-1929.
Poor's Manual of Railroads, 1880-1909, New York: H. V. & H. W. Poor.
Who's Who in America, 1899-1900, edited by John W. Leonard, Chicago: A. N. Marquis and Company, 1899.

OFFICIAL DOCUMENTS

Report on Transportation Business in the United States at the Eleventh Census, Part I, *Transportation by Land* (Henry C. Adams, special agent), Washington: Government Printing Office, 1895.
United States Industrial Commission Report (including review of evidence, topical digest of evidence, testimony and conclusions of the Commission), 20 volumes, 1898-1902.
United States Interstate Commerce Commission Annual Reports, 1887-1903.
United States Interstate Commerce Commission Annual Statistics, 1887-1903.
United States Interstate Commerce Commission, *Report on Intercorporate Relationships of Railways in the United States as of June 30, 1906.*
United States Interstate Commerce Commission: *Hearings in the matter of consolidations and combinations of carriers, relations between such carriers, and community of interest therein, their rates, facilities and practices*, begun November, 1906. No. 943.
United States Interstate Commerce Commission: *Investigation of facts as to combination or arrangement between the Pennsylvania Railroad and other railroads*, by Martin A. Knopf, February 2, 1906.

343

United States Supreme Court: *Northern Securities Case* (transcript of evidence), 4 volumes.

United States Courts: *Union Pacific Receivership Records,* 4 volumes (1893?).

United States Congress: *Congressional Record,* XXVII, Part 2, pp. 1539-1540, 53rd Congress, 3rd Session (Reilly Bill).

United States Congress: *A Bill* Directing the foreclosure of the Government lien on the Pacific railroads, and for other purposes (introduced by Mr. Allen in Senate January 7, 1896), no. 777, 54th Congress, 1st Session.

United States Congress: *A Bill* Directing the foreclosure of the Government lien on the Pacific railroads and for other purposes (introduced by Mr. Sulzer in House, July 22, 1897), H. R. 3946, 55th Congress, 1st Session.

United States Congress: *Investigation of Alleged Coal Combination, H. R. Report 2278,* 52nd Congress, 2nd Session.

United States Congress: *Views of the Minority of the House Committee on Pacific Railroads on the Reilly Bill* (includes as appendix Pattison's minority report submitted in 1888 together with report of majority of the committee to investigate the Pacific railroads), *H. R. Report 1290,* 53rd Congress, 2nd Session.

United States Congress: Letter from the Attorney-General transmitting pursuant to House Resolution dated October 14, 1893, a draft of a bill to reorganize the Union Pacific Railway Company, and to readjust and secure the claims of the United States against said company, *H. R. Executive Document 203,* 53rd Congress, 2nd Session.

United States Congress: *Report* of Mr. Brice, chairman of the Senate Pacific Railroads Committee, recommending a solution of the problems raised by the Government's claims against the roads, *Senate Report 830,* 53rd Congress, 3rd Session.

United States Congress: *Notes of hearings before the Committee on Pacific Railroads of the Senate on the subject of the indebtedness of the Pacific Railroads to the Government, Senate Document 314,* 54th Congress, 1st Session.

United States Congress: *Report from majority of Committee on Pacific Railroads,* with statement and hearing thereon by C. P. Huntington in appendix (submitted by Mr. Gear, May 1, 1896), *Senate Report 778,* 54th Congress, 1st Session.

United States Congress: *Report from Committee on Pacific Railroads* (submitted April 25, 1896), *H. R. Report 1497,* 54th Congress, 1st Session.

United States Congress: *Agreement with Reorganization Committee of the Union Pacific Railroad Company* (submitted to Senate January 25, 1897), *Senate Document 283,* 54th Congress, 2nd Session.

United States Congress: *Report of the Government Directors of the Union Pacific Railway for year ending June 30, 1896, Senate Document 12,* 54th Congress, 2nd Session.

United States Congress: *Report from the majority of the House Committee on Pacific Railroads* (submitted by Mr. Harrison, February 11, 1897), *H. R. Report 2906*, 54th Congress, 2nd Session.

United States Congress: *Hearings before the Senate Committee on Interstate Commerce*, May, 1900 (testimony of Frank Parsons), *Senate Document 420*, 56th Congress, 1st Session.

United States Congress: *Investigation of Financial and Monetary Conditions in the United States*, before the Subcommittee of the Committee on Banking and Currency (*Pujo Investigation*), 1912-13.

United States Congress: *New York, New Haven and Hartford Railroad: Evidence taken before the Interstate Commerce Commission relative to the financial transactions of the New York, New Haven and Hartford Railroad Company*, together with the report of the Commission thereon, *Senate Document 543*, 63rd Congress, 2nd Session.

United States Congress: *Investigation of Railroads* (St. Louis and San Francisco and its purchase of the Chicago and Eastern Illinois and the St. Louis, Brownsville and Mexico, and its later failure) by the Interstate Commerce Commission, *Senate Document 26*, 63rd Congress, 2nd Session.

United States Congress: *Hearings before the Joint (Newlands) Committee of the Senate and the House of Representatives on Interstate and Foreign Commerce to investigate Government control, regulation and ownership of interstate public utilities and the argument of Alfred P. Thom, counsel for the Railway Executives' Advisory Committee*, November 23, 24, 25, 27, 28, 29, December 1, 2, 1916.

United States Congress: *Hearings before the Senate Committee on Interstate Commerce upon matters relating to revenues and expense of railroads which report to the Commission*, 5 volumes, 67th Congress, 2nd Session.

United States Congress: *Regulation of Stock Ownership in Railroads*, 3 volumes, *H. R. Report 2789*, 71st Congress, 3rd Session.

United States Attorney-General: *Report* for the year ending November 30, 1897, *H. R. Document 9*, 55th Congress, 2nd Session (includes report of final settlement of Union Pacific debt to Government).

Messages and Papers of the Presidents, a compilation by James D. Richardson, Washington: Government Printing Office, 1897-1925.

New York State Legislature: *Testimony taken before the Special Senate Committee relative to the coal monopoly* (Reading combination), transmitted to the legislature February 1, 1893, *Document 5*, I, 1893.

New York State Legislature: *Report of the Senate Special Committee on the Coal Combination*, transmitted February 1, 1893, *Document 21*, IV, 1893.

New York State Legislature: *Report of the Joint (Armstrong) Committee of the Senate and Assembly of the State of New York appointed to investigate the affairs of life insurance companies*, transmitted to the legislature February 22, 1906, 11 volumes.

General Works

Adams, Henry C., "A Decade of Federal Railway Regulation," *Atlantic Monthly*, April, 1898, LXXXI, pp. 434-443.

Adler, Cyrus, *Jacob H. Schiff, His Life and Letters*, 2 volumes, Garden City: Doubleday, Doran and Company, Inc., 1928.

Alexander, E. P., "Railway Management," *Scribner's Magazine*, V, 1889, pp. 27-48.

Bogart, E. L., *Economic History of the American People*, New York: Longmans, Green and Company, 1930.

Bogen, Jules I., *The Anthracite Railroads*, New York: The Ronald Press Company, 1927.

Brandeis, Louis, *Other People's Money*, Washington: National Home Library Foundation, 1933.

Bureau of Railway Economics, *A Brief Survey of Railway Taxation*, 28-page pamphlet, Washington, 1930.

Burr, Anna Robeson, *Portrait of a Banker*, James Stillman, New York: Duffield and Company, 1927.

Cleveland, F. A. and Powell, F. W., *Railroad Promotion and Capitalization*, New York: Longmans, Green & Company, 1909.

Clews, Henry, *Fifty Years in Wall Street*, New York: Irving Publishing Company, 1908.

——, "Railroad Stocks and Bonds," *The Independent* (New York), June 1, 1893.

Corey, Lewis, *The House of Morgan*, New York: G. Howard Watt, 1930.

Cunniff, M. G., "Increasing Railroad Consolidation," *World's Work*, III, 1902, pp. 1775-1780.

Cushing, Harry A., *Voting Trusts*, New York: The Macmillan Company, 1915.

Daggett, Stuart, *Railroad Reorganization*, Boston: Houghton, Mifflin and Co., 1908.

Demands of the Railroad Employees, 15-page pamphlet, New York, 1910.

Depew, Chauncey, *My Memories of Eighty Years*, New York: Charles Scribner's Sons, 1922.

Eckenrode, H. J. and Edmunds, P. W., *E. H. Harriman, The Little Giant of Wall Street*, New York: Greenberg, 1933.

Edwards, E. J., "Men Behind the Railroads," *Booklovers' Magazine*, I, 1903, pp. 335-342.

Gibbon, John, "Railroad Consolidation," *North American Review*, 1892, pp. 251-4.

Graser, F. H., "The Voting Trust in Railway Finance," *Railway World*, 1904, pp. 547-8.

Greene, Thomas L., "Changes in the Form of Railroad Capital," *Quarterly Journal of Economics*, IV, 1890, pp. 449-457.

——, *Corporation Finance*, New York: G. P. Putnam's Sons, 1897.

——, "Railway Accounting," *Political Science Quarterly*, VII, 1892, pp. 598-612.

——, "Railroad Stock Watering," *Political Science Quarterly*, VI, 1891, pp. 474-492.

Hadley, Arthur T., "The Prohibition of Railroad Pools," *Quarterly Journal of Economics*, IV, 1889-90, pp. 158-171.

——, "Railroad Problems of the Immediate Future," *Atlantic Monthly*, March, 1891, pp. 386-393.

——, "Remedies for Railway Troubles," *Forum*, V, 1887, pp. 429-435.

Haney, Lewis, *A Congressional History of Railways in the United States*, Carnegie Institute of Washington, 1915.

Harriman, E. A., "Voting Trusts and Holding Companies," *Yale Law Journal*, XIII, 1904, pp. 109-123.

Hedges, J. B., *Henry Villard and the Railways of the Northwest*, New Haven: Yale University Press, 1930.

Henry and West (Bankers), *The Railroads and the Necessity for Higher Rates*, 9-page pamphlet, Philadelphia, 1913.

Hirschl, A. J., *Combination, Consolidation and Succession of Corporations*, Chicago: Callaghan and Company, 1896.

Hovey, Carl, *Life Story of J. P. Morgan*, New York: Sturgis and Walton Company, 1912.

Hungerford, Edward, *The Modern Railroad*, Chicago: A. C. McClurg and Company, 1911.

Johnson, Emory R., "The Principle of Governmental Regulation of Railways," *Political Science Quarterly*, XV, 1900, pp. 37-49.

Jones, Eliot, *The Anthracite Coal Combinations*, Cambridge: Harvard University Press, 1914.

——, *Principles of Railway Transportation*, New York: Macmillan Company, 1925.

Josephson, Mathew, *The Robber Barons, The Great American Capitalists, 1861-1901*, New York: Harcourt, Brace and Company, 1934.

Kennan, George, *Biography of Edward H. Harriman*, 2 volumes, Boston: Houghton, Mifflin Company, 1922.

Keys, C. M., "An Era of Better Railroads," *World's Work*, IX, 1905, pp. 5816-5822; X, 1905, pp. 6302-6313; XIII, 1907, pp. 8437-8445, 8455-8464, 8536-8552, 8651-8664, 8791-8803; XVII, 1909, pp. 11238-11243; XX, 1910, pp. 13045-13056, 13187-13204.

Kirkland, F. S., *A History of American Economic Life*, New York: F. S. Crofts and Company, 1934.

Langstroth, Charles S. and Stilz, Wilson, *Railway Cooperation*, Philadelphia: University of Pennsylvania, 1899.

Laut, Agnes C., *The Romance of the Rails*, New York: Tudor Publishing Company, 1936.

McVey, Frank L., *Railroad Transportation*, Chicago: Cree Publishing Company, 1910.

Meade, E. S., "The Great American Railway Systems," *Railway World,* 1903, pp. 1327-1328, 1355-1357, 1383-1385, 1411-1413, 1467-1468; 1904, pp. 147-149, 175-176, 203-204, 231-232, 257-259, 433-435, 491-493, 687-688, 723-724, 843-845, 871-872, 899-900, 1039-1041, 1095-1096, 1207-1209, 1235-1236, 1263-1264, 1291-1292, 1487-1489; 1905, pp. 7-8, 27-28, 47-48, 171-172, 195-196, 215-216, 235-236, 356-358, 397-399, 417-418, 437-438, 615-617, 635-636, 675-676, 695-697, 895-897.

——, "The Reorganization of Railroads," *Annals of the American Academy for Political and Social Science,* March, 1901, 205-243.

Meyer, B. H., *A History of the Northern Securities Case,* Bulletin of University of Wisconsin, no. 142, Madison, 1906.

Meyer, Hugo R., "The Settlements with the Pacific Railways," *Quarterly Journal of Economics,* XIII, 1899, pp. 426-444.

Miller, Sidney L., *Inland Transportation, Principles and Policies,* New York: McGraw-Hill Book Company, Inc., 1933.

Moody, John, *The Railroad Builders,* New Haven: Yale University Press, 1921.

——, *The Truth about the Trusts,* New York: Moody Publishing Company, 1904.

Myers, Gustavus, *Great American Fortunes,* New York: Modern Library, 1936.

Newcomb, H. T., "The Concentration of Railroad Control," *Annals of the American Academy,* XIX, 1902, pp. 89-107.

——, "The Progress of Federal Railway Regulations," *Political Science Quarterly,* XI, 1896, pp. 201-221.

——, *The Proposed Radical Railway Legislation,* an address delivered before the faculty and students of the University of Missouri, October 20, 1905. 32-page pamphlet, Washington, 1905.

——, "The Present Railway Situation," *North American Review,* November, 1897, pp. 591-599.

——, "The Recent Great Railway Combinations," *Review of Reviews,* XXIV, 1901, pp. 163-174.

Nimmo, Joseph, *The Railroad Problem,* 1901-1902, volume of pamphlets in Interstate Commerce Commission Library, Washington, D. C.

Noyes, Alexander D., *Forty Years of American Finance,* New York: G. P. Putnam's Sons, 1909.

Parsons, Frank, *The Railways, The Trusts and The People,* Philadelphia: C. F. Taylor, 1906.

——, "The People's Highways," *The Arena,* XII, 1895, pp. 218-232, 393-410.

Pliny Fisk Statistical Library of Princeton University and Bureau of Railway Economics, *Catalogue of Railroad Mortgages,* Washington, 1919.

Prouty, Charles A., *National Regulation of Railways,* American Economic Association Publications, 3rd series, IV, no. 1, February, 1903. Proceedings 15th Annual Meeting, Philadelphia, December 26-29, 1902.

Pyle, J. G., *The Life of James J. Hill,* 2 volumes, New York: Doubleday, Page & Company, 1917.

Raushenbush, H. S. and Laidler, H. W., *Power Control*, New York: New Republic, Inc., 1928.

Raper, C. L., *Railway Transportation*, New York: G. P. Putnam's Sons, 1912.

Rice, Isaac L., "Bribery in Railway Elections," *Forum*, VII, 1888, pp. 106-112.

———, "Legalized Plunder of Railroad Properties: The Remedy," *Forum*, XVII, 1894, pp. 676-689.

Riegel, R. E., *The Story of the Western Railroads*, New York: Macmillan Company, 1926.

Ripley, Edward P., *Railroads: Finance and Organization*, New York: Longmans, Green and Company, 1915.

———, *Railroads: Rates and Regulation*, New York: Longmans, Green and Company, 1912.

Rosewater, Edward, *Railroad Regulation in the Light of Past Experience (1885-1905)*, 23-page pamphlet containing Rosewater's testimony before Senate Select Committee in 1886.

Sakolski, A. M., *American Railroad Economics*, New York: Macmillan Company, 1916.

Sharfman, I. Leo, *Railway Regulation*, Chicago: LaSalle Extension University, 1915.

Snyder, Carl, *American Railways as Investments*, New York: The Moody Corporation, 1907.

Some Legal Phases of Corporate Financing, Reorganization and Regulation, New York: Macmillan Company, 1917; a symposium containing: "Preparation of Corporate Bonds, Mortgages, Collateral Trusts and and Debenture Indentures," by Francis Lynde Stetson.

Spearman, Frank H., *The Strategy of Great Railroads*, New York: Charles Scribner's Sons, 1904.

Sterne, Simon, "Railway Reorganization," *Forum*, X, 1889-90, pp. 37-53.

———, "Recent Railroad Failures and their Lessons," *Forum*, XIII, 1894, pp. 19-38.

Stickney, A. B., *The Railway Problem*, St. Paul, Minn.: D. D. Merrill and Company, 1890.

Swain, H. H., "Economic Aspects of Railroad Receiverships," *Economic Studies of the American Economic Association*, April, 1898.

Thompson, Slason, *A Short History of American Railways*, New York: D. Appleton and Company, 1925.

Tittman, Edward D., "The Masters of Our Railways," *National Magazine*, XXII, 1905, pp. 65-82.

Van Oss, S. F., *American Railroads as Investments*, New York: G. P. Putnam's Sons, 1893.

———, "Recent American Railway Reorganizations," *The Journal of Finance*, April, 1898, pp. 345-355.

Warman, Cy, *The Story of the Railroad*, New York: D. Appleton and Company, 1898.

ATCHISON, TOPEKA AND SANTA FE

Plan and Agreement for the Reorganization of the Atchison, Topeka and Santa Fe Railroad Company. Dated June 19, 1894, 6-page pamphlet.

Report of Stephen Little on the Overstatement of the Income of the Atchison, Topeka and Santa Fe and the St. Louis and San Francisco systems respectively for the four years ended June 30, 1894. A typed copy addressed to R. Somers Hayes, Chairman and the Reorganization Committee; signed by Little.

General Reorganization Committee of the Atchison, Topeka and Santa Fe Railroad Company: Report of Stephen Little, dated November 2, 1894. 9-page pamphlet containing complete report.

Plan and Agreement for the Reorganization of the Atchison, Topeka and Santa Fe Railroad Company, dated March 14, 1895. 27-page pamphlet.

Report of Aldace F. Walker, and John J. McCook, Receivers of the Atchison, Topeka and Santa Fe Railroad. Dated July 1, 1896. *And Statement to the Directors of the Atchison, Topeka, and Santa Fe Railway Company by Aldace F. Walker, Chairman of the Board.* Dated July 1, 1896. 13-page pamphlet.

Annual Reports, 1890-1893.

BALTIMORE AND OHIO

Hungerford, Edward, *The Story of the Baltimore and Ohio,* New York: G. P. Putnam's Sons, 1928.

Reorganization Committee of the Baltimore and Ohio Railroad Company: Report of Stephen Little, dated New York, July 11, 1896, 27-page pamphlet.

Review and Analysis of Reports on the Baltimore and Ohio Railroad Company to November 30, 1895, dated New York, April 26, 1897, by Patterson and Corwin. 21-page pamphlet.

Reorganization of the Baltimore and Ohio Railroad Company: Plan and Agreement, dated June 22, 1898. 25-page pamphlet.

Reorganization of the Baltimore and Ohio Southwestern Railway Company: Plan and Agreement, dated December 15, 1898, 21-page pamphlet.

Annual Reports of the Baltimore & Ohio, 1890-1895.

ERIE

Mott, E. H., *Between the Ocean and the Lakes; the Story of the Erie,* New York: Ticker Publishing Company, 1908.

Circular Letter to Holders of New York, Lake Erie and Western Railroad Company's Second Consolidated Mortgage Bonds, etc., signed by Board of Directors, dated January 2, 1894.

Circular Letter to Holders of New York, Lake Erie and Western Railroad Company's Second Consolidated Mortgage Bonds, etc., signed by Drexel, Morgan and Company and J. S. Morgan and Company, dated January 2, 1894.

Circular Letter to Holders of New York, Lake Erie and Western Railroad Company's Second Consolidated Mortgage Bonds, etc., signed by Drexel, Morgan and Company and J. S. Morgan and Company, dated March 6, 1894.

RICHMOND TERMINAL AND SOUTHERN

Richmond and West Point Terminal Railway and Warehouse: Plan of Reorganization, dated March 1, 1892. 28-page pamphlet.

Plan and Agreement for the Reorganization of the Richmond and West Point Terminal Railway and Warehouse Company, the Richmond and Danville Railroad Company and system, the East Tennessee, Virginia and Georgia Railway and system, dated May 1, 1893. 49-page pamphlet.

Circular Letter May 22, 1893, to Security Holders of the Richmond and West Point Terminal Railway and Warehouse Company, the Richmond and Danville Railroad Company and system and the East Tennessee, Virginia and Georgia Railway Company and system, signed by Drexel, Morgan and Company.

Central Railroad and Banking Company of Georgia, the Southwestern Railroad Company of Georgia and the Macon and Western Railroad Company: Bondholders Protective Agreement, dated February 3, 1894. 11-page pamphlet.

Richmond and West Point Terminal Railway and Warehouse Company and its Subordinate Companies, including the Richmond and Danville Railroad Company and system, the East Tennessee, Virginia and Georgia Railway Company and system: Plan of Reorganization as Modified, dated February 20, 1894.

PHILADELPHIA AND READING

The Philadelphia and Reading Railroad Company: Plan of Readjustment and Explanatory Statement, Adopted by the Board of Managers, May 27, 1893. 20-page pamphlet.

Circular Letter to General Mortgage Bondholders and Junior Security and Stock Holders of Philadelphia and Reading Railroad Company, dated September 19, 1894, signed by General Mortgage Bondholders' Committee.

Philadelphia and Reading Railroad Company, Philadelphia and Reading Coal and Iron Company: Readjustment Agreement, dated October 1, 1894, 11-page pamphlet.

Plan and Agreement for the Reorganization of the Philadelphia and Reading Railroad Company and the Philadelphia and Reading Coal and Iron Company, dated December 14, 1895. 27-page pamphlet.

A Statement of Isaac L. Rice Concerning the Affairs of the Philadelphia and Reading Railroad Company (1895?). 41-page pamphlet.

Reading Reorganization: Opinion of H. C. McCormick, Attorney-General of Pennsylvania, January 2, 1897, declaring National Company charter may be adopted by Reading Company.

Charter and Organization of the National Company, Constructing the National Railway from Philadelphia to New York, with Statement in Relation thereto; Charter Perpetual, dated Philadelphia, 1873. And Agreement January 18, 1873, Between the National Railway Company and the Excelsior Enterprise Company Now Called the National Company. 119 and 13-page pamphlet.

NORTHERN PACIFIC

Villard Papers in the Harvard College Library; a collection containing copies of many of the published pamphlets concerning the Northern Pacific as well as Villard's private papers.

Villard, Henry, *Memoirs*, 2 volumes, Boston: Houghton, Mifflin and Company, 1904.

Report of the Special Committee to the Stockholders of the Northern Pacific Railroad Company, February, 1893. 30-page pamphlet.

Open letter to the Stockholders of the Northern Pacific Railroad Company signed by President Thomas F. Oakes by order of the Board of Directors, dated February 28, 1893. A rebuttal to the Report of the Special Committee. 12-page pamphlet.

Northern Pacific Railroad Company: Report of Receiver Henry C. Rouse, December 11, 1893. 20-page pamphlet.

Northern Pacific Railroad Company Third Mortgage Bondholders' Protective Committee Agreement, dated August 15, 1894. 7-page pamphlet.

Northern Pacific Railroad Company Bondholders' Reorganization Agreement, dated February 19, 1894. 8-page pamphlet.

First Mortgage Five Per cent Bonds of the Wisconsin Central Company: Bondholders' Agreement of January 23, 1895. 12-page pamphlet.

Message to the Stockholders of the Northern Pacific Railroad Company from Brayton Ives, President, dated October 17, 1895.

Reorganization of the Northern Pacific Railroad Company, dated March 16, 1896. 29-page pamphlet.

Circular Letters to Northern Pacific Railroad Company security holders from J. P. Morgan and Company, Drexel and Company and Deutsche Bank, dated March 16, 1896, April 4, 1896, April 24, 1896, June 1, 1896.

Official Statement of the Northern Pacific Railway Company, dated December 1, 1896. 21-page pamphlet.

Reorganization of the Wisconsin Central System, dated April 10, 1899. 27-page pamphlet.

GOVERNMENT-AIDED PACIFIC ROADS (SOUTHERN PACIFIC, CENTRAL PACIFIC, UNION PACIFIC)

Davis, J. P., *The Union Pacific Railway*, Chicago(?): S. C. Griggs and Company, 1894.

——, " The Union Pacific Railway," 91-page pamphlet reprinted from article in *Annals of the American Academy*.

Dodge, G. M., *How We Built the Union Pacific Railway and other Railway Papers and Addresses*, Washington: Government Printing Office, printed as *Senate Document 447*, 61st Congress, 1st Session.

Kahn, Otto H., " Edward Henry Harriman," an address delivered before the Finance Forum in New York, January 25, 1911. 47-page pamphlet.

Trottman, Nelson, *History of the Union Pacific*, New York: Ronald Press Company, 1923.

White, H. K., *History of the Union Pacific Railway*, Chicago: University of Chicago Press, 1895.

The Journal of Finance, A Monthly Review, IV, 1898, pp. 885-894 (London), The Union Pacific Railroad Company.

Scrapbook of Newspaper Clippings Relating to S. H. H. Clark and the Union Pacific Railroad (New York Public Library pamphlet collection).

Answer of the Union Pacific Railway Company to the Specifications of the Minority Commissioner of the United States Pacific Railway Commission, 1888(?). 119-page pamphlet.

The Union Pacific System Receivers' Office: Outstanding Bonds and Stock as of June 30, 1894 and Particulars re Defaults, revised November 1, 1894. 112-page pamphlet.

Reorganization of the Union Pacific Railway Company, Plan and Letter of Submittal to Security Holders, dated October 15, 1895. 35-page pamphlet.

Plan and Agreement for the Reorganization of the Oregon Short Line and Utah Northern Railway Company, dated February 20, 1896. 29-page pamphlet.

Agreement of Holders of Collateral Notes of Union Pacific Railway Company, dated February 15, 1897.

Reorganization of the Union Pacific, Denver and Gulf: Plan and Agreement, dated September 29, 1898. 39-page pamphlet.

The Central Pacific Railroad Company in Equitable Account with the United States, growing out of the Issue of Subsidy Bonds in Aid of Construction, etc. (argument of Roscoe Conkling and William D. Shipman reviewing testimony and exhibits presented before the Pacific Railway Committee Appointed according to the Act of Congress Approved March 3, 1887). 134-page pamphlet.

Stevens, Richard F., *Recommendations for a Basis of Settlement of the United States Claims against the Central Pacific Railroad Company*. An open letter to Honorable Rufus Blodgett, United States Senator From New Jersey. 16-page pamphlet.

As to Refunding the Central Pacific Debt: Quotations from Huntington's letters to Colton, May 1875 to January 1878 proving the building frauds, to corroborate statements made in the California memorial against refunding the Central Pacific debt. 10-page pamphlet.

A Memorial Against Refunding the Claim of the United States upon the Central Pacific Railroad Company for $70,000,000, signed by Committee (Charles A. Sumner, J. M. Barrett, F. B. Perkins) appointed

in pursuance of unanimous vote of mass meeting of citizens of San
Francisco May 25, 1894. 14-page pamphlet.

*The Central Pacific Railroad: Its Relations with the Government: It Has
Performed all its Obligations,* argument of Creed Hammond, its gen-
eral solicitor, before a Select Committee of the United States Senate
March 17, 26, April 7, 1888. 18-page pamphlet.

*Relations between the Central Pacific Railroad Company and the United
States Government: Summary of Facts, 1889.* 70-page pamphlet.

*Central Pacific Railroad Company: Facts Regarding its Past and Present
Management* (by a stockholder and former employee. Robert S.
Graham?), 1889. 40-page pamphlet.

*Arraignment, Demands and Resolutions Adopted by Mass Meeting of
Citizens of San Francisco in Metropolitan Temple,* Tuesday Evening,
June 18, 1894, signed by William C. Little, secretary. 12-page pamphlet.

Henry E. Highton to the Attorney-General: An open Letter on the Subject
of the Policies and Power of Congress to enact a law Funding the Debt
of the Central Pacific Railroad, dated June 25, 1894. 19-page pamphlet.

*Memorial of the People of California Against Refunding Pacific Railroad
Debt,* addressed to Congress and signed by Committee of Fifty appointed
by monster meeting at Metropolitan Temple, December 7, 1895. 4-page
pamphlet.

*The Central Pacific Railroad Debt: California's Remonstrance Against
Refunding It,* Addressed to Senate and House of Representatives, and
signed by Committee of Fifty and Adolph Sutro, Mayor of San Francisco, dated December 26, 1896. 29-page pamphlet.

*A Report on the Physical and Financial Condition of the Southern Pacific
Company and an Analysis of its Operation for the Past Five Years,*
dated August 1, 1902, submitted by White and Kemble. 74-page pamphlet.

The Pacific Railroad Debts: Letter to the Secretary of the Treasury from
John T. Doyle, San Francisco, May 31, 1895. 8-page pamphlet.

The Pacific Railroad Debts: Letter to a Senator, Honorable John Sherman,
from John T. Doyle, Menlo Park, January 29, 1896. 8-page pamphlet.

*A Comparison of the Results of Operation of the Several Transcontinental
Railway Systems for year ended June 30, 1900,* by Lee, Higginson and
Company. 10-page pamphlet.

Annual Reports of the Southern Pacific, 1890-1899.

Annual Reports of the Union Pacific, 1890-1893.

MISCELLANEOUS ROADS

Dozier, Howard Douglas, *A History of the Atlantic Coast Line Railroad,*
Boston: Houghton, Mifflin Company, 1920.

Consolidated Railroad of Vermont Five Per Cent Mortgage Bonds: Agreement for Deposit of Bonds, dated April 7, 1896. 9-page pamphlet.

Kerr, J. L., *The Missouri Pacific, An Outline History,* New York: Railroad
Research Society, 1928.

BIBLIOGRAPHY

——, *Story of a Southern Carrier* (Louisville and Nashville Railroad), New York: Young and Ottley, 1933.

Reorganization of the Norfolk and Western Railroad Company: Plan and Agreement, dated March 12, 1896, and letter of submittal from the Reorganization Committee. 21-page pamphlet.

Schotter, H. W., *Growth and Development of the Pennsylvania Railroad Company*, 2 volumes, Philadelphia: Allen, 1927.

Annual Reports of the Norfolk & Western, 1890-1894.

Annual Reports of the New York, New Haven & Hartford, 1890-1899.

Annual Reports of the New York Central & Hudson River Railroad Company, 1890-1899.

Annual Reports of the Lake Shore & Michigan Central, 1890-1899.

Annual Reports of the Central Railroad of New Jersey, 1890-1899.

Annual Reports of the Lehigh Valley Railroad, 1890-1899.

Annual Reports of the Chicago, Burlington & Quincy, 1890-1899.

Annual Reports of the Missouri Pacific, 1890-1899.

Annual Reports of the Denver & Rio Grande Railroad Company, 1890-1899.

Annual Reports of the Wabash Railroad Company, 1890-1899.

INDEX

357

Gould Interests, 237, 285-291
Gowen, Franklin B., 107, 109
Grand Canon of the Arkansas, 13
Grand Forks, N. D., 294
Grand Rapids & Indiana Railroad, 269
Grand Trunk, 176, 258, 291, 305-310
Grant, U. S., 9
Great Lakes, 108, 111, 112, 199, 295
Great Northern, 11, 13, 43, 49-50, 51, 52, 195, 196, 197, 198, 199, 205, 250, 265, 282, 292-297, 328, 332, 342
Gulf of Mexico, 285
Gutenberg Bible, 55

Hallgarten & Company, 163, 184
Hambleton, Messrs. & Company, 157
Hamburg, 245
Hammond, Ind., 290
Hanford, Judge C. H., 193, 194
Hannibal, Mo., 285
Harding, J. H., 190
Harlan, Justice John M., 194
Harmon, Judson, 241
Harriman, E. H., 32, 145, 160, 164-165, 213, 214, 217-255, 277, 281, 301, 328, 332, 333, 334, 340, 341, 342
Harriman, E H. & Company, 163, 330-331
Harris, Joseph S., 173, 175, 186
Harris, Robert, 190
Hartford Railroad, 256
Hartley, Marcellus, 190
Haven, George C., 218, 222
Hayes, R. Somers, 218, 222
Heidelback, Ockelheimer & Company 98
Hempstead, N. Y., 246
Hepburn Act, 339
Hewitt, Abram S., 170
Higginson, H. L., 233
Hilgard, Ferdinand Heinrich Gustav, see Villard, Henry
Hill, James J., 49-50, 147, 160, 189, 190-216, 250, 251, 266, 282, 292-297, 328, 331, 332, 333, 342
Hoffman, L. A. von, 218
Hollins, H. H. & Company, 98, 101
Honesdale, Pa., 272
Hope & Company, 222
Hopkins, Mark, 297
Housatonic Railroad, 256
Houston, Tex., 285
Hoyt, Colgate, 57
Hudson River, 271, 272; see North River

Hughitt, Marvin, 237
Hunt, Wilson G., 146
Huntington, C. P., 147, 217, 250, 277-278, 297-301, 317

Idaho Central, 249
Illinois, 282, 284, 334
Illinois Central Railroad, 32, 164, 246, 247, 265, 276-278, 317, 330, 342
Indian Territory, 284
International & Great Northern, 286
Interstate Commerce Act, 17-23, 32, 33, 338
Interstate Commerce Commission, 12, 20-23, 26-27, 33, 81, 113, 247, 303, 323, 325, 331, 336, 339, 340
Inman, John H., 98-99, 100, 101, 102, 103
Inman, Swann & Company, 98
Iowa, 165, 282, 284
Iron Mountain Railroad, 290
Iselin, Adrian, jr., 183, 218, 222
Iselin, A., & Company, 184
Italian railroads, 335
Ives, Brayton, 42, 45, 55, 57, 191, 192, 193, 194, 195, 199, 203

Jackson, Andrew, 9
Jefferies, Edward T., 289
Jenkins, Judge James G., 57, 191
Jersey City, N. J., 167
Johnston, Joseph E., 9
Joint Traffic Association Case, 338n
Journal of Finance, 86, 244
Juneau, Swann & Company, 98

Kansas, 71, 87, 282, 284
Kansas Central Company, 91
Kansas City, Mo., 285
Kansas Pacific, 83, 89, 238, 242
Kentucky, 154, 311
Kessler & Company, 98
Kimball, F. J., 216
King, Edward, 222, 225
King, John, 63
Kittson, Norman W., 293
Knowles, Judge Hiram, 194
Knoxville, Tenn., 154
Kuhn, Abraham, 245
Kuhn, Loeb & Company, 163, 196, 209, 238, 245, 271, 321, 340

LaFollette, Robert M., 325
La Junta, Col., 13
Lake Champlain, 306
Lake Erie, 273

Pacific Coast Jobbers Association, 298
Packer, Asa, 274
Packer Estate, 189, 275
Pardee Brothers & Company, 177
Paris, 245
Parkersburgh, W. Va., 143
Parson, Charles, 259
Patterson & Corwin, 141
Pattison, Robert, 89
Paxson, Judge Edward M., 172
Payne, Henry C., 46, 193, 194
Peabody, J. C., & Company, 163
Pennsboro & Harrisville Railroad, 291-292
Pennsylvania, 113, 114, 272, 273
Pennsylvania Coal Company, 189
Pennsylvania Company, *see* Pennsylvania Railroad.
Pennsylvania Finance Company, 118, 180
Pennsylvania Railroad Company, 12, 108, 112, 130, 132, 143, 189, 214, 246, 259, 264, 265, 266-271, 274, 276, 291, 329, 330, 331, 332, 333, 342
Pere Marquette, 329
Perkins, William H., 94
Petersburg Railway, 315
Philadelphia, Pa., 107, 108, 130, 131, 136, 142, 170, 187, 195, 203, 272, 275
Philadelphia & Reading Coal & Iron Company, 108-129, 172-189
Philadelphia, Reading & New England Railroad, 115
Philadelphia & Reading Railroad, 25, 30, 34, 35, 92, 106-129, 147, 172-189, 190, 259, 262, 271, 272, 273, 274, 276, 303, 327, 329, 332
Pierce, H. Clay, 213
Pierce, Winslow S., 238, 240, 245
Pike's Peak, 56
Pittsburgh, Pa., 107, 113, 133, 136, 264, 267, 270, 271, 291
Pittsburgh & Connellsville, 142
Pittsburgh & Western, 132, 136
Poor, Henry W., 313
Portland, Ore., 193, 297, 330, 331
Port Reading, N. J., 111
Port Reading Railroad, 111, 114
Porter, H. H., 32
Portsmouth, Great Falls & Conway, 262
Pothonier, C. Sligo de, 222
Potomac River, 154
Pottsville, Pa., 274
Poughkeepsie Railroad, 115

Price, Waterhouse & Company, 40
Prince & Company, 119, 120, 179
Probst, John D., 46, 195, 199
Prouty, Charles A., 333
Providence, R. I., 257
Pueblo, Col., 14, 15, 289
Puget Sound, 11, 42
Pujo Committee, 160, 329
Pullman Company, 130
Pullman, George M., 32
Pullman Strike, 25

Quintard, George W., 170

Railroad capitalization, 12-13, 320-323
Railroad combination, 11-12, 17-18, 110-111, 326-334
Railroad efficiency, 334-337
Railroad Gazette, 140
Railroad mileage in United States, 9-11, 28
Railroad profits, 23-24, 27-28, 301-302
Railroad Securities Commission of 1911, 325
Railway Age and Northwestern Railroader, 134
Railway World, 125, 136, 188, 215
Ralston, R. G., 46
Ramsey, Joseph, 291
Rates, 15-17, 19-22, 23, 323-325, 333-334, 337-340
Read, William A., 137, 209
Reading, Pa., 186
Reading Company, 186; *see* Philadelphia & Reading Railroad
Ream, Norman B., 213, 214
Rebates, 15-16, 19-21, 22-23
Reconstruction, 9, 314
Red River Valley, 49
Reilly, James A., 233, 239-240
Reinhart, J. W., 69-70, 72, 73, 74, 78-82
Rensslaer Polytechnic Institute, 270
Reorganization methods, 148, 319-328; *see* Morgan, J. P.
Rice, Isaac L., 98. 117, 119, 175-176, 178-179, 182
Richmond & Allegheny, 70
Richmond & Danville, 92, 93, 94, 95, 98, 100, 105, 106, 150-151
Richmond, Fredericksburg and Potomac, 215
Richmond, Nicholasville, Irwin & Beattyville, 310-312
Richmond & Petersburg, 315

Swiss railroads, 336n
Syndicate profits in reorganizations, 321-322

Taft, William H., 325
Talcott, T. M. R., 105-106
Tappen, Frederick D., 94
Taylor, William R., 119
Tennant, Sir Charles, 170
Tennessee, 154
Tennessee Coal, Iron & Railroad Company, 98
Terre Haute & Indianapolis Railroad, 267
Texas, 71, 284
Thaelman, Ernst, 195, 199
Thomas, Anthony J., 150
Thomas, Eben B., 170, 203
Thomas, George C., 187
Thomas, Samuel, 311-312
Thomas, Samuel T., 155-156
Thurman Act, 235, 255
Tod, J. Kennedy, 94, 183, 213, 214, 230
Tod, J. Kennedy, & Company, 184
Toledo, Peoria & Western, 267
Toledo, Wabash & Western, 290
Topeka, Kan., 68, 77
Tower, Charlemagne, jr., 195, 199, 203
Tracy, Charles E., 148
Trans-Missouri Freight Association Case, 338n
Tyler, Sidney F., 183

Union Pacific, 10, 11, 13, 19, 30, 34, 35, 62, 73, 78n, 83-91, 145, 217, 232-252, 282, 288, 297, 301, 303, 321, 326, 331, 332, 333, 334, 340
Union Pacific, Denver & Gulf, 30, 250
Union Steamboat Company, 65
United States Express Company, 130
United States Government, 83-85, 88, 89, 90, 91, 233-245, 251-255, 300
United States Industrial Commission, 105, 158, 188-189, 298, 332
United States Investor, 144
United States Steel Corporation, 98
United States Supreme Court, 18, 19, 20, 21, 199, 235, 300, 311-312, 324, 325, 338, 340
University of Virginia, 151
Utah Northern Railroad, 83

Vanderbilt, Cornelius, 11, 263

Vanderbilt Interests, 115, 119, 132-133, 146, 189, 190, 238, 258, 263-266, 272, 274, 276, 283, 329, 330, 333, 342
Vanderbilt, William H., 146
Vanlandingham, A. J., 297
Van Oss, S. F., 316
Vermilye Brothers, 137, 163, 211
Vermont, 170, 258
Vermont & Canada, 305
Vermont legislature, 309
Villard, Henry, 42, 43, 46, 51, 54, 55-60, 191, 195
Virginia, 36, 153, 315
Virginia legislature, 36

Wabash Case, 19
Wabash Railroad, 127, 290-291
Wall Street, 45, 55, 72, 97, 138, 163, 164, 187, 188, 196, 219, 246, 251
Wall Street Journal, 146, 152, 158, 169, 185, 201, 211, 219, 240, 296
Walter, Alfred, 275
Washington, 51
Washington, D. C., 25, 56, 93, 143, 154, 298, 317
Waterbury, John I., 260
Waverly, N. Y., 63
Webb, W. Seward, 308
Webster, Sidney, 164n
Weehawken, N. J., 167
Weld, B. Rodman, 218
Welsh, J. Lowber, 170, 172, 187
West Stockbridge Railroad, 259
West Virginia, 36, 131, 292
Western Freight Association, 22, 32, 71
Western National Bank, 55
Western New York & Pennsylvania Railroad, 268-269
Western Union, 130, 137
Western University of Pennsylvania, 70
Wheeler, William R., 298
Wheeling, O., 136
Wilkes-Barre, Pa., 272
Wilbur, E. P., 172, 275, 276
Williams, J. B., 46
Williamson, Samuel E., 170
Willis, James D., 203
Wilmington, Columbia & Augusta, 315
Wilmington & Weldon, 315
Winter, Edwin, 203
Wisconsin, 282, 325